# 50 Concepts for a Critical Phenomenology

# 50 CONCEPTS FOR A CRITICAL PHENOMENOLOGY

EDITED BY GAIL WEISS
ANN V. MURPHY
GAYLE SALAMON

NORTHWESTERN UNIVERSITY PRESS
EVANSTON, ILLINOIS

Northwestern University Press
www.nupress.northwestern.edu



Printed in the United States of America

10 9 8 7 6 5 4 3 2 1

Library of Congress Cataloging-in-Publication Data

Names: Weiss, Gail, 1959– editor. | Murphy, Ann V., editor. | Salamon, Gayle, editor.
Title: 50 concepts for a critical phenomenology / edited by Gail Weiss, Ann V Murphy, Gayle Salamon.
Other titles: Fifty concepts for a critical phenomenology
Description: Evanston, Illinois: Northwestern University Press, 2019. | Includes index. | Summary: "This volume is an introduction to both newer and more established ideas in the growing field of critical phenomenology from a number of disciplinary perspectives"— Provided by publisher.
Identifiers: LCCN 2019022558 | ISBN 9780810141148 (paperback) | ISBN 9780810141155 (cloth) | ISBN 9780810141162 (ebook)
Subjects: LCSH: Phenomenology.
Classification: LCC B829.5 .A314 2019 | DDC 142.7—dc23
LC record available at https://lccn.loc.gov/2019022558

This volume is dedicated to critical phenomenologists: past, present, and future.

# Contents

# Acknowledgments

We wish to thank the societies that have nurtured us as critical phenomenologists, particularly the Society for Phenomenology and Existential Philosophy, the International Merleau-Ponty Circle, and philoSOPHIA: A Society for Continental Feminism. Not only academic venues, but also scholarly communities, they have fostered the friendships we share with each other and with the volume's contributors.

Thanks to Northwestern University Press for enthusiastically supporting this project from its inception. We are grateful to Jane Bunker, to whom we originally pitched this idea, to Trevor Perri, who shepherded it all the way through, and to Anne Gendler for her skillful handling of the final production process. We thank RL Goldberg for his invaluable assistance formatting a long manuscript and Cathy Hannabach for the book's index.

Finally we thank our contributors, whose collective support and enthusiasm was our greatest inspiration. We are grateful to each of them for their dedication to the project and for their wonderful work.

# Introduction: Transformative Descriptions

How could an anthology possibly have a central perspective?

—MAURICE MERLEAU-PONTY, *Signs*

Maurice Merleau-Ponty's *Phenomenology of Perception* begins with a question: "What is phenomenology?" Nearly three-quarters of a century later, this question remains unanswered. Our volume does not propose to answer it but rather to honor its generative insight, an insight that Merleau-Ponty inherits from Edmund Husserl's *Crisis of European Sciences and Transcendental Phenomenology*, namely that the philosopher is a "perpetual beginner." As a philosophical tradition, phenomenology has privileged wonder, ambiguity, and curiosity over the Cartesian drive toward certainty, determinacy, and indubitability. One of phenomenology's most axiomatic methodological commitments is the refusal to accept the taken-for-grantedness of experience. This commitment entails the perpetual interrogation of the most familiar features of our everyday experiences, not to deny them but in order to know them better. Like literature, history, and anthropology, phenomenology has yielded rich descriptions of lived experience. Phenomenology is marked by a faith that such descriptions can disclose the most basic structures of human existence, including temporality, perception, language, and intersubjectivity. As these structures are brought into relief, our understanding of our own experiences is transformed, and our deepest assumptions about our very being in the world may be challenged.

The fifty concepts that appear in this volume exemplify the continuing fecundity of attunement to lived experience and its structuring conditions that have been a hallmark of the phenomenological method. Together they also expand our understanding of phenomenology's potential far beyond its classical horizons. Our intellectual landscape has now been significantly shaped by disciplines that did not exist when phenomenology's foundational texts were being written. It is our conviction as phenomenologists that the diverse disciplinary perspectives offered by feminist theorists, critical race theorists, queer theorists, decolonial and indigenous scholars, disability studies scholars, and others are crucial for phenomenology's future. They are also producing exciting readings of the phenomenological canon from marginalized perspectives that breathe new life into its foundational texts. By illuminating constitutive aspects of human existence that challenge the universalizing tendencies of philosophy, they bring new accountability and new promise to the practice of phenomenology.

A central Husserlian tenet is that an experience can never be understood or described in isolation. This means not only that our experiences are interconnected but also that they are always generated from particular places, times, and cultural milieus. More specifically, Husserl claims that there is a dynamic and reversible figure/ground structure to all experience whereby in focusing on an individual phenomenon, all else necessarily recedes into a more or less indeterminate background. This holds true not only for perceiving and conceiving but also for imagining, judging, willing, valuing, and feeling, that is, for the many different ways we are intentionally oriented toward the world around us. The figure/ground structure, he asserts, is itself situated within multiple horizons of significance, including temporal, spatial, social, historical, cultural, political, and institutional horizons. These horizons actively inform our experience and for the most part do so prereflectively, without our explicit awareness. Nonetheless, they exert substantial influence in determining what becomes the figure and what remains the ground. Merleau-Ponty, focusing on the primacy of perception, describes the ways in which perceptual patterns become sedimented over time as embodied habits. Habits can render the world comfortable, familiar, and predictable even though, as several entries in this volume remind us, they necessarily limit our horizons, foreclosing some perspectives and possibilities by privileging others.

Contemporary phenomenologists increasingly recognize that these foreclosures are a function of structural, political, and institutional inequities that are internalized as personal biases and habits. This insight has inspired a critical phenomenology, one that mobilizes phenomenological description in the service of a reflexive inquiry into how power relations structure experience as well as our ability to analyze that experience. Critique is not critical if it refuses to situate itself, to recognize the limitations and liabilities of its own perspective. A critical phenomenology draws attention to the multiple ways in which power moves through our bodies and our lives. It is also an ameliorative phenomenology that seeks not only to describe but also to repair the world, encouraging generosity, respect, and compassion for the diversity of our lived experiences. Such a project can never be an individual endeavor, moreover, but requires coalitional labor and solidarity across difference.

The authors collected in this volume range from distinguished scholars revisiting some of the terms they have coined or made famous to newer voices who are actively working to expand the boundaries of what counts as philosophical inquiry. These thinkers bear varying degrees of fidelity to phenomenology as a method and a tradition; however, as their entries reveal, each offers rich phenomenological insights that open up new horizons for critical phenomenology. This volume is intended as a resource and also as an invitation to you, our readers, to join us in the interrogation of both the familiar and the unfamiliar, whether in experience, thought, or perception. In so doing, we make the familiar newly strange and bring the unfamiliar in closer, even while preserving its alterity. Such a critical phenomenology—whatever it may become—disrupts sedimented patterns of thinking and perceiving, creating the conditions of possibility for new and unpredictable futures.

Gail Weiss, Ann V. Murphy, and Gayle Salamon
Santa Fe, New Mexico, November 2017, and North Pomfret, Vermont, March 2018

# 50 Concepts for a Critical Phenomenology

# 1 The Phenomenological Method

Duane H. Davis

If, just over one hundred years after its initial development, we ask what the meaning and significance of the phenomenological method could be for us today, it is imperative that the articulation of this position be fundamentally situated within the intersectionality that is human existence. From its beginnings in Husserl's thought, phenomenology has consistently been defined as a response to crisis—a critical inquiry into the very nature of our being. There is no doubt that Husserl's phenomenological method famously or infamously invokes a transcendental turn that is grounded in the reflective power of the transcendental ego, but surely all of this matters to us only if it pertains to matters-at-hand. Husserl noted that *all subjectivity is intersubjectivity*; now we must consider such differentials not only *among* our diverse selves but *within* the selves we are becoming. Transcendental subjectivity must be redescribed in terms of intersectionality to develop a critical phenomenology. As we shall see, the phenomenological method provides the basis for us to do so. Another, more direct way of emphasizing the praxial promise of this project is to describe intersectionality as the occasion for the *redeployment* of phenomenology. Thus, race, gender, and class and their intersection are not ancillary to phenomenology if it is to be relevant today for addressing the ongoing crises we face daily.

I will begin with a general account of the phenomenological method—more conjuring its spirit than explicating any specific philosopher's incarnation of it. There are great differences in the senses ascribed to the phenomenological method among the various philosophers who are associated with the phenomenological movement.[1] Given the brevity of this essay, we do not have the luxury of exploring the nuances of any phenomenologist's position; however, in the latter portion of this essay, I would like to call attention briefly to one small aspect of Husserl's thought that might help us see the promise of a critical phenomenology in a direction similar to the vision of Patricia Hill Collins.

## The General Sense of the Phenomenological Method

The phenomenological method is an attempt to offer prescriptive descriptions of the world in which we live.[2] It involves the transformation of the way we understand our world such that we can be astonished before it—the attempt to see our world as if for the first time, through unjaded eyes. This transformation is to be affected by suspending our habitual and theoretical presuppositions and thus allowing the world to appear as it becomes what it is and as it matters to us.

When we read that phenomenology is the account of *appearances*, we see that there is something at stake here that does not come down to *subjective* perspective or worldview—the way something appears to some*one*, to *one*'s culture, or even to any *one* culture. Appearances in the phenomenological sense are not psychic constructions. Likewise, the account of appearances-as-they-are does not connote an *objective* account. Appearances in the phenomenological sense are not abstractions bereft of a world. The phenomenological method is not an attempt to purge subjective bias to reveal objective truth—instead it regards the pretense of traditional objectivity as a bias every bit as much as the caprice of subjectivity. As we shall see, it is helpful to remember that phenomenology seeks to give accounts of appearances as *processes*—of the coming-to-appear. The principal aspects of the phenomenological method we shall consider here include *intentionality*, the *epochē*, the *phenomenological and eidetic reductions*, and *transcendental subjectivity*. Each of these aspects of the phenomenological method is intertwined with the others, yet we should attempt to distinguish these aspects in order to reveal the promise of critical phenomenology.

Undoubtedly the foundational insight of the phenomenological method is *intentionality*: our understanding is always engaged within the world. We stand in the world we are understanding. This means that neither subjectivity nor objectivity is an epiphenomenal illusion determined at the exclusion of the other, but both are instead ineluctably bound together. The principle of intentionality thus offers a new standpoint to seek understanding of the world, since we are no longer equating consciousness with some interiority standing over against some exteriority which must be related through metaphysical sleight of hand. Instead, phenomenological intentional consciousness is the relation itself such that consciousness is always "consciousness of" something. As existential phenomenologists (i.e., Heidegger, Merleau-Ponty, Beauvoir, and Sartre) expanded upon Husserl's position, they explored intentionality as an intimate relation and explored its significance in ways not restricted to its epistemological formulation. That is, consciousness is not merely a knower-known relation but is also "being-in-the-world" or "the flesh of the world."

However it is construed, this phenomenological intentional consciousness is not easy to come by; it is an achievement—a radical alteration of everyday and theoretical consciousness. Our most common ways of understanding are motivated by biases and habits that can originate individually or culturally. Phenomenology is, as the name implies, an account of appearances, and it begins as a reflection upon experiences as we live them. Lived experience (*Erlebnis*) is transient, fleeting, and not intrinsically reliable as a form of understanding. Yet this is the kind of understanding that prevails in our everyday ways of acting and interacting in the world. Husserl's name for this uncritical affirmation of the world is the *natural standpoint*, to which he contrasts the *phenomenological standpoint*. Phenomenology involves a radical alteration of consciousness—a complete shift in attitude toward what appears that involves a suspension of the natural attitude.[3] Yet this "mere change of standpoint" holds "the key to all genuine philosophy."[4]

According to Husserl, at least, phenomenology was to be a presuppositionless philosophy. In order for phenomena to appear in an unencumbered way as the intentional relations of phenomenological consciousness, we must suspend our everyday assumptions about phenomena as well as our theoretical predispositions. This process of "bracketing" or "putting out of play" is what Husserl adopted a term from the ancient Greek skeptics to describe: the *epochē*. Only through this arduous critical exercise can we reveal phenomena as they are.

The *phenomenological and eidetic reductions* are the other side of the same coin, so to speak, of the *epochē*. Implementing the *epochē* is the first step in the phenomenological reduction. (It is first logically rather than temporally.) We can think of the word *reduction* in its culinary sense such that a sauce is reduced to its essence: its defining character becomes unmistakably manifest. By setting aside habitual biases, the phenomenological reduction provides free access to real and potential experience of phenomena conceived within the intentional relationship, while the eidetic reduction provides access to "invariant essential structures" of phenomena.[5] These ideals or essential structures are possible only through transcendental reflection. That is, the conditions of the possibility of the appearances are disclosed through this intense reflection.

And so, by implementing the skeptical attitude of the *epochē* and at once engaging in the phenomenological and eidetic reductions, a field of *transcendental subjectivity* is revealed as the condition of the possibility of the appearance of phenomena within intentional relations.[6] It is important to note here that Husserl did not equate transcendental subjectivity with the sovereign subjectivity of early modern Western philosophy's models of the individual. Transcendental reflection reveals that the subjectivity of the Cartesian "I think," for example, is but one psychological aspect of the intentional relation of consciousness in all its possibilities.

So phenomenology is a rigorous quest asking after the essential structures of appearances. They can be disclosed only within the context of intentionality. By bracketing out the natural attitude—the aforementioned habitual biases and theoretical biases—the phenomenon is reduced to its essence. The disclosed structures of phenomena bespeak a certain propriety. For Husserl, especially, the phenomenological method leads us to the things themselves.[7]

Husserl's phenomenology developed constantly throughout his career, yet its status as a purification project remained constant. The purification process of knowledge is achieved only through transcendental phenomenology. It is to be "won," as Husserl frequently states. This rhetoric of *winning out against* the limitations, biases, errors, and vicissitudes of everyday experience and theoretical presuppositions alludes to a crisis in our understanding of the world. Husserl believed that these crises, both theoretical and practical, could be addressed only through employing the phenomenological method. Now we must consider anew the value of critical phenomenology in addressing contemporary crises that we understand in terms of intersectionality.

## The Praxial Promise of Critical Phenomenology

Now that we have a general sense of the phenomenological method, let us briefly give specific attention to one aspect of the aforementioned problem of the suspension of the natural standpoint in Husserl's phenomenology. Husserl seems to be claiming at once that we are engaged within the world of lived experience and that we are not.[8] Yet this apparent contradiction could also provide a way of showing the praxial promise of an intersectional phenomenology.

The phenomenological method is too often superficially dismissed as harboring an ineradicable idealism despite the fact that it was intended to provide a critical, enworlded account from the beginning. Husserl addressed this even in what is generally regarded as his most idealistic moments of his career in *Ideas, Volume 1*. Husserl indicated that when one employs the phenomenological method, one remains in the world about which one is concerned. In other words, when one takes the transcendental turn, the world goes on turning. More specifically, Husserl stated that even though the phenomenological method involves a suspension of the general thesis of the natural standpoint in favor of the phenomenological standpoint, the world of the natural standpoint is where this all takes place.

According to Husserl, the phenomenological method strives for knowledge that is apodictic, both necessary and certain. Of course, this goal was called into question by the aforementioned existential phenomenologists. Merleau-Ponty put it succinctly when he said that "the most important lesson of the reduction is the impossibility of a complete reduction."[9] Nonetheless, orthodox Husserlian or existential phenomenologies alike ascribe to the phenomenological method. And the phenomenological method purports to seek apparently contradictory goals in its attempt to offer prescriptive descriptions.

Phenomenologists sometimes speak of the intentional objects revealed in the transcendental field through the *epochē* and reduction as "objects-as-intended" or "objects-as-meant." Clearly phenomenology is keen to disclose the essential structures of phenomena situated in a matrix of relations sometimes referred to as a ground for a figure, an intentional horizon, or as the lifeworld. In every case, the aforementioned propriety obtains here in prescriptive descriptions such that a phenomenon manifests "its universal relatedness-back-to-itself."[10] Husserl wants this reflexivity to be metaphysically adequate yet critical.

The problem is that the limitation of the natural standpoint is that it can speak only of the experience of the natural world, while the phenomenological standpoint reveals the essential transcendental structures of our experience, yet, at the same time, the transcendental reflection of the phenomenological method is said to take place in the world of the natural standpoint. We need to take a closer look at how these two attitudes can be compossible.

At the end of the first chapter of *Ideas, Volume 1*, Husserl states that the domains of empirical science (i.e., the natural attitude) and the eidetic science (i.e., the phenomenological attitude) are quite distinct, yet "the radical distinction in no way bars out intercrossing and *overlapping* [*überschiebung*]."[11] The word *überschiebung* is a technical geological term that describes the sliding of one tectonic plate over another. It is interesting that the root verb *schieben* means "to shove or move" but also has an idiomatic sense of sloughing off or deflecting blame—putting the blame on someone.[12]

Husserl's manner of explaining this overlapping is that the world remains present for us, only its objective nature is "bracketed." Everything hinges upon the overlapping of the thesis of the natural attitude and the phenomenological attitude if the phenomenological method is to have practical relevance. The general thesis of the natural standpoint is a tacit and necessary connectedness within the world that is obviously consistent with the intentionality of consciousness. Husserl points out that the world is present whether or not we focus on aspects of it, but this presence is indeterminate, like a "misty horizon" whose presence is not only as a world of facts but "with the same immediacy, as a *world of values*, a *world of goods*, a *practical world*."[13]

Within this indeterminate but necessarily present world, the natural attitude, we might adopt a variety of other attitudes. Husserl gives an example of phenomenology in practice in the world. He illustrates this overlapping when he describes how the arithmetical attitude *overlaps* with the natural attitude. I might be aware that there are books on the desk. If I turn my attention to the pile of books, I see that there are ten. But I might adopt an arithmetical attitude and consider the number 10 itself rather than the ten books beside me. Husserl points out that the attitudes overlap. The world of the natural attitude remains present "*undisturbed by the adoption of new standpoints*."[14] Husserl states that "we put out of action the general thesis which belongs to the essence of the natural standpoint": the world is "there" for us even as we put it in brackets. Pure phenomenological consciousness is the residue of the disconnection from the thesis of the natural standpoint, and it remains situated in the world. This is the transcendental turn where my attitudes or standpoints overlap.

The general context seems to indicate that the transcendental phenomenological attitude overlaps with the natural attitude in such a way that it is right at home in the natural world, that it is grounded, that it has the ability to slide over the natural attitude without disturbing it even as the thesis is altered. We engage in a certain suspension of the thesis. While Husserl uses the word *Aufhebung* to describe this alteration, he makes it clear that he does not mean to oppose the general thesis of the presence of the world with its antithesis of non-being. The thesis undergoes a modification "whilst remaining in itself what it is."[15] There seems to be little doubt that these sections illustrate a peaceful, stable overlapping of the attitudes.

Metaphors hold infinite meanings in keep, some of which we release through our careful attention—with or without regard to the purported intentions of the author. Husserl's geological metaphor resonates in many ways. We must suspend our uncritical attitude toward Husserl's text, even while it remains present for us, indefinite as a misty horizon. . . .

Let us pursue other resonances of this geological metaphor. The idea that this *overlapping* (*überschiebung*) should be the occasion for truths that are "unshakeable" is a very interesting choice of metaphor. Plate tectonics teaches that when one plate slides over another, the results are anything but stable. One plate encroaches upon another, resulting in profound and widespread instability such that we mistrust the very ground upon which we stand. And regardless of what Husserl might have thought about this, new ways to appreciate the phenomenological method might open up just where it bespeaks instability and generates awe and wonder about the ever-shifting, trembling ground.

Following the existential phenomenologists, let us recognize the praxial promise of this instability and encroachment rather than regarding it as something to be overcome through a purification process.[16] Most important, let us recognize that encroachment and overlapping of differences both among us all and as the intersectionality of differences *which we are*. In order to achieve a critical phenomenology, phenomenology must be seen as a philosophy of difference rather than identity. Or, to put it another way, when our personal identity is disclosed to be intersectional, we can come to disclose our sociopolitical identities as the difference of differences. True to the spirit of the phenomenological method, this allows us to see our identities, personal and public, as intersectional phenomena—as coming-to-appear as encroachment or overlapping. This would better suit Husserl's hope that all subjectivity is intersubjective and that our relations with others were "co-transcendental."[17]

Patricia Hill Collins's landmark work in intersectional theory is instructive in helping actualize the praxial promise of critical phenomenology. Collins addresses intersectionality as situated within the power relations it examines, as a strategy useful for revealing social phenomena anew, as well as a critical praxis. She defines intersectionality succinctly: "The term intersectionality references the critical insight that race, class, gender, sexuality, ethnicity, nation, ability, and age operate not as unitary, mutually exclusive entities, but rather as reciprocally constructing phenomena."[18] She turns to racial formation theory to show how its intersectionality does not conflate discourses about race with the power relations it describes.[19] "Both are held separate yet interconnected."[20] To invoke the Husserlian metaphor, they *overlap*. But Collins's solution embraces the tumult and encroachment of differences in intersectionality. The consequences of facing up to this limitation include that we approach ourselves—our identities—as subjectivities subject to the same sorts of contingencies we see when considering intersubjective relations. When Collins concludes that intersectionality must maintain its "critical edge" by examining the way it speaks to people in various disciplines,[21] she also provides a model for how phenomenology can contribute to this autocritical project. But this requires that phenomenology must situate itself within the same critical domain.

In this way, one might say that intersectionality shows us the complement to Husserl's observation: *all intersubjectivity is subjectivity*. The transcendental ground upon which our reflections stand is not holy ground. Subjectivity is always subject to the structures it cares about and describes critically.[22] Perhaps this manifests the spirit of intentionality: to in-tend, to care about that within which one appears as phenomenon.

## Notes

1. There have been a variety of important resources written from diverse orientations providing overviews of phenomenology, of which I will mention only two here. For an important comprehensive report on the early figures of the phenomenological movement, see Herbert Spiegelberg, *The Phenomenological Movement* (The Hague: Martinus Nijhoff, 1960). For a later critical retrospective and selective assessment, see Jean-François Lyotard, *Phenomenology*, trans. B. Beakley (Albany: State University of New York Press, 1991).

2. In his early idealistic work, Husserl warns that phenomenology offers pure description, yet his own phenomenology is critical insofar as it offers descriptions that reveal truths, and thus which are at once prescriptive.

3. The suspension of the natural standpoint is problematic insofar as Husserl also claims that we remain engaged within the world even as we work to alter that engagement. We will have more to say about this topic below.

4. Edmund Husserl, "Author's Preface to the English Edition," in *Ideas, Volume 1*, trans. W. Gibson (New York: Macmillan, 1931), 16. Also see Edmund Husserl, "Phenomenology," *Encyclopedia Britannica* (1927), in Joseph J. Kockelmans, *Edmund Husserl's Phenomenology* (West Lafayette, Ind.: Purdue University Press, 1994), 113.

5. Husserl, "Phenomenology," 129–31.

6. Husserl is following Kant's transcendental turn here. The universal nature of phenomenological truths is achieved through the eidetic reduction and would be impossible through any finite series of determinate lived experience.

7. Husserl, *Ideas*, 35.

8. Though he did not formulate it precisely in these terms, this contradiction is at the heart of the preface of Merleau-Ponty's *Phenomenology of Perception*, where he announces his departure from Husserlian phenomenology.

9. Maurice Merleau-Ponty, *Phenomenology of Perception*, trans. D. Landes (New York: Routledge, 2014), lxxvii.

10. Husserl, *Ideas*, 301.

11. Husserl, *Ideas*, 79, my emphasis.

12. That is, . . . *die Schuld auf einen schieben*. . . .

13. Husserl, *Ideas*, 103.

14. Husserl, *Ideas*, 104.

15. Husserl, *Ideas*, 108.

16. Merleau-Ponty, especially, never tired of making sweet lemonade out of bitter lemons. We have since come to acquire a taste for lemons. Though it is possible to make only a few gestures in this direction here, I see the greatest potential for developing a critical phenomenology by working from the encroachment (*empiétement*) and divergence (*écart*) Merleau-Ponty sometimes celebrated in his notion of the flesh of the world.

17. Husserl, *Ideas*, 21.

18. Patricia Hill Collins, "Intersectionality's Definitional Dilemmas," *Annual Review of Sociology* 41 (August 2015): 1.

19. Collins, "Intersectionality's Definitional Dilemmas," 1.

20. Collins, "Intersectionality's Definitional Dilemmas," 4.

21. Collins, "Intersectionality's Definitional Dilemmas,"17.

22. See Étienne Balibar on this point: *Citizen Subject*, trans. S. Miller (New York: Fordham University Press, 2016).

# 2 Critical Phenomenology

Lisa Guenther

Phenomenology is a philosophical practice of reflecting on the transcendental structures that make the lived experience of consciousness possible and meaningful. It begins by bracketing the natural attitude, or the naive assumption that the world exists apart from consciousness and "reducing" an everyday experience of the world to the basic structures that constitute its meaning and coherence. The purpose of this reduction is not to abstract from the complexity of ordinary experience but rather to lead back (*reducere*) from an uncritical absorption in the world toward a rigorous understanding of the conditions for the possibility of any world whatsoever. The most basic of these conditions is the transcendental ego; there is no experience, and hence no meaningful experience, without *someone* who does the experiencing. This "someone" is not a bare cogito or "I think"; it is, in its most basic formulation, a relation or orientation of the thinker to the thought. In other words, the cogito is always already a cogito *cogitatum*; I do not just think, I think *thoughts*, feel *feelings*, remember *memories*, and so forth.

This discovery has consequences for how we understand ourselves as subjects. If I am not just a bare cogito, but the relation or orientation of an intentional act (thinking) to an intentional object (thought), then even at the level of absolute individuality, I do not exist as an isolated point, but rather as a vector or arrow that gestures beyond itself in everything it thinks and does. If we take this dynamic orientation as our philosophical starting point, then a range of seemingly intractable problems dissolve. It becomes nonsensical to wonder how the cogito gets outside itself to connect to a world or whether "other minds" exist, because the act of thinking always already implies a range of thoughts, the open horizon of which defines the phenomenological concept of world. Rather than bumping our philosophical heads against the bell jar of solipsism, classical phenomenology gives us a language to articulate the relationships without which we could not be who we are or understand what we experience. It lights up the transcendental structures that we rely upon to make sense of things but which we routinely fail to acknowledge. In other words, phenomenology points us in a critical direction.

But where classical phenomenology remains insufficiently critical is in failing to give an equally rigorous account of how contingent historical and social structures also shape our experience, not just empirically or in a piecemeal fashion, but in what we might call a quasi-transcendental way. These structures are not a priori in the sense of being absolutely prior to experience and operating the same way regardless of context, but they do play a constitutive role in shaping the meaning and manner of our experience. Structures like patriarchy, white supremacy, and heteronormativity permeate, organize, and reproduce the natural attitude in ways that go beyond any particular object of thought. These are not things to be seen but rather *ways of seeing*, and even ways of *making the world* that go unnoticed without a sustained practice of critical reflection. There is nothing necessary or permanent about these structures, and they don't even operate in stable, consistent ways across all contexts; even within a given historical moment, differently positioned subjects are likely to have divergent relations to overlapping structures. And yet these structures generate the norms of the lifeworld and the natural attitude of those who inhabit them. We overlook them at our peril, even if our project is transcendental, because they are part of what we must bracket to get into the phenomenological attitude.

The prospect of critical phenomenology[1] raises a number of questions: What, if anything, can phenomenology teach us about the lived experience of power and oppression and the role of quasi-transcendental social structures in shaping this experience? What would it take for phenomenology to become critical, not only of the naive assumption that the world exists apart from consciousness, but also of the naive assumption that one could give a rigorous account of consciousness without addressing the contingent social structures that normalize and naturalize power relations in any given world? And if phenomenology does become critical, what does it have to contribute to ongoing discourses and practices of social-political critique? Is critical phenomenology just catching up with these conversations, or can it open new and powerful directions for thought and action?

## Traces of Critical Theory in Phenomenology

A crucial difference between classical and critical phenomenology is the degree to which intentionality is understood as the *orientation* of an intentional act (noesis) toward an intentional object (noema), where noesis constitutes noema without being reciprocally constituted by it, or as a *relation* in which feedback loops interweave noetic processes with a noematic field and vice versa. Husserl takes the former position, Merleau-Ponty the latter. Husserl's account of the absolute priority of noesis allows him to argue that consciousness is not just "a little *tag-end of the world,*"[2] or an object that is causally determined by forces outside of itself. But his transcendental idealism leads Husserl to make some rather unhelpful claims for the project of critical phenomenology, such as his thought experiment that even if a "universal plague" had destroyed every other subject, leaving me utterly alone, I would still have access to "a unitarily coherent stratum of the phenomenon world" as "the correlate of continuously harmonious, continuing world-experience."[3] As the experience of people in solitary confinement suggests, even a relatively short period of extreme isolation from others has a profound effect on one's experience of the world as a "continuously harmonious" context for meaningful experience.[4] The capacity of material, historical changes in the world to affect not just *what* I perceive but *how* I perceive it, and even to erode my capacity to experience the world in a coherent, harmonious fashion, suggests that noesis is not absolutely prior to noema, but rather implicated in a complex reciprocity through which the world really can influence my capacity to perceive it.

The logic of "influence" here is not causal but conditional; to acknowledge the quasi-transcendental effect of the world on consciousness is not to reduce the latter to a tag-end of the former, but rather to acknowledge the concreteness of embodied Being-in-the-world as well as the agency of the world as an interhuman and more-than-human web of possibilities and tendencies. Merleau-Ponty's account of the *relation* between noesis and noema, and his later account of the chiasmatic structure of intercorporeal Being-in-the-world, offers a more promising starting point for critical phenomenology because it acknowledges the weight of the world without treating it as an inexorable determinative force. In other words, Merleau-Ponty shows how the world shapes consciousness, without depriving consciousness of the agency to shape the world in return. I don't think critical phenomenology can get off the ground without these two insights.

Once we have established a philosophical basis for acknowledging that contingent but persistent social structures influence our capacity to experience the world, not just in isolated instances but in a way that is deeply constitutive of who we are and how we make sense of things, we need to develop and refine a set of conceptual tools and methods for tracking this influence. Husserl's concepts of transcendental intersubjectivity and the lifeworld are useful here, as are Heidegger's account of mood, interpretation, and historicality and Merleau-Ponty's account of operative intentionality, body schema, intercorporeality, and perceiving according to others.

For example, the body schema is a useful concept for critical phenomenology because it plays a constitutive role in the emergence of meaning, and yet it remains historically contingent and open to reconfiguration in a way that an *eidos*, or essence, is not. For Merleau-Ponty, the body schema is not just an image in my mind of what my body looks like; it is a dynamic organizational matrix or template, both for my proprioceptive sense of embodiment and for embodied action. When I reach for my laptop or negotiate a curb on my bicycle, I rely on my body schema to perform the action; for the most part, I don't need conscious thought to do this. But I was not born typing on laptops; I had to learn, and the historical process of acquiring skills, incorporating technologies, and negotiating landscapes remains sedimented in my body schema as traces that are activated to various degrees. The body schema is not just a program that I run to accomplish tasks; it is a historical record of experience, context, emotion, taboos, and desires. As such, the body schema is an invaluable resource for critical phenomenology, not only as an archive of the natural attitude in particular lifeworlds, but also as the site of a dynamic process through which habits and norms are reconfigured.

In recent years, critical phenomenologists have developed, expanded, and reworked Merleau-Ponty's concept of the body schema to account for gendered and sexual schemas (Simone de Beauvoir, Iris Marion Young, Talia Mae Bettcher, Gayle Salamon), racialized schemas (Frantz Fanon, Lewis Gordon, Sara Ahmed, George Yancy, Alia Al-Saji), disability schemas (Kay Toombs, Lisa Diedrich, Havi Carel), and other aspects of embodied lived experience.

## Traces of Phenomenology in Critical Theory

Many thinkers write about experience. But what makes an account of experience phenomenological? More specifically, what makes it a useful resource for critical phenomenology? In her landmark essay, "Poetry Is Not a Luxury," Audre Lorde defines poetry as "a revelatory distillation of experience":

> The quality of light by which we scrutinize our lives has direct bearing upon the product which we live, and upon the changes which we hope to bring about through those lives. It is within this light that we form those ideas by which we pursue our magic and make it realized. This is poetry as illumination, for it is through poetry that we give name to those ideas which are—until the poem—nameless and formless, about to be birthed, but already felt.[5]

While Lorde does not identify her method as phenomenology, or even as philosophy, her reflections on experience offer a powerful inspiration for critical phenomenology. Her account of the "quality of light by which we scrutinize our lives" speaks to the conditions of critical reflection, both in the sense of a condition of possibility and also in the sense of an atmosphere or context that shapes what can be seen and how it is seen. For Lorde, the practice of critical scrutiny is motivated by the feeling of something that matters to someone, and it is in following this feeling and struggling to name it that poetry (and arguably philosophy) emerges. For Lorde, poetry is both a descriptive practice of illuminating and articulating one's experience and also a transformative practice of changing the conditions under which one's experience unfolds. The descriptive and transformative dimensions of this practice reciprocally invoke one another; there is no meaningful change without an interrogation of meaning, and yet the process of scrutinizing and naming one's experience already begins to change its meaning. A poetically expressed feeling is not the same as a nameless and formless one; when the quality of light by which we scrutinize our lives becomes an object of reflection itself, its quality has already started to change.

In phenomenological terms, we could think of this "quality of light" as the affective tonality or mood that both motivates and contours one's meaningful experience as an embodied Being-in-the-world. This affective tonality cannot be understood apart from one's social location in a specific historical lifeworld, and yet social location is not reducible to a causal or determinative force. For example, an affective investment in whiteness as property, whether conscious or unconscious, will bring a different quality of light to one's experience and generate a different understanding of the world, than a Black, Indigenous, or Latinx investment in abolishing white supremacy. But the structure of whiteness as property is not an inexorable destiny condemning white people to racism and absolving us of the responsibility to become otherwise. Rather, a critical phenomenology of whiteness inspired by Lorde's account of poetry would have to scrutinize the quality of light that illuminates the world from a white perspective and to name the feelings that motivate this perspective, with the hope of bringing about a change, not only in the structure of whiteness but in the shape of the world that white supremacy has built. This is poetry as illumination *and* transformation: a way of making otherwise inchoate but powerful feelings available for further scrutiny, not just as a process of individual introspection but as a collective practice of critical interrogation and social change. The emotional work of critical scrutiny is not just a matter of disinterested theoretical reflection; the meaning of our lives and the shape of our world depend upon this scrutiny, and it can be exhausting. There are many reasons to avoid or derail critical scrutiny, and yet the motivation to persist is also powerful, since the meaning and materiality of our lives is at stake.

There is much for an aspiring critical phenomenologist to learn from Lorde's account of poetry as "a revelatory distillation of experience." Lorde shares some core insights with classical phenomenology: namely, that experience is lived, that it presupposes a subject whose perspective matters, that this perspective is partial, and that it is both possible and necessary for a subject of experience to scrutinize or reflect on the meaning and motivation of its experience. But Lorde also moves beyond the descriptive agenda of classical phenomenology in ways that are instructive for critical phenomenology; reflection or critical scrutiny is not an end in itself for Lorde, but part of a process of moving from feeling to language to action, without leaving any of these moments behind.

## What Is Critical Phenomenology?

Critical phenomenology goes beyond classical phenomenology by reflecting on the quasi-transcendental social structures that make our experience of the world possible and meaningful, and also by engaging in a material practice of "restructuring the world" in order to generate new and liberatory possibilities for meaningful experience and existence.[6] In this sense, critical phenomenology is both a way of doing philosophy and a way of approaching political activism.

As a philosophical practice, critical phenomenology suspends commonsense accounts of reality in order to map and describe the structures that make these accounts possible, to analyze the way they function, and to open up new possibilities for reimagining and reclaiming the commons. It is a way of pulling up traces of a history that is not quite or no longer there—that has been rubbed out or consigned to invisibility—but still shapes the emergence of meaning.

As a political practice, critical phenomenology is a struggle for liberation from the structures that privilege, naturalize, and normalize certain experiences of the world while marginalizing, pathologizing, and discrediting others. These structures exist on many levels: social, political, economic, psychological, epistemological, and even ontological. They are both "out there" in the world, in the documented patterns and examples of hetero-patriarchal racist domination, and they are also intrinsic to subjectivity and intersubjectivity, shaping the way we perceive ourselves, others, and the world. In other words, they are both the patterns that we see when we study something like incarceration rates, and also the patterns *according to which* we see. As a transformative political practice, critical phenomenology must go beyond a description of oppression, developing concrete strategies for dismantling oppressive structures and creating or amplifying different, less oppressive, and more liberatory ways of Being-in-the-world.

In other words, the ultimate goal of critical phenomenology is not just to interpret the world, but also to change it.

## Notes

1. My approach to critical phenomenology is unrelated to Max Velmans's concept of the same name in "Heterophenomenology versus Critical Phenomenology: A Dialogue with Dan Dennett," *Cogprints*, 2001, http://cogprints.org/1795/. However, it does bear a resemblance to Michael Marder's account of critical phenomenology in *phenomena-critique-logos: The Project of Critical Phenomenology* (London; Rowman & Littlefield, 2014), and to anthropologist Robert Desjarlais's method of critical phenomenology in "Movement, Stillness: On the Sensory World of a Shelter for the 'Homeless Mentally Ill,'" in *Empire of the Senses: The Sensual Culture Reader*, ed. D. Howes (Oxford: Berg, 2005), 369–70.

2. Edmund Husserl, *Cartesian Meditations: An Introduction to Phenomenology*, trans. Dorian Cairns (Dordrecht: Kluwer Academic, 1991), 24.

3. Husserl, *Cartesian Meditations*, 93, 96.

4. I develop a critical phenomenology of solitary confinement in *Solitary Confinement: Social Death and Its Afterlives* (Minneapolis: Minnesota University Press, 2013).

5. Audre Lorde, *Sister Outsider: Essays and Speeches* (Berkeley, Calif.: Crossing Press, 2007), 37, 36.

6. Frantz Fanon, *Black Skin, White Masks*, trans. Charles Lam Markmann (New York: Grove Press, 1967), 82.

# 3 Bad Faith

Lewis R. Gordon

*Bad faith* has a colloquial and a philosophical history. They, in turn, offer two meanings. The first is linked to law. There, one could testify or enter a contract in bad faith, where the meaning involves entering agreements with false intentions. The second, philosophical meaning has a circuitous history emerging primarily through reflections from French existential philosophy. This is not to say that the phenomenon described in French existentialism was created by it. Chronicles of that form of bad faith are perhaps as old as mythic reflection.[1]

The philosophical form of bad faith addresses the problem of lying to oneself. Unlike the legal model, which involves a lie to others, the philosophical one does not require another being deceived. What is crucial is the focus on the self.

In existential phenomenology, which focuses on how problems of existence relate to those of consciousness, bad faith surfaces as a free act of consciousness. In phenomenological terms, consciousness is always *of* something. This is the intentionality view of consciousness. The something of which there is consciousness is that which appears. In existential terms, it stands out. This is, as well, what *existence* means, from the Latin *ex sistere*. To stand out is to emerge or to appear.

Turned back onto itself, the question posed to consciousness is whether consciousness appears. The problem is that consciousness must then become a thing, even though things are objects of consciousness. What kind of thing could consciousness be for it to be an object for itself? Existential phenomenologists, from Simone de Beauvoir and Jean-Paul Sartre through to others outside of the European tradition, such as Nishitani Keiji in Japan or Noël Chabani Manganyi and Mabogo P. More in South Africa, argue that consciousness is not a *thing*.[2] It is at best a relationship to things. This offers a core understanding of philosophical treatments of bad faith. It involves attempting to take consciousness out of the relationships through which things appear. Put differently, it's the imposition of nonrelationality onto relations.

The contradictory element of bad faith leads to many important observations. The first is that for consciousness to be of something, the thing must be *there* through which the relationship of being conscious of it is *here*. This here-there relationship means consciousness must be embodied. If it weren't so, it would be everywhere without a there or here through which to be anywhere. This means, then, that disembodiment is something to which we could commit ourselves only through denying the perspective or embodied standpoint from which we do so. It would be a form of bad faith.

One of the reasons French thinkers brought the concept of bad faith to the fore as an explicit philosophical problem is because of the subtlety of the expression in the French language. *Mauvais* means "false" or "worthless," and in the feminine, *mauvaise*, "bad." *Foi*, generally translated as "faith," also means "belief," "confidence," "pledge," or "trust." Thus, *la mauvaise foi* refers to a wide range of attitudes or dispositions that are not immediately apparent in the English expression "bad faith."

Bad faith, philosophically understood, is coextensive. It refers to a variety of distinct yet connected phenomena. Belief, for example, could be a manifestation of bad faith. To believe, instead of to know, requires an element of doubt. Yet in epistemology or theory of knowledge there is the notion of a true, justified belief or *perfect belief*. If it were perfect, however, it would have no reason for doubt and would thus not properly be belief. Such a version of belief collapses into bad faith.

There is a famous example Sartre offers in response to the phenomenalist, the proponent of there being no distinction between imagination and perception, ideas and things. He asks for the phenomenalist to count the columns of the imagined Parthenon versus doing so in the presence of the actual one. The number of the former is uncertain, whereas that of the latter is specific and certain. The agent creates the image of the imagined Parthenon; the real one resists what the agent may wish it to be.[3]

The ability to imagine, creating images, hints at a special ability of consciousness. The agency involved is an expression of freedom. It means that consciousness could always reach beyond what is given. This ability has many names in the philosophical literature, from *nihilating* to *transcending* to *taking flight*. The main thing is that it could reach beyond itself. It is thus responsible for whether it stands still or takes flight.

If it attempts to take flight from itself, consciousness does so through attempting to be what it isn't. This is paradoxical because the ordinary response—Then what is it, really?—doesn't work because that would require its being a thing. Even the possessive pronoun *its* is metaphorical here.

This philosophical insight leads to a variety of descriptions of bad faith. It is:

- an attempt to hide from responsibility
- an attempt to flee freedom
- an evasion of displeasing truths through investing in pleasing falsehoods
- an effort to believe what one does not believe
- an effort to see without being seen—that is, to be a perspective that cannot be seen
- an effort to be seen without seeing—that is, to be seen without a point of view
- an effort to be a thing
- an effort to flee responsibility for values
- an effort to become a god or Absolute

There are many famous examples associated with these manifestations of bad faith. Beauvoir and Sartre's famous one of the approached woman on a dinner date that's not supposed to be a date is one instance. Critics take the example as a negative judgment on the woman who disembodies herself as her suitor holds her hand.[4] They miss the point of the example. The point was to illustrate the capacity for *disembodiment*. In holding her hand, her suitor was outwitted by supposedly holding a thing, not her. In existential phenomenology, there is no separation of mind and body because consciousness, as having to be somewhere, is properly lived or "in the flesh." Thus, the approached woman must convince herself that her suitor is touching her hand but not *her*.

It would be a mistake to read the example of the approached woman as a *moral* allegory. There are, after all, conditions under which one would have good reasons to be in bad faith. It's not a good idea to be fully embodied during an experience of rape, for instance. The same applies to experiences of torture and trauma. Flight into the pleasing falsehood of "That's not being done to *me*" makes sense for the sake of survival. The approached woman, as I prefer to call her (instead of "coquette," as some critics have interpreted her actions), is an example whose many possibilities offer what Beauvoir calls "ambiguity."[5] The basic point of disembodiment reveals a philosophical point in which only part of a story is revealed.

We should ask, as well, about the suitor's experience of the hand he is holding. An important phenomenological insight is that one could experience another's disembodiment. He could *notice* her hand appears devoid of lived agency. This is an important observation because it brings to the fore a crucial element of bad faith. It is *social*. All of the examples Sartre offers in *Being and Nothingness* are such. The waiter who attempts to be a *waiter-thing* or object, the accuser who asks the homosexual to admit he is a homosexual, the champion of sincerity, all the way through to the sadists and masochists, dominating and possessive lovers, emerge in social relationships infected with an effort to undermine the conditions of what makes them possible. The lies that undergird what the characters in these examples assert are that they are things in some instances, ethereally disembodied in others. The problem is that "things" cannot be social. They are pure externalities. They are without points of view. Neither can pure subjects that see without being seen. Without the possibility of being a *there*, they cannot be a *here*. To be social, there must be intersubjectivity or communicated points of view.

We come, then, to the philosophical insight that the opposite of bad faith is not good faith, which is a form of sincerity, or "authenticity," which often appeals to a form of "wholeness," but, instead, critical relationships to *evidence* and, in the case of seriousness, play. Bad faith works if one can lie to oneself. To do so requires eliminating one's relationship to what makes lies appear as lies: evidence. One must disarm the evidentiality of evidence—that is, its ability to appear. Rendered impotent, evidence cannot interfere with our believing what we want to believe.

Philosophers and social theorists have used the concept of bad faith to describe a variety of social phenomena. In famously arguing one "becomes a woman," Beauvoir in *The Second Sex* inaugurated philosophical challenges to whether anatomy constitutes destiny.[6] The long line of debates through to the present appears in critical theoretical work that may at first not seem existential. Judith Butler transformed this question in

*Gender Trouble*, for instance, into the challenge of whether one must be a subject and a call to explore the possibility of agency without agents.[7]

Before Beauvoir, Friedrich Nietzsche interrogated this question of subjects by questioning the values through which they are made.[8] Taking responsibility for such values releases them from their "seriousness." Such seriousness, at times called the spirit of seriousness, is a form of bad faith. Nietzsche's transvaluation of values, or bringing value to our values, taking responsibility for them, is a rallying cry against bad faith. Additionally, seriousness, turned onto the self, collapses into taking oneself too seriously. Opposing bad faith there involves play in the sense of realizing agency at work in the construction of the rules through which life's games or values are played. Not taking ourselves too seriously entails, then, taking responsibility for and a mature attitude toward values and at least what we take to be ourselves.

Similar arguments emerged earlier in African diasporic philosophy and social thought as well. Richard Wright was a source of inspiration for Beauvoir.[9] He was part of a long line of African diasporic thinkers who observed the contradiction of whites identifying blacks and other racialized groups as human beings whose humanity they deny. Racism, understood in this way, is an attempt to flee the displeasing truth of systemic dehumanization of certain groups of human beings. Relatedly, W. E. B. Du Bois's formulation of double consciousness, where black people see themselves as what antiblack racist societies claim they "are," is similar to Nietzsche's argument about the materialization of values.[10] The spirit of seriousness is manifested in the notion of black people *being* problems. The moment of realizing they are human beings who face problems is transformative. Instead of being problems, they question the society that treats them as such. The sociologist and philosopher Paget Henry calls this *potentiated second sight*, which Jane Anna Gordon later expanded into *potentiated double consciousness*.[11] This critique of a society that makes people into problems requires identifying its contradictions. For instance, if the options of increased human relations are available to one group but are barred to another, expectations of equal outcomes become ludicrous. If the unfair options are presumed "natural" or "intrinsic," we are on the terrain of seriousness. Demonstrating the contradictions is a form of dialectical critique in that one moves from the self as a problem to the systemic sources of what affects how the self is constructed. Where the society denies culpability, the critique unveils societal bad faith. Frantz Fanon similarly argued that the black as understood in an antiblack society is a white construction and that a colonial and racist society is one that attempts to force human beings outside of human relationships.[12]

Peter Caws, in his work on structuralism, makes an observation similar to Fanon's in his analysis of Claude Lévi-Strauss's debate with Sartre.[13] Structuralism, as Caws sees it, is an acknowledgment of relationships and rules through which intelligibility results. It thus need not be incompatible with existential phenomenological thought since relations follow from distinctions. Lived reality is, in other words, relational. This argument is also the basis of Caws and other philosophers, this author included, arguing for the compatibility of Marxism, transcendental phenomenology, and existential thought. Existential Marxism and existential phenomenology are not oxymoronic because each is relational. They address alienation through arguing against the closing off of flourishing. Thinking, learning, doing, praxis, and all manifestations of *human living* require meaning, and those require being able to affect reality. Of course, there are many kinds of Marxism. Those that assert an ontological or reductive materialism, from this perspective, simply exemplify efforts to take freedom away from the struggle against human alienation. Material*ism* is, after all, as Sartre argued in his *Critique of Dialectical Reason*, a form of bad faith through the elision of a basic fact: matter in and of itself leaves no room for its conceptualization. To be a reductive materialist requires hiding the relations through which even matter becomes intelligible.[14]

More recently, the concept of bad faith is used as a diagnosis of bad disciplinary methodological practices. Where a discipline treats itself as the world, as all of reality, and its methods as "complete," its practitioners forget it's a human-created practice. This form of bad faith I call *disciplinary decadence*. Similar to the transvaluation of values, a response to it requires what I call a teleological suspension of disciplinarity. Put differently, practitioners of a discipline get into trouble when they take their discipline too seriously. Doing so takes it out of relations with reality. They turn their discipline inward into itself as the world and treat it as closed. In the human sciences, the result is asserting as problems those who do not "fit" the dictates of the discipline.

Another form of bad faith recently discussed in philosophical and social thought is imposed purity. Such a notion could emerge only by eliminating all external relationships, because they would be "contaminants," and retreating into sterile nonrelations. Impurity, however, follows from standing out and coming into contact with that which transcends the self. The human being, as a social being, is in a communicative enterprise that affects every relationship. Jane Anna Gordon and Michael Monahan refer to this communicative interactive relationship with reality as *creolization*.[15] It is to say that mixture is at every moment of communication and intention.

There are many other creative directions in which analyses of bad faith have been taken. For instance, in theology, the desire to become a god is one example. Although theologians advise against such hopes, because they are forms of idolatry, there is the problem of theodicy. In an effort to secure the goodness of the gods, the notion of a good or values beyond human comprehension is one instance. Another points to the notion of human beings as intrinsic sources of evil. The problem with both is that they fail to explore the implications of freedom.

If human beings are free, this means we have the capacity not only to commit terrible acts but also *not to do so*. As Fanon put it, we are not only a no but also a *yes*.

Second, as Sartre suggests, even if the gods or G-d exists, either would be a bad idea. The reasons are twofold. The first is logical: a complete incompleteness amounts to a full consciousness. Relations would collapse since there would no longer be something *of which to be conscious* because of the elimination of negations. The second is axiological. Human beings would still face whether to obey or disobey them, which makes them, Him, Her, or It ultimately irrelevant.

I should like to add, however, that Sartre's argument works only where the sacred is interpreted ontologically. The reader should notice, for example, my use of the Jewish formulation "G-d." Under that model, the fundamental point transcends Being. Indeed, the question of the openness of G-d as an obligation of humanity taking responsibility for the ethical face of reality is consistent with Nietzsche's and Sartre's challenge for human maturity.

Third, and finally, beyond the theological and theodicean is the basic question of freedom. Some critics claim bad faith is a useless concept since it appears impossible for human beings to avoid it or sustain not being in it.[16] The existential response is that such critics miss the point. The argument isn't that human beings must be in bad faith. It is that we cannot be free without our ability to attempt evading freedom. We are capable of being in bad faith because we are free. It doesn't follow that all our decisions would be done in bad faith. It only means we are responsible for the decisions we make. Radicalizing this philosophical insight, we learn also that such responsibility doesn't come from the "outside," as it were. This means we are also responsible for it. Freedom entails responsibility also for responsibility.

This brings us to a closing observation. Some critics of existentialism confuse freedom with an absence of constraints. This confuses human beings with gods. Freedom doesn't entail the ability to do whatever we wish, where desire, will, and deed become one without responsibility. That would be license. Instead, freedom involves taking responsibility for living in a world with others.

## Notes

1. I elaborate on much of the discussion offered here in such books as Lewis R. Gordon, *Bad Faith and Antiblack Racism* (Atlantic Highlands, N.J.: Humanities International Press, 1995), *Fanon and the Crisis of European Man: An Essay on Philosophy and the Human Sciences* (New York: Routledge, 1995), *Existentia Africana: Understanding Africana Existential Philosophy* (New York: Routledge, 2000), and *Disciplinary Decadence: Living Thought in Trying Times* (New York: Routledge, 2006). The reader should also consult Joseph Catalano's studies: *A Commentary on Jean-Paul Sartre's "Being and Nothingness"* (Chicago: University of Chicago Press, 1980), *A Commentary on Jean-Paul Sartre's "Critique of Dialectical Reason: Volume 1, Theory of Practical Ensembles"* (Chicago: University of Chicago Press, 1986), and *"Good Faith" and Other Essays* (Lanham, Md.: Rowman and Littlefield, 1996), and Gail Weiss, *Body Images: Embodiment as Intercorporeality* (New York: Routledge, 1998).

2. See Simone de Beauvoir, *The Ethics of Ambiguity*, trans. Bernard Frechtman (New York: Citadel, 2000); Jean-Paul Sartre, *Being and Nothingness: A Phenomenological Essay on Ontology*, trans. Hazel V. Barnes (New York: Washington Square Press, 1956); Nishitani Keiji, *Religion and Nothingness*, trans. Jan Van Bragt (Berkeley: University of California Press, 1982); Noël Chabani Manganyi, *Being-Black-in-the-World* (Johannesburg: Ravan Press, 1973) and *Alienation and the Body in Racist Society: A Study of the Society That Invented Soweto* (New York: NOK, 1977); and Mabogo Percy More, *Looking through Philosophy in Black: Memoirs* (London: Rowman and Littlefield International, 2018).

3. See Jean-Paul Sartre, *L'Imaginaire: Psychologie phénomenogique de l'imagination* (Paris: Gallimard, 1940).

4. See, e.g., Julien S. Murphy, ed., *Feminist Interpretations of Jean-Paul Sartre* (State College: Pennsylvania State University Press, 1999), and Margaret Simons, ed., *Feminist Interpretations of Simone de Beauvoir* (State College: Pennsylvania State University, 1995).

5. See Beauvoir, *The Ethics of Ambiguity*.

6. Simone de Beauvoir, *The Second Sex*, trans. Constance Borde and Sheila Malovany Chevallier (New York: Vintage, 2011).

7. Judith Butler, *Gender Trouble: Feminism and the Subversion of Identity* (New York: Routledge, 1990).

8. Friedrich Nietzsche, *On the Genealogy of Morals*, trans. W. Kaufmann and R. J. Hollingdale, introduction by W. Kaufmann (New York: Vintage, 1989).

9. See Beauvoir's concluding chapter of *The Second Sex*.

10. See W. E. B. Du Bois, "The Study of Negro Problems," *Annals of the American Academy of Political and Social Science* 11 (January 1898): 1–23 and *The Souls of Black Folk: Essays and Sketches* (Chicago: A. C. McClurg, 1903).

11. For "potentiated second sight," see Paget Henry, "Africana Phenomenology: Its Philosophical Implications," in *Journeys in Caribbean Thought: The Paget Henry Reader*, ed. Paget Henry, Jane Anna Gordon, Lewis R. Gordon, Aaron Kamugisha, and Neil Roberts (London: Rowman & Littlefield International, 2016), 27–58; for "potentiated double consciousness," see Jane Anna Gordon, "The General Will as Political Legitimacy: Disenchantment and Double Consciousness in Modern Democratic Life," Ph.D. dissertation, University of Pennsylvania, 2005, "The Gift of Double Consciousness: Some Obstacles to Grasping the Contributions of the Colonized," in *Postcolonialism and Political Theory*, ed. Nalini Persram (Lanham, Md.: Lexington Books, 2007), 143–61, and *Creolizing Political Theory: Reading Rousseau through Fanon* (New York: Fordham University Press, 2014). I offer discussion of varieties of double consciousness in many of my writings, but see *An Introduction to Africana Philosophy* (Cambridge, U.K.: Cambridge University Press, 2008), for summaries, especially 77–79 and 117. There is also the concept of "doubled double consciousness," as Nahum Dimitri Chandler formulates it in his *X—The Problem of the Negro as a Problem for Thought* (New York: Fordham University Press, 2014).

12. Frantz Fanon, *Peau noire, masques blancs* (Paris: Éditions du Seuil, 1952). For discussion, see Lewis R. Gordon, *What Fanon Said: A Philosophical Introduction to His Life and Thought* (New York: Fordham University Press, 2015).

13. Peter Caws, "Sartrean Structuralism?," in *The Cambridge Companion to Sartre*, ed. Christina Howells (Cambridge, U.K.: Cambridge University Press, 1992), 293–317 and *Structuralism: The Art of the Intelligible* (Atlantic Highlands, N.J.: Humanities International Press, 1988).

14. See Jean-Paul Sartre, *Critique of Dialectical Reason, Volume 1: Theory of Practical Ensembles*, trans. Alan Sheridan-Smith, ed. Jonathan Rée (London: Verso, 1991).

15. See Jane Anna Gordon, *Creolizing Political Theory* and Michael J. Monahan, *The Creolizing Subject: Race, Reason, and the Politics of Purity* (New York: Fordham University Press, 2011).

16. See some of the critical responses to Sartre's conceptions of bad faith and freedom in Arthur Schilpp, ed., *The Library of Living Philosophers: The Philosophy of Jean-Paul Sartre* (LaSalle, Ill.: Open Court, 1981). See as well Gabriel Marcel's *The Philosophy of Existentialism*, trans. Manya Harari (New York: Citadel, 1968).

# 4 Being and beings: The Ontological/Ontic Distinction

John D. Caputo

*Ontological Difference*. This expression refers to the distinction between Being (*Sein*) and beings (*Seienden*) in the work of Martin Heidegger. Tracking the fortunes of this expression provides a valuable insight into the development of Heidegger's work and, beyond Heidegger, into continental philosophy today, including the genesis of a post-theistic theology after the death of God. While the distinction is central to *Being and Time*, the expression itself does not appear there, evidently being reserved for "Time and Being," the famous missing part,[1] and ultimately yields to a more radical formulation in the 1940s.

Being and beings are distinct: Being is not a being—but not separate: Being is always the Being *of* beings, and beings are beings only *in* their Being. They belong together in a circular relation. Being is not a first being, like God. To God, as to every being, there belongs a proper Being, in virtue of which it appears. Being does not differ from beings ontically, as one being differs from another, but ontologically, as the condition under which beings appear. Without Being, no beings appear; when beings do appear, Being is not one of them.

Being is not the sum total of all beings but the horizon or framework within which beings are encountered, the "clearing" (*Lichtung*) where the light breaks through, the "open" where beings are "freed" or "released" into appearance. We say of Being not that it "is," but "there is" Being. Marking the difference between Being and beings puts a stress on language, which is oriented to beings and their ontical relationships. Anything we say about Being is prone to distortion, the way anything theologians say about God is prone to idolatry. This is a structural feature: Being of itself withdraws and we are inclined to be preoccupied with beings. This "forgottenness" or "oblivion" (*Vergessenheit*) of Being's difference from beings is an ontological not a psychological point. While Being remains out of explicit cognizance, it is implicitly presupposed. Thinking Being makes the implicit explicit, re-cognizing it, recollecting it.

The ontological difference is *phenomenological*, concerned with how beings are given and with the ontological sense of truth (disclosedness), where phenomenology means letting (*legein*) the things that appear in the light (*phainomena*) appear. It is *hermeneutical*, since any given understanding of Being determines whether beings appear *as* this or that. It is *transcendental*, in both the *Aristotelian* sense that Being crosses over all the regions of beings, and the *Kantian* sense, where Dasein's understanding of Being provides the condition under which phenomena (beings) are possible. In "What Is Metaphysics?" (1929), Heidegger exploits the paradoxes that his line of thinking invites. Since Being is *not* a being, this *not* is no thing, hence "nothing," and Dasein's transcendence means to be stretched out into (the) Nothing. This essay aroused the ire of Rudolph Carnap, whose attack—along with the "Nazi affair"—forever scorched Heidegger's reputation in Anglo-America.

*Regional Ontologies.* But Carnap was mistaken. Positivism proved to be epistemologically bankrupt, while the ontological difference proved to be immensely fertile. The various disciplines, like physics and history, are organized under "basic concepts," understandings of the Being proper to their field, which are the subject of the "regional ontologies." The advances that take place *inside* the regional field without disturbing the prevailing framework (ontic changes) differ from more radical changes in the basic concepts themselves (ontological shifts). This distinction cuts across *all* disciplines—Luther in theology, Einstein in physics—and undercuts the old divide between the *Geisteswissenschaften* and the *Naturwissenschaften*.[2] Thomas Kuhn's theory of the revolutionary change occasioned by (ontological) "paradigm shifts" effectively confirmed Heidegger's analysis, one of the most important insights afforded by the ontological difference.

Beyond the "regional ontologies" lies the question of the meaning of Being as such, the subject of "fundamental ontology." This introduces a third thing: beings, their Being, and its "meaning," which is called the "upon which of a projection," a time-function which fixes the parameters of the projection of the Being of beings. For example, the distinction between time and eternity is itself a time-function, taking its lead from (is "projected upon") the "now." Eternity is conceptualized as an unchanging now, and time is conceived as a flowing now, a moving image of the changeless now. "Eternity" is not timeless; it is the effect of temporalizing in terms of the now. Hence, the "meaning of Being" is *time*. That is an *ontological* not an *ontic* determination; it is a *transcendental* answer, not a transcendent one. It explains how the understanding of Being is formally constituted, and it does not offer material content to the meaning of Being, like saying Being is God or the One.

*Two Ontological Differences.* Max Müller reports a first draft of "Time and Being" which distinguishes *two* forms of the ontological difference: (1) "the '*transcendental*' or ontological difference in the narrow sense: the difference of beings from their beingness [*Seiendheit*, abstracted, universalized is-ness]"; (2) "the '*transcendentish*' (*transcendenzhafte*) or ontological difference in the wider sense: the difference of beings *and* their beingness from Being itself."[3] Heidegger's path of thought is a search for this third thing, the root of the ontological difference, variously named Being itself, or *Seyn* (with a y), or Being crossed out, or Being's "unconcealment." Müller further reports a third difference:

(3) "the '*transcendent*' or theological difference in the strict sense: the difference of God from beings, from beingness and from Being." The discourse on God takes place entirely outside the jurisdiction of the ontological difference in either sense. Heidegger might have meant what Husserl meant, that God is simply transcendent to phenomenological experience, or what Luther (whose work Heidegger knew well) meant, that God chose what is not (*ta me onta*) to reduce to nothing the things that are (1 Cor:18–31). Never mention "God" and "Being" in the same breath.

*Being and Time* is largely confined to working out the difference between the Being of Dasein, whose Being (*Wesen*) is "existence" (*Existenz*), and its ontical (*existentiell*) characteristics. That caused huge confusion. The French assumed that *was* the ontological distinction, and, after the war, Heidegger became the guru of French "Existentialism," remarkably despite his association with National Socialism.

*Ontotheology*. By 1940,[4] the ontological difference came to constitute the very metaphysics which it is the task of thinking to overcome. Metaphysics reduces Being to some version of beingness—*eidos, ousia, actus*—but the difference as such, "infinitely different from Being,"[5] is left unthought. "Difference" is then detached from the expression in order to think the differing *itself*, the Dif-ference (*Unter-Schied*) or the *Austrag*. *Austrag*, ordinarily meaning the issue of a decision, literally translating the Greek *dia* + *phorein* and the Latin *dif* + *ferre*, "to carry off," "to carry out," describes the ontological circle. Being is carried over or "comes over" (to) beings (*Überkommnis*), thereby un-concealing (*ent-bergend*) beings in their Being, even as beings arrive or "come-into" Being (*Ankunft*) while concealing Being. Being and beings "are borne away from and toward each other" (*auseinander-zueinander-tragen*).[6] Metaphysics is the issue of the *Austrag*, itself unthought. Thinking takes the "step back"—as opposed to Hegel's step up (*Aufhebung*)—into this unthought Dif-ference, which "sends" (*Geschick, schicken*) Being to beings, the "event" (*Ereignis*) which "gives" Being (*es gibt*) to beings.

Metaphysics is onto-*theo*-logical. In ontotheology, *logos* degenerates into *ratio* and *Grund*, an explanatory ground. Being provides the common ground of beings (ontology), while the supreme being supplies the causal ground of other beings (theology). To the God who enters the onto-theo-logical circle, the *causa sui*, "humanity can neither pray nor sacrifice," "neither fall to its knees in awe nor play music and dance." A "god-less thinking" would be closer to "the truly divine God (*dem göttlichen Gott*) than onto-theologic would like to admit." [7] The truly divine God is not the crucified God (Luther) but (Christianity a thing of his prewar past), the God of the poets, Hölderlin's Greek divinities.

*Tillich's Ground of Being*. A god-less atheism closer to the truly divine God is a perfect introduction to the theology of Paul Tillich, for whom the Supreme Being is a "half-blasphemous and mythological concept" to which "atheism is the right religious and theological reply."[8] For Tillich, God is not a being (ontic) but Being itself, the inexhaustible (ontological) "ground of Being" from which beings emerge and into which they pass away. The blasphemy is to reduce Being itself to a being; the mythology is to think God an inscrutable super-person. Atheism about the *causa sui* is not the end of theology but the beginning—of a post-theistic, pan*en*theistic God-in-all and all-in-God (the circularity between Being and beings described by Heidegger). For Tillich, the ontological difference *is* (or *absorbs*) the theological difference, because God is Being itself, showing the way out of idolatry. For Karl Barth—twentieth-century theology divides between Tillich and Barth—the ontological difference *is* idolatry, to which theology is a sustained *Nein!* God is not contaminated by Being; the ontological difference is *abolished* by the theological difference.

For Tillich religion is a matter of ultimate (unconditional) concern. God is the ground that sustains us, the Being surmounting nonbeing that gives us the *courage to be*. That is our faith—and our ontology. Religion in this *ontological* sense can be found *wherever* human beings engage themselves unconditionally ("authentically")—in art or science, politics or personal life—and differs from religion in the ordinary sense of the confessional bodies (*ontical* and regional), thereby displacing the usual "regional" distinction between the religious and the secular. Religion is a matter not of finding an ontic stranger but of overcoming our *ontological estrangement* from God, "in whom we live and move and have our being."

*Derrida and Différance.* If Barth's neo-orthodoxy faced backward and Tillich was forging a religion for the postmodern world, it remained for Derrida to uproot Tillich's residual German idealist metaphysics. For Derrida, linguistic difference is the most formal difference, constituted by the sheer "differential space" between signifiers. The ontological difference is one difference among many (dialectical, transcendental, sexual,[9] etc.); it is a "signified," an effect produced by a rule-governed use of signifiers. *Différance* signifies not an effect of the linguistic system but its constituting, transcendental condition.[10] Because the Derridean "little a" in *différance* can only be seen not heard, exploiting both spatial-visible spacing (differing) and temporal-audible spacing (deferral), *différance* is prior to both, a kind of archidifference (archiwriting). This is not mysticism but antiessentialism. *Différance* is not the truly divine God. "Being" and "God" are constituted textual effects, always recontextualizable not stable essences, yet ever subject to the pressures of sedimentation. The process of de-sedimentation is called "deconstruction." In Derrida, Heidegger's "destruction" of "the history of ontology" on the basis of the ontological difference becomes the "deconstruction" of the "metaphysics of presence," on the basis of *différance*.

The theological implication is not (Christian Neoplatonic) negative theology but a (quasi-Jewish) messianic without a Messiah, a structural ("ontological") expectancy, whatever the ("ontic") historical context. The effect of *différance*, putting pressure on any purportedly stable presence, is to keep the future open, pressuring it to the limits of the possible, to the possibility of *the* impossible. In early Heideggerian terms, deconstruction tracks the disruptive pressure exerted by the ontological upon the ontic. The opposite of deconstruction is to arrest this unrest (which is truly destructive). The Messiah means the coming of what we cannot see coming, the "event" (*événement, l'à venir*) shattering the horizon of expectation. "God" is one of the best names for the possibility of the impossible itself, which demands a faith (*foi*) in an event irreducible to any doctrinal belief (*croyance*). This constitutes an underlying (ontological) "religion without (ontical) religion," found wherever the inbreaking possibility of the impossible may break out.

*Post-theistic Theology*. Like Tillich's, Derrida's religion is not an onticoregional but an underlying ontological category, concerned with an "unconditional" that can be found anywhere. Any given (ontical) order is inwardly and structurally exposed to ontological disturbance, made restless by the expectation and memory of something unconditional. Augustine's ontically "restless heart" (*cor inquietum*) is made restless by an ontological desire. Every restlessness is an ontico-ontological disturbance. But unlike Tillich, where the unconditional is an ontological ground, which buoys up beings in their Being, Derrida takes a *second* and decisive step. The ground becomes a groundless ground, no longer ontological but "hauntological," belonging to the order not of Being but of the call or the promise. The *ontological difference* becomes the *hauntological difference*. The unconditional is not a *Geist* but a ghost, not a Spirit but a specter, the issue of the in/stability of *différance*, of the *memory* and the *promise* lodged in a complex legacy, without *ontological* support. We are disturbed by a dif-ference, an uncanny (*unheimlich*) visitor, an unanticipatable *tout autre*. This "unconditional without sovereignty" is neither a being nor Being itself, neither finite nor infinite. It does not exist; it insists, it calls for existence. The promise is a pure promise, exposed in all its powerless power, without a panentheistic ground, without theistic omnipotence to protect it.

This theology, coming after the death of God,[11] descends from the ontological difference in two steps: (1) the ontologization of the ontic (Tillich): God as the First Being yields to the ontological ground of being, demythologizing the Supreme Being; religion as an onticoregional category yields to being-seized by something of unconditional depth; (2) the de-ontologization of the ontological (Derrida): the spectralization of the ontological ground of being in favor of the unconditional call without sovereign authority. Radical theology is "weak" theology coming after the death of both an omnipotent theistic super-being and a deep ground of being, a theology not of the Almighty but of the might-be, a theology of the event, of the dangerous perhaps (Nietzsche). Weak does not mean anemic but the weakening of Being into may-being, not spineless indecision but a weak messianic force (Benjamin), where the Messiah cannot change the past but the meaning of the past. Post-theistic theology is a spectralization of the ontological difference.

## Notes

1. It first appears in print in Martin Heidegger, "On the Essence of Ground" (1928), in *Martin Heidegger: Pathmarks*, ed. William McNeill (Cambridge, U.K.: Cambridge University Press, 1998), 105; it was first announced in a 1927 lecture course, Martin Heidegger, *The Basic Problems of Phenomenology*, trans. Albert Hofstadter (Bloomington: Indiana University Press, 1978), 227–30. Both texts are projected versions of "Time and Being."

2. Martin Heidegger, *Being and Time*, trans. John Macquarrie and Edward Robinson (New York: Harper & Row, 1962), 28–31 (§3).

3. Max Müller, *Existenzphilosophie im Geistigen Leben der Gegenwart* (Heidelberg: Kerle Verlag, 1964), 67.

4. Martin Heidegger, "The Ontological Difference," in *Nietzsche*, Vol. 4: *Nihilism*, trans. David Krell (New York: Harper & Row, 1993), 150–59; "The Onto-theo-logical Constitution

of Metaphysics," in *Identity and Difference*, trans. Joan Stambaugh (New York: Harper & Row, 1969), 42–76.

5. Martin Heidegger, "Der Spruch des Anaximander," in *Gesamtausgabe*, Vol. 5: *Holzwege*, ed. F.-W. von Herrmann (Frankfurt/Main: Klosterman, 1977), 364 note d.

6. Heidegger, *Nietzsche*, 155.

7. Heidegger, *Identity and Difference*, 72.

8. Paul Tillich, *Theology of Culture* (Oxford: Oxford University Press, 1959), 25.

9. In "Geschlecht I: Sexual Difference, Ontological Difference," trans. Ruben Berezdivin, *Research in Phenomenology* 13, no. 1 (1983): 65–83, Derrida showed the difficulty Heidegger had in maintaining the sexual neutrality of the ontological difference.

10. Jacques Derrida, "Différance," in *Margins of Philosophy*, trans. Alan Bass (Chicago: University of Chicago Press, 1982), 1–27.

11. While I am describing my own idea of "weak theology," comparably radical views are found in varying ways in Richard Kearney, Catherine Keller, Emmanuel Levinas, Jean-Luc Marion, Mark C. Taylor, Gianni Vattimo, and Slavoj Žižek. For two complementary surveys, see Christina Gschwandtner, *Postmodern Apologetics?* (New York: Fordham University Press, 2013), and Graham Ward, ed., *The Postmodern God* (Oxford: Blackwell, 1997). See also the comprehensive *The Palgrave Handbook of Radical Theology*, eds. Christopher D. Rodkey and Jordan E. Miller (Cham, Switzerland: Palgrave MacMillan, 2018).

# 5 Being-in-Itself, Being-for-Itself, and Being-for-Others

Kris Sealey

In *Being and Nothingness*, Jean-Paul Sartre grounds his phenomenology of the human in three basic structures: (1) being-in-itself, (2) being-for-itself, and (3) being-for-others. The first, being-in-itself, describes that which is void of self-consciousness (or what we might understand as a capacity to be self-aware). This would include those inert objects that populate our world: chairs, computers, trees, the ocean. The "in" in the "being-in-itself" is meant to convey that fullness of being is actually *in* these inert objects. They are full of what they are and, as a consequence, cannot be anything other than what they are.

Being-for-itself would be (as the name suggests) a kind of being that can be *for* itself, that can be aware of itself. For Sartre, this mode of being captures the human. As human beings, we possess a kind of reality that allows us to turn around, as it were, to face ourselves. In that move, we are (oddly enough) never *in* ourselves but always outside of ourselves in order to reflectively encounter who we are. This self-reflective encounter means that our existence in the world is always coupled by an *awareness* of ourselves existing in the world. This capacity for self-reflection is important for Sartre's phenomenological account, since he identifies this as the very structure (or foundation) of human freedom. Unlike a "being-in-itself" (the chair, the ocean, a tree) that can be only what it is, a "being-for-itself"—a human being—is not tethered to her being in a way that compels her to be permanently one thing. Being-for-itself can be *more than* or *other than* who I currently am, since I can choose to be more than or other than who I currently am. For Sartre, being-for-itself is the structure of the human, because the structure of the human is its capacity for choice (or freedom to choose).

Being-for-others adds complexity to this structure of human freedom, primarily because humans must enact their freedom in a world that is populated by other free humans (and shaped through their collective choices). Sartre writes that my freedom is inseparable from what he names my "being-for-others"—the meanings that my embodied existence takes on for the other. The fact that I must grapple with, in some shape or form, a being that I have *for* the other is what Sartre wants to convey by naming this "being-for-others" as the third structure of his phenomenological account of the human.

In what follows, I situate Sartre's phenomenological analysis of our being-for-others alongside Fanon's account of the lived experience of the colonized in *Black Skin, White Masks*. Specifically, I discuss the ways in which Fanon's exposition of this condition demonstrates a certain failure in the phenomenology of being-for-others (at least insofar as it has been developed by Sartre). In particular, there are moments in Fanon's analysis (particularly in the fifth chapter of *Black Skin, White Masks*) that call to mind a Sartrean analysis of the look, and of shame, in order to underscore the sense in which this Sartrean account fails to capture the phenomenological moments particular to the condition of the colonized.

Fanon addresses this in a footnote toward the end of the fifth chapter of *Black Skin, White Masks*: "Though Sartre's speculations on the existence of The Other may be correct . . . their application to a black consciousness proves fallacious. This is because the white man is not only The Other but also the master, whether real or imagined."[1] In this way, Fanon's analysis of the lived experience of the black is always already politicized, or at the very least connected to a cultural horizon that is not acknowledged in Sartre's *Being and Nothingness*. The difference between the Sartrean and the Fanonian account seems relevant to what it might mean to bring phenomenology's method to bear in critical ways. Can a structure like Sartrean being-for-others capture a colonially constituted intersubjectivity, such that being-for-itself and being-for-the Other continue to be meaningful across the power differential of racism and imperial epistemology? Elena Flores Ruíz's delineation of the important differences between European and decolonial existentialism is helpful here, insofar as it describes the "methodological racism"[2] of the phenomenological method, whereby the failure to account for the multiplicities of human conditions is coded in the very conceptual tools deployed. Though her analysis pertains specifically to existentialism, a meaningful analogy can be drawn to phenomenology since phenomenology also presupposes certain truths about the world, about our encounter with others in the world, and about what it means to be a subject in the world, which simply do not hold in the context of colonial domination. Ruíz writes, "Since we do not choose the social matrix into which we are born, there is a certain amount of alienation (as self-estrangement) that is required for socialization. . . . Yet what is distinctive about this kind of basic grounding alienation is that it . . . establishes a kind of *continuity* of experience that is not present in the colonized subject's experience of being thrown into the world."[3] Fanon's engagement with Sartre's conception of being-for-itself not only underscores similar methodological presuppositions but also opens up avenues through which to think about an alternative (and perhaps decolonial) phenomenology. My hope is that through the following engagement between Fanon's and Sartre's accounts, the possibility of a critical phenomenology might emerge.

As noted earlier, Sartre shows that the for-itself structure is always already mediated through its being-for-others. Alongside my apprehension of the meaningful world that I create for myself, I also exist concretely in the world of *other* consciousnesses, all of whom are engaging in the same negating transcendence of being. For Sartre, the most original apprehension of my being for the Other is through the experience of shame, which is the experience of being looked at, in order to be judged, by the Other.[4] In the section of *Being and Nothingness* devoted to "The Look," Sartre describes shame as a "non-positional" self-consciousness through which I "[realize] an intimate relation of myself to myself."[5] As nonpositional, the object of one's shame-consciousness is not encountered as an object of knowledge, which is to say, I cannot *know* the version of myself encountered in the moment of shame. At the same time, there is a gap of sorts, between the nonpositional shame-consciousness, which does the encountering (on the one hand) and the self that is encountered (on the other). This "gap that does not facilitate a relation of knowledge" will be important for Sartre's determination of shame and, ultimately, for his determination of the truth of consciousness's being-for-others.

Before the other's look, I acquire an exteriority through which the other apprehends me as an object in her world. Though mine, this exteriority is not for me (the way my world is for me), but rather for the other. "Thus I, who in so far as I am my possibles, am what I am not and am not what I am—behold now I am somebody!"[6] Though my being-for-the other means that I am this "somebody" for him, in his world I am alienated from this version of myself, given that its source lies "on the outside," from and for the Other. However, despite this estrangement, my being-for the Other is nonetheless my being, and the self that I am for the other is ultimately "me."

On this reading, it may seem that the empty structure of consciousness as "no-thing" or as pure intentional activity is compromised by its being inhabited by a self (the self that is *for* someone else). However, on Sartre's account, this doesn't seem to undermine the fundamental truth of consciousness's structure, which is that it is a transcendence of (and in) being. The look of the Other serves as a "mediator between me and myself."[7] Across such mediation, I am able to recognize who I am in a world with others. In other words, despite my being-for-others having its source in the other (or outside of me), I am able to apprehend it, give it meaning, include this being-for-others in *my* network of a meaningful world. So, despite the alienation in discovering myself to be endowed with meaning that I didn't choose, my being-for-others is an integral part of my experience of myself and the world. For this reason, Sartre asks us to understand the moment of shame (the moment in which I encounter that truth) as ultimately a "confession"[8]—the truth of who I am as a free transcendence of being remains right alongside this other truth, "that I *am* as the Other sees me."[9]

On this account, given in terms that are abstracted from colonial power structures that make for a racialized comportment in the world, recognition across intersubjectivity is a necessary component of human freedom. Through this recognition, human freedom is existentially meaningful in a world with others. However, when applied to recognition across racialized bodies (as Fanon does), my being-for-others signifies as a mechanism for oppression that does not make freedom meaningful. Rather, it radically limits human freedom.

Drawing on Fanon, Ruíz describes the experience of alienation in noncolonial existential contexts as follows:

> [The] "self" in European existentialism is a very different self than the one in decolonial existentialism. In the former there exists a whole self within a life story who is perhaps fragmented, dislocated, and estranged by the conditions she finds herself in, but there is still a there-ness to her narrative identity that can engage in critical

> introspection and narrative repair through articulating and rearticulating her life story (to herself and others) with tools that show up as tools and do not further alienate her.[10]

In this description of a noncolonial experience of alienation, Ruíz captures the ways in which certain fragmentations and ruptures brought on as a consequence of discovering oneself with meaning given by the other do not undermine one's fundamental sense of grounding in the world. This noncolonial account of intersubjectivity has it that my being-for-others is *integral* to my transcendence as a being-for-itself, and not destructive of it. The "continuity of experience" Ruíz references is a continuity that protects the integrity of the structure of being-for-itself. Despite my being-for-others, I continue to be "precisely the one by whom there is a world."[11] In the fifth chapter of *Black Skin, White Masks*, Fanon powerfully shows that this is not the case in the lived experience of the colonized and racialized subject.

In his foreword to *Black Skin, White Masks*, Homi Bhabha describes Fanon's phenomenological account as a "colonial depersonalization."[12] In determining the possibility of a critical phenomenology, it is important to raise the question of colonial depersonalization alongside the structure of consciousness's being-for-others put forth by Sartre. In other words, do Sartre's descriptions of how my being-for-itself is invaded by meaning constituted by (and *for*) the other capture the depersonalization structuring the colonial experience of being looked at? In reading the fifth chapter of *Black Skin, White Masks*, it becomes clear that, as racialized in the political context of colonial representation, the lived experience of the colonized calls for something more than the relationship given to us by Sartre, that is, the relationship between being-for-itself and being-for-others. In the colonial context, the colonized subject does not encounter herself as "the one by whom there is a world." Rather, Fanon shows us that the world she encounters—the "white world, the only honorable one"[13]—is a world that is constituted by and for the white colonizer. The meaning of a lived experience of colonial depersonalization must start from there.

Fanon writes that this white world "barred [him] from all participation."[14] As such, the mediating game between consciousness and the other, through which I am able to discover myself (my being-for-others) before the look, is precisely the game the colonial power matrix reserves for whites. This power matrix constructs the racialized other as a depersonalization that does not participate. It is for this reason that Fanon describes such lived experiences not in terms of inferiority, but rather in terms of nonexistence: "A feeling of inferiority? No, a feeling of nonexistence."[15] What this means is that the lived experience of the colonized calls on phenomenology to generate a fourth conceptual framework alongside being-for-itself, being-for-others, and being-in-itself. The feeling of nonexistence proposed by Fanon points to a zone of nonbeing. Out of this zone, the racialized and colonized consciousness navigates its being-for-others, and it is upon this *colonial* negation that the racialized other is barred from all participation.

Framed as such, the colonized black encounters something heavier than shame before the other when confronted by the look of the white colonizer. He finds a strangeness that is much stranger than the alienation that structures Sartre's phenomenological account. Under the weight of this strangeness, Fanon determines that this racialized other encounters himself and the world across a "racial epidermal schema," and not the "corporeal schema" that might facilitate a transcending relationship between being-for-itself and its body. In the racial epidermal schema, we find a phenomenological structure that is always already politicized. It necessarily includes the cultural framework out of which the lived experience in question emerges. In other words, the political and cultural determinations of colonial domination are inseparable from the lived experience that Fanon describes. "[He] was hated . . . not by the neighbor across the street or [his] cousin on [his] mother's side, but by an entire race."[16] Hence, the eyes from which the look reaches Fanon are explicitly political and are "the only real eyes"[17] in the colonial scheme of things.

This intimacy between lived experience and the political might account for the heaviness of what the colonized encounters in himself before the look of the white colonizer. It might also account for the fundamental strangeness of that encounter as well. Whereas I discover that I am a "somebody" before the other's look, according to Sartre's account, Fanon discovers that he is "battered down by tom-toms, cannibalism, intellectual deficiency, fetishism" and "woven . . . out of a thousand details, anecdotes, stories."[18] In these descriptions, there is a fullness of being, brought on by the look of the colonizer. How might we understand this fullness within the frame of colonial depersonalization? Does this fullness make Fanon a "somebody" for the little child on the train who cries to his mother, "Look at the nigger! . . . Mama, a Negro"?[19]

In these concrete descriptions, Fanon conjures the idea of the racialized consciousness as a fullness that is nevertheless (and quite significantly) empty. Before the Look, Fanon does not become the "purely established transcendence [or the] given transcendence" that he would have become in Sartre's account.[20] The lived experience of the colonized is such that he is never a transcendence to begin with. Hence, according to Ruíz, Fanon's task, the task of the colonized, is to "[work] one's way out of alienation as a dehumanized object that is not yet even an alienated subject,"[21] not yet even a "given transcendence."

In her work *Black Looks*, bell hooks writes that "for black people, the pain of learning that we cannot control our images, how we see ourselves . . . or how we are seen is so intense that it rends us. It rips and tears at the seams of our efforts to construct self and identity."[22] The pain that hooks describes here replaces the continuity of experience assumed in the Sartrean conception of my being-for-others. In other words, there is no continuity of experience for Fanon when, upon being looked at, he finds himself in "triple person . . . responsible at the same time for [his] body, for [his] race, for [his] ancestors."[23] That for which Fanon is called to be responsible—himself in these three registers—breaks him up (he references processes of amputations and excisions to give meaning to his being-for-others). It is not simply a matter of being alienated from his being for the other, but of being ripped and torn apart (to return to hooks's words) so that no one remains who might experience alienation. Torn asunder in a zone of nonbeing, Fanon *doesn't* encounter his being-for-others, because his freedom (his being-for-itself) is permanently stalled in the context of colonial violence. Hence, when Fanon writes, "All I wanted was to be a man among other men," we see what is most fundamentally violating in colonial domination.[24] We see, in this violence, conditions for the impossibility of being-for-itself.

Fanon's analysis in *Black Skin, White Masks* offers us a critical phenomenology. His deployment of the structures of being-for-itself, being-in-itself, and being-for-others is, indeed, phenomenological. But through their application in the colonial context, Sartre's categories are strained by their failure to account for the experience of the colonized. We might see this strain in terms of the failure of Sartre's account to apply universally. However, this strain also indicates, more positively, the need for critical applications of phenomenology's concepts. That is to say, in using the phenomenological method critically, we are called to be vigilant of certain unwarranted assumptions we might make about what it means to be human and about the breadth of experiences available to the condition of being human. Given that this vigilance is undermined when we become blind to the plurality of ways in which encounters with power determine the meaning of "being human," a critical phenomenology inevitably calls for an intersectional phenomenology. Criticality comes out of a multidimensional and heterogeneous understanding of the human. To be sure, this intersectional way of engaging phenomenology must be open-ended, available always to take on the strain of some other lived experience excluded by a provincial (and not sufficiently critical) analysis. Ultimately, this is the safeguard we possess against provinciality masking itself in the universal.

## Notes

1. Frantz Fanon, *Black Skin, White Masks*, trans. Charles Ian Markmann (London: Pluto Press, 1986), 138.
2. Elena Flores Ruíz, "Existentialism for Postcolonials: Fanon and the Politics of Authenticity," *APA Newsletter/Hispanic Issues in Philosophy* 15, no. 2 (Spring 2016): 19–22.
3. Ruíz, "Existentialism," 20.
4. Sartre notes that this moment of shame is not dependent on the actual presence of looking eyes. Rather, it is the possibility that my actions (indeed, my very being in the world) is looked at by another consciousness that brings on the experience of shame.
5. Jean-Paul Sartre, *Being and Nothingness: An Essay on Phenomenological Ontology*, trans. Hazel E. Barnes (New York: Philosophical Library, 1956), 221.
6. Sartre, *Being and Nothingness*, 263.
7. Sartre, *Being and Nothingness*, 221.
8. Sartre, *Being and Nothingness*, 261.
9. Sartre, *Being and Nothingness*, 222.
10. Ruíz, "Existentialism," 20.
11. Sartre, *Being and Nothingness*, 257.
12. Fanon, *Black Skin, White Masks*, xi.
13. Fanon, *Black Skin, White Masks*, 114.
14. Fanon, *Black Skin, White Masks*, 114.
15. Fanon, *Black Skin, White Masks*, 139.
16. Fanon, *Black Skin, White Masks*, 118.
17. Fanon, *Black Skin, White Masks*, 115.
18. Fanon, *Black Skin, White Masks*, 112, 111.
19. Fanon, *Black Skin, White Masks*, 113.

20. Sartre, *Being and Nothingness*, 262.
21. Ruíz, "Existentialism," 19.
22. bell hooks, *Black Looks, Race and Representation* (Boston, South End Press, 1992), 3–4.
23. Fanon, *Black Skin, White Masks*, 112.
24. Fanon, *Black Skin, White Masks*, 112.

# 6 Being-toward-Death

Mark Ralkowski

It is not an exaggeration to say that "being-toward-death" (*Sein zum Tode*) is the most important concept in Heidegger's *Being and Time*. As John Haugeland has argued, "Death . . . is not merely relevant but in fact the fulcrum of Heidegger's entire ontology."[1] There are at least two reasons for this. First, it sheds light on the ontological structures of Dasein, disclosing its "futurity" and finitude. Second, it is crucial to the text's analysis of authenticity (*Eigentlichkeit*), Heidegger's problematic nonmoral ideal, which itself brings together several other important concepts in Heidegger's philosophy (e.g., guilt, thrownness, anxiety, projection, anticipation, and resoluteness). However, to say that "death" is important to Heidegger's thought is not to say that its meaning is undisputed. As a matter of fact, there is a lot of scholarly disagreement about what exactly he meant by "death" and "being-toward-death."[2] One reason for this confusion is Heidegger's technical use of the words *death* (*Tod*) and *dying* (*Sterben*), which he distinguishes from related words such as *demising* (*Ableben*) and *perishing* (*Verenden*). Our challenge here is to understand what it means to say that "death is a way to be, which Dasein takes over as soon as it is" (245).[3]

Heidegger sets up his discussion of death by suggesting that Dasein can become whole only through authentic being-toward-death. This follows from the fact that Dasein's care structure is partly characterized by "being-ahead-of-itself"—we are always reaching out beyond ourselves and our circumstances toward open possibilities; as long as we are making choices and engaged with projects, our life stories are incomplete. "The 'ahead-of-itself,' as an item in the structure of care, tells us unambiguously that in Dasein there is always something *still outstanding*. . . . As long as Dasein *is* as an entity, it has never reached its 'wholeness.' But if it gains such 'wholeness,' this gain becomes the utter loss of Being-in-the-world" (236). We *are* our possibilities. Heidegger says Dasein is "being-possible" (*Möglichsein*) and an "ability-to-be" (*Seinkönnen*) because "it *is* existentially that which, in its potentiality-for-being, it is *not yet*" (145). Our essence is to be incomplete and open toward a future. The moment all of our possibilities are closed and there is no longer anything still outstanding in our lives, we are no longer Dasein (*nicht-mehr-Dasein*) (236). *Authentic* Being-toward-death solves the problem of wholeness, not by actualizing all of our possibilities, and not by ending our life stories prematurely, but by enabling us to achieve a kind of integrity in our way of being that is compatible with our "thrown projection" and makes us capable of "existing as a *whole ability-to-be*" (264).

Heidegger distinguishes between *dying, demising,* and *perishing* because he wants us to see (1) that the end of a human life is different from the end of an animal's or plant's life, and (2) that *death* refers to neither of these endings; it is one of Dasein's possibilities. All other creatures perish, but when Dasein's life comes to its end "it does not simply perish" (247); it loses a world (of meanings, projects, and relationships) and concludes a life story—this permanent loss of a world and conclusion of a life story is what Heidegger calls *demise*. Death, by contrast, is "a way to be" (245); it is "the possibility of no-longer-being-able-to-be there"; it is "the possibility of the absolute impossibility of Dasein" (250). Heidegger calls "death" Dasein's "uttermost" possibility because it shapes *every other possibility,* rendering them finite, and it determines the significance of our choices because it means they are adding up to something—they are shaping a life story—rather than opening on to other possibilities indefinitely. Whether or not we acknowledge it, our lives are *always* structured by death because our possibilities are "determined by the *end* and so are understood as finite [*endliche*]" (264).[4] Our possibilities are *ending-* or *terminal*-possibilities. This is true when we make our choices while lucidly aware of our finitude, but it is also true when we are in the "mode of evasion" that characterizes our everyday being-in-the-world (254). As Heidegger suggests famously, we flee death constantly and in any number of ways, including when we treat it as a future event, i.e., when we reduce "death" to "demise" and treat it as something we will eventually have to deal with, rather than as the possibility that shapes *all of our possibilities*. This "constant *fleeing in the face of death*" is what Heidegger calls "falling" (*Verfallen*), and "falling" is our default state (it is an existential structure of our being), which means our everydayness is shaped by inauthentic being-toward-death. We lose ourselves in the everyday social world because we are fleeing from the task of selfhood that authentic being-toward-death discloses.

"Falling" allows us to ignore the fact that our lives are adding up to something, because it encourages us to focus on the instrumental reasoning of the everyday. Instead of giving our lives unity and direction by taking ownership of them, we do "what one does"; we go with the flow of *das Man,* allowing ourselves to be dispersed in practical tasks, unreflectively satisfying the "manipulable rules and public norms" of "the They" (288).[5] But this means we lose sight of *ourselves*: "everyone is the other, and no one is himself" (128). In rare moments, we can be returned to ourselves by an experience of anxiety (*Angst*), which disrupts the tranquility of the everyday world by emptying it of its usual significance and meaning. In these moments, none of our projects or commitments makes sense to us anymore, and we see that we are committed to roles prescribed to us by *das Man*. As the author of Ecclesiastes says, looked at from this point of view, life appears to be nothing more than the "vanity of vanities" (1:2), one means-ends strategy after another. We experience our *worlds collapsing*: "the world has the character of completely lacking significance" (186), and we are reintroduced to ourselves as self-interpreting beings with fundamental choices to make: "Anxiety thus takes away from Dasein the possibility of understanding itself, as it falls, in terms of the 'world' and the way things have been publicly interpreted. Anxiety throws Dasein back upon that which it is anxious about—its authentic potentiality-for-Being-in-the-world. Anxiety individualizes Dasein for its ownmost Being-in-the-world, which as something that understands, projects itself essentially upon possibilities. Therefore, with that which it is anxious about, anxiety discloses Dasein *as Being-possible*" (187–88). Anxiety gives us a kind of self-knowledge because it brings us "face to face with the world as world" (i.e., as the source of possibilities that we must appropriate and update for ourselves) (188), and "it brings Dasein back from its falling, and makes manifest to it that authenticity and inauthenticity are possibilities of its Being" (191).[6] In these rare moments, we experience ourselves as we really are—we see our "naked Dasein . . . the pure 'that-it-is' of our ownmost individualized thrownness" (343)—because the experience of world collapse makes us feel "uncanny" (*unheimlich*), like we don't really belong in the world, *and yet we continue* (now unsuccessfully) *to project ourselves into the possibilities it opens up for us*. We are "thrown back upon" ourselves and "individualized" (188) by this anxiety. It takes the world away from us, not letting us flee into the publicly approved "anyone" roles of *das Man*, and in doing so it discloses our "being-possible," showing us that, *as Dasein*, we must *decide* our existence by "seizing upon or neglecting" (*Ergreifens oder Versäumens*) our possibilities (12).[7]

Heidegger says famously that "real anxiety" is not about anything in particular (like a job interview or a difficult conversation); it is about our "being-in-the-world as such" (186). We are anxious over the fact that we must make something out of our finite lives, and that we must do so without any guidance from nature or the structure of the self.[8] Our choices are life-shaping; they are essential in defining who we are and what we think life is all about—*and yet we have no basis for them*: Dasein is the "null basis" of a "null projection" (287). We can never *fully* justify our choices, and so our projects, commitments, and roles—in short, our identities and sense of meaning and purpose in life—are constantly vulnerable to being undermined by anxiety, which "is always latent in being-in-the-world" (189). What authentic being-toward-death does is *maintain* this anxiety (266),[9] and so it is *anxiety about death* that brings us back from our falling and individualizes us (263). In doing so, it also shows us that while we can never give a full justification for our lives or choices, because there is no human telos to follow, we can ensure that our lives are *our own*.

By making our choices in the light of death, we see their full significance (they are shaping a life) and recognize their ultimate baselessness (we cannot account for them). This doesn't necessarily cause us to change the *contents* of our lives (298), although it could lead to that—e.g., a change of career, lifestyle, or relationship. But it does involve a transformation in *the way* we understand and live our lives. When Dasein owns up to its finitude, "stands before itself" (287), is individualized "down to itself" (263), and recognizes the inescapability of death *as a possibility*, it "shatters all one's tenaciousness to whatever existence one has reached" (264). We are freed from our complacent acceptance of "those possibilities which may accidentally thrust themselves upon one, and one is liberated in such a way that for the first time one can authentically understand and choose among the factical possibilities lying ahead" (264). Living this way is risky, since one's grip on the world is much weaker than we like to pretend: the anticipation of death "opens [Dasein] to a constant threat arising out of its own 'there'" (265)—one's world is *always* on the verge of collapse, and one is always at risk of losing everything.[10] But Heidegger also thinks we can give our lives a clarity, intensity, and direction that they ordinarily lack when we "run ahead into" (*Vorlaufen in*) death. "Once one has grasped the finitude of one's existence," he suggests, "it snatches one back from the multiplicity of possibilities which offer themselves as closest to one—those of comfortableness, shirking, and taking things lightly" (384). We become "free for [our] ownmost possibilities, which are determined by the end" (264), and so we truly become what we are: free, world-disclosing beings who must take a stand on ourselves, and then have our lives defined by that stand.[11]

This is why death is a way of living for Heidegger. The possibility of death is ineluctable; it structures our lives, making all of our possibilities finite. When we anticipate death, we relate to our possibilities as "determined by the end," which allows us to reflect on ourselves and our situations from the perspective of "the 'nothing' of the possible impossibility of [our] existence" (266). We see what our lives are adding up to and recognize our responsibility in authoring those stories. This is both liberating and anxiety-inducing. It is liberating because it frees us from our complacency and from the "dimmed down" possibilities afforded us by *das Man* (194–95). And it is anxiety-inducing because it discloses the contingency of our commitments and identities. There is no *single* right thing to do or life to live; there aren't any absolute standards for us to follow. Human life is shaped by a constant vulnerability *to world collapse* that calls for resoluteness and promises "an unshakeable joy" (310) to those who listen to the call of conscience and "run ahead into" death.

The concept of being-toward-death has been the subject of scholarly controversy for many decades. Hubert Dreyfus lays out some of these interpretations in his foreword to Carol White's *Time and Death: Heidegger's Analysis of Finitude.*[12] Some of these authors implausibly turn "death" into "demise," treating death as the end of a human life and ignoring Heidegger's efforts to distinguish "demise" from the existential "death" of Dasein;[13] others interpret death to mean either the closing down of possibilities[14] or the paralysis of Dasein's "ability-to-be" in rare experiences of profound anxiety;[15] a third group treats death as a structural feature of Dasein's being[16] and interprets "dying" as "the resigned, heroic acceptance of this condition";[17] a final pair of scholars equates death with the kind of world-collapse that characterizes *a culture* when it undergoes an epochal change in its understanding of being, which allows these authors to connect *Being and Time* with Heidegger's later thought and argue for unity and development in Heidegger's philosophy as a whole.[18] Many of these views do not capture Heidegger's idea of death *as possibility*, or of "being responsible for the task of making something of our lives"[19] while accepting existence in "its finitude" (384).

One of the most fruitful developments of Heidegger's concept of being-toward-death is in Iain Thomson's article "Heidegger's Perfectionist Philosophy of Education in *Being and Time*," where he unearths an implicit "perfectionist" philosophy of education in Heidegger's account of the self's return to itself in authenticity. On this view, Heidegger adopted Aristotle's teleological framework for thinking about the human essence (according to which human life is structured by purposes), and then used it to develop his analytic of Dasein, in which *Eigentlichkeit* replaces *eudaimonia*. For Aristotle, the greatest human fulfillment comes from perfecting *nous* (intellect); for Heidegger,

Dasein's greatest fulfillment is conceived of "practically, in terms of an embodied stand—'authenticity'—that each of us is capable of taking on our own being."[20] Authenticity is made possible by anticipatory resoluteness, one of Heidegger's "metavalues,"[21] and "names a double movement in which the world lost in anticipation is regained in resolve, a (literally) *revolutionary* movement by which we are involuntarily turned away from the world and then voluntarily turn back to it, in which the grip of the world upon us is broken in order that we may thereby gain (or regain) our grip on this world."[22]

The goal of education in this sense is to bring the self back to itself in a "transformative journey," one that first turns us away from the everyday world in an experience of anxiety, and then turns "us back to this world in a more reflexive way."[23] As Heidegger says in his 1940 essay on the allegory of the cave, "Plato's Doctrine of Truth," "real education lays hold of the soul itself and transforms it in its entirety by first of all leading us to the place of our essential being [i.e., the *Da* of our *Sein*] and accustoming us to it."[24] It involves "leading the whole human being in the turning around of his or her essence."[25] If Thomson is right, Heidegger thought of education as a kind of "secular conversion," one that (1) reintroduces us to the task of selfhood and (2) teaches us to recognize and challenge the nihilistic ontotheology of our age.[26] And if *that* is right, being-toward-death is not just the fulcrum of Heidegger's ontology. It is essential to any philosophy of the good life, and *death* is one of our most important educators, because when it is embraced and anticipated, it teaches us *how to live with our ineluctable anxiety* and use it to *make our lives our own*.

## Notes

1. John Haugeland, "Truth and Finitude: Heidegger's Transcendental Existentialism," in *Heidegger, Authenticity, and Modernity: Essays in Honor of Hubert L. Dreyfus*, vol. 1, ed. Mark Wrathall and Jeff Malpas (Cambridge, Mass.: MIT Press, 2000), 44.

2. For examples of these differences, see Jean-Paul Sartre, *Being and Nothingness: A Phenomenological Essay on Ontology*, trans. Hazel E. Barnes (New York: Citadel Press, 2001); Paul Edwards, *Heidegger's Confusions* (New York: Prometheus, 2004); Herman Phillipse, *Heidegger's Philosophy of Being: A Critical Interpretation* (Princeton, N.J.: Princeton University Press, 1998); Piotr Hoffman, "Death, Time, History: Division II of *Being and Time*," in *The Cambridge Companion to Heidegger*, ed. Charles B. Guignon (Cambridge, U.K.: Cambridge University Press, 1993); Michael Zimmerman, *The Eclipse of the Self: The Development of Heidegger's Concept of Authenticity* (Athens: Ohio University Press, 1986); Stephen Mulhall, "Human Mortality: Heidegger on How to Portray the Impossible Possibility of Dasein," in *A Companion to Heidegger*, ed. Hubert L. Dreyfus and Mark A. Wrathall (Oxford: Blackwell, 2005); Charles B. Guignon, "Authenticity, Moral Values, and Psychotherapy," in Guignon, *The Cambridge Companion to Heidegger*; William J. Richardson, *Through Phenomenology to Thought* (New York: Fordham University Press, 2003); Taylor Carman, *Heidegger's Analytic: Interpretation, Discourse, and Authenticity* (Princeton, N.J.: Princeton University Press, 2003); William Blattner, "The Concept of Death in *Being and Time*," *Man and World* 27 (1994): 49–70; Haugeland, "Truth and Finitude"; Julian Young, *Heidegger's Philosophy of Art* (Cambridge, U.K.: Cambridge University Press, 2001); Carol J. White, *Time and Death:*

*Heidegger's Analysis of Finitude*, ed. Mark Ralkowski (Aldershot, U.K.: Ashgate, 2005); Carol J. White, "Heidegger on Death: A Deflationary Critique," *The Monist* 59, no. 2 (April 1976): 161–86; Carol J. White, "Dasein, Existence, and Death," *Philosophy Today* 28 (Spring 1984): 52–65; John Richardson, *Heidegger* (London: Routledge, 2012); Iain Thomson, "Heidegger's Perfectionist Philosophy of Education in *Being and Time*," *Continental Philosophy Review* 37 (2004): 439–67; Iain Thomson, "Death and Demise in *Being and Time*," in *The Cambridge Companion to Heidegger's* Being and Time, ed. Mark A. Wrathall (Cambridge, U.K.: Cambridge University Press, 2013). For an overview of these interpretive differences, see Dreyfus, foreword in White, *Time and Death.*

3. Unless otherwise noted, all of the parenthetical citations in this entry refer to the German pagination given in the margins of Martin Heidegger's *Being and Time*, trans. J. Macquarrie and E. Robinson (New York: Harper & Row, 1962).

4. As W. J. Richardson (*Through Phenomenology to Thought*, 75) puts this crucially important point, Dasein "already is what it can-be, hence what it not-yet-is, sc. its end. Since the potentiality of There-being includes already interior to itself in existential fashion its end, then the death of There-being must be described not as a being-at-its-end . . . [this is demise] but as the Being-unto-end . . . of There-being, indicating thereby that the end always penetrates the whole existence."

5. For further discussion of Heidegger's concept of *Das Man*, see Nancy Holland's essay in this volume, "The They."

6. As Heidegger says, "resoluteness is what first gives authentic transparency to Dasein" (299).

7. This is Stambaugh's translation. See Martin Heidegger, *Being and Time*, trans. Joan Stambaugh (Albany, N.Y.: SUNY Press, 1996), 10. One's "naked Dasein" is what and who one is "when stripped of all modifications and associations with others, left to the empty individuality of a being whose only characteristic is to-be-in-the-World" (W. J. Richardson, *Through Phenomenology to Thought*, 73).

8. As W. J. Richardson (*Through Phenomenology to Thought*, 73) says, Dasein is anxious "about the complete indetermination of the world." The structure of Dasein might suggest that authenticity is the deepest fulfillment of our being, as Thomson ("Heidegger's Perfectionist Philosophy of Education in *Being and Time*") suggests, but authenticity does not give us guidance on *what* to choose; it guides us only, if at all, in *how* we make our choices—namely, by running ahead into death. It is up to us, and the "disclosive projection" of our resolution (298), to figure out what to do and who to be.

9. Heidegger says anxiety "holds open the utter and constant threat to itself arising from Dasein's ownmost individualized Being" (265–66) because anxiety is *about* death (the death that is inscribed in the being of Dasein)—"being-towards-death is essentially anxiety" (266).

10. As Haugeland ("Truth and Finitude," 352) puts this point, "authentic Dasein faces up to and takes over the ultimate *riskiness* of its life as a whole—it lives resolutely as and only as *vulnerable*."

11. See Hubert L. Dreyfus, *Being-in-the-World: A Commentary on Being and Time, Division I* (Cambridge, Mass.: MIT Press, 1991), 23. As Guignon ("Authenticity, Moral Values, and Psychotherapy," 283) puts the point, "it is by taking a stand on one's life as a whole that one satisfies Pindar's counsel to 'become what you are.'"

12. Dreyfus, *A Companion to Heidegger*, ix–xxxvi.

13. See the previously cited works by Sartre, Edwards, and Phillipse.

14. Carman, *Heidegger's Analytic*, 282.

15. Blattner, "The Concept of Death in *Being and Time*," 314. Iain Thomson develops a version of this view in the two articles cited above. As he says, "this strange experience of being in a way in which we are not able to be anything is precisely what Heidegger calls *death*" ("Death and Demise in *Being and Time*," 281). This is an illuminating account of *Angst*, but it is not the "death" that we are anxious about in anticipatory resoluteness. That would mean we were anxious about anxiety, which leads to a regress. As we have seen, for Heidegger death is "the possibility of the *impossibility* of Dasein" (250, emphasis added; cf. 266), whereas in an experience of *Angst* Dasein is *still being-possible*; it is still Dasein. It just cannot connect to any of its projects or commitments. Dreyfus, Carman, Balttner, and Thomson are correct not to conflate "death" and "demise," but death *as a possibility* is not demise. As Heidegger says, "we must characterize Being-towards-death as a *Being towards a possibility*. . . . In such Being-towards-death this possibility must not be weakened; it must be understood *as a possibility*, it must be cultivated *as a possibility*, and we must *put up with* it *as a possibility*" (261).

16. See Young, *Heidegger's Philosophy of Art*, 127–34.

17. Dreyfus, *A Companion to Heidegger*, xxxi.

18. See the previously cited works by Haugeland and White.

19. See Guignon, "Authenticity, Moral Values, and Psychotherapy," 282. Which is why Carman (*Heidegger's Analytic*, 271–79) and Dreyfus (*A Companion to Heidegger*, xviii, xxxi) are wrong to include Guignon in their critiques of interpreters who mistake "death" for "demise." The interpretation presented in this entry is closest to Guignon's ("Authenticity, Moral Values, and Psychotherapy"), J. Richardson's (*Heidegger*), and W. J. Richardson's (*Through Phenomenology to Thought*).

20. Thomson, "Heidegger's Perfectionist Philosophy of Education in *Being and Time*," 447.

21. See Guignon, "Authenticity, Moral Values, and Psychotherapy," 283. Like Thomson, Guignon finds a special kind of virtue "ethics" in *Being and Time*, despite Heidegger's insistence that he isn't making value judgments. He suggests that *Eigentlichkeit* is made possible by certain character traits, such as resoluteness, steadiness, courage, integrity, openness to change, and "above all, clear-sightedness about one's own life as a finite, thrown projection." These character traits don't point toward any particular moral values—e.g., they don't tell us to be a liberal or a conservative—but they do guard against self-deception, and Dasein's historicity points beyond atomistic liberal individualism by reminding us of our communal and historical context, the source of our possibilities for self-interpretation. As J. Richardson (*Heidegger*, 168) says, authenticity appears to be a "second-order value, which has indirect authority over other values, via that acid test of anxiety."

22. Thomson, "Heidegger's Perfectionist Philosophy of Education in *Being and Time*," 456.

23. Thomson, "Heidegger's Perfectionist Philosophy of Education in *Being and Time*," 457.

24. Martin Heidegger, "Plato's Doctrine of Truth," in *Pathmarks*, ed. William McNeill (Cambridge, U.K.: Cambridge University Press, 1998), 167.

25. Heidegger, "Plato's Doctrine of Truth," 166.

26. Thomson develops this second point in his book *Heidegger on Ontotheology: Technology and the Politics of Education* (New York: Cambridge University Press, 2005). See especially chapters 3 and 4.

# 7 Borderlands and Border Crossing

Natalie Cisneros

## Theorizing Borderlands: Introduction and History

Though the popularity of border studies in the academy has increased in recent years, with the formation of new journals, conferences, and academic programs, theoretical work on the lived experience of border crossing has existed both inside and outside of the academy for decades. Indeed, since at least the 1960s, the identities, practices, and experiences of border spaces have been explored by Chicana/o activists, organizers, artists, and writers. These thinkers have over this time developed distinctive and diverse theoretical frameworks and methodologies for theorizing their own lived experiences of borders and border crossing.[1]

Chicana feminists in particular have led the way in conceiving of borderland as both an object and a site of theoretical practice.[2] Indeed, feminist border thinkers have for decades been philosophizing about existence on the borderlands, despite the great difficulty of theorizing experiences that "often fell outside the dominant cultural constructions of selfhood or normative identity."[3] Indeed, though feminist border thought emerged in and through progressive movements of the 1960s, the lived experiences of Chicanas required different theoretical frameworks and political practices than were offered by either Anglophone feminist movements or racial justice movements dominated by cisgendered men.[4] Chicana feminism has often been marginalized relative to two of the major spaces that these movements gave birth to within the U.S. academy: Chicano studies and women's studies.[5] As a result, the long and complex tradition of feminist border thought has frequently gone unacknowledged in mainstream academic spaces.

The history of theorizing borderlands and border crossing is, thus, a history of a kind of doubly precarious theoretical practice; at the same time that dominant languages and ways of knowing have rendered the lived experiences of borderlands inarticulable, the work of creating new theoretical frameworks and linguistic practices has often not been documented or cited (even as it has sometimes been appropriated by mainstream feminist theory).[6] It is from this site of doubled precarity that Chicana feminist work on borderlands has emerged and evolved not as a unified theory but as "a series of conversations and overlapping political, literary, scholarly and artistic movements."[7] There is, therefore, no single theoretical conception of borderlands or border crossing, but instead a dynamic and long-standing tradition of theorizing these lived experiences from a multiplicity of perspectives and through a variety of forms. Theorizing done from the borderlands is often based in "contentious confrontation" rather than consensus.[8]

In what follows, I focus on a contribution to these doubly precarious, contentious conversations that has been particularly generative within Chicana feminism and influential beyond it: Gloria Anzaldúa's *Borderlands/La Frontera*. This text has been cited more than many others in the field and has influenced scholarship across a wide variety of disciplines, including Chicano/a studies and feminism, as well as American studies, literary studies, queer theory, and cultural theory.[9] *Borderlands*, along with Anzaldúa's other work, has also inspired and informed activists and organizers in the decades since its publication in 1987.[10] Accordingly, I reflect on some of the central conceptual, methodological, and political contributions of *Borderlands* in order to point toward the significance of this text for the possibility of addressing lived experiences that have been largely marginalized within the phenomenological tradition. Ultimately, I suggest that the conceptual frameworks, theoretical methodologies, and political practices that characterize Anzaldúa's work on borderlands and border crossing are inextricably linked. That is, in order to account for lived experience in the borderlands, it is necessary not only to understand particular concepts but also to engage in specific methodological and political practices. Ultimately, for Anzaldúa, theorizing borderlands and border crossing demands a rethinking of what it means to "study" or account for lived experiences on the border and elsewhere.

## Conceptualizing Borders and Borderlands

In *Borderlands/La Frontera*, Anzaldúa offers a new conceptual framework for understanding identities, experiences, and spaces that have been occluded by dominant theoretical frameworks. Alongside her more widely known theories of "Borderlands" and "mestiza consciousness," she develops many other theories throughout *Borderlands* and her later work, including "autohistoria/autohistoria-teoría," "Nepantla," "La Facultad," "El Mundo Zurdo," "conocimiento," the "Coyolxauhqui imperative," "Nos/Otras," and "spiritual activism."[11] While I focus here on *Borderlands*, and in particular on how Anzaldúa theorizes borderlands and the experiences of crossing borders and dwelling in the borderlands—including her conception of "mestiza consciousness"[12]—it is important to note that many of these concepts are closely related to one another and that "the boundaries between them are fluid, at times blurring into each other."[13]

Anzaldúa begins to explain her theory of borderlands in the first line of her preface to the first edition of the text: "The actual physical borderland that I'm dealing with in this book is the Texas–U.S. Southwest/Mexican border."[14] On Anzaldúa's account, then, borderlands should be understood as physical, historical, and geopolitical spaces. Indeed, this text explicitly centers on Anzaldúa's own lived experiences as well as the experiences of those most affected by the violent settler colonial, imperialist, and neoliberal forces that have constituted these border spaces: indigenous people, migrants, immigrants, and other Tejanos and Chicanos. Anzaldúa describes the U.S.-Mexico border as an open wound, "una herida abierta where the Third World grates against the first and bleeds," and it is through this hemorrhaging that a "third country—a border culture" is formed. The literal, physical border between these two states creates a liminal space, and this "place of contradictions" is the subject of Anzaldúa's reflections in this text.[15]

While she roots her theory of borders, border crossing, and border culture within a particular time and space, Anzaldúa's theory of the borderlands also goes beyond this specific political and physical border between states. For Anzaldúa "borderlands are physically present wherever two or more cultures edge each other, where people of different races occupy the same territory, where under, lower, middle and upper classes touch, where the space between two individuals shrinks with intimacy." She thus conceives of multiple kinds of intersecting and overlapping spaces, including psychic, spiritual, and sexual borderlands. Although these borderlands are not coextensive with those formed by the more literal U.S.-Mexican border, these other borders also have real physical, historical, and geopolitical presence for those who live in and through them. It is in this sense that Anzaldúa characterizes borders in general as instruments of division that "are set up to define the places that are safe and unsafe, to distinguish *us* from *them*." Though there exist important differences among the borderlands that she theorizes, all of the borders that she describes in this text divide and render particular bodies—including Anzaldúa's own body—unsafe. The borders between nations, as well as classes, genders, races, and spiritual practices, are, for Anzaldúa, all unnatural boundaries, and the borderlands that are created in their wake are tense, unstable, violent, and even deadly places.[16]

## Theorizing Border Consciousness: The New Mestiza

Anzaldúa coins the term "new mestiza" in order to theorize her own lived experiences of many different and overlapping border spaces.[17] Drawing on—and critically rereading—the concept *mestizaje*, or racial mixing, she conceives of the "new mestiza" as a form of identity that results from crossing over or passing through borders. While there are many different kinds of borders, and thus many different ways to "cross over, pass over, or go through the confines of the normal," Anzaldúa's theory of the mew mestiza emphasizes how cultural, ethnic, racial, sexual, and gender borderlands overlap and intersect with one another for Chicanas living on the U.S.-Mexico border in particular.[18] At the same time, Anzaldúa's account of the new mestiza is meant to capture the experiences of those who live outside of this particular physical and geopolitical space, but whose identities are constituted by other borders, like those that circumscribe gender and sexuality. As Mariana Ortega notes, neither of these aspects of the mestiza identity can be jettisoned, as doing so either narrows Anzaldúa's account to the Chicana experience or leads to the "erasure of the importance of the actual conditions of those who inhabit the borderlands."[19]

The new mestiza experiences the borderlands as a "risky home," a place of contradictions, characterized by "hatred, anger, and exploitation," but also "certain joys."[20] Central among these joys, according to Anzaldúa, is a new form of consciousness. Like W. E. B. Du Bois's conception of "double consciousness," mestiza consciousness is characterized by a unique awareness of the functions of power that construct this form of subjectivity. In the case of mestiza consciousness, this means that those who are constituted as abnormal transgressors have gained a tolerance not only for duality but for multiplicity and ambiguity.[21] That is, by virtue of her identity as a border crosser, the new mestiza "can't hold concepts or ideas in rigid boundaries." As a result she has a "more whole perspective," and her thinking resists binaries that structure dominant ways of knowing, including subject-object, normal-abnormal, and English-Spanish.[22]

It is from this perspective, from Anzaldúa's situatedness in a place of contradictions, that her account of borderlands, border crossing, and border consciousness in *Borderlands* emerges: "This book, then, speaks of my existence, My preoccupations with the inner life of the self, and with the struggle of that Self amidst adversity and violation; with the confluence of primordial images; with the unique positionings consciousness takes at these confluent streams; and with my almost instinctive urge to communicate, to speak, to write about life on the borders, life in the shadows."[23] Anzaldúa's painful and complex lived experiences as a "border woman" inform—and make possible—her theoretical work in *Borderlands*. Her existence in the liminal space of the borderlands compels her to sketch the contours of this reality and of the violent bordering forces that constitute it. In doing so, she makes visible forms of violence, as well as sources of creativity that dominant ways of knowing relegate to the shadows. And it is through theorizing the lived experiences of border dwellers that the new mestiza resists the very borders that constitute her as abnormal, transgressive, and forbidden.

In a way resonant with the Chicana feminist tradition within and from which she writes, in *Borderlands/La Frontera* Anzaldúa demands a rethinking of what counts as knowledge and of what the practice of theory looks like. Throughout the text, she makes clear that accounting for the lived experiences of borderlands and border dwellers means resisting dominant ways of seeing, describing, understanding, and knowing. And because the borders she describes are often drawn through literal and symbolic violence, the project of theorizing mestiza consciousness is a political practice of survival. For Anzaldúa, then, the process of seeing, describing, and understanding borderlands, border crossing, and border consciousness is an always already political project.

## Notes

1. Adela de la Torre and Beatriz M. Pesquera, eds., *Building with Our Hands: New Directions in Chicana Studies* (Berkeley: University of California Press, 1993), 1; Elena Ruíz, "Feminist Border Thought," in *Routledge International Handbook of Contemporary Social and Political Theory*, ed. Gerard Delanty and Stephen P. Turner (London: Routledge, 2013),

352; Aída Hurtado, "Sitios y Lenguas: Chicanas Theorize Feminisms," *Hypatia* 13, no. 2 (May 1, 1998): 149, https://doi.org/10.1111/j.1527-2001.1998.tb01230.x.

2. Hurtado, "Sitios y Lenguas," 149; Torre and Pesquera, *Building with Our Hands*, 1. Elena Ruíz marks an important distinction between "border thought," a term used to describe Walter Mignolo's conceptual framework which is rooted in world-systems analysis and "feminist border thought," which originated in and through the beginning of the Chicano/a movement of the 1960s. Following Ruíz both terminologically and conceptually, my present discussion of borderlands and border crossing focuses on the central contributions of feminist border thought in "articulating the complex workings of intersectional oppression such as race, class, gender, and ethnicity on women of color" ("Feminist Border Thought," 352).

3. Ruíz, "Feminist Border Thought," 352.

4. Ruíz, "Feminist Border Thought," 352; Chéla Sandoval, "The Struggle Within: A Report on the 1981 N.W.S.A. Conference," in *Making Face, Making Soul/Haciendo Caras: Creative and Critical Perspectives by Feminists of Color*, ed. Gloria Anzaldua (San Francisco: Aunt Lute Books, 1995).

5. Ruíz, "Feminist Border Thought"; Sandoval, "The Struggle Within"; Torre and Pesquera, *Building with Our Hands*, 2.

6. Ruíz, "Feminist Border Thought," 350; Paula M. L. Moya, *Learning from Experience: Minority Identities, Multicultural Struggles* (Berkeley: University of California Press, 2002), 29; Torre and Pesquera, *Building with Our Hands*, 2.

7. Ruíz, "Feminist Border Thought," 352.

8. Hurtado, "Sitios y Lenguas," 148.

9. Maria Lugones, "From within Germinative Stasis: Creating Active Subjectivity, Resistant Agency," in *Entre Mundos / Among Worlds: New Perspectives on Gloria Anzaldua*, ed. AnaLouise Keating (New York: Palgrave Macmillan, 2006), 3; Sonia Saldívar-Hull, *Feminism on the Border: Chicana Gender Politics and Literature* (Berkeley: University of California Press, 2000), 12–13; Ruíz, "Feminist Border Thought," 351.

10. Deena J. González, "Gender on the Borderlands: Re-Textualizing the Classics," in *Gender on the Borderlands: The Frontiers Reader*, ed. Antonia Castaneda et al. (Lincoln: University of Nebraska Press, 2007), 17–18; Ruíz, "Feminist Border Thought," 355.

11. Keating, *Entre Mundos / Among Worlds*, 5; Ruíz, "Feminist Border Thought," 355.

12. See "Mestiza Consciousness" by Elena Ruíz in this volume.

13. Lugones, "From within Germinative Stasis" 5.

14. Gloria Anzaldúa, *Borderlands/La Frontera: The New Mestiza*, 3rd edition (San Francisco: Aunt Lute Books, 2007), 19.

15. Anzaldúa, *Borderlands/La Frontera*, 19.

16. Anzaldúa, *Borderlands/La Frontera*, 19, 3, 4.

17. Elsewhere in her work, and especially during what Keating calls Anzaldúa's "late period," she develops other theoretical frameworks and metaphors for theorizing borderland identity, including la nepantlera and la naguala. For more on how Anzaldúa's theory of border subjectivity changes throughout her work, see Mariana Ortega, *In-Between: Latina Feminist Phenomenology, Multiplicity and the Self* (Albany, N.Y.: SUNY Press, 2016), and AnaLouise Keating, "Re-envisioning Coyolxauhqui, Decolonizing Reality: Anzaldúa's Twenty-First-Century Imperative," in Gloria Anzaldua, *Light in the Dark: Luz en lo Oscuro: Rewriting Identity, Spirituality, Reality* (Durham, N.C.: Duke University Press, 2015).

18. As Anzaldúa explains in the opening lines of chapter 7 of *Borderlands/La Frontera*, Vasconcelos "envisaged una raza mestiza. . . . He called it a cosmic race, la raza cósmica, a fifth race embracing the four major races of the world" (99). Vasconcelos's conception of la raza cósmica has been a problematic and much critiqued, if also generative, concept in Latin American and Latina/o history and thought. In contradistinction to Anzaldúa's account of mestiza consciousness, for instance, Vasconcelos's work on mestizaje has been rightfully criticized for failing to take into account oppressive power functions surrounding gender and sexuality, which is particularly problematic given pervasive sexual violence that characterizes the history of racial mixing in Latin America and elsewhere (Marilyn Grace Miller, *Rise and Fall of the Cosmic Race* (Austin, T.X.: University of Texas Press, 2004), 37). For more on Anzaldúa's critical use of this term, see Theresa Delgadillo, *Spiritual Mestizaje: Religion, Gender, Race, and Nation in Contemporary Chicana Narrative* (Durham, N.C.: Duke University Press, 2011); Ortega, *In-Between*, 25; Rafael Pérez-Torres, *Mestizaje: Critical Uses of Race in Chicano Culture* (Minneapolis: University of Minnesota Press, 2006), 45; Andrea Pitts, "Toward an Aesthetics of Race: Bridging the Writings of Gloria Anzaldúa and José Vasconcelos," *Inter-American Journal of Philosophy* 5, no. 1 (2014): 80–100.

19. Ortega, *In-Between*, 25–26.

20. Lugones, "From within Germinative Stasis," 87; Anzaldúa, *Borderlands/La Frontera*, 19.

21. Anzaldúa, *Borderlands/La Frontera*, 52; Ruíz, "Feminist Border Thought"; W. E. B. Du Bois, *The Souls of Black Folk* (Oakland, Calif.: Eucalyptus Press, 2013).

22. Anzaldúa, *Borderlands/La Frontera*, 52.

23. Anzaldúa, *Borderlands/La Frontera*, 19

# 8 Collective Continuance

Kyle Whyte

Theory and philosophy from indigenous peoples and indigenous studies often describe experience and time in ways that relate to what I am calling collective continuance. Collective continuance considers existence as emanating from relationships between humans and nonhumans that are in constant motion, embracing of diversity and constituted by reciprocal responsibilities. When these relationships flourish, they can facilitate a society's resilience or its members' capacity to self-determine how to adjust to changes and challenges in ways that avoid preventable harms and support their freedom and aspirations (including those of nonhumans). Yet relationships of collective continuance are among those most harmed by systematic domination, such as U.S. settler colonialism. Collective continuance, as a philosophical framework, puts in relief some aspects of the nature of injustice.

While I have mainly written about collective continuance as providing insights on what makes up the fabrics of our societies, some of the foundations of my philosophy are rooted in Anishinaabe philosophies of experience and time that privilege motion, diversity, and reciprocal responsibility as critical dimensions of our existence. *Anishinaabe* is an autonym used by indigenous communities of the Great Lakes region, namely Ojibwe, Potawatomi, Odawa, and Mississauga, among others. Anishinaabe territory is bisected by the Canada-U.S. border. Concepts of motion, diversity, and reciprocal responsibility convey an understanding of existence that is at once fluid and systematically organized. I will start by sharing some of these philosophies of experience and time and then move on to the more social and political dimensions of collective continuance and injustice. Here I just offer some examples that show the range of scales on which motion, diversity, and reciprocal responsibility are considered as figuring into our existence as individuals and members of collectives. Though I am unable to cover the subject in this writing, readers should look further at Gerald Vizenor's philosophy of *survivance* in relation to much of what I am about to discuss.[1]

One entry point to begin with is language. Anishinaabe philosophies of language emphasize an understanding of experience as involving motion and diversity. Anton Treuer discusses how the lexicon is at least two-thirds verbs. This predominance of verbs orients existence, as experienced through language, toward constant action or motion.[2] Margaret Noodin writes that "action is always central and speakers constantly think about how to communicate what is happening."[3] Yet, for Noodin, the motion/action orientation of the language is coupled with having to cope with infinite diversity: "Anishinaabemowin is a language of options so diverse and extreme that the act of seeking a center is the focus. In a world of snowflakes, agates, and leaves there are patterns premised on individuality, and the view from a distance shows unity, while a look up close reveals infinite variety."[4] For Noodin, then, the philosophy of language highlights how experience is about being in motion toward a center or unified pattern that neither remains fixed nor aims to overcome endless diversity. Linguistically mediated experience is fluid.

Time too can be understood as fluid. Sherry Copenace and Dylan Miner have discussed with me in separate conversations the Anishinaabemowin expression *aanikoobijigan*.[5] The expression means "ancestor" and "descendent" at the same time. This meaning suggests an Anishinaabe perspective on intergenerational time—a perspective in which lived time is more like experiencing spiraling motion, where we live alongside diverse narratives of future and past relatives simultaneously as we walk forward. Kimberley Blaeser, in a conversation with Jennifer Andrews, writes about the philosophy of time involved in her work:

> BLAESER: There's the circular shape, but there's also the lateral, the different strands on the spider's web, and then I envision what happens when a fly lands and there's a vibration. So we're talking about the vibration, the motion, the movement, and I guess it's that idea of being in the essence of movement that is in a continuum; we're in a constant evolution and yet at the same time it reconnects us, and so it folds back, and maybe it's like a . . .
>
> ANDREWS: An accordion.
>
> BLAESER: Yeah! When you talk about a circle, you're still restricting it to a single dimension.[6]

Blaeser introduces a diversity of types of time, discussing circularity, laterality, strands on a spider's web, vibration, motion and movement, and folding back, among others. Dolleen Manning, in intergenerational dialogue with her mother, Rose Manning, writes of two dimensions of existence that can be described as the "fish" (individual or basic group) and "shoal" (navigational acuity). These dimensions "gather and break apart rather like a shoal of fish or a flock of birds—in other words, with an eye for the immediate and a pulse in time with the infinite."[7]

Manning, Blaeser, and Noodin philosophize about experience and time using concepts like strands on a spider's web, snowflakes, or shoals. These concepts point to a fluid understanding of how the fabric of society is woven through relationships that involve our individual senses of and perspectives on existence but that also scale up to the level of our relationships to others as members of collectives. What has most interested me about collective continuance is that it is a social and political philosophy based in concepts of constant motion and diversity. For example, the ancient migration story of Anishinaabe people moving from the East Coast to the Great Lakes region of North America is primarily about how people develop new relationships to the beings and places of each stopping point and learn certain lessons before opting to leave or stay. Scott Lyons interprets migration as "[producing] *difference*."[8]

Lyons writes that "the Great Migration also speaks of home. There was always a destination in view . . . but . . . it kept changing! One moment the Great Migration had come to an end; the next moment people were telling stories about the last two, three, four stopping points they encountered. Home is a stopping point, for there is no sense in the migration story that there will be only one home for only one people forever."[9] Similar to Noodin's philosophy of language, political and social organization for Lyons is understood as involving systematic processes of focusing on "a center" or "a home" or "a stopping point" that is known to be nonfixed, temporary, and changeable—out of a multiplicity or diversity of options and possibilities.

The idea of migration, as expressing motion and diversity, is critical in Anishinaabe social and political philosophy. Michael Witgen discusses the territory of Anishinaabewaki in the Great Lakes region during the transatlantic fur trade period. In this territory, beings approximating people today actually are complex identities associated with the *many* places where they engaged in economic and cultural activities throughout the year in their seasonal rounds (harvesting, ceremonial, and political systems that are designed to respect the dynamics of ecosystems). At once, someone could be associated with certain animal ancestors (i.e., clan memberships), families, bands/tribes, lodges, ceremonial communities, romantic and parental ties, and diplomatic roles. At a particular place and a particular point in time during the calendar year, someone might primarily be known as a "trader" or a member of "clan y." But that was just that person's identity at that place and that time of year. Identity was always shifting.[10]

Gender is another example pertaining to social and political philosophy. Consider people who today are coded and/or code themselves as women—though, just to note, Anishinaabe societies did not historically privilege binary, hetero-patriarchal gender systems. In seasonal round governance, women exercised a range of leadership roles, whether as knowledge keepers (experts) of particular plants and animals, visible leaders and diplomats, or servant leaders (such as through participation in the selection of visible leaders). Women also did not see their relationships to men, such as through marriage, as among their most important relationships.[11]

The seasonal round is sometimes called an "accordion" system of governance in its constant expansion and contraction in response to environmental change,[12] resonating with my earlier discussion of language, time, and migration. The seasonal round governance system, while grounded in motion and diversity, is also, at another level, highly organized. Brenda Child writes that the seasonal round governance system is not an accidental arrangement of fluid relationships: "It was a way of life passed down by the generations and required study, observation of the natural world, experimentation, relationships with other living beings on the earth, and knowledge-generating labor."[13]

When Anishinaabe people discuss how the seasonal round is organized systematically they often focus on relationships of reciprocal responsibilities across humans and nonhumans. Robin Kimmerer, referring to intimate relationships between humans and nonhumans, writes about their morality as part of a "covenant of reciprocity,"[14] which she sees as relationships of gift-giving and gift-receiving responsibilities across all beings. "In Potawatomi, we speak of the land as *emingoyak*, that which has been given to us," a gift that must be reciprocated with our own.[15]

Deborah McGregor, in her work with Josephine Mandamin and Anishinaabe women's water movements, suggests that we need to think systematically about the different lives that water supports "(plants/medicines, animals, people, birds, etc.) and the life that supports water (e.g., the earth, the rain, the fish)." The system is based on responsibilities such that "water has a role and a responsibility to fulfill, just as people do."[16] She writes, "All beings have responsibilities to fulfill, and recognizing this contributes to a holistic understanding of justice. Our interference with other beings' ability to fulfill their responsibilities is an example of a great environmental injustice, an injustice to Creation."[17]

Anishinaabe philosophies of diplomacy also feature a focus on reciprocal responsibility. Leanne Simpson has reinvigorated awareness of the *Dish with One Spoon* treaty between Anishinaabe and Haudenosaunee peoples in the Great Lakes region. She writes that "*Gdoo-naaganinaa* [the dish] acknowledged that both the Nishnaabeg and the Haudenosaunee were eating out of the same dish through shared hunting territory and the ecological connections between their territories. . . . Both parties were to be responsible for taking care of the dish. . . . All of the nations involved had particular responsibilities to live up to in order to enjoy the rights of the agreement. Part of those responsibilities was taking care of the dish."[18] For Kimmerer, McGregor, and Simpson, a fabric of society woven of reciprocal responsibilities is one whose members have an appreciation for one another's unique contributions and are committed to ensuring that all relatives (parties to relationships of reciprocal responsibilities) can carry out their responsibilities.

For me, the philosophies of existence I have discussed so far call attention to—among many other things—how any social fabric must be able to be fluid *and* invested in moral relationships (e.g., reciprocal responsibility) in order to be best prepared to adjust to changes and threats and sustain its members' freedoms and aspirations. They describe both the fabric of such a conception of society and the senses of experience and time that emanate from being entangled in such relationships. When we zoom in on experience and time, *collective continuance* refers to an understanding of existence as living through diverse, constantly changing relationships with different species, ancestors, future generations, and spiritual and ecological beings (e.g., water). These relationships are infused with responsibilities. So *continuance* refers to living through constant motion and diversity within a *collective* of responsibility-laden relationships.

When we zoom out to the scale of systematic social and political organization, collective continuance considers a society's resilience as conditioned by its members' capacities to self-determine how they will adjust to changes in ways that best avoid preventable harms and support their freedoms and aspirations—whether human or nonhuman. In my own view, societies with high degrees of collective continuance are societies rich in reciprocal responsibilities across human and nonhuman members, as Kimmerer, McGregor, and Simpson discuss. Yet moral relationships are constantly in motion and embedded in conditions that are infinitely diverse, shoal-like, and folding back, as Blaeser, Noodin, and Manning show us. Parties or relatives in these relationships embrace migration, motion, fluidity, vibration, and expansion/contraction as experiences and temporalities that should be respected and celebrated, not avoided or denied.

Even though collective continuance privileges, in a sense, adaptive capacity and fluidity, this way of thinking can also help ground trenchant and uncompromising criticisms of colonial and other forms of anti-indigenous domination that commit violence and trauma on experiential,[19] social, and political scales.[20] Consider U.S. settler colonialism against indigenous peoples. *Settler colonialism* refers to complex social processes in which at least one society seeks to move permanently onto the terrestrial, aquatic, and aerial places lived in by one or more other societies who already derive economic vitality, cultural flourishing, and political self-determination from the relationships they have established with the plants, animals, physical entities, and ecosystems of those places.

The settlers' aspirations are to transform indigenous homelands into settler homelands. Settlers create moralizing narratives about why it is (or was) necessary to destroy other peoples (e.g., military or cultural inferiority), or they take great pains to forget or cover up the inevitable violence of settlement. Settlement is deeply harmful and risk-laden for indigenous peoples because settlers are literally seeking to erase indigenous economies, cultures, and political organizations for the sake of establishing their own.[21]

Settler colonialism, then, is a type of injustice driven by settlers' desire, conscious and tacit, to erase indigenous peoples.[22] What they seek to erase is our collective continuance. Historic and contemporary settler colonialism uses tactics that directly target the reciprocal responsibilities, fluidity, and diversity of Anishinaabe and other indigenous peoples. Broken treaties, reservations, and other types of land dispossession fix indigenous mobility and migration for the sake of the interests of U.S. settlement. Boarding schools, banning indigenous ceremonies, U.S. government definitions of indigeneity, commodity foods, and standardized government programs reduce human and nonhuman diversity and detach us from our relatives, making it hard to carry out reciprocal responsibilities. The U.S.'s lack of accountability to the security of indigenous peoples and its imposition of sexist and patriarchal norms on communities undermine reciprocal responsibility, diversity, and fluidity. Injustice, under this lens, is an affront to our existence.

Settler colonial injustice occurs when one society undermines the conditions that make up the fabric of a society's collective continuance, denying the dimensions of our existence based on constant motion, diversity, and reciprocal responsibility. Ironically, the goal of U.S. settler colonialism, of course, is to establish conditions for the "collective continuance" of the different people within the U.S. sphere. Yet, as problems of sexual violence, racism, and climate change demonstrate today, the relationships constituting what we might call "U.S. collective continuance" are based on extraction (e.g., of natural resources) and fixity (i.e., of property ownership), lack commitment to reciprocity, and privilege exclusion and discrimination. These are very different types of relationships and give rise to different senses of experience and time for those peoples whose existence emanates from these relationships. So while the U.S. has sought to create itself as a resilient settlement in North America, it has done so at the expense of undermining indigenous collective continuance and establishing its own version of collective continuance based on morally troubling and ecologically unsustainable relationships.

## Notes

1. Gerald Vizenor, *Survivance: Narratives of Native Presence* (Lincoln: University of Nebraska Press, 2008).

2. Mark Bernstein, "When Language Is More Than Words," *Princeton Alumni Weekly*, 117, no. 6 (January 11, 2017): 28–33.https://paw.princeton.edu/article/when-language-more-words; Anton Treuer, *Living Our Language: Ojibwe Tales and Oral Histories* (St. Paul: Minnesota Historical Society Press, 2008).

3. Margaret Noodin, *Bawaajimo: A Dialect of Dreams in Anishinaabe Language and Literature* (East Lansing: Michigan State University Press, 2014), 16–17.

4. Noodin, *Bawaajimo*, 16–17.

5. Sherry Copenace, personal discussion, July 7, 2017; Dylan Miner, *Aanikoobijigan*, installation, Artspace, Peterborough, Ontario, 2017.

6. Jennifer Courtney, Elizabeth Andrews, and Kimberly M Blaeser, "Living History: A Conversation with Kimberly Blaeser," *Studies in American Indian Literatures* 19, no. 2 (2007): 1–21.

7. Dolleen Tisawii'ashii Manning, "The Murmuration of Birds," In *Feminist Phenomenology Futures*, ed. H. Fielding (Bloomington: Indiana University Press, 2017), 155.

8. Scott Richard Lyons, *X-Marks: Native Signatures of Assent* (Minneapolis: University of Minnesota Press, 2010), 4.

9. Lyons, *X-Marks*, 4.

10. Michael Witgen, *An Infinity of Nations: How the Native New World Shaped Early North America* (Philadelphia: University of Pennsylvania Press, 2011).

11. Susan Sleeper-Smith, *Indian Women and French Men: Rethinking Cultural Counter in the Western Great Lakes* (Amherst: University of Massachusetts Press, 2001); Richard White, *The Middle Ground: Indians, Empires, and Republics in the Great Lakes Region, 1650–1815* (Cambridge: Cambridge University Press, 1991); Priscilla K. Buffalohead, "Farmers Warriors Traders: A Fresh Look at Ojibway Women," *Minnesota History* 48, no. 6 (1983): 236–44.

12. Regna Darnell, "Rethinking the Concepts of Band and Tribe, Community and Nation: An Accordion Model of Nomadic Native American Social Organization," *Algonquian Papers-Archive* 29 (1998): 90–105; Witgen, *An Infinity of Nations*.

13. Brenda J. Child, *Holding Our World Together: Ojibwe Women and the Survival of Community* (New York: Penguin, 2012), 30.

14. Robin Kimmerer, "The Covenant of Reciprocity," In *The Wiley Blackwell Companion to Religion and Ecology*, ed. J. Hart (New York: John Wiley and Sons, 2017).

15. Robin Kimmerer, "The Giveaway," In *Moral Ground*, ed. K. D. Moore and M. P. Nelson (San Antonio, Texas: Trinity University Press, 2010), 143–44.

16. Deborah McGregor, "Honouring Our Relations: An Anishnaabe Perspective on Environmental Justice," in *Speaking for Ourselves: Environmental Justice in Canada*, ed. J. Agyeman, P. Cole, and R. Haluza-Delay (Vancouver: University of British Columbia Press, 2009), 37–38.

17. McGregor, "Honouring Our Relations," 40.

18. Leanne Simpson, "Looking after Gdoo-Naaganinaa: Precolonial Nishnaabeg Diplomatic and Treaty Relationships," *Wicazo Sa Review* 23, no. 2 (2008): 37.

19. K. P. Whyte, "Indigenous Experience, Environmental Justice and Settler Colonialism," in *Nature and Experience: Phenomenology and the Environment*, ed. B. Bannon (New York: Rowman and Littlefield, 2016).

20. K. P. Whyte, "Food Sovereignty, Justice and Indigenous Peoples: An Essay on Settler Colonialism and Collective Continuance," In *Oxford Handbook on Food Ethics*, ed. A. Barnhill, T. Doggett, and A. Egan (Oxford: Oxford University Press, 2018).

21. K. P. Whyte, "The Dakota Access Pipeline, Environmental Injustice and U.S. Colonialism," *Red Ink—An International Journal of Indigenous Literature, Arts and Humanities* 19, no. 1 (2017): 154–69.

22. Whyte, "The Dakota Access Pipeline, Environmental Injustice and U.S. Colonialism."

# 9 Compulsory Able-Bodiedness

Robert McRuer

The concept of *compulsory able-bodiedness* now circulates widely in disability studies, queer and feminist theory, and theories of the body, especially theories such as phenomenology attuned to the ways in which the body is oriented in space and time. I first used the concept of compulsory able-bodiedness in passing at the 1999 American Studies Association conference, and then in a more fully developed presentation at the 1999 Modern Language Association convention. The feminist disability studies scholar Rosemarie Garland-Thomson had invited me to write about the intersections of queer theory and disability studies, and I initially began to respond to that invitation in collective, interdisciplinary spaces where disability studies, in particular, was emerging as a force capable of reshaping the humanities as we entered the twenty-first century.

## Feminist Foundations of Compulsory Able-Bodiedness

*Compulsory able-bodiedness* is an explicit adaptation of the concept of *compulsory heterosexuality*, most fully developed by Adrienne Rich in her landmark 1980 essay, "Compulsory Heterosexuality and Lesbian Existence."[1] Rich herself did not coin the phrase, which feminist theorists and activists were using throughout the 1970s, but her essay did codify it as an important component of a critical feminist theory. Rich's intent in "Compulsory Heterosexuality" was to draw attention to the ways in which heterosexuality was not truly an "option" for women (as, perhaps, the term *sexual preference* might imply), but rather a compulsory identification, reinforced through virtually all institutions of society. Rich provided a range of examples of compulsory heterosexuality from various cultural contexts, even as she simultaneously posited an oppressive patriarchal society that could be understood as cross-cultural and cross-temporal, and hence as fairly monolithic. Heterosexuality, in Rich's analysis, was sustained as dominant within patriarchy because it passed as a "universal" status. It was, in other words, made compulsory by a patriarchal order and subsequently naturalized. Heterosexuality's naturalization makes it well-nigh invisible and difficult to talk about; it has been the unspoken norm that stands opposed to a range of substantialized "deviations." Rich offered "lesbian existence" as a form of resistance to the patriarchal imposition of compulsory heterosexuality, famously suggesting that *all* women might be part of what she theorized as a "lesbian continuum." Her discussion of a lesbian continuum marked a perhaps necessary moment of intragender political solidarity, although it paradoxically opened the essay to the charge that, in its attempt to unify all women, it diluted the experiences of women who actually identified as lesbians or literally shaped sexual bonds with other women.

My own article "Compulsory Able-Bodiedness and Queer/Disabled Existence" was first published in 2002, in one of the defining anthologies of disability studies in the humanities, *Disability Studies: Enabling the Humanities*.[2] It later became a part of the introduction to my 2006 monograph, *Crip Theory: Cultural Signs of Queerness and Disability*.[3] I thus sought to position a critical attention to compulsory able-bodiedness as a key component of the critical project that has come to be called *crip theory*, a project that draws on artistic, activist, and academic reclamations and reinventions of the word *crip*. In putting forward compulsory able-bodiedness as a term deeply related to compulsory heterosexuality, I had several goals. First, I intended to assert that able-bodiedness is in many ways even more naturalized and subsequently invisibilized and difficult to analyze in contemporary culture than heterosexuality. Although it is essentially founded on a logical contradiction—able-bodiedness is simultaneously assumed to be the supposed "natural state" of any body *and yet* is a state that all of us are striving to attain or maintain—no sustained critical attention had been directed toward the ways in which able-bodied hegemony is secured in a culture that marginalizes, stigmatizes, and oppresses disability. Second, and related, I wanted to interrogate the cultural dominance of able-bodiedness by linking it to histories of normalcy that were then emerging in both queer theory and disability studies.[4] Able-bodiedness, like heterosexuality, I contended, is able to pass as the natural state of things due to its uninterrogated attachment, for more than two centuries, to ideas of what is "normal." Indeed, by the end of the nineteenth century, the *OED* explicitly codified "physically and mentally sound; free from any disorder; healthy" as one of the primary meanings for *normal*.[5] Ideas of what is "normal" of course emerge in a particular system of labor, and my contention was that industrial capitalism's need for able-bodied workers helped sediment the unconscious association of able-bodiedness and normalcy. Later, in *Crip Theory*, I attempted to specify some of the ways in which compulsory able-bodiedness takes particular forms in neoliberal capitalism, generally through a "tolerance" or even contained "celebration" of disabled or queer minorities that nonetheless sustains the subordination of disability and queerness to the desired states of heterosexuality and able-bodiedness.

Third, I wanted to suggest that compulsory able-bodiedness was actually a *necessary component* of compulsory heterosexuality (and vice versa). For this, I turned from Rich to the work of Judith Butler. Butler's theory of gender trouble famously argues that heterosexuality is constituted performatively through repeated, compulsory acts or imitations.[6] This compulsory repetition of a dominant masculinity and femininity, and of heterosexuality, produces, or literally materializes, heterosexuality as the supposed foundation or origin of all gender identifications. This *origin*, however, is clearly only established paradoxically, as the *outcome* of repeated acts. My argument about compulsory able-bodiedness registered what was arguably a lacuna in Butler's theory: the most successful heterosexual subject, I argued, compelled to repeat dominant gender identities, *is already an able-bodied subject*, capably engaged in the repetition of dominant gender identifications, just as the most successful able-bodied subject *is already a heterosexual subject*, free from "deviance" or "perversion" that might somehow manifest itself on the body. Queerness broadly conceived, I argued, is regularly understood or positioned in contemporary culture as always a bit disabled. This was literally true when homosexuality remained a diagnosis but remains true in the homophobic cultural imaginary (and indeed, "gender identity disorder" remained a diagnosis until the most recent addition of the *Diagnostic and Statistical Manual of Mental Disorders*, when it was reclassified as "gender dysphoria").[7] Disability, likewise, is regularly perceived in contemporary culture as always a bit queer or perverse, as stereotypes of disabled people without or with an excess of sexuality make clear. Stigmaphobic queer or disabled attempts to distance one identity from the other ("We may be disabled [or queer] but we're not *that*!") contribute to the ongoing, performative consolidation of both heterosexual and able-bodied dominance.

Finally, arguably following both Rich's and Butler's leads, I offered up "queer/disabled existence" as a form of resistance to compulsory able-bodiedness. Michael Warner had noted a gap in Butler's theory, "let us say, between virtually queer and critically queer."[8] Everyone is virtually queer in the sense that the dominant identities Butler traces are impossible to embody without contradiction and incoherence. "Critically queer" perspectives, however, might be positioned in ways that *mobilize* heterosexuality's necessary failures, collectively "working the weakness in the norm," in Butler's words.[9] I concluded by theorizing playfully (given the recoil that "critical" or "severe" disability invariably produces in an ableist culture) how *critically disabled*, or *severely disabled*, perspectives might actually be those best positioned to undermine the workings of compulsory able-bodiedness.

## Crip Extensions of Compulsory Able-Bodiedness

Alison Kafer appears to be the first to specifically use *compulsory able-mindedness* alongside *compulsory able-bodiedness* in her important study *Feminist, Queer, Crip*.[10] The field of disability studies has shifted significantly during the second decade of the twenty-first century; the 2011 publication of Margaret Price's *Mad at School: Rhetorics of Mental Disability and Academic Life* might serve as a convenient marker for that shift.[11] What Price terms "mental disability" has certainly been at the forefront of various movements (antipsychiatry, mad pride) for decades, but her study was nonetheless one of the first book-length interventions into disability studies attempting to center mental disability, considering the different questions that emerge when we do so. Price usefully deploys the concept of *bodymind* "to emphasize that although 'body' and 'mind' usually occupy separate conceptual and linguistic territories, they are deeply intertwined."[12]

Read through Price's transformative understanding of bodymind, one might insist that compulsory able-bodiedness obviously already generates disciplines/compulsions connected to the mind, emotions, and behavior as much as it generates disciplines/compulsions connected to corporeality more directly. Kafer's *Feminist, Queer, Crip*, however, deploys *compulsory able-mindedness* alongside *compulsory able-bodiedness* in order to mark her commitment to thinking expansively and intersectionally: "If disability studies is going to take seriously the criticism that we have focused on physical disabilities to the exclusion of all else, then we need to start experimenting with different ways of talking about and conceptualizing our projects."[13] Kafer's project as a whole extends this commitment to thinking across many other vectors of difference, linking disability to transgender identity, race, class, and a variety of contemporary feminisms. Rabia Belt's recent work also uses *compulsory able-mindedness*, considering how actual contemporary laws and institutions are undergirded by it. Belt argues that these compulsory systems of power literally impede citizens' right to vote; hers is thus one of the first studies to excavate the at times very concrete effects of compulsory able-bodiedness and compulsory able-mindedness.[14]

In an earlier article that was part of a special issue of the *Journal of Women's History* on Rich's legacy, Kafer reads Rich's work backward through compulsory able-bodiedness. In "Compulsory Bodies: Reflections on Heterosexuality and Able-bodiedness," Kafer registers some useful cautions regarding the use of compulsory able-bodiedness as a new term that has emerged from feminist deployments of compulsory heterosexuality.[15] First, the use of compulsory able-bodiedness should not obscure the fact that feminists at the time of Rich's essay, and Rich herself, were generally turning to "disability" only as a negative metaphor. Second, a logic of "substitution," Kafer argues, might obscure the specific ways in which homophobia and ableism function. Third, a move toward discussions of compulsory able-bodiedness might redirect attention away from the ongoing need to talk about how compulsory heterosexuality constrains women's lives and freedoms. In the context of these cautions from "Compulsory Bodies," it's important to remember that my own initial theorization of compulsory able-bodiedness insisted on talking about able-bodiedness and heterosexuality together; my point was, again, that the two systems depend upon each other. Moreover, if there was a logic of substitution at play in my own work with Butler, it was in the interest of drawing out something that was missing in her theory—namely, an attention to how gender trouble is always already haunted by ability trouble.

Sara Ahmed is another feminist thinker, more specifically emerging from feminist phenomenology, who is very much in conversation with developments in disability studies and who has consequently also productively deployed compulsory able-bodiedness in her work. Ahmed's theorization of "willfulness," in particular, examines how the "willful subject" resists the ways in which compulsory able-bodiedness is related to "the idea of a body as a machine" and is a system that puts forward "'being able' as a corporeal and regulative norm."[16] In what we might understand as a crip alternative, Ahmed offers the willful subject generating "wiggle room." Queer and disabled existence can be discerned in Ahmed's description of "the will as wiggle room," as she conjures up desirable deviation and ruin: "The will is also the name we give to possibility . . . the room to deviate, a room kept open by will's incompletion, a room most often in human history designated as ruin."[17] I call all of this work "crip extensions" of compulsory able-bodiedness because it highlights the ways in which a crip analytic reaches for other queer/disabled possibilities.

## Locating and Displacing Compulsory Able-Bodiedness in History

As I have indicated, my initial use of *compulsory able-bodiedness* argued that it consolidated over the course of the nineteenth century with the rise of industrial capitalism. Other scholars, however, have subsequently done even more work to analyze the ways in which compulsory able-bodiedness has functioned at particular moments in history, so I will conclude this very brief survey by looking backward, a critical gesture that is, José Esteban Muñoz suggests, a way of "cruising utopia."[18] Looking backward entails both specifying how compulsory able-bodiedness might function in different times and places and considering how compulsory able-bodiedness might be useful as an analytic for thinking about earlier periods, including periods not as obviously organized around an able-bodied/disabled binary (as the world of industrial capitalism, with its explicit demand for the materialization of "able-bodied workers," is). Julie Passanante Elman's study *Chronic Youth: Disability, Sexuality, and U.S. Media Cultures of Rehabilitation*, in particular, is an example of the first mode of looking backward. Elman historicizes the ways in which compulsory able-bodiedness works in relation to shifting understandings of youth from the 1970s forward.[19] Surveying how adolescence had congealed as a "problem" to be managed in the contemporary United States, she overviews the historical emergence of what she calls "rehabilitative citizenship" and "rehabilitative edutainment."[20] Rehabilitative citizenship generated cultural and emotional attachment to an increasingly privatized political sphere where personal responsibility and regulation of individualized behavior were prioritized. In this late twentieth-century context, the problem of adolescence needed to be addressed in ways that could vouchsafe "a linkage of heterosexuality and able-bodiedness as the 'healthy' or natural outcome of development."[21] Rehabilitative edutainment—afterschool specials, young adult literature, and other cultural forms—emerged as specific biopolitical technologies of compulsory able-bodiedness, often teaching the heterosexual/able-bodied proto-citizen to be accepting of LGBT or disabled others, even as those others were not understood as the ideal neoliberal citizen-subject.

Richard Godden and Jonathan Hsy's "Analytic Survey: Encountering Disability in the Middle Ages" is a good example of the second mode of looking backward.[22] Their historicist survey opens with the clear assertion that "neither 'disability'—nor even a broad notion of 'normalcy'—existed as a fixed term in the medieval West."[23] As scholars of the past themselves resist the demands of compulsory able-bodiedness in our present, they approach somatic difference—or bodies, minds, and behaviors that might be perceived as unusual or atypical—in new ways. Godden and Hsy explicitly draw on crip theory (and its thick connection to queer theory) as an analytic: "To 'crip' as a verb—much as one deploys 'queer' as a verb—is to adopt an orientation toward the world that asserts the potential for radical transformation of so-called normative social scripts, desires, and ways of life."[24] Godden and Hsy's project might be understood as generating Ahmedian "wiggle room" within medieval scholarship, and as offering a model for scholars of virtually any period: how does thinking beyond compulsory able-bodiedness allow us to break out of more mechanical approaches to the past? How might cripping the past help us locate the many and varied locations where the will to deviate from compulsory able-bodiedness and other so-called normative social scripts—a will that Ahmed's feminist phenomenology conjures up in the present—has appeared?

I am spotlighting here, of course, only a few of the crip extensions or historical interrogations of the concept of compulsory able-bodiedness. I concluded my initial introduction of compulsory able-bodiedness by insisting that the perspective it affords us should be about "collectively transforming (in ways that cannot necessarily be predicted in advance) the substantive uses to which queer/disabled existence has been put by a system of compulsory able-bodiedness . . . and about imagining bodies and desires otherwise."[25] Compulsory able-bodiedness marginalizes or minimizes queer/disabled existence. Since the time of my initial article, however, feminists, queer theorists, disability studies scholars, and theorists of the body have indeed collectively worked to think both with and beyond compulsory able-bodiedness, generating transformative, severely disabled perspectives in the process. Rich herself, eventually living with disability and moving beyond disability as only a negative metaphor, announces in a late poem, "I write this / with a clawed hand."[26] With clawed hands and other queer/crip modes of cultural production and analysis, a critical phenomenology should continue to extend Rich's legacy, unraveling compulsory able-bodiedness alongside compulsory heterosexuality, accessing in the process new ways of thinking, feeling, and being in common.

## Notes

1. Adrienne Rich, "Compulsory Heterosexuality and Lesbian Existence," *Signs: Journal of Women in Culture and Society* 5, no. 4 (1980): 631–60.

2. Robert McRuer, "Compulsory Able-Bodiedness and Queer/Disabled Existence," in *Disability Studies: Enabling the Humanities*, ed. Sharon L. Snyder, Brenda Jo Brueggemann, and Rosemarie Garland-Thomson (New York: MLA, 2002), 88–99.

3. Robert McRuer, *Crip Theory: Cultural Signs of Queerness and Disability* (New York: NYU Press, 2006), 1–32.

4. See, for example, Lennard J. Davis, *Enforcing Normalcy: Disability, Deafness, and the Body* (New York: Verso, 1995); Michael Warner, *The Trouble with Normal: Sex, Politics, and the Ethics of Queer Life* (New York: Free Press, 1999).

5. Quoted in Robert McRuer, "Normal," in *Keywords for American Cultural Studies*, 2nd edition, ed. Bruce Burgett and Glenn Hendler (New York: NYU Press, 2014), 184.

6. Judith Butler, *Gender Trouble: Feminism and the Subversion of Identity* (New York: Routledge, 1990).

7. American Psychiatric Association, *Diagnostic and Statistical Manual of Mental Disorders*, 5th edition (Arlington, Va.: APA, 2013).

8. Michael Warner, "Normal and Normaller: Beyond Gay Marriage," *GLQ: A Journal of Lesbian and Gay Studies* 5, no. 2 (1999): 168–69n87.

9. Judith Butler, "Critically Queer," *GLQ: A Journal of Lesbian and Gay Studies* 1, no. 1 (1993): 26.

10. Alison Kafer, *Feminist, Queer, Crip* (Bloomington: Indiana University Press, 2013).

11. Margaret Price, *Mad at School: Rhetorics of Mental Disability and Academic Life* (Ann Arbor: University of Michigan Press, 2011).

12. Price, *Mad at School*, 240n9.

13. Kafer, *Feminist, Queer, Crip*, 16.

14. Rabia Belt, "Mental Disability and the Right to Vote," Ph.D. dissertation, University of Michigan, 2015, 3.

15. Alison Kafer, "Compulsory Bodies: Reflections on Heterosexuality and Able-bodiedness," *Journal of Women's History* 15, no. 3 (2003): 77–89.

16. Sara Ahmed, *Willful Subjects* (Durham, N.C.: Duke University Press, 2014), 109.

17. Ahmed, *Willful Subjects*, 191–92.

18. José Esteban Muñoz, *Cruising Utopia: The Then and There of Queer Futurity* (New York: NYU Press, 2009).

19. Julie Passanante Elman, *Chronic Youth: Disability, Sexuality, and U.S. Media Cultures of Rehabilitation* (New York: NYU Press, 2014).

20. Elman, *Chronic Youth*, 7.

21. Elman, *Chronic Youth*, 7.

22. Richard Godden and Jonathan Hsy, "Analytic Survey: Encountering Disability in the Middle Ages," *New Medieval Literatures* 15 (2013): 313–39.

23. Godden and Hsy, "Analytic Survey," 314.

24. Godden and Hsy, "Analytic Survey," 318.

25. McRuer, "Compulsory Able-Bodiedness," 97.

26. Adrienne Rich, "Circum/Stances," in *Collected Poems: 1950–2012* (New York: Norton, 2016), 1001.

# 10 Confiscated Bodies

George Yancy

The concept of confiscated bodies is used to describe phenomenologically disruptive and violative encounters endured by the black body across various racially saturated social spaces, often quotidian social spaces, where black bodies are encountered by or confronted by the white gaze.[1] More specifically, the concept of confiscated bodies provides a phenomenologically rich and thick account of an experience that black bodies undergo within sociohistorical contexts of antiblack racism, where black bodies are "defined" or "scripted" through procrustean white gazes that ontologically truncate or racially essentialize them. Hence, within the context of discussing the confiscation of racialized black bodies, the phenomenon of the white gaze, its performative, habituated structural force, is presupposed. Furthermore, the white gaze presupposes the larger historical accretion of white semiotic material and institutional power and hegemony. On this score, whiteness functions as what I call *the transcendental norm*, or that according to which black bodies or bodies of color are deemed "deviant," "different," "ersatz," "raced," and "marked" against the normative, unmarked background of whiteness. Being "defined" in relationship to whiteness, which constitutes the unnamed and unmarked background, the black body further undergoes profound *lived* experiential forms of disorientation, disruption, ontological distortion, and corporeal malediction.

By *transcendental* norm, I do not mean whiteness to be construed as an *ahistorical*, necessary, or universal category. Rather, whiteness is historically contingent and functions as a teleological site of global, colonial usurpation. W. E. B. Du Bois insightfully asks, "But what on earth is whiteness that one should so desire it?" He responds, "I am given to understand that whiteness is the ownership of the earth forever and ever, Amen!"[2] Structurally, whiteness functions as a site of "manifest destiny," and white people are constituted as "humans qua humans" or "persons qua persons." Whiteness functions as the grand metanarrative regarding the "superiority" of white beauty, intelligence, and governance. And characteristic of power, more generally, the metanarrative structure of whiteness attempts to obfuscate the fact that its origin is historically contingent and actively maintained as opposed to an ahistorical given. More specifically, despite the historical contingency of whiteness, Du Bois argues that white people masquerade as "super-men and world-mastering demi-gods."[3] As a site of colonial desire, a site of institutional power, and a site of unmarked privilege, the power of the white gaze has historically, and within our contemporary moment, confiscated black bodies, rendering them as problematized, distorted, and transmogrified *objects*. Describing the hegemonic structure of the white gaze within the context of a larger white supremacist, asymmetrical social and political world, Jean-Paul Sartre writes, "For three thousand years, the white man has enjoyed the privilege of seeing without being seen: he was only a look—the light from his eyes drew each thing out of the shadow of its birth; the whiteness of his skin was another look, condensed light."[4] Elaborating on whiteness in terms of its various tropes, Sartre adds, "The white man—white because he was man, white like daylight, white like truth, white like virtue—lighted up the creation like a torch and unveiled the secret white essence of beings."[5]

It is this privilege and power of seeing without being seen that bespeaks the structural hegemonic orders that position the white body as the bearer of the white gaze and the black body as the object of the white gaze, the *seen*, the *looked at*. The relationship between the bearer of the look (the white body) and the *looked at* (the black body) is governed by an antiblack white racism whose logics are also informed by the white racist imaginary within which the black body constitutes the inverse image of whiteness. Hence, the black body is deemed "dangerous," "defiled," "hypersexual," "evil," "uncivilized," "perverse," and "monstrous." In short, the performative power of the white gaze is inextricably linked to the sedimentation of white racist phantasmagoric productions that are socially and institutionally shared and "validated" by white people.

It is important to provide this brief account of whiteness as the transcendental norm and to define the structure of the white gaze because these sociohistorical phenomena are inextricably linked to the process of confiscated black bodies; their confiscation takes place within contexts of sociality and historicity where they undergo processes in which their meaning and their integrity are *stolen* or *taken* and thrown back to them as that which they are presumed *to be*, presumed *to own*. Etymologically, the term *confiscation* denotes being seized by *authority*. Within the context of antiblack white racism, the black body is marked, for example, as "criminality" through white historical authority, its discursive power, its power of interpellation whereby the black body is hailed as always already "guilty."

The following are a few examples of this phenomenon. Cornel West describes a powerful experience when he was driving from New York to teach at Williams College in Massachusetts. He was stopped by a white police officer on concocted charges of trafficking cocaine. After looking over West's driver's license, the police officer said that he was the "Nigger we been looking for."[6] As Frantz Fanon writes, reflecting on being labeled as a Negro, "'Look, a Negro!' The circle was drawing a bit tighter. I made no secret of my amusement."[7] The interpellation "Nigger" or "Negro" involves "a pointing which circumscribes a dangerous body."[8] West says that he told the police officer that he taught "philosophy and religion at Williams."[9] The police officer replied, "And I'm the flying Nun."[10] Within this context, West's racialized embodied "culpability" is deemed "self-evident." Furthermore, the first-person account that West provides to the white police officer—that he teaches philosophy and religion at Williams—is belied by the violence of the white police officer's white gaze, which, as stated, is part of a larger historical accretion of white semiotic, material, and institutional power and hegemony. As Fanon writes, "No exception was made for my refined manners, or my knowledge of literature, or my understanding of the quantum theory." Fanon understands the power of the white gaze to confiscate his body, returning it as ontologically forlorn or even as "a new genus": "I am being dissected under white eyes, the only real eyes. I am fixed."[11] Similarly, regarding West's predicament, what the white gaze "sees" is all that there is to see. The white police officer's gaze is not an inaugural event, though, but the site of white historical iterative perceptual practices.

The point here is not to argue that first-person accounts are free of historically embedded meanings. West is not a presocial, atomic self whose meaning is solely self-legislated. None of us are created ex nihilo. Judith Butler, who offers a poststructuralist-inspired critique of the ideology of the neoliberal subject, argues that our being is inextricably linked "to a sociality that exceeds" each of us.[12] She writes, "The body has its invariably public dimension. Constituted as a social phenomenon in the public sphere, my body is and is not mine."[13] The body, for Butler, is given over within the space of sociality; the body bears the imprint of others and "is formed within the crucible of social life."[14] Butler's critique is marshaled against a certain conception of the embodied self as a site of absolute autonomy, what she calls "a fantasy of impossible mastery."[15] For Butler, our embodiment is a site of a certain kind of dispossession. Butler's social ontology, however, does not presuppose the historical necessity of the emergence of specific contexts. For example, within the context of white supremacy, specific embodied subjects are given over from the beginning vis-à-vis a certain racialized epistemic, scopic, hegemonic order. Hence, there is no necessity that preconfigures the specifically historical and violent ways in which the black body's meaning vis-à-vis the white gaze constitutes a site of confiscation, which is a different kind of *racialized* dispossession.

When the white police officer stops West, it is as if West is a priori not to be trusted. After all, according to white racist logic, West is a black man and thereby the quintessential "drug dealer." The lived experience of West's embodiment (as nonexternalized) is confiscated, seized, and West is externalized, reduced to his epidermis, his black embodied being distorted and phenomenologically returned to him as something other than how he defines himself or lives his embodiment outside the existential stressors of the white gaze. Instead, however, West's embodied integrity has been confiscated and thereby becomes the *externalized* black criminal, the black male stereotype of the white imaginary. Confiscated, his black body is returned as reified, a peculiar object. West describes how, before he was stopped, his time spent at Williams College was an amazing intellectual experience, one where he inhabited a "stratospheric atmosphere."[16]

One can imagine West's feeling elated, where his black embodiment was not, at that moment, a *thing* to contend with. Prior to being stopped, West was not "battered down" by white racist assumptions and stereotypes.[17] Immediately prior to being stopped, there isn't the experience of being confiscated, of being somatically imprisoned by white myths. West might be said to have been, prior to being stopped, moving lithely through space, which implies moving with effortless grace. Prior to being stopped, West's body constitutes the background—*not the foreground*—in terms of which the world is made available to him. As Merleau-Ponty writes, "I am not in front of my body, I am in my body, or I am my body."[18] West's body, prior to the stop, is unthematized. As he drives his car, he does so familiarly; his "being-in" the car is one of dialectical smoothness. If he wants to turn on the indicator light, like Fanon reaching for his cigarettes,[19] West doesn't locate his hand in space and then move it toward the indicator lever. Sara Ahmed writes, "The body is habitual insofar as it 'trails behind' in the performing of action, insofar as it does not pose 'a problem' or an obstacle to the action, or is not 'stressed' by 'what' the action encounters." She continues, "For Merleau-Ponty, the habitual body does not get in the way of an action: it is *behind the action*."[20] Yet, once stopped, West's black body stands out as an impediment, it undergoes a process of thematization whereby it is phenomenologically returned as an "extraneous object," which might invoke the question for West: Where is my body?

To pose such a question presupposes a form of embodiment that has been confiscated/taken, where one feels alienated from that sense of being one's body or not being in front of one's body. West's body is no longer behind this action. For West, his black body has become something to be dealt with, like an object thrown into his path. As Fanon writes, once making contact with the white gaze, he is "sealed into that crushing objecthood": "My body was given back to me sprawled out, distorted, clad in mourning in that white winter day." Note the affective intensity, the mourning, the lament, involved in the confiscation, how the black body is taken, torn away, and then thrown back, *spread out* before Fanon as the "Nigger" that the white gaze objectifies him to be. Like West's inhabiting a "stratospheric atmosphere," Fanon writes about coming into the world "imbued with the will to find a meaning in things, my spirit filled with the desire to attain to the source of the world, and then I found that I was an object in the midst of other objects" Or he talks about having his joy *slashed* (cut, hacked, taken) away by a white world.[21] Both West and Fanon undergo sociogenic processes of confiscation whereby the logics of the white gaze render their bodies surface-like, objectively present before them; where they undergo the *lived* experience of having their bodies occupy a spatial position of being, as it were, "over there." There is also that powerful sense of rupture experienced after having their bodies confiscated and thrown forward, especially within the context where their bodies, as Ahmed says, ought to trail behind their actions.

Du Bois also provides an account when his young black body is confiscated vis-à-vis the white gaze and describes the sudden recognition that his black body is foregrounded as a problem. He writes about an early school experience where "something put it into the boys' and girls' heads to buy gorgeous visiting cards—ten cents a package—and exchange." He says that the exchange went fine until one white girl, who he describes as "a tall newcomer," refused to exchange with him. She refused his "card peremptorily, with a glance. Then it dawned upon [him] with a certain suddenness that [he] was different from the others; or like, mayhap in heart and life and longing, but shut out from their world by a vast veil."[22] Note that Du Bois emphasizes the authoritative way in which she casts her glance; unlike with West and Fanon, there are no words spoken. And notice how he moved from the *lived* experience of a sense of belonging, or *Mitsein*, how, like West and Fanon, there is a sense of being-lithe-in-the-world and then the sudden confiscation, the somatic jolt, the rupture, the abrupt manifestation of one's self as an *object*.

It is important to note that the phenomenon of confiscated black bodies needn't be preceded by what is spoken; it is enough that there is some form of performative act that derives from the white body. Hence, as I walk by cars with white people in them, it is customary to hear the sudden sound of car doors locking—*click, click, click*. White women have pulled on their purses as I've moved in their direction, though minding my own business. White people have moved to the side of the street as they've seen me walking in their direction. And both black men and black women have shared the "elevator effect," whereby white people perform all manner of gesticulations that function to confiscate black bodies of their embodied integrity, whereby within the short ride on the elevator, their black bodies are thrown back to them as *things* a bit too close, a bit too scary, a bit too black. The point here is that the *clicks* and the gesticulations are also sites of white performative power that reduce black bodies to *threatening objects*.

Young Du Bois painfully came to realize—through a glance—that he was *seen* as different, a "difference" that disclosed his black body as "untouchable," fixed in its "monstrosity," and where his body might be said to be "surrounded by an atmosphere of certain uncertainty."[23] Du Bois, West, and Fanon all undergo shared phenomenological processes of coming to *appear* to themselves differently, as barred. It is an experiential violation; they move from a sense of the familiar to the unfamiliar, "taken outside" of themselves and *returned*. With Fanon in mind, Ahmed writes, "The black man, in becoming an object, no longer acts or extends himself; instead, he is amputated, *losing his body*."[24]

Charles Johnson locates this confiscation, this *loss* within the context of walking down Broadway in Manhattan, "platform shoes clicking on the hot pavement, thinking as I stroll of, say, Boolean expansions. I turn, thirsty into a bar. The dimly-lit room, obscured by shadows, is occupied by whites. Goodbye Boolean expansions. I am *seen*." The process of "being seen" is really one of not being seen at all. Johnson describes the epidermalization of his world as a process where his "subjectivity is turned inside out like a shirt cuff." There is a process of emptying, of something having gone missing or having been taken by force—stolen: "Our body responds totally to this abrupt epidermalization; consciousness for the subject is violently emptied of content." Even as Johnson walks down the hallway of his university and encounters a white professor he knows well, his black embodiment stands out as a fungible *object*: "Passing, he sees me as he sees the fire extinguisher to my left, that chair outside the door. I have been seen, yet not seen, acknowledged as present to him, but in a peculiar way."[25] Being seen, Johnson is reduced to that which is *simply* seen as an object; it is a case where his lived embodied *here* is experienced as an occurrent bodily *there*.

Merleau-Ponty writes, "To say that my body is always near to me or always there for me is to say that it is never truly in front of me, that I cannot spread it under my gaze, that it remains on the margins of all of my perceptions, and that it is with me."[26] Yet within the context of the examples that I have briefly provided, the white gaze, whether or not accompanied by verbal iterations, visually foregrounded the black body—for those who undergo the racialized experience of having their bodies confiscated and returned and for those doing the actual confiscating.[27] In the situations of confiscation experienced by West, Fanon, Du Bois, and Johnson, each experienced the *lived* dimension of losing his way, of being stopped, of being reoriented toward his body as a suddenly distorted *object* and of having his embodied motility and aspirations arrested within a world where social affordances are always already white. Indeed, as Ahmed writes, "to be black in 'the white world' is to turn back towards itself, to become an object, which means not only not being extended by the contours of the [white] world, but being diminished as an effect of the bodily extensions of [white] others."[28]

While there are other, less subtle and more *overtly* violent and vicious contexts within which confiscated black bodies undergo forms of racialized foregrounded objectification—stolen and enslaved black bodies that functioned as *objects* of market value notated in a ledger and forced into the dis-eased holds of slave ships during the transatlantic slave trade or brutally lynched black bodies that functioned as *objects* of white racist bloodlust and perverse white desire—I limited my consideration here to black male embodied experiences within social spaces of white meaning construction whereby the black body is ontically mapped as problematic and reduced to an objective epidermal surface, and returned to itself as fundamentally distorted. Black bodies and bodies of color continue to endure everyday acts of confiscation ("As Chinese, you speak English so well"). Such everyday acts of confiscation are sites of pain, frustration, and even death—think here of Trayvon Martin, Renisha McBride, Eric Garner, Tamir Rice, and so many others. While not theorized here, the concept of confiscated bodies holds additional descriptive significance within the context of disability and LGBT communities where embodied diversity is rendered a site of the "physically monstrous" or the "sexually deviant," where such bodies undergo forms of confiscation against the normative axiological backdrop of ableism and heteronormativity—where, indeed, the integrity of such forms of embodiment is confiscated and those bodies violently returned as *disposable*.

## Notes

1. George Yancy, *Black Bodies, White Gazes: The Continuing Significance of Race in America*, 2nd edition (Lanham, Md.: Rowman & Littlefield, 2017).

2. W. E. B. Du Bois, "The Souls of White Folk," in *W. E. B. Du Bois: A Reader*, ed. David Levering Lewis (New York: Henry Holt, 1995), 454.

3. Du Bois, "The Souls of White Folk," 456.

4. Jean-Paul Sartre, "Black Orpheus," in *Race*, ed. Robert Bernasconi (Malden, Mass.: Blackwell, 2001), 116.

5. Sartre, "Black Orpheus," 116.

6. Cornel West, with David Ritz, *Brother West, Living and Loving Out Loud: A Memoir* (New York: Smiley Books, 2009), 124.

7. Frantz Fanon, *Black Skin, White Masks*, trans. Charles Lam Markmann (New York: Grove Press, 1967), 112.

8. Judith Butler, "Endangered/Endangering: Schematic Racism and White Paranoia," in *Reading Rodney King, Reading Urban Uprising*, ed. Robert Gooding-Williams (New York: Routledge, 1993), 18.

9. West, *Brother West*, 124.

10. West, *Brother West*, 124.

11. Fanon, *Black Skin, White Masks*, 117, 116.

12. Judith Butler, *Giving an Account of Oneself* (New York: Fordham University Press, 2005), 36.

13. Judith Butler, *Precarious Life: The Powers of Mourning and Violence* (New York: Verso, 2006), 26.

14. Butler, *Precarious Life*, 26.

15. Butler, *Giving an Account of Oneself*, 65.

16. West, *Brother West*, 124.

17. Fanon, *Black Skin, White Masks*, 112.

18. Maurice Merleau-Ponty, *Phenomenology of Perception*, trans. Donald A. Landes (New York: Routledge, 2012), 151.

19. Fanon, *Black Skin, White Masks*, 111.

20. Sara Ahmed, "A Phenomenology of Whiteness," *Feminist Theory* 8, no. 2 (2007): 156.

21. Fanon, *Black Skin, White Masks*, 109, 113, 109, 114–15.

22. W. E. B. Du Bois, *The Souls of Black Folk* (New York: New American Library, 1982), 44.

23. Fanon, *Black Skin, White Masks*, 110–11.

24. Ahmed, "A Phenomenology of Whiteness,"161, my emphasis.

25. Charles Johnson, "A Phenomenology of the Black Body," in *America and the Black Body: Identity Politics in Print and Visual Culture*, ed. Carol E. Henderson (Madison, N.J.: Fairleigh Dickinson University Press, 2009), 258, 259, 256.

26. Merleau-Ponty, *Phenomenology of Perception*, 93.

27. Helen Ngo, *The Habits of Racism: A Phenomenology of Racism and Racialized Embodiment* (Lanham, Md.: Lexington Books, 2017). See Ngo's brilliant first-person phenomenological account of how her "Asian body" is confiscated through various forms of verbal interpellation, especially 55–56.

28. Ahmed, "A Phenomenology of Whiteness," 161.

# 11 Controlling Images

## Patricia Hill Collins

In the 1990 edition of *Black Feminist Thought,* I introduced the idea of controlling images as an important concept for black feminist thought in the United States. I identified four interrelated controlling images of black femininity: (1) the mammy, the faithful, obedient domestic worker who accepts subordination as her rightful place in American society; (2) the matriarch, the too strong black mother whose failure to conform to mainstream gender norms emasculates African American men, thus damaging African American families; (3) the welfare mother whose irresponsible childbearing places unjust burdens on the state; and (4) the jezebel, a sexually aggressive woman whose claims of ownership over her own body threaten the social order.[1] In *Black Sexual Politics,* I provide a more finely tuned analysis of how these core controlling images of black femininity articulate with African American social class structure, namely, how working-class African American women are more likely to be stigmatized as "bitches," prostitutes and bad mothers, whereas middle-class African American women encounter updated images as modern mammies, Black ladies and "educated bitches."[2]

Understanding the content of these controlling images as well as their changing contours over time, I argue, illuminate the broader workings of political domination and resistance. For example, the controlling images of black femininity all invoke ideas about African American women's bodies, motivations, behaviors, appearance, achievements, and suitability as lovers, wives, mothers, daughters, workers, leaders, and citizens, making these ideas potential sites of domination and resistance. Such images provide a window into the function of representations in sustaining hierarchical power relations as well as the resilience of controlling images across different historical eras.

Yet African American women's efforts to shape and resist the content, use, and effectiveness of controlling images of black femininity point to how controlling images circulate within black feminist thought and similarly subordinated knowledges. Controlling images can provide shared texts for crafting resistant knowledges, offering meaningful thinking tools that help individual African American women see the workings of power in their everyday lives. Moreover, because African American women experience hierarchical power relations holistically, black feminist thought understands power relations as intersectional. Historically, black feminist thought has investigated various intersections of race, class, gender, sexuality, age, ethnicity, ability, and nationality as intersecting systems of power that in turn affect the changing contours of controlling images. Rather than trying to parse out the workings of race, class, gender, sexuality, and ethnicity as distinctive systems of power, understanding black femininity within intersecting power relations has been especially useful.

Viewing social relations of domination and resistance as organized via intersecting systems of power suggests that other social groups also encounter controlling images that are tailor-made for them. One can draw these social groups broadly, e.g., controlling images applied to white American men, or more narrowly, e.g., those applied to middle-class, white American, straight women. In this sense, the case of African American women can be extrapolated to multiple, interconnected social groups that also participate in the same social context. More broadly, the concept of controlling images may be a central organizational principle of intersecting power relations.

## Some Characteristics of Controlling Images

Controlling images have several distinguishing features. First, the overarching purpose of controlling images lies in normalizing and naturalizing social hierarchies within a given social context. The aforementioned controlling images applied to African American women are less meaningful outside the specific U.S. social context where race, class, gender, sexuality, age, ability, and nationality constitute salient social categories. Other social groups within the U.S. context also encounter distinctive constellations of controlling images that articulate with their placement within intersecting power relations. A comparable set of controlling images of black masculinity for African American men resembles yet differs from those associated with African American women. Similarly, Latinas, Asian women, Muslim women, and indigenous women have distinct controlling images of a racialized femininity that serve similar purposes.

Second, controlling images resemble stereotypes yet differ in how each conceptualizes social interaction. Stereotypes assume a certain causal relationship between prejudiced beliefs and human behavior. People who hold erroneous stereotyped beliefs ostensibly act on their beliefs through discriminatory behavior. Addressing racial or sexual discrimination, for example, requires helping individuals shed racist or sexist stereotypes. Yet this approach assumes that people are passive consumers of erroneous information and that their behavior can be countered by exposure to truth. Redressing the harm done by stereotyping requires a moral discourse of good and bad that manages stereotyping through reeducating misinformed individuals and, if that doesn't work, censuring them. Stereotypes also offer scant guidance for how stigmatized, stereotyped groups can resist domination; the best way to resist discrimination lies in fostering tolerance among more powerful actors by recruiting subordinated groups to eschew acting in stereotypical ways.

In contrast, viewing society as shaped by controlling images focuses less on the truth or falsity of the images themselves than on the work they do in structuring unequal power relations. Controlling images are malleable, and the meanings that individuals make of them are under their control. Individuals do not simply accept the truth or falsity of the images themselves, implicitly viewing the images as located somewhere "out there" in hierarchical power relations. Instead, because individuals actively construct their social lives by how they interpret and use controlling images, they are accountable for the social phenomena they engender. Reducing social hierarchy does not yield to simple moral discourses of replacing negative images with more positive ones. Instead, when individuals make meaning of their experiences using controlling images, their beliefs and actions structure power itself. In this sense, moving from seeing images of African American women as just stereotypes and conceptualizing black femininity through the lens of controlling images constitutes an important theoretical shift.

Third, controlling images are hegemonic and, if they are seen at all, are evaluated differently by different social actors. African Americans, indigenous peoples, and other subordinated groups with long histories in the U.S. may be more apt to identify and criticize the controlling images that they encounter because such images are uniformly negative. Yet the content of controlling images need not be negative in order to reproduce prevailing power hierarchies. Some controlling images are positive, holding up societal ideals that are seemingly embodied by the experiences of privileged groups but that serve a similar function as their negative counterparts. The controlling images that are reserved for elite groups are uniformly positive, leaving the impression that these images do not exert control over members of such groups or, more often, that no controlling images apply to them at all. Yet when individuals who benefit from controlling images violate the implicit privileges that accrue to them, the case, for example, of white women who engage in interracial love relationships, their peers may brand them as "race traitors" precisely because their actions undermine the norms of white femininity. Regardless of the individual analysis of controlling images that are applied to them, individuals within groups experience varying degrees of penalty and/or privilege that are associated with the categories to which they are assigned.

Fourth, individuals demonstrate varying degrees of awareness regarding the contours and significance of the controlling images applied to themselves and others. The presence of a complex array of controlling images does not mean that individual social actors can perceive them or that social groups recognize the images that characterize other groups. Within a given social setting, some controlling images are more visible than others. For example, the controlling images that are applied to elite, straight, white men concerning intelligence, morality, and leadership ability are so well-known that they may not be identified as controlling images at all. Despite the heterogeneity in how individual white men choose to perform white masculinity, the controlling images of white masculinity constitute such a deep cultural root that their effects are unavoidable. Similarly, controlling images of black femininity may be ubiquitous, yet individual African American women may not see them as such. Regardless of individual awareness, controlling images are hegemonic—they are part of the fabric of power relations regardless of individual consciousness of their scope, content, and effects.

Fifth, people bring varying degrees of awareness to how controlling images shape their everyday experiences. An individual may be knowledgeable about representations of white masculinity and black femininity yet believe that controlling images do not apply in his or her everyday life. In this sense, controlling images refer not just to external social scripts but also to internal processes of individual subjectivity. Controlling images constitute filters that reflect on one's own worldviews as well as explanations for one's experiences within social hierarchies. Each individual decides the ways in which he or she will perform the social scripts suggested by controlling images. The responses to one's own controlling images as well as those that apply to others are as varied as are individuals themselves. Theoretically, as individuals, we each possess the existential freedom to make ourselves anew, but practically, as members of multiple social groups, we must also take controlling images into account while doing so. Decisions of whether to accept, refuse, reform, and/or transform dimensions of the controlling images that are applied to each of us constitute the bedrock of individual and collective political awareness and action.

Finally, by providing interconnected social scripts for understanding the particular social hierarchies of a given society, controlling images are inherently relational. The specific content of one set of controlling images is intelligible primarily through its connection to others. For example, the controlling images applied to African American women and Latinas gain meaning from one another. Both sets of images provide conceptual tools that are designed to structure a similar subordination. The controlling images applied to groups that routinely have more power, e.g., heterosexual, elite white men with U.S. citizenship, may be hegemonic, yet changing either the status of this group or the controlling images applied to them often has a broader, ripple effect. Because negative controlling images applied to African American women give meaning to an entire set of interrelated controlling images, many other groups have a stake in maintaining or resisting the status quo that sustains controlling images of black femininity. In this sense, both the content of controlling images as well as their ability to shape intersecting power hierarchies are relational.

## Controlling Images and Intersecting Power Relations

Intersecting power relations of race, class, gender, sexuality, age, ability, and ethnicity have structural and interactional dimensions. Controlling images articulate with vertical, social structural conceptions of power, e.g., within power as domination that is organized through social hierarchies); and horizontal, interactional conceptions of power, e.g., within power as a web-based, relational entity among individuals and social groups. Situating controlling images in this juncture of structured social hierarchies and dynamic social interactions provides an angle of vision on the relational nature of structural and web-based forms of political domination.

Structurally, social structures of racism, sexism, and similar forms of domination require controlling images for reproducing social hierarchy. Specifically, power relations are embedded in the built environment. Housing discrimination in U.S. cities and suburbs against African Americans, Latinx, and similarly racialized groups does not rest solely on the actions of individuals who hold racist beliefs. Rather, the urban landscape is structured via neighborhoods and social institutions that represent sedimented societal beliefs concerning race, ethnicity, class, and citizenship. Leveling these physical structures in order to replace the housing, roads, schools, office parks, stores, hospitals, and other aspects of the built environment is impossible. The social environment is similarly durable and structured. Societal rules may make scant mention of categories of race, class, gender or sexuality, yet nonetheless manage to reproduce longstanding hierarchies. Structural power relations can seem so intractable that they leave little room for political resistance.

Controlling images offer a way of analyzing one's own participation in reproducing these structural power relations. Even when controlling images seem hegemonic, elite social actors rarely exercise total "control" exclusively from the top down. Because controlling images are always performed and never finished, the ways in which subordinated social actors criticize, perform, and provide counternarratives matters. This suggests that power from below consists of the bottom-up use of the same controlling images to craft political acquiescence and/or resistance to seemingly durable structural power relations. In this sense, struggles over the meaning of controlling images constitute contested political sites where social actors seek to shape the social structures that organize their everyday lives.

The interactional dimensions of power also shape power relations. Within web-based networks of power, patterned social interactions rarely occur among equals. The interactional dimension of power relations encompasses the myriad ways that individuals use controlling images to create and re-create their own subjectivities in relation to others within intersecting power relations. In a power-laden social context, controlling images constitute a language of social interaction that implicitly or explicitly takes power into account. Individuals may imagine they are the same, with the same interests, beliefs, and experiences, yet make differential use of controlling images to make sense of their shared social worlds. Here understandings of race, class, gender, sexuality, age, ability, and ethnicity as intersecting phenomena influence what a given individual will deem relevant in her or his everyday experiences. In the interpretive context discussed thus far, controlling images justify social hierarchy via hegemonic, interrelated social scripts, foster patterned social interactions, and provide conceptual tools that can help individuals make sense of their experiences.

Controlling images also inform how disciplinary power works at this convergence of structural and interactional power relations. Disciplinary power constitutes a form of social interaction whereby individuals watch one another by keeping one another under surveillance. Whether from positions of authority within bureaucracies or the microaggressions of everyday life, social actors participate in processes of mutual policing, using the ideas of controlling images as the social scripts against which people are evaluated. Yet this kind of disciplinary power cannot remain static—its ideas must change in order to be useful. The growing significance of popular culture in a global context illustrates the significance of controlling images to disciplinary power. Collectively, a broader culture industry draws upon controlling images to create interdependent social scripts. Such scripts in turn inform individual, group-based and institutional behavior within intersecting power relations. Social actors use these social scripts as well as the constellation of interdependent controlling images on which they rest to evaluate and manage their own actions and that of others. Social institutions are highly influenced by such images, as evidenced by public policies that disproportionately benefit some groups to the detriment of others.

Because controlling images are so durable and permeate popular culture and everyday social interaction, they may appear to be permanent. Yet resistance occurs when individuals recognize that controlling images are malleable and can be recast for many different political purposes. When one looks for creative uses of controlling images to upend social scripts, they too permeate popular culture and everyday social interactions. How social actors take up social scripts and perform them can vary considerably from one individual to the next. By claiming the role of "Mom-in-Chief," former first lady Michelle Obama simultaneously invoked controlling images of middle-class white femininity and skillfully sidestepped the controlling images of black femininity. Oprah Winfrey made strategic use of the controlling image of the mammy, recognizing the power of this image for her viewing audience. Few of her viewers, however, had illusions that Oprah was their personal mammy.

These high-profile examples suggest that individuals can take charge of their consciousness of and actions in relation to the controlling images in their everyday lives. With its focus on individual consciousness, intentionality, and experiences from the point of view of the individual, phenomenology offers a rich set of conceptual tools for imagining how individuals might use controlling images in political resistance. Conversely, focusing on controlling images might counter phenomenology's assumption that individual thought and action are unencumbered by power relations. When an individual woman unpacks the tailor-made controlling images that justify her subordination, she brings a changed consciousness to her past, present, and future experiences. Controlling images offer a set of concepts that become meaningful only in relation to power relations.

Simply criticizing the content of controlling images, while necessary, by itself is unlikely to reduce social hierarchy or change human social interactions. Instead, disrupting the authority granted to controlling images requires sustained social action. Because controlling images are collectively created and endorsed, collective action is also needed. Social movements have long aimed to disrupt both controlling images and the power relations they uphold. In this sense, ideas and political resistance are intimately linked. Changing our understandings of controlling images can change behavior, and these changes in turn fosters different possibilities for the social world.

## Notes

1. Patricia Hill Collins. *Black Feminist Thought: Knowledge, Consciousness, and the Politics of Empowerment* (New York: Routledge, 2000), 69–96.

2. Patricia Hill Collins. *Black Sexual Politics: African Americans, Gender, and the New Racism* (New York: Routledge, 2004), 119–48.

# 12 Corporeal Generosity

Rosalyn Diprose

In the context of virtue ethics, generosity is understood as an individual virtue that contributes to human well-being. However, within critical phenomenology generosity takes on an ontological sense as openness toward, or being-given to, others characteristic of human subjectivity, interrelationality, and justice within social and political relations. The "corporeal" component of the concept *corporeal generosity* highlights both the affective basis of the generosity by which human beings are interrelated and the significance of bodily markers of differences between human beings. The ethical dimension of corporeal generosity lies in its sense as potentiality toward equitable and just social relations; conversely, forgetting the generosity of others through the discriminatory evaluation or erasure of these corporeal markers of difference is the locus of injustice.

The notion of corporeal generosity owes something to Aristotle's discussion of magnanimity in book 4 of his *Nicomachean Ethics*.[1] Here generosity is a habituated, cultivated character trait that guides a person toward giving to others beyond the call of duty. But within contemporary social relations underscored by ontological individualism and the logic of an exchange economy, the gift is understood as a commodity, and generosity is subject to calculation of benefit to the giver and the recipient. In this economy of give-and-take what seems generous to some may, paradoxically, be parsimonious to others, and, once subject to calculation, generosity seems to run counter to social justice. While Aristotle seems to tie generosity to calculation and attention to outcomes (the generous person "will give to the right persons the right amounts at the right times"),[2] he also says the generous act must be done *tou kalou heneka* (for the sake of the noble)[3] rather than for some other benefit to the giver or to the recipient. Generosity depends on the noble *proairesis* of the giver, and, while Aristotle defines *proairesis* as "a desire, guided by deliberation,"[4] as Robert Bernasconi explains, "if one's *proairesis* is noble (*kalon*) then one seeks to give more and without measuring this more by reference to what has been received. . . . The gift . . . has the character of an excess (*hyperbole*) such that it cannot be measured by any calculation of its value."[5]

*Corporeal Generosity* develops the concept by connecting this "noble desire" to questions of subject-formation, human relationality, and social justice, thus moving away from understanding generosity as an individual virtue governed by choice and deliberation.[6] Corporeal generosity challenges the assumption that the individual is constituted prior to giving as a reflexive, self-present, autonomous subject who is entirely separate from others. It pertains to a level of interrelationality more primordial than, and perverted by, sociality based on an economy of contract and exchange. Central to the development of this idea of corporeal generosity is Emmanuel Levinas's idea of "radical generosity."[7] Also important are Nietzsche's ontology of "will to power" and "self-overcoming," Merleau-Ponty's phenomenology, and various feminist philosophies of embodiment and difference. In light of such considerations, corporeal generosity can be understood, not as the expenditure of one's possessions but the dispossession of oneself *for the other*; it is not one virtue among others, but the primordial condition of personal, interpersonal, and communal existence. While understanding generosity as this prereflexive corporeal openness to others may not guarantee social justice, it is a necessary move in that direction. Explaining how requires saying more about the development of the concept.

The sociologist Marcel Mauss, through his 1925 essay *The Gift,* is usually credited with the idea that giving, rather than commodity transactions, establishes social bonds and the relational social identities of the community members.[8] Arguably, Nietzsche's philosophy has been equally important for a notion of human interrelations based on generosity: "self-overcoming" involves the noble gift-giving virtue that undercuts the *ressentiment* characteristic of sociality modeled on the creditor-debtor paradigm.[9] Nietzsche aside, Mauss argues that in some "archaic" societies (and underlying modern societies) a gift can function on the order of a "potlatch" (to nourish or consume), where its circulation determines the social rank and identity of a society's members and establishes social bonds between them in the form of a moral obligation toward the giver.[10] Importantly, a gift has the power to establish a social relationship between persons only if the possession given to another carries the significance of being part of the personhood of the giver such that its circulation is one which seeks a return to the place of its birth.[11] So, contrary to the logic of identity in an economy of contract and exchange, identity and sociality are accomplished through giving, not prior to it.

Alan Schrift suggests that it was Jacques Derrida's discussions of the impossibility of the gift (e.g., in *Given Time*),[12] along with earlier analyses by feminist philosophers of the relation between generosity and sexual difference, that have rekindled interest in the topic since the 1980s.[13] While Derrida emphasizes the importance of the gift in opening human existence and sociality, he follows Lévi-Strauss in criticizing Mauss for remaining caught within the logic of exchange and contract with the consequence of envisaging social bonds in terms of obligation of the recipient to the donor.[14] It is this logic that makes the gift and gift-giving impossible: once *recognized as a gift* (hence, a commodity), the gift bestows a debt on the recipient and is annulled as a gift through obligation, gratitude, or some other form of return.[15] The gift is possible only if it goes unrecognized, if it is not commodified, if it is forgotten by the donor and donee. Only then is presence (the gift as [a] present and the presence of both the donor and the donee) deferred such that difference and relationality as giving are maintained.[16]

Derrida then, following Heidegger, ties the aporia of the gift to the gift-event of Being that defers self-presence. The nonreciprocity of the gift matters existentially and ethically because no relation to Being is generated without the production of an "interval" or indeterminate difference (*différance*) between the self and the other that defers the full presence of meaning and being.[17] For giving to engender a relation with the other, the order of being based on exchange must be disrupted, the gift cannot be returned, the (temporal) circle cannot be closed, difference cannot be erased. Giving is what puts the circle of exchange in motion and what exceeds and disrupts it, and, if self-present identity is claimed in being-given to the other, a debt to the other is incurred.

Derrida's accounts of giving echo Levinas on radical generosity, although Levinas places greater emphasis on its ethical dimension. Crucially, Levinas also explains what prompts the "noble desire" of generosity in the first place. It is not one's virtuous character but the other's "ineradicable difference," "*signified* in the nakedness of the face . . . in the expressivity of the other person's whole sensible being" (also in the other's "destitution"), that "inspires" the "handshake" of sociality.[18] And the handshake signifies, not the transmission of knowledge or distant compassion for another but the nonvolitional gift of my "possessions," including time, the fruits of my labor, the "bread from one's mouth," language, and the possibility of a common world.[19] But the most fundamental possession I give to the other is my self-possession; corporeal generosity is the gift of myself for the other through sensibility, the "saying" as "exposure to another" with "indifference toward compensations in reciprocity."[20] For Levinas, only by understanding intersubjectivity in these terms of the nonvolitional opening of the self to another through sensibility "beyond being" (beyond ontology and politics), in terms of a bond lying in "the non-indifference of persons toward one another," can we conceive of a sociality that "does not absorb the difference of strangeness."[21] This sociality also founds my uniqueness as both a "non-coinciding with oneself"[22] and the "here I am" for the other (responsibility for the other, including not erasing alterity through the "said" of language).

Levinas pits his notion of corporeal generosity against any morality or philosophy that grounds our relation to exteriority in knowledge or norms that we already embody, which would eradicate difference in building a common world where nothing remains foreign.[23] Similarly, politics, says Levinas, which involves judgment, evaluation, and knowledge of differences, "represses" generosity, or the "*saying* [as] an ethical openness to the other"; the moral-political order is inspired and directed by "the ethical norm of the interhuman," not the other way around.[24]

While granting much of Levinas's philosophy of generosity, the way he separates politics and ontology from radical generosity presents a problem for political philosophy and its concerns about social justice. The distinction between the two orders implies that the repression of the ethical relation by politics is uniform, whatever form politics takes. This does not easily admit to "degrees" of ethical openness to others depending on *how* the "said" of language and politics organizes social relations. Similarly, the way Derrida ties the gift to its radical forgetting and its operation to the deferral of self-presence overlooks how, in practice, the "gifts" of some (property owners, men, wage earners, "whites") tend to be recognized, remembered, and valued more often than the generosity and gifts of others (the landless, women, the unemployed, indigenous peoples, refugees, and immigrants), which tend to be taken for granted. It is in the *systematic asymmetrical forgetting of the gift*, where only the generosity of the privileged is memorialized, that social inequities and injustice are based. In attending to the connection between generosity and social justice, it is necessary to shift the emphasis away from, while keeping in mind, the aporia of the gift to consider how the asymmetrical forgetting of generosity allows the constitution of hierarchical relations of domination within economies of contract and exchange.

One predominant kind of systematic asymmetrical forgetting of the gift occurs in the social constitution of sexual difference. As Luce Irigaray argues, because "woman" is defined conventionally as either man's Other (as Beauvoir famously argued in *The Second Sex*) or a lack, the "economy of the interval" between the (male) subject and the other is such that sexual difference does not take place.[25] As mother, woman "represents the place of man" (she is the "envelope" by which man delimits himself) such that she is "separated from [her] own 'place.'" Or, as object of sexual desire, woman is not the subject or recipient of generosity; she *is* the "gift" commodified and exchanged between men.[26] Translating this analysis into the paradigm of corporeal generosity, it can be shown how contemporary legal and moral discourses on maternity and the sexual relation assume that women's bodies by definition are already open to and given to the other at least with regard to the gifts of procreation and sexual pleasure.[27] That nonvolitional, unconditional generosity is assumed to be the natural disposition of some women may explain why, in the eyes of the law, rape is so hard to prove and why women's reproductive self-determination is so hard to achieve and maintain. Instead of positing two orders of interrelationality—the order of unconditional generosity and the conditional order of the ontological and political, which Hélène Cixous differentiates in terms of a "feminine" economy of generosity and a "masculine" economy of contract and exchange of property [28]—it would seem that unconditional generosity of exposure is already distributed inequitably within the political organization of society in ways that demand self-sacrifice of the subordinated and their openness to colonization by the privileged.

Attending to the *politics* of corporeal generosity is aided by adding consideration of salient insights from Anglophone feminist philosophers of embodiment and difference and from Merleau-Ponty's ontology of interrelationality in terms of the intertwining of "the flesh." There are two reasons for this refocus on the corporeal dimension of generosity with regard to the ontological-political order. First, the injustice that inflects asymmetrical forgetting of generosity is governed by the way social norms and ideas about bodily markers of difference designate which bodies are recognized as possessing property that can be given and which bodies are devoid of property and already given over to others or open to colonization; which bodies are worthy of gifts and which are not. These norms are embedded in what phenomenologists call the "common world," the "said" of language (Levinas), in "the flesh" of the world (Merleau-Ponty), or what Moira Gatens calls "imaginary bodies," those culturally specific "images and symbols through which we make sense of social bodies and which determine, in part, their value, their status and what will be deemed their appropriate treatment."[29] While these ideas about bodies inflect the political organization of society, they also impact on the formation of subjectivities, which on Merleau-Ponty's account means we embody social imaginaries insofar as we live through the bodies of others who are already social beings: "perception" and, hence, subjectivity—which takes place in the "flesh" or the "interworld" of affective prereflective sensibility—is "cultural-historical" because "the . . . imaginary is in my body."[30] While this is where the discriminatory evaluation of differences takes place, contrary to Levinas's reading of Merleau-Ponty, the intercorporeal realm of "the flesh" does not involve the uniform effacement of alterity: we are open to the bodies of others by degrees, depending on the extent to which prejudicial ideas about different bodies have taken hold of one's perception.

Nor is the intercorporeal world of "the flesh" devoid of generosity. Indeed, the second reason for this refocus on the ontological-political is that just as the interrelation between bodies can effect an ontological closure to the other, the "flesh of the world" is also fundamentally an openness inspired by the "strangeness of difference." Hence, corporeal generosity engenders the *overcoming of the closure of relationality*. While Merleau-Ponty does not discuss generosity explicitly, we can extrapolate from his ontology to say that the generosity of intercorporeality rests on the ambiguity or the instituted-instituting feature of "the flesh."[31] This means that existing ideas that govern social relations and that we embody are open to transformation. Hence, sociality is open to new paths of thinking and modes of living through corporeal generosity provoked by the other's alterity. A politics of corporeal generosity also includes a thoroughgoing critique of prejudicial ideas about bodies that promote an ontological closure to alterity and some character building in generosity though education in civic virtues.

Locating generosity within corporeal intersubjectivity, where generosity is irreducible to either volitional acts or passive sensibility, grounds an active politics that aims for justice. For instance, the concept underscores campaigns for giving hospitality to refugees and it supports critical analyses of colonization of indigenous peoples and suggests means of achieving decolonization.[32] Others have worked with the concept of corporeal generosity to reimagine maternity while arguing for greater reproductive self-determination for women.[33] It has some currency in environmental politics in projects for reenvisaging the human-nonhuman relation.[34] Within organizational studies corporeal generosity features in schemes for developing a more multicultural and equitable working environment.[35]

## Notes

1. Aristotle, *The Nicomachean Ethics*, trans. Hippocrates Apostle (Dordrecht: Reidel 1975), hereafter referred to as NE followed by standard notation, then page numbers to this edition.

2. Aristotle, NE, 1120a, 26.

3. Aristotle, NE, 1120a, 14.

4. Aristotle, NE, 1113a, 11.

5. Robert Bernasconi, "What Goes Around Comes Around: Derrida and Levinas on the Economy of the Gift and the Gift of Genealogy," in *The Logic of the Gift: Toward an Ethic of Generosity*, ed. Alan D. Schrift (New York: Routledge, 1997), 267.

6. Rosalyn Diprose, *Corporeal Generosity: On Giving with Nietzsche, Merleau-Ponty, and Levinas* (Albany: State University of New York Press, 2002).

7. Discussed in these terms in Emmanuel Levinas, *Totality and Infinity: An Essay on Exteriority*, trans. Alphonso Lingis (Pittsburgh, Pa.: Duquesne University Press, 1969), 50–51, 168–74, 208; Emmanuel Levinas, "Meaning and Sense," in *Emmanuel Levinas: Collected Philosophical Papers*, trans. Alphonso Lingis (Dordrecht: Martinus Nijhoff, 1987), 92; Emmanuel Levinas, "On Intersubjectivity: Notes on Merleau-Ponty," in *Outside the Subject*, trans. Michael B. Smith (Stanford, Calif.: Stanford University Press, 1994), 101–3; Emmanuel Levinas, *Otherwise Than Being or Beyond Essence*, trans. Alphonso Lingis (The Hague: Martinus Nijhoff, 1981), 48–51 and 72–4.

8. Marcel Mauss, *The Gift: Forms and Functions of Exchange in Archaic Societies*, trans. Ian Cunnison (New York: Norton Library, 1967).

9. For two accounts of Nietzsche's approach to generosity, see Alan Schrift, "On the Gift-Giving Virtue: Nietzsche's Unacknowledged Feminine Economy," *International Studies in Philosophy* 26, no. 3 (1994): 33–44; and Diprose, *Corporeal Generosity*, chapters 1 and 8.

10. Mauss, *The Gift*, 6

11. Mauss, *The Gift*, 10, 19.

12. Jacques Derrida, *Given Time, 1: Counterfeit Money*, trans. Peggy Kamuf (Chicago: University of Chicago Press, 1992).

13. Alan Schrift, "Introduction: Why Gift?," in Schrift, *The Logic of the Gift*, 1.

14. Derrida, *Given Time*, 24.

15. Derrida, *Given Time*, 12–14.

16. Derrida, *Given Time*, 23–4.

17. Derrida, *Given Time*, 20, 27. Also Jacques Derrida, "Différance," in *Margins of Philosophy*, trans. Alan Bass (Chicago: University of Chicago Press, 1982).

18. Levinas, "On Intersubjectivity," 102.

19. Levinas, *Totality and Infinity*, 168–74; Levinas, *Otherwise Than Being*, 74.

20. Levinas, *Otherwise Than Being*, 47–48; Levinas, "On Intersubjectivity," 101.

21. Levinas, "On Intersubjectivity," 103.

22. Levinas, *Otherwise Than Being*, 56.

23. Levinas is also critical of Heidegger and Merleau-Ponty for remaining within the order of being that would eradicate alterity and the ethical relation. For a defense of Merleau-Ponty against this criticism, see *Corporeal Generosity*, chapter 9.

24. Emmanuel Levinas, "Dialogue with Emmanuel Levinas," in *Face to Face with Levinas*, ed. Richard A. Cohen (Albany: State University of New York Press, 1986), 29–30.

25. Luce Irigaray, "Sexual Difference" (1984), in *An Ethics of Sexual Difference*, trans. Carolyn Burke and Gillian C. Gill (London: Athlone Press, 1993), 6, 10.

26. Luce Irigaray, "Women on the Market" (1977), in *This Sex Which Is Not One*, trans Catherine Porter with Carolyn Burke (Ithaca, N.Y.: Cornell University Press, 1985), 170–91.

27. See Diprose, *Corporeal Generosity*, chapters 2, 4.

28. Hélène Cixous, "Castration or Decapitation?," trans. Annette Khun, *Signs* 7, no. 1 (1981): 41–55. See Alan Schrift's critical appraisal of Cixous's approach to generosity in "Why Gift?"

29. Moira Gatens, *Imaginary Bodies: Ethics, Power and Corporeality* (London: Routledge, 1996), viii.

30. Maurice Merleau-Ponty's works referred to here are "Eye and Mind," trans. Carleton Dallery in *The Primacy of Perception*, ed. James M. Edie (Evanston, Ill.: Northwestern University Press, 1964), 159–90; *Signs*, trans. Richard McCleary (Evanston, Ill.: Northwestern University Press, 1964), 159–81; and *The Visible and the Invisible*, trans. Alphonso Lingis (Evanston, Ill.: Northwestern University Press, 1968).

31. Diprose, *Corporeal Generosity*, chapter 9.

32. For example, Diprose, *Corporeal Generosity*, chapter 8.

33. See, for example, Myra Hird, "The Corporeal Generosity of Maternity," *Body & Society* 13, no.1 (2007): 1–20.

34. For example, Gay Hawkins, *Ethics of Waste: How We Relate to Rubbish* (Lanham, Md.: Rowman & Littlefield, 2006), 110–5; Clive Barnett and David Land, "Geographies of Generosity: Beyond the 'Moral Turn,'" *Geoforum* 38 (2007): 1065–75.

35. See Philip Hancock, "Embodied Generosity and an Ethics of Organization," *Organization Studies* 29, no. 10 (2008): 1358–73; Alison Pullen and Carl Rhodes, "Corporeal Ethics and the Politics of Resistance in Organizations," *Organization* 21, no.6 (2014): 782–96.

# 13 Decolonial Imaginary

Eduardo Mendieta

The locus classicus for the first articulation of the philosopheme of the "decolonial imaginary" is Emma Pérez's 1999 book, *The Decolonial Imaginary: Writing Chicanas into History*.[1] While Pérez is a historian and her text is a pointed intervention in the practice of writing history, it is nonetheless a text that is very much influenced by philosophy in general, and in particular the work of philosopher of history Hayden White and philosopher Michel Foucault. In fact, one of Pérez's goals is to unearth, rescue, restore, and reactivate the "subjugated" knowledges of Chicanas in general, and Chicana lesbians in particular. What also makes Pérez's book a key text is her distinct intersectional approach. This is evident in the way the book is divided into three methodological sections: "Archaeology: Colonialist Historiography, Writing the Nation into History"; "From Archaeology to Genealogy: Discursive Events and Their Case Studies"; and "Genealogy: History's Imprints upon the Colonial Body." Thus, Pérez traces an intersectional research agenda by digging and sifting through the sediment of a colonial and colonizing imaginary, traversing through a genealogy that foregrounds Mexican diasporic and postrevolutionary identities, so as to arrive at what she calls "third space feminist (re)vision."

Pérez defines the decolonial imaginary in the following way:

> I believe that the time lag between the colonial and postcolonial can be conceptualized as the decolonial imaginary. Bhabha names the interstitial gap between the modern and the postmodern, the colonial and the postcolonial, a time lag. This is precisely where Chicano/a history finds itself today, in a time lag between the colonial and the postcolonial. If we are dividing history into these categories—colonial relations, postcolonial relations, and so on—then I would like to propose a decolonial imaginary as a rupturing space, the alternative to that which is written in history. I think that the decolonial imaginary is that time lag between the colonial

> and postcolonial, the interstitial space where differential politics and social dilemmas are negotiated.[2]

This reading offers a disruptive transcription, or transposition, of Homi Bhabha's own Lacanian/Fanonian psychoanalytic disruption of the modern/postmodern, colonial/postcolonial dyad, to the temporal-spatial border of the U.S. Pérez refocuses our locus of attention and the locus of enunciation from Europe and its colonies to the U.S. and its own colonial/imperial shadows. Pérez, however, also conceives the decolonial as a "time lag," as the practice of disrupting the world-clock of empire. If we understand colonialism as a practice of colonizing time, then in Pérez's articulation, the decolonial imaginary aims to disrupt and shatter colonial and colonizing temporalities as they manifest in historiography. Another point of reference for Pérez's coinage of "colonial imaginary" is Jacques Lacan. She writes, "In the Lacanian sense, the imaginary is linked to the mirror stage, at which a child identifies the 'I' of the self in a mirror, an image is reflected back, and the subject becomes object. For my purposes, the imaginary is the mirror identity where coloniality overshadows the image in the mirror."[3] The imaginary in this Lacanian reading, then, is a distorting mirror, a framed space of alienation and disidentification, but also, at the same time, the mirror that projects an impossible and unreal image of who we are not but are commanded to become. In Pérez's generative articulation of the decolonial imaginary, then, we have the lineaments of what she elsewhere calls a "decolonial project" and "decolonial tool."[4]

There is another, if neglected and lesser known locus classicus for the performance and enactment of a decolonial imaginary, I would argue. This is Guillermo Gómez-Peña, Enrique Chagoya, and Felicia Rice's visually arresting and rhetorically powerful *Codex Espangliensis: From Columbus to the Border Patrol,* a sui generis "codex" that was begun in 1992, finished in 1998, and published in 2000.[5] Gómez-Peña, Chagoya, and Rice reveal the decolonial imaginary as not simply a project but the actual projecting of an image or images that may begin to conjure a decolonial subject. That is to say, we can think of the decolonial imaginary as a drafting, drawing, imaging that may interpellate not just postcolonial but, most importantly, decolonizing agencies. Like most of the classical Aztec codices of the sixteenth century, the book is designed to be unfolded. It opens up into two folds: the one on the left unfurls to be read from the left to the right; the fold on the right unfurls to be read from the right to the left. This right fold is made up of texts, images, drawings, and cut-outs that draw from the visual archive of the pre-Columbian past, up through our more recent visual repertoire. The text was composed by Gómez-Peña, the images and collages were designed by Chagoya, and the formatting of the codex was designed by Rice. It was deliberately composed and designed as an act of resistance to the anti-Mexican fervor of the early 1990s, but also as a decolonial intervention to question the quincentennial celebrations of the so-called discovery of the New World. I want to argue that along with Pérez's inaugural text, where the concept of decolonial imaginary is explicitly articulated, we should consider the *Codex Espangliensis* as an exemplar of what such an imaginary may begin to look like. While the terms *imaginary* and *decolonial* are not explicitly evoked in the text, it is evident from Gómez-Peña's numerous performances and texts that his work is decolonial and decolonizing and explicitly directs our attention to the interaction among image, imagination, and imaginary.[6] Gloria Anzaldúa's paradigm-shifting text *Borderlands/La Frontera: The New Mestiza* enacts linguistically and poetically what the *Codex Espangliensis* does visually. It sketches the contours of a "decolonial imaginary" through her corporeal cartographies of *La Frontera*. Inchoate in her poetics of resistance we also find a radical imaginary.[7]

If I had the space, I would close this synopsis by turning to María Lugones's placental essay, "Towards a Decolonial Feminism,"[8] which takes up the work of many other Latina and Chicana feminists to elaborate what she calls "decolonial feminism." Here, Lugones confronts critically and generatively the work of both Aníbal Quijano, who coined what has become a *Punctum Archimedis* for decolonial philosophizing, the coloniality of power, and Walter Mignolo, who coined the term *colonial difference*.[9] But this must remain a promissory note, or better, an invitation. It would also be important to catalogue those imaginaries against which, through which, and with which the decolonial imaginary wrestles, toils, rubs, mimics, and mocks. And so we begin: pre-Columbian, colonial, postcolonial, imperial, postimperial, modern, postmodern, premodern, medieval, ancient, Orientalist, Occidentalist, civilizational, religious, Protestant, Baroque, racial, gender, sexual, temporal-spatial, geographical, chronotopological, futurological, revolutionary, and so on imaginaries.[10] Thus the "decolonial imaginary" is a radical imaginary, to use that felicitous expression by Cornelius Castoriadis. It aims to work upon the past so as to awaken us from our colonial amnesia and engage us in an orthopedics of our imperial aphasia so as to forge paths toward a common future.[11] A "decolonial imaginary" intervenes in how we think, give, or take time away, if time is the horizon of redemption, memory, transformation, and ultimately liberation.[12]

In keeping with the contestational, disruptive, shattering, disidentifying dimensions and aspects of the "decolonial imaginary," I would like to offer a typology of ways of mapping/locating/tracking the imaginary and how they are contested, confronted, dislocated, and refracted by thinkers of what Nelson Maldonado-Torres has called the "decolonial turn."[13] The following are not imaginaries per se, but rather ways of thinking and localizing them. The most elemental and immediate way of offering a cartography of the imaginary is through the analysis of what Michèle LeDoeuff calls, *l'imagineire philosophique* (the philosophical imaginary). By this, LeDoeuff means that even the driest and most rationalist philosophy is populated by a "whole pictorial world" that includes "rocks, clocks, horses, donkeys and even a lion."[14] Philosophy is not only the staging of logos but also a panoply of imagined beings, among them the figure of the woman and the barbarian.[15] On the side of a "decolonial philosophical imaginary" we would find Enrique Dussel, María Lugones, and Walter Mignolo. Dussel, in particular, offers cartographies of Western and Eurocentric imaginaries that legitimate colonialism. Among his most important insights is his critique of the Cartesian *cogito* as requiring Hernán Cortés's *ego conquiro* as its material condition of possibility. "I conquer" is thus the practical foundation of "I think."[16] The philosophical project of "Enlightenment" requires that some cultures and peoples be relegated to a culpable, immature (*verschuldeten Unmündigkeit*) past.[17]

What Dussel did for early modern philosophy and contemporary philosophy, Mignolo did for the Renaissance in his work, *The Darker Side of the Renaissance: Literacy, Territoriality and Colonization*, in which he diagnoses how Amerindian ways of writing, recording historical memory, and configuring social space were colonized by

Renaissance configurations of literacy, history, and space.[18] In *The Idea of Latin America*, Mignolo maps the ways in which "Latin" America was invented in order to provide geopolitical alibis for Eurocentric and Anglocentric colonial and imperial projects.[19] A key argument in this book is that coloniality is constitutive of modernity. In other words, the Anglo-Eurocentric imaginary is predicated on a colonial/modernizing/capitalist project. Lugones furthers this contribution to the cartographies of the philosophical imaginary by engaging the concept of the coloniality of power through the material production of sex/gender and the colonizing gaze.[20] If, to argue along with Dussel and Mignolo, coloniality is constitutive of both the Enlightenment and modernity, for Lugones, the invention/production of sex/gender is foundational to both. The coloniality of power—i.e., the coloniality of modernity/imperialism—is always already the coloniality of gender. We could thus rephrase Dussel's philosophical dictum about the "ego conquiro" through Lugones's key insight: "ego sexum" is co-originary with the Cortésian "ego conquiro."

With respect to *sociopsychological* mappings of the imaginary, an obvious point of reference is Jacques Lacan, whose *Écrits* remains the de rigueur point of reference for any thinking about the imaginary.[21] Charles Taylor, Homi Bhabha, and Kalpana Seshadri-Crooks also contribute to these distinct mappings; Seshadri-Crooks's *Desiring Whiteness: A Lacanian Analysis of Race* is particularly significant because it offers one of the most in-depth and comprehensive Lacanian analyses of race, and how it configures our social imaginaries.[22]

Alongside decolonial and sociopsychological mappings of the imaginary are what I would call *chronotopological imaginaries*[23] associated with figures such as Henri Lefebvre, David Harvey, Derek Gregory, and Stuart Elden. Lefebvre's analytics of spatiality distinguishes among spatial practices, representations of space, and representational spaces. He links this tripartite differentiation to the phenomenological differentiation among the perceived, the conceived, and the lived, in such a way that "the triad perceived-conceived-lived, along with what is denoted and connoted by these three terms, contributes to the production of space through interactions which metamorphose those original *intuitus* into a quasi-system."[24] In other words, spatial practices, ways of representing space, and the ways in which we inhabit representational spaces, including the imaginary geographies of the colonial imagination (such as those, for instance, of Joseph Conrad and William Faulkner and those catalogued by Edward Said in *Orientalism*)[25] transform habits into conceptual matrices. The "decolonial chronotopological imaginary" might describe thinkers such as Aníbal Quijano, Ramón Grosfoguel, Nelson Maldonado-Torres, Santiago Castro-Gómez, Walter Mignolo, and Fernando Coronil.[26] What is distinctive about their cartographies of the colonial/imperial/capitalist imaginary is that they simultaneously link the invention of continents, that is, geographies of barbarism and backwardness, with what Johannes Fabian has called "the denial of coevalness," that is, the process of temporally segregating peoples and cultures through the creation of an epistemic matrix or framework that conditions the intelligibility of the human sciences in general.[27] In this way, these authors link colonial/imperial/capitalist imaginaries to the epistemic imaginary of the West that de-authorizes non-Western cultures to make credible knowledge claims.

The imaginary may be portrayed as the "final frontier" of our philosophical critique, yet it has remained neither uncharted nor unexplored. It has been approached through the mappings of philosophical, sociopsychological, and chronotopological cartographies on the many sides of the colonial/modern divide. The "decolonial imaginary" rivets us to the axis where we are held together by the images, imaginations, and imaginaries that both possess us and inform the ways in which we refuse identification with others and also enable moments of liberating disidentification. The "decolonial imaginary" is a radical imaginary precisely because it illuminates how we are both possessed by a coloniality/modernity/imaginary that could not be imagined without those who were colonized and in need of modernization and enlightenment, and, at the same time, how that same imaginary is the very site of resistance, liberation, and solidarity.

## Notes

1. Emma Pérez, *The Decolonial Imaginary: Writing Chicanas into History* (Bloomington: Indiana University Press, 1999).
2. Pérez, *The Decolonial Imaginary*, 6.
3. Pérez, *The Decolonial Imaginary*, 6.
4. See Emma Pérez, "Queer Subaltern Citizens: Agency through Decolonial Queer Theory," draft of paper delivered at the Subaltern Citizens and Their Histories conference at Emory University, October 12–14, 2006, page 4 of the manuscript. See also her "Queering the Borderlands: The Challenges of Excavating the Invisible and Unheard," in "Gender on the Borderlands," special issue of *Frontiers: A Journal of Women Studies* 24, nos. 2–3. (2003): 122–31. I want to thank Emma Velez for bringing to my attention these later essays.
5. Guillermo Gómez-Peña, Enrique Chagoya, Felicia Rice, *Codex Espangliensis: From Columbus to the Border Patrol* (San Francisco: City Lights Books, Moving Parts Press, 2000). See my interview with Guillermo Gómez-Peña, "Eduardo Mendieta and Guillermo Gómez-Peña: A Latino Philosopher Interviews a Chicano Performance Artist," *Nepantla: Views from the South* 2, no. 1 (2001): 539–54.
6. See Guillermo Gómez-Peña, *New World Border: Prophecies, Poems, and Loqueras for the End of the Century* (San Francisco: City Lights Books, 1996). See also my essay, "The Bio-technological *scala naturae* and Interspecies Cosmopolitanism: Patricia Piccinini, Jane Alexander, and and Guillermo Gómez-Peña," in *Biopower: Foucault and Beyond*, ed. Vernon Cisney and Nicolae Morar (Chicago: University of Chicago Press, 2015), 158–79.
7. Gloria Anzaldúa, *Borderlands/La Frontera: The New Mestiza* (San Francisco: Spinsters/Aunt Lute, 1987).
8. Maria Lugones, "Toward Decolonial Feminism," *Hypatia* 25, no. 4 (Fall 2010): 742–59. See also her essay "Methodological Notes towards a Decolonial Feminism," in *Decolonizing Epistemology: Latina/o Philosophy and Theology*, ed. Ada María Isasi-Díaz and Eduardo Mendieta (New York: Fordham University Press, 2012), 68–86.
9. Here I would direct the reader to Mariana Ortega, "Decolonial Woes and Practices of Un-knowing," *Journal of Speculative Philosophy* 31, no. 3 (2017): 504–16, in order to follow up on some immanent criticisms.

10. I would be remiss if I failed to mention the important background works of Gruzinski, Todorov, and Eduardo Subirats. See Serge Gruzinski, *The Conquest of Mexico: The Incorporation of Indian Societies into the Western World, 16–18th Centuries*, trans. Eileen Corrigan (Cambridge, U.K.: Polity Press, 1993). It is important to underscore that the original French title was *La colonization de L'imaginaire* (1988)—the colonization of the imaginary. See also Tzvetan Todorov, *The Conquest of America: The Question of the Other*, trans. Richard Howard (1984; Norman: University of Oklahoma Press, 1999); Eduardo Subirats, *El continente vacío: La conquista del Nuevo Mundo y la conciencia moderna* (Ciudad de México: Siglo XXI, 1994). It is unfortunate that Subirats's text has not been translated as it is a resource for thinking the way the colonial imaginary invented a continent that was empty of peoples and cultures meriting respect.

11. See Cornelius Castoriadis, "Radical Imagination and the Social Instituting Imaginary" (1994), in *The Castoriadis Reader*, ed. David Ames Curtis (Malden, Mass.: Blackwell, 1997), 319–37. See also Cornelius Castoriadis, *World in Fragments: Writings on Politics, Society, Psychoanalysis, and the Imagination*, ed. and trans. David Ames Curtis (Stanford, Calif.: Stanford University Press, 1997), especially "The Discovery of the Imagination" 213–45; and his *The Imaginary Institution of Society*, trans. Kathleen Blamey (Cambridge, U.K.: Polity Press, 1987). All indispensable work for anyone working on the concept of the "imaginary."

12. See my essay "Postcolonialism, Postorientalism, Postoccidentalism: The Past That Never Went Away and the Future That Never Arrived," in *Emerging Trends in Continental Philosophy, Volume 8: History of Continental Philosophy*, ed. Todd May, general editor Alan D. Schrift (Durham, U.K.: Acumen, 2010), 149–71.

13. Nelson Maldonado-Torres, *Against War: Views from the Underside of Modernity* (Durham, N.C.: Duke University Press, 2008), 6–7.

14. Michèlle LeDoeuff, *The Philosophical Imaginary*, trans. Colin Gordon (London: Continuum, 2002), 1.

15. See also the interview with LeDoeuff in Raoul Mortley, *French Philosophers in Conversation: Levinas, Schneider, Serres, Irigaray, LeDoeuff, Derrida* (London: Routledge, 1991), 80–91.

16. Enrique Dussel, *Philosophy of Liberation*, trans. Aquilina Martinez and Christine Morkovsky (Maryknoll, N.Y.: Orbis Books, 1985), 3.

17. Enrique Dussel, *The Invention of the Americas: Eclipse of "the Other" and the Myth of Modernity*, trans. Michael D. Barber (New York: Continuum, 1995), 19.

18. Walter Mignolo, *The Darker Side of the Renaissance: Literacy, Territoriality and Colonization* (Ann Arbor: University of Michigan Press, 1995).

19. Walter Mignolo, *The Idea of Latin America* (Malden, Mass.: Blackwell, 2005).

20. María Lugones, *Pilgrimages/Peregrinajes: Theorizing Coalition against Multiple Oppressions* (Lanham, Md.: Rowman & Littlefield, 2003).

21. Jacques Lacan, *Écrits: The First Complete Edition in English*, trans. Bruce Fink in collaboration with Héloïse Fink and Russell Grigg (New York: Norton, 2005).

22. Charles Taylor, *Modern Social Imaginaries* (Durham, N.C.: Duke University Press, 2004); Homi Bhabha, *The Location of Culture* (London: Routledge, 1994); Kalpana Seshadri-Crooks, *Desiring Whiteness: A Lacanian Analysis of Race* (London: Routledge, 2001).

23. See my essay "Chronotopology: Critique of Spatio-Temporal Regimens," in *New Critical Theory: Essays on Liberation*, ed. Jeffrey Paris and William Wilkerson (New York: Rowman & Littlefield, 2001), 175–97.

24. Henri Lefebvre, *The Production of Space,* trans. Donald Nicholson-Smith (Malden, Mass.: Blackwell, 1991), 246.

25. Edward W. Said, *Orientalism,* 25th anniversary edition (New York: Vintage Books, 1994).

26. Aníbal Quijano is now a key figure in what Maldonado-Torres called the "decolonial turn," which in his genealogy goes back as far as W. E. B. Du Bois. Unfortunately, Quijano is not as well-known as he should because he has mostly published essays. Now, however, we have an indispensable resource with Aníbal Quijano, *Cuestiones y Horizontes: Antología Esencial,* selección y prólogo a cargo de Danilo Assis Clímaco (Ciudad Autónoma de Buenos Aires: CLACSO, 2014). The rest of these authors can be found in Mabel Moraña, Enrique Dussel, and Carlos A. Jáuregui, eds., *Coloniality at Large: Latin America and the Postcolonial Debate* (Durham, N.C.: Duke University Press, 2008).

27. See Johannes Fabian, "Of Dogs Alive, Birds Dead, and Time to Tell a Story," *Chronotypes: The Construction of Time,* ed. John Bender and David E. Wellberry (Stanford, Calif.: Stanford University Press, 1991), 185–204.

# 14 *Durée*

Alia Al-Saji

*Durée* (duration) has come, after Henri Bergson, to be synonymous with *lived time*, with what it is to endure and live time (in both passive and active senses). While an initial reading of Bergson might take *durée* to be equivalent to the internal time or flow of consciousness—or, more broadly, mind (*esprit*)—and to be contrary to materiality, sociality, and space (especially if limited to Bergson's early work),[1] this way of reading *durée* falters with subsequent texts (*Matière et mémoire* onward) and as soon as one begins to think through the lived implications of enduring.[2] For not only should we avoid predetermining who or what is living time; lived time is not reducible to consciousness for Bergson, nor are *durées* limited to human, or even animal, lives. Taking seriously what it means to endure and live time impels us to think *durée* not only as substantive (*la durée*) but as verbal (*durer*), to take the ontological sense of being as becoming.[3] I want to argue that what appears to be a quantifiable period or continuum—the *durée* of a phenomenon or life—is felt as an intensive and affectively differentiating process, *for which the weight of its own duration makes a difference*. This is to say that *durée* is not a linear flow that moves on from the past toward an indiscriminately "open" future, but is one that carries the past with it in relational and nonlinear ways—for which the past remains operative, neither closed book nor completed being. The duration of pastness continues to push on, or weigh down, the present but in differential and affective ways.

My purpose in rethinking *durée* is to make visible its sometimes sidelined ethical and political dimensions, while also putting under pressure the categories and distinctions according to which its phenomenological and ontological senses have seemed self-evident (e.g., future/past, quality/quantity, continuity/discontinuity). I want to retool the term so as to allow an understanding of the *longue durée*[4] of racism and the afterlives of colonialism and slavery whose "rot remains," instituting the phenomenological field of possibility and enduring in the material, embodied, and affective life of the present (differentially, for differently positioned subjects).[5]

## Zigzagging Senses of *Durée*

The common sense of *durée* (in French) takes it to belong to something, a relation of possession. It is the *durée of* consciousness, of a life, of things, or of historical events. *Durée* is delimited and periodized within the life of things to which it applies. Because of the stability of the thing or the self-identity of the phenomenon projected behind it, *durée* is taken to measure the interval *in which* they take place, perceived as a continuum.[6] What is missed is not only the way in which *durée* escapes quantification while grounding measure, but also how *durée* generates intervals through its rhythmic punctuation and hesitation—how its perceived continuity, or flow, relies on structuring discontinuities and differentiations, how *durée* is a kind of multiplicity.

More than a simple reversal, the Bergsonian sense of *durée* deepens and destabilizes the common understanding in three ways. First, it makes *durée* an absolute: rather than time belonging to us, we belong to it. This recalls Deleuze's argument, in his reading of Bergson, that reducing *durée* to subjective, interior life misses its radical immanence: we live, move, and change within time.[7] But this relation should not be read as that of container to content. *Durée*, to borrow a Merleau-Pontian expression, is an invisible yet structuring dimension *according to which* we live; it is not a thing but that through or against which things and events appear.[8] Thus *durée* lies before measure—a grounding dimension that makes measure possible.

It is commonplace to describe Bergsonian *durée* as a qualitative flow, which is falsified if spatialized (e.g., clock-time); time is taken to be opposed to spatial extension and quality to quantity. This misses, however, the second, deeper import of the Bergsonian turn in thinking time as *durée*. While Bergson often emphasizes the risks of spatialization (in addition to its practical and utilitarian functions), it should be noted that spatializing schemas skew not only how we understand life, consciousness, and time but also how we see matter and extension. The spatial schema is an abstract, homogeneous grid projected onto material extension that freezes its movements and empties out its temporal rhythms; this cuts up the flow of the material universe and solidifies it into (countable) objects, while condensing sensations into (qualitative) attributes.[9] Rather than simply reversing the quantity/quality distinction, then, *durée* comes prior to this distinction and is the source of both terms.[10]

Third is the understanding of *durée* as continuum. Gaston Bachelard famously criticized Bergsonism for eliding the discontinuity and negativity that must ontologically undergird *durée*; what results is a confused flow, where interruptions are epiphenomenal, unable to do justice to either the phenomenology of the passage of time or the instant.[11] Bergson's early account of *durée* as interpenetrating, heterogeneous flow (*Essai*) sometimes lends itself to this interpretation. By overemphasizing the role of succession over coexistence in structuring *durée*, dimensional and vertical relations that organize the flow are presented vaguely in terms of overlap or "interpenetration."[12] But if this interpenetration remains undifferentiated, then heterogeneity disappears in a fog where moments blend and where differences in kind between past and present are subsumed to a presentist and linear continuum. Rather than taking *durée* to simply *flow*, then, I think that pastness and memory must be understood to form the invisible, and unconscious, infrastructure of *durée*. Moreover, the past should be conceived as dynamic and nonrepresentational—as tendency and affect rather than sediment or aggregate of fractionable instants. This is born out by Bergson's accounts of the past in *Matière et mémoire* and *L'évolution créatrice*. The implication (in response to Bachelard) is that Bergsonian *durée* weaves together *both* discontinuity *and* continuity, one through the other.

## Nonlinear *Durée*: Hesitation and the Affective Weight of the Past

That *durée* is neither linear succession nor uninterrupted continuity puts under pressure the idea of time as progress. *Durée* should not be construed as a seamless movement of progress oriented toward the future, *moving on and leaving the past behind* (with closure determining the past and openness located only in the future). This misses the intensively accumulating and differentiating force of the past. While *durée* may initially appear as flow, that flow is immanently structured through hesitation: "Time is . . . hesitation, or it is nothing at all," says Bergson.[13] Such hesitation may be understood from three angles. (1) Phenomenologically, hesitation is the interval within *durée*, the delay in perception, opened up in the sensorimotor schema of the body by its affective thickness and complexity; living bodies feel rather than simply react, allowing memory to flood in and differentially inform the course of action. But (2), ontologically, the zone of indetermination that is my hesitating body is a rhythm of *durée* that embodies an intensive configuration of pastness—materialized in my habitualities, actualized in my recollections, and felt in the unconscious weight of the past that pushes down upon me or buoys me up. (3) The import of pastness reminds us that, structurally, *durée* involves a dissymmetrical splitting of time (more fountain than flow): ever *passing* on the cusp to futurity, the present is sustained by the *coexistence of the past* that it falls into and reconfigures.[14]

Thus *my durée*—how I live or endure time, how or that I hesitate—is linked to the affective weight of the past for me (which is more than just *my* past).[15] Ways of living pastness shape the field of the present while opening intervals of indeterminacy that ripple through time. This coexistence of past with present—the past's nonrepresentational, affective, and dimensional work—(un)grounds continuity while making hesitation and transformation possible. To say that the past endures in or remains with the present is neither to make it another presence, nor is it nostalgic retrieval. What can be consciously recollected are fragments. But to remain unconscious and nonobjectivated is not equivalent to erasure or active disregard, for unconsciousness is part of the power of the past. It is how the contingent past becomes general, dimensional, atmospheric, and enveloping.[16] In this way, the past as a multiplicitous whole—as a nonlinear system of relations—forms the virtual atmosphere, milieu, or texture of our lives; it insinuates itself into the present *as past*, without becoming actual.[17] Unrepresented, yet differentially felt in its magnetizing effects and orienting force, the past is a structuring dimension *according to which* we perceive and live.

Although it is difficult to think the past beyond the dichotomy of conservation and negation, a third way is suggested by Maurice Merleau-Ponty when he notes, in *Le visible et l'invisible*, that "its absence counts in the world."[18] Here, absence is operative, orienting (and potentially disorienting); it acts indirectly through motivation rather than efficient causality. *Durée* has the power of *institution*. This points, on the one hand, to the past's grounding function and normative weight in experience and, on the other hand, to how the past makes possible a sequel, which can also be a shift in sense and difference.[19] This is because *durée* institutes dimensions, a system of differences, *according to which* meaning can be made; change in how meaning is made (or in how one perceives and feels) takes the instituted past as pivot.

To complicate the concept of institution, *durée* should also be understood as *tendency*. To describe the *durée* of a life and the *durée* of life, Bergson opens *L'évolution créatrice* with the image of a snowballing past, meant to show how the enduring past is felt as changing weight, pressure, and tendency (*tendance*).[20] Breaking with linear teleology and undoing the solidity of institution, tendencies meander, changing intensively and diverging through the contingency of their own duration. Events endure and are conserved not simply as contents but in how they relate to and reconfigure the past as a whole. It is in this sense that we can understand the *irreversibility* of the past within a nonlinear theory of *durée*. The past snowballing on itself is not the accumulation of events in a disorganized mass, but a past in continual movement, *immanently reconfigured through its own duration*.[21] This past remains incomplete: because it is haunted by the memory of tendencies, diverged from but not actualized—traces of what might have been[22]—and because it is open to the creation of possibility, when the circle of the social imaginary is disrupted, so that hitherto foreclosed meaning-making ripples through time.[23]

## Colonial *Durée*

To take seriously the *durées* of colonialism is to recognize their enveloping waters, their stifling atmospheres. Colonial and racial formations endure and are rephrased—or, more precisely, in enduring are rephrased, without losing hold.[24] Such an understanding of their *durée* presents an antidote to the idea of linear progress, in which the grip of oppressions is supposed to loosen in a present that overcomes, and has moved on from, the past. Indeed, the linear time of progress could be conceived as a ruse of empire—a way of hiding and exculpating present racism by positing racism to belong to the defunct past. This is where my rethinking of *durée* meets the concept of "coloniality" in Latin American philosophies (from Aníbal Quijano): the idea that colonialism is not a bygone event but a world system whose effects and affects continue to perdure and to structure our present.[25]

So far I have drawn on several watery, atmospheric, and ghostly metaphors to describe *durée*. Such images powerfully capture the work of the past as a fluid milieu that overflows objectification, but also aptly describe how the past may immerse us or offer us buoyancy, how memories may flood in or remain nebulous, how my body may anchor me in the present, and how events may create ripples through time. Bodies of water affectively pull us into the past: the Middle Passage, the Black Atlantic, refugee crossings and drownings of the Mediterranean, the Persian (Arabian) gulf, the Tigris and Euphrates. Colonialism, Frantz Fanon says, occupies not only the land but also our bodies and our breathing;[26] racism is not only institutional but, through the weight of its own duration, it becomes atmospheric.[27] Colonizations and stereotypes of the past *bog down* racialized subjects.[28] While searching in the archives of slavery and finding only spectral figures, silences, and evasions, Saidiya Hartman tries to conjure and give voice to the lives of ghosts (all the time wary of reproducing the specular enjoyment of suffering that was part of slavery).[29] Hortense Spillers goes back to the belly of the slave ships where gender was quantified and flesh made "cargo," the journey through which African female flesh is "ungendered" and its racial afterlives.[30] Christina Sharpe charts the afterlives of slavery through the wake, ship, hold, and weather, interweaving present and past wakes, dead and living, in a methodology of "wake work."[31] And Alexander Weheliye exposes the racialization of the flesh in constructions of the "human" and appeals to its viscosity to rethink subjection.[32]

We are reminded that the very duration of colonialism and white supremacy makes a difference: that they intensify through time, even while being rephrased. Its "retrograde movement," or feedback loop, institutes a history that naturalizes and justifies colonial conquest by scapegoating the bodies and cultures of those who came to be colonized. But this is also a duration that needs to be shored up and maintained by active forgetting and disregard in the present and by reiterations and reinventions of colonial formations through other means. For the colonized and racialized—or the "formerly" colonized—to live under the weight of what I am calling *colonial durée (colonial duration)* is to experience a "painful sense of time."[33]

What is elided in colonial *durée* is the simultaneity and "coevalness" of *durations*, of multiple ways of living time.[34] The racialized subject feels herself coming *too late*, projected back to a perpetual past, in a linear timeline that begins with ancient Greece and where Eurocentric civilization constitutes modernity.[35] As Fanon shows, such allochronism may be lived as bodily fragmentation or "tetanization."[36] At the same time, persisting legacies of white supremacy and colonialism are expressed in the "affective ankylosis" and indifference of colonial bodies[37]—racial pathologies of ignorance that sustain sites of white and neocolonial privilege.[38] Despite them both outwardly resembling paralysis, tetanization and "affective ankylosis" reveal very different ways of living colonial *durée*, feeling the weight of the colonial past, and hesitating; they map different positionalities. *Tetanization* points to the hypersensibility and bodily sensitivity of colonized subjects.[39] But *ankylosis* describes the affective indifference of *colonial subjects*, their ability to disregard, compartmentalize, or "forget" the histories from which they stem; it captures the recalcitrance and lack of hesitation of racializing habits of perception.

That racism wears and bogs us down—differentially—through its duration, means that it cannot be shrugged off. To move on, leaving it unchallenged in the background, allows its colonial construction of the past to become normative—adherent, generalized, and atmospheric. Critique requires not only the recognition of simultaneous, multiple *durées*, but resistance at the level of the past: reconfiguring its relations to generate intervals of buoyancy, ebb and flow, to make the past hesitate.

## Notes

1. Henri Bergson, *Essai sur les données immédiates de la conscience* (1889; Paris: Presses Universitaires de France, 1927).

2. Henri Bergson, *Matière et mémoire: Essai sur la relation du corps à l'esprit* (1896; Paris: Presses Universitaires de France, 1939).

3. Henri Bergson, *L'évolution créatrice* (1907; Paris: Presses Universitaires de France, 1941), 298.

4. Fernand Braudel's historical term differs from lived time, but I also see convergences with Bergson. Braudel, "Histoire et Sciences Sociales: La longue durée," *Annales. Économies, Sociétés, Civilisations* 13, no. 4 (1958): 725–53.

5. Ann Laura Stoler, ed., *Imperial Debris: On Ruins and Ruination* (Durham, N.C.: Duke University Press, 2013), 1–2. Stoler quotes "the rot remains" from the poem "Ruins of a Great House" by Derek Walcott. There, Walcott describes empire as "ulcerous crime" and "rotting lime," making palpable its corrosive duration.

6. This is the first (nonphilosophical) sense of *durée* in *Le Nouveau Petit Robert: Dictionnaire alphabétique et analogique de la langue française* (Paris: Dictionnaires Le Robert, VUEF, 2003). The second (philosophical) sense is "temps vécu," opposed to spatialization and derived from Bergson. Also, *La Trésor de la Langue Française informatisé*, www.cnrtl.fr/definition/durée, accessed December 14, 2017. *Duration* in English shares this sense of "the time during which a thing . . . continues." "Duration, n.," *OED*, 2017, www.oed.com, accessed December 14, 2017.

7. Gilles Deleuze, *Cinéma 2: L'image-temps* (Paris: Les Éditions de Minuit, 1985), 110.

8. Maurice Merleau-Ponty, *L'Œil et l'esprit* (Paris: Éditions Gallimard, 1964), 23; Maurice Merleau-Ponty, *L'Institution, La Passivité, Notes de cours au Collège de France, 1954–1955* (Paris: Éditions Belin, 2003), 249–50.

9. Bergson, *Matière et mémoire*, 231–36; Bergson, *L'évolution créatrice*, 299–307.

10. Witness Bergson's attempt to *think with* the duration of matter in *Matière et mémoire* (chapter 4) and his genetic account of materiality as the relaxation and inversion of *élan vital* in *L'évolution créatrice* (201–11).

11. Gaston Bachelard, *La dialectique de la durée* (Paris: Presses Universitaires de France, 1950), vii, 7–8.

12. Bergson, *Essai*, 75–77.

13. Henri Bergson, *La pensée et le mouvant* (1934; Paris: Presses Universitaires de France, 1938), 101, translation mine.

14. Henri Bergson, *L'énergie spirituelle* (Paris: Presses Universitaires de France, 1919), 131–2; Deleuze, *Cinéma 2*, 109.

15. I read the Bergsonian past-in-general as more than any personal past, even though it is the past from the perspective of my body in the world. Alia Al-Saji, "The Memory of Another Past," *Continental Philosophy Review* 37 (2004): 203–39.

16. In *L'Institution*, Merleau-Ponty argues that, since the past is the level *according to which* one perceives, it cannot itself be perceived. This invisibility assures ubiquity or generality.

17. Bergson, *L'évolution créatrice*, 5, 20.

18. Maurice Merleau-Ponty, *Le visible et l'invisible*, ed. C. Lefort (Paris: Éditions Gallimard, 1964), 281.

19. Merleau-Ponty, *L'Institution*, 38–41.

20. Bergson, *L'évolution créatrice*, 2, 4–6.

21. *Reconfiguration* is my term. I use it to capture how the past changes along with the present, without rewriting or erasure, and while retaining an organic memory of transformations it has undergone. Al-Saji, "Hesitation as Philosophical Method—Travel Bans, Colonial Durations, and the Affective Weight of the Past," *Journal of Speculative Philosophy* 32, no. 3 (2018): 331–59.

22. In Bergson's hypothesis of *élan vital*, life holds a multiplicity of tendencies that, insofar as they are virtual, coexist in mutual implication. As they grow, however, tendencies become incompatible and diverge. Nonactualized tendencies are not erased; they remain as *virtual memories* or *traces* that haunt other lines of evolution and could lead to different materializations (*L'évolution créatrice*, 53, 90, 100, 119–20).

23. "In duration, considered as a creative evolution, there is perpetual creation of possibility and not only of reality" (Bergson, *La pensée et le mouvant*, 13).

24. Ann Laura Stoler, *Duress: Imperial Durabilities in Our Times* (Durham. N.C.: Duke University Press, 2016), 237–65.

25. Aníbal Quijano, "Coloniality of Power, Eurocentrism, and Latin America," *Nepantla: Views from the South* 1, no. 3 (2000): 533–80. Indeed, coloniality molds our concept of being. Nelson Maldonado-Torres, "On the Coloniality of Being," *Cultural Studies* 21, nos. 2–3 (2007): 240–70. Critically, this requires rethinking the coloniality of gender, as María Lugones argues in "Heterosexualism and the Colonial/Modern Gender System," *Hypatia* 22, no. 1 (2007): 186–209.

26. Frantz Fanon, *L'an V de la révolution algérienne* (1959; Paris: La Découverte, 2001), 49.

27. Frantz Fanon, *Pour la révolution africaine: Écrits politiques* (1964; Paris: La Découverte, 2006), 48–49; Frantz Fanon, *Les damnés de la terre* (1961; Paris: La Découverte, 2002), 279.

28. Fanon says "engluer" in *Peau noire, masques blancs* (Paris: Éditions du Seuil, 1952), 32, 224.

29. Saidiya Hartman, *Lose Your Mother: A Journey along the Atlantic Slave Route* (New York: Farrar, Straus and Giroux, 2007) and *Scenes of Subjection: Terror, Slavery and Self-Making in Nineteenth-Century America* (Oxford: Oxford University Press, 1997).

30. Hortense J. Spillers, "Mama's Baby, Papa's Maybe: An American Grammar Book," *Diacritics* 17, no. 2 (1987): 64–81.

31. Christina Sharpe, *In the Wake: On Blackness and Being* (Durham, N.C.: Duke University Press, 2016).

32. Alexander Weheliye, *Habeas Viscus: Racializing Assemblages, Biopolitics, and Black Feminist Theories of the Human* (Durham, N.C.: Duke University Press, 2014).

33. Edouard Glissant, *Le discours antillais* (Paris: Éditions Gallimard, 1997), 226, translation mine.

34. Johannes Fabian, *Time and the Other: How Anthropology Makes Its Object* (New York: Columbia University Press, 1983).

35. Fanon, *Peau noire,* 118–19.

36. Fanon, *Peau noire,* 110. *Damnés* describes the muscle contractions and spasms of colonized subjects (279–80). ("Allochronism" is Fabian's term for the temporal othering and denial of coevalness to other cultures.)

37. Fanon, *Peau noire,* 118–19.

38. Charles Mills diagnoses this "epistemology of ignorance" in *The Racial Contract* (Ithaca, N.Y.: Cornell University Press, 1997), 18. (See Mills's entry, "Epistemological Ignorance," in this volume.) Stoler captures this ambivalence in the concept of "colonial aphasia" (*Duress,* 122).

39. Fanon, *Peau noire,* 110, 114. Fanon uses *tetanization* in medical and metaphorical senses at once. If colonization is *tetanus,* then it infects colonized bodies through colonial *wounds* (33, 94, 181); its toxicity provokes muscle spasms which may externally look like paralysis but betray excessive activity.

# 15 Epistemological Ignorance

Charles W. Mills

## I

*Know thyself*, the Delphic motto charges us, and in the Western philosophical tradition, at least from Socrates onward, this is taken up as a central theme and imperative. The ideal becomes self-transparency, both for its own sake and as a step toward self-mastery. The epistemological and the ethical are to work in tandem, eliminating self-deception and other obstacles to appropriate moral behavior and guiding our analysis of and intervention in social situations. In both the Platonic and the Aristotelian tradition, albeit in different ways, self-understanding is linked to self-control, and such individual virtue at the micro level is a prerequisite, at the macro level, for the construction of the just polis. The good state, whether Plato's ideal republic or Aristotle's aristocracy, is inhabited by good citizens, seeing, knowing, and acting rightly.

But the strictly limited class of those eligible for "individual" status (male Athenian citizens) makes unnecessary, or even proscribes, any general dissemination of these norms. The Guardians and the *aristoi* need to be far-seeing and to be self-transparent; those in the lower orders do not, and opacity is perfectly licit for such nonequals. Political inequality is straightforwardly linked with cognitive inequality: it is because of their cognitive inferiority that Plato's silver and brass classes, and Aristotle's women and natural slaves, do not share political power. Epistemic and political deference to their superiors is all that is required of them. And if medieval Christianity would later affirm a spiritual community of souls, all equal in God's eyes, it would not repudiate, in the temporal realm, the necessary hierarchies of ecclesiastical and noble authority over the bodies of the lower orders.

In the standard narrative, it is the advent of modernity that radically disrupts and overturns this system of deeply imbricated and hierarchically ranked social and political, moral and epistemic "estates": the Protestant Reformation, the emergence of the individual, the discrediting of ascriptive hierarchy, the bourgeois revolutions, the moral and epistemic egalitarianism promised in the manifestos of equal rights and an anti-authoritarian Cartesian program to put all beliefs into question. Suddenly—at least on paper—the epistemic was to be democratized, opening the door to all to know not merely themselves but the sociopolitical systems supposedly requiring their consent. In Plato's republic, far from societal transparency being an overarching ideal for all, even the golden Guardians were to be inculcated in the "noble lie" of the Myth of the Metals. But now transparency could at last become a global and unqualified norm, applicable both at the individual and the sociopolitical level.

Particularly in the liberal social contract tradition, supposedly based on the equal rights and nonfungibility of equal individuals—unlike a later consequentialist liberalism prone to "Government House" utilitarian calculations, hidden from the public eye, that maximize aggregate social welfare at the expense of the unfortunate—equal epistemic access to the political is foundational. Thus even Thomas Hobbes—who would, perversely, use the new modern individualist ontology to argue for premodern absolutism—introduces *Leviathan* with the injunction that for the creation of the "Artificiall Man" that is the state, one need only "Nosce teipsum, Read thy self," since all "men" can learn to read "Man-kind" in themselves, given their "similitude of *Passions*, which are the same in all men."[1] In "the faculties of the mind" there is "yet a greater equality amongst men, than that of strength," so that—contrary to Aristotle's claims about some being innately "more worthy to Command, meaning the wiser sort (such as he thought himselfe to be for his Philosophy)"—the "Lawes of Nature" governing the creation of the Commonwealth are rationally apprehensible by and equally binding on all.[2] For John Locke, the defender of limited government, it is likewise the case that "the *State of Nature* has a Law of Nature to govern it, which obliges every one: And Reason, which is that Law, teaches all Mankind . . . that [all are] equal and independent," "a Law . . . as intelligible and plain to a rational Creature . . . as the positive Laws of Common-wealths, nay possibly plainer."[3] Jean-Jacques Rousseau's radically transformed political community, different as it is from both absolutism and liberal democracy, nonetheless rests on a symmetrical and reciprocal alienation of individual selves to the whole that presupposes equal cognitive and moral capacities in the creation of the general will.[4] And Immanuel Kant, for whom the contract is "merely an *idea* of reason," declares that the "civil state" is based on the a priori principles of freedom, equality, and independence, with "freedom to make *public use* of one's reason in all matters" being all that is necessary for people to overcome their "immaturity" and achieve "enlightenment."[5]

For all four of the contract theorists, then, the ostensible starting point—in seeming sharp contrast with premodern status and cognitive hierarchy—is moral and epistemic equality. In Locke and Kant, the two contractarians most central to the liberal tradition, this egalitarian commitment is preserved in the promised transparency of the political order, not to be trumped by considerations of realpolitik, though Locke's citizens retain the right to revolution, while Kant's do not. And even when it is denied or qualified, as in the case of the two nonliberals—the Hobbesian citizenry who alienate their rights to an absolutist sovereign empowered to censor, or the Rousseauian citizenry who may require a superhuman "Legislator" equipped with a deceptive and manipulative "civic religion" to bring them to political readiness—this limitation does not rest on their innate cognitive inequality as such but on their shortsighted selfishness and immaturity. It would seem, then, that in modernity in general, and liberal modernity in particular, we have a transition to a world of self- and sociopolitical "knowing" in which the Delphic injunction, guided by a democratized, nonelitist, and nondiscriminatory epistemology, could finally be fulfilled.

But the promise was illusory. As Marxist and other class theorists, as first- and second-wave feminists, as critical race theorists (avant la lettre), have been pointing out for hundreds of years now, liberal modernity's break with an illiberal premodernity, putatively in radical and sharp contrast to it, is very partial indeed.[6] In some cases matter-of-factly stated in the text itself, in some cases tacitly assumed or implied, liberalism turns out to be systematically illiberal. Even the white male working class is sometimes formally denied equal standing (Locke's proprietarian polity, Kant's relegation of the non-self-supporting to "passive citizen" status), and is at all times materially subject to the dictates of capital. Possibly equal in the state of nature for Hobbes and Rousseau, but not Locke and Kant, white women—constituting half or nearly half the population in the Euro-states—become sociopolitical inferiors for all four contract theorists, not at all liberated from patriarchy by modernity but subordinated through the new form of what Carole Pateman calls "fraternal" patriarchy (the contractual rule of the brothers rather than the fathers).[7] And people of color, a category largely marginal to ancient and medieval thought (except in the Christian iconography of the "Monstrous Races"),[8] enter the global Euro-polity as natural subordinates, conquered by the expansionist Euro-empires that are also integral to modernity (Hobbes's and Locke's incompetent Native Americans, unable to leave the state of nature on their own or appropriate it efficiently; Rousseau's feckless "savages"; Kant's biological racial hierarchy of Europeans–Asians–Africans–Amerindians).[9]

Rather than an unqualified egalitarian liberalism, then, what we actually have is a bourgeois, patriarchal, and racial/imperial liberalism, where the supposedly generic "men" are propertied, male, and white.[10] It is their moral status that is equalized; it is their cognitions that are recognized; it is their selves and the polities which privilege them that determine what can be "known." The actual social contract, far from leveling all premodern hierarchies, puts some on a different basis (class, gender) while establishing new ones (race); it is a domination contract.[11] And its epistemology is necessarily accordingly altered. If in premodernity the overtly subordinated, denied even the pretensions to equality, could simply be ignored, now—in an epoch nominally marked by a commitment to equal rights, equal cognitive powers, and equal political consent—those excluded by an inferiority at least facially in tension with supposedly egalitarian and universalist pronouncements *must be actively denied* "knowings" that contradict the established order. Knowing thyself, knowing thy society, would mean coming to "know" one's identity as a victim of an oppressive classist/patriarchal/white-supremacist sociopolitical order. But such truths cannot be *known* if the system is to preserve itself.

So modern epistemology, as a set of norms for guiding cognition, must perforce also include norms that guide it *away* from any openness to the potentially subversive perspectives of the subordinated. These cannot be partitioned processes but rather different aspects of the same process. Particularly in states pretending to be liberal, whether Western or Western-implanted, which do claim to uphold transparency as a norm, actual transparency would be fatal. What is required instead is a structural opacity denying its actual identity, predicated, in Miranda Fricker's terminology, on a "principled" testimonial and hermeneutical injustice to dangerous "knowers": the systemic refusal of credibility to their potentially antisystemic claims and conceptual frameworks.[12] Given the actual class, gender, and racial hierarchies of nominally inclusive and egalitarian liberal democracies, an epistemology of knowledge-seeking must simultaneously constitute itself as an epistemology of knowledge-avoidance: an epistemology of ignorance.[13] *Knowing as a general cognitive ideal will thus require, whenever necessary, knowing to not-know.*

## II

What, then, are the phenomenological implications for the individual of this apparent practical contradiction, this schedule of cognitive norms divided against itself? Imagine that you are one of these flawed cognizers moving through the world. (It shouldn't be difficult—you are!) You are a body in space, but not a space that is featureless or homogeneous in character, symmetrically invariant around any chosen pivotal point or axis, but rather a space structured through and through by relations of power and hierarchy. You are a body in the body politic, a part, let us say (since he is the most materialist of the four major contract theorists), of Hobbes's great LEVIATHAN, the artificial man, the macrobody composed of millions of microbodies.

As such, you are, in Gail Weiss's formulation, intercorporeally linked with other bodies,[14] your perceptions and conceptions shaped by them, so that your knowledges are always (in the broader, trans-sexual sense, though including the sexual) carnal knowledges, and also, as emphasized, carnal nonknowledges, carnal ignorances, things your body is not supposed to know, not permitted to know, because of their incongruity with the official norms of self-knowing and self-ignoring, of the macrobody. Epistemology, as the mainstream of the tradition has finally, belatedly, discovered, must be *social*. Hobbes analogized different sociopolitical functions to different parts and functions of the body (the sovereignty, the soul; the magistrates, the joints; reward and punishment, the nerves, etc.),[15] and some parts and functions (ruling) are more esteemed than others (reproduction, labor). Women, the subordinate classes, natural slaves, nonwhite "natives" cannot have an equal role in determining the authorized perceptions and cognitions of the macrobody. So the rules that positively valorize the status of being class-respectable, male, and white must also negatively valorize the status of being lower class, female, and nonwhite. In learning the rules, then, one is adopting both patterns of behavior and patterns of cognition, deference to certain kinds of testimony and disregard of others, reflexively approbative or reflexively critical judgments on one's own self-monitored reactions.

So you see, you hear, you feel, you smell, you taste, and all the time, to a significant extent without your conscious control, you are conceptualizing, you are admitting for entry and you are filtering out, you are considering and accepting, you are considering and rejecting, mini theories and mini explanations linked to larger meso and macrotheories and explanations about these perceptions, about what is going on, about what is *happening*. And in your corporeal human density as a perceiver, a knower, you are not, of course, an android or robot or other affectless entity but an organism moved by emotions, desires, fears, feelings of repugnance and attraction, some deeply embedded and embodied, all of which are factored into, combined with, the inputs you are receiving, not just shaping them but in a sense making them (since some are simply filtered out of the spotlight of your perception, while those that are noticed are noticed in a certain way, perceptually and conceptually precolored). The picture (but it is broader than the visual) of society and self that you have been given requires that *you know better* than to take seriously apparently conflicting perceptions, conceptions, explanations. In knowing to not-know, the official epistemology (which is also an epistemology of ignorance) legitimizes, indeed demands our cognitive dismissal of potentially subversive counterknowings.

But sometimes . . .

Sometimes the noetic system fails, the clash (even dimly perceived) between official and actual reality is too great, the filters malfunction, the body resists its imposed incorporation. The tensions inherent in such an exercise snap the process the other way, and knowing to not-know reveals its ambiguity, its Janus-facedness. Could it be—could it just be—that we should instead endorse, *know*, these derogated perceptions and conceptions *as* the veridical ones, and then, as a corollary, *not-know*, reject, the official epistemology, the prescribed norms of cognition that directed us to ignore them? And what would it then mean for the story we have been told of ourselves and society, the relation of our body to the body politic, and the possibility of developing from these incipient and perhaps still inchoate countercognitions an alternative perspective on both?

So across oppositional political theories of class, race, and gender, and also in their explicitly intersectionalist incarnations, we find the thematization of this potential. The Italian Marxist Antonio Gramsci characterizes workers' consciousness as "contradictory," simultaneously containing "prejudices from all past phases of history" and "intuitions of a future philosophy," "principles of a more advanced science."[16] The "common sense" that is shaped by bourgeois class domination nonetheless contains a nucleus of "good sense," "which deserves to be made more unitary and coherent."[17] W. E. B. Du Bois, in the first essay of his most famous book, *The Souls of Black Folk*, classically describes black American situatedness in a racist white world "which yields him no true self-consciousness, but only lets him see himself through the revelation" of that world, resulting in a "double consciousness," a "sense of always looking at one's self through the eyes of others . . . look[ing] on in amused contempt and pity." But he is still confident that a veridical "second-sight" will ultimately enable the black American "to attain self-conscious manhood, to merge his double self into a better and truer self."[18] From around the United States, indeed around the world as I write this in December 2017, the #MeToo movement has empowered women of all classes and races to recognize that what happened to them, what routinely happens to them, from sexual harassment and groping to outright assault and rape, is not singular, not their own fault, not something that they asked for by their dress, their behavior, something they said, but an entrenched and widespread wrong embedded in their inferior position in a body politic controlled by male bodies for whom they are to be permanently sexually accessible.[19] By rejecting the socio-epistemic pressures to say nothing, to keep it to themselves, to recognize that "boys will be boys," to accept as falling on them, if anyone, any shame that might attach to the parties involved in the event, women as a group can come to know differently, to *not-know* "his" story and to affirm the suppressed truths that their own bodies are telling them: "If something feels wrong, it is wrong—and it's wrong by my definition and not necessarily someone else's."[20] And the hope is that one day, from these multiple intersecting oppositional sources, an "epistemology of resistance"[21] can be synthesized to achieve a genuinely Enlightened modernity in which opacity—prescribed nonknowing to obfuscate systemic sociopolitical oppression—will no longer be necessary.

## Notes

1. Thomas Hobbes, *Leviathan*, ed. Richard Tuck (New York: Cambridge University Press, 1991), 9–10.

2. Hobbes, *Leviathan*, 87, 107.

3. John Locke, *Two Treatises of Government*, student edition, ed. Peter Laslett (New York: Cambridge University Press, 1988), *Second Treatise* §6, 12 (271, 275).

4. Jean-Jacques Rousseau, The Social Contract *and Other Later Political Writings*, ed. and trans. Victor Gourevitch (New York: Cambridge University Press, 1997).

5. Immanuel Kant, *Political Writings*, 2nd edition, ed. Hans Reiss, trans. H. B. Nisbet (New York: Cambridge University Press, 1991), 79, 74, 54–55.

6. Domenico Losurdo, *Liberalism: A Counter-History*, trans. Gregory Elliott (New York: Verso, 2011).

7. Carole Pateman, *The Sexual Contract* (Stanford, Calif.: Stanford University Press, 1988).

8. Debra Higgs Strickland, *Saracens, Demons, and Jews: Making Monsters in Medieval Art* (Princeton, N.J.: Princeton University Press, 2003).

9. Charles W. Mills, *The Racial Contract* (Ithaca, N.Y.: Cornell University Press, 1997).

10. Jean-Jacques Rousseau, "Discourse on the Origin and Foundations of Inequality among Men," in *The* Discourses *and Other Early Political Writings*, ed. and trans. Victor Gourevitch (New York: Cambridge University Press, 1997); Pateman, *Sexual Contract*; Mills, *Racial Contract*; Jennifer Pitts, *A Turn to Empire: The Rise of Imperial Liberalism in Britain and France* (Princeton, N.J.: Princeton University Press, 2005).

11. Charles W. Mills, "The Domination Contract," in Carole Pateman and Charles W. Mills, *Contract and Domination* (Malden, Mass.: Polity, 2007), chapter 3.

12. Miranda Fricker, *Epistemic Injustice: Power and the Ethics of Knowing* (New York: Oxford University Press, 2007).

13. Mills, *Racial Contract*. In the book itself, and in my later "White Ignorance," in *Race and Epistemologies of Ignorance*, ed. Shannon Sullivan and Nancy Tuana (Albany: State University of New York Press, 2007), my focus is on race, but the concept is obviously generally applicable to all systems of domination.

14. Gail Weiss, *Body Images: Embodiment as Intercorporeality* (New York: Routledge, 1999).

15. Hobbes, *Leviathan*, 9.

16. Antonio Gramsci, *Selections from the Prison Notebooks*, ed. and trans. Quintin Hoare and Geoffrey Nowell Smith (New York: International Publishers, 1971), 333, 324.

17. Gramsci, *Prison Notebooks*, 328.

18. W. E. B. Du Bois, *The Souls of Black Folk* (1903; New York: Signet Classic/New American Library, 1969), 45.

19. Charlotte Alter, Susanna Schrobsdorff, Sam Lansky, Kate Samuelson, Maya Rhodan, and Katy Steinmetz, "The Silence Breakers: The Voices That Launched a Movement," *Time*, December 18, 2017, 30–70.

20. Ashley Judd, recalling the attempted 1997 assault on her by Harvey Weinstein, cited in Alter et al., "The Silence Breakers," 34.

21. José Medina, *The Epistemology of Resistance: Gender and Racial Oppression, Epistemic Injustice, and Resistant Imaginations* (New York: Oxford University Press, 2013).

# 16 Eros

Tamsin Kimoto and Cynthia Willett

## Poetry as Phenomenology

Audre Lorde would hardly have described herself as a phenomenologist; indeed, she often resisted the claim that she was a theorist at all and preferred instead to be called a poet. However, her reflections on poetry offer helpful insights for critical phenomenologists. If the work of critical phenomenology is both to expose and to critique norms and institutions that structure our experiences in the world through mechanisms of domination and subordination, then Lorde's insistence on poetry as a "revelatory distillation of experience"[1] can aid us in this project. On Lorde's account, living under conditions of white heteropatriarchy produces distortions and unintelligibility in the lives of women, especially women of color. Poetry gives us the space to illuminate those experiences through the insistence that we attend first to what is felt but is still "nameless and formless."[2] What is so vital for this understanding of poetry as a kind of critical phenomenological work is Lorde's insistence on the imbrication of description and transformation. Her visionary practice contributes to a critical phenomenology through an appeal to an immediacy that explodes white heteropatriarchy's mythical norms. These mythical norms enshrine privileged, white, heterosexual, male standards of beauty and value. As both intersectional and critical, her approach to poetry does not map directly onto a European tradition or otherwise limit itself to the "master's tools."[3] Instead, her phenomenological musings on the erotic draw on and contribute to a black feminist tradition of "visionary pragmatism."[4] Patricia Hill Collins explains visionary pragmatism as an undertaking "symbolized by an ongoing journey."[5] The poetic description of what is felt allows us to pinpoint those structures of our experience that are oppressive and to imagine the world otherwise.

Lorde's insistence on the felt or affective valences of our experiences is crucial for the critical force of her work. She explains what is at stake for such a project in political terms: when we understand "living . . . only as a *problem to be solved*," we are relying "solely upon our ideas to make us free."[6] Understanding living as a problem to be solved prevents us from approaching it as a situation to be lived because such an understanding turns us to ideas that may not, or cannot, in fact, speak to our particular experiences.[7] To avoid this restricted approach to life, she urges reformulating the Cartesian *cogito*'s "I think, therefore I am" as "I feel, therefore I can be free."[8] Lived experience is first felt experience for Lorde, and acknowledging this, she suggests, can point us toward the limitations of the ideas we have inherited under white heteropatriarchy, thus opening up the possibility for the development of new modes of experiencing and knowing the world.

## The Lived Experience of the Erotic

Lorde's poetic description of the erotic is rich with language familiar to phenomenology, beginning with her claim that "the erotic cannot be felt secondhand."[9] The phenomenological attention to first-person experience and Lorde's insistence on a "disciplined attention to the true meaning of 'it feels right to me'"[10] both turn on the idea that our own particular experiences, when viewed through the proper lens, can reveal a great deal about how the world and our encounters with it are structured. At the heart of the inchoate experience of feelings, Lorde's poetry conjures what she calls a lifeforce. Following Plato and Freud, she names that force after the mythic male figure Eros: "The very word *erotic* comes from the Greek word *eros*, the personification of love in all its aspects—born of Chaos, and personifying creative power and harmony."[11] Plato's *Symposium* takes up the question of eros and its relationship to philosophy, and his *Phaedrus* specifically poses the question of how to manage eros and the mania it inspires.[12] Whereas for Plato and Freud, the sublimation of the erotic accounts for creative activity, for Lorde, the erotic itself *is* creative energy. More specifically, she argues that the erotic, "the knowledge and use of which we are now reclaiming in our language, our history, our dancing, our loving, our work, our lives," is an "assertion of the lifeforce of women."[13] In this respect, Lorde aligns with other feminists in the 1970s who also reexamine the erotic based on women's experiences. In her criticisms of psychoanalysis, Luce Irigaray charges that the erotic experiences of women have been ignored; instead, psychoanalysis has offered us an account of sexual development that reduces woman to the status of an object.[14] She traces heterosexual passion to the mother-child relationship, aiming to alter the association of the mother with the womb or womb-like functions. Her placental imagery replaces libidinal cycles of narcissistic fusion and repressive separation with a biosocial dynamic of mediation and connection.

Lorde too searches for new myths and visions, invoking narratives of reconnection and shared experience rather than separation and independence. But for Lorde, this erotic dynamic does not revolve around the nuclear family's heterosexual couple. Instead, eros as a visionary force carries her back to ancient African spiritual and ancestral sources and forward to queer couples, flourishing workers, and the intersectional politics of struggle and solidarity. In this erotic vision, society is held together not by rational self-interest but by a collective responsibility for a future where all children across social differences can fulfill themselves in meaningful work and shared passions.[15]

Lorde notes that there is a "hierarchy" of experiences of the erotic: not all experiences of the erotic are equally illuminating. For this poet with working-class sensibilities, the difference between "painting a back fence and writing a poem" is one of degree rather than kind.[16] Both activities are experiences of the erotic because, if we attend to them as poet-phenomenologists, each can point to those gaps in our conceptual frameworks where there is something felt and known but in need of new modes of expression. Importantly, the erotic is not expressed just in exceptional experiences; when we attend to our everyday, life-sustaining, and joy-affirming practices as erotic experiences, they are newly enlivened with meaning. In this way, the erotic is a phenomenological "lens through which we scrutinize all aspects of our existence" for the feelings they inspire and what they make possible.[17]

According to Lorde, the erotic as a lifeforce connects first-person embodied experience to the shared genealogy of women with whom we live and who lived before us. When understood as a lifeforce—that is, vital energy and passion—eros draws on the mysteries of shared myths, symbols, and rhythms. On this account, eros is the locus of the social bond that holds together lovers, friends, and workers in solidarity. It is also the source of resistance to oppressive systems that threaten to appropriate our erotic energy. Such an appropriation occurs, Lorde observes, in the objectification of women, where the erotic is stripped of these larger meanings.

## The Lived Politics of the Erotic

As a mode of connecting to a lifeforce that sustains the creative and political practices of women, the erotic places us in a shared endeavor of world-making. It does so, Lorde maintains, by insisting on the "interdependence of mutual (nondominant) differences" and "different strengths" rather than on mere sameness. "Difference," she asserts, "is that raw and powerful connection from which our personal power is forged."[18] In order to understand the erotic as an experience that is lived politically, we must recognize differences and "share the power of each other's feelings" rather than manipulating these differences for our own ends.[19] The critical task of an erotic politics is resisting the temptation to a heroic and isolated struggle; instead, Lorde urges us to feel ourselves as "part of an ever-expanding community of struggle."[20] Though primarily associated with joy, the erotic, especially in its political manifestations, can also appear as anger. Anger, Lorde claims, is an experience of the erotic that binds us to others and "is loaded with information and energy."[21] It is not the same as hatred, which comes from the desire to dominate and destroy others.[22]

As a way of experiencing the political as it is lived, eros reinforces the feminist tenet that "the personal is political." Ultimately, for Lorde, the erotic is how we care for ourselves and others. In her reflections on living with cancer, Lorde speaks to the resonance between living through breast cancer and myriad social oppressions.[23] In a world that aims to produce death at varying speeds and modes, caring for oneself "is not self-indulgence, it is self-preservation, and that is an act of political warfare."[24] Sustaining ourselves depends on developing a sense of attunement to our lived, felt experience. As Haunani-Kay Trask puts it, the "recognition of these feelings is the beginning of a new knowledge which empowers, which carries us out of alienation, the numbing of our feelings, into courageous living."[25]

For Lorde, the transformation of feeling into action at stake in poetic description and the erotic entails an insistence on altering the material realities of our situations. More important, in her reflections on anger, she reminds us that the task of critically describing and transforming our experience is open to constant revision as we engage in the work of coalition with others. Our goal must be to eliminate oppressive forces as well as to generate new worlds through affirming, rather than covering over, our differences.[26] The personal is political not only because of the ways in which our personal experiences are shaped by oppressive conditions, but also because it is in attending to them that we can work toward a different world in common.

## Notes

1. Audre Lorde, "Poetry Is Not a Luxury," in *Sister Outsider* (Berkeley: Crossing Press, 2007), 37.
2. Lorde, "Poetry Is Not a Luxury," 36.
3. Audre Lorde, "Age, Race, Class, and Sex: Women Redefining Difference," in *Sister Outsider*, 123.
4. Abena Busia and Stanlie James, *Theorizing Black Feminisms: The Visionary Pragmatism of Black Women* (New York: Routledge, 1993).
5. Patricia Hill Collins, *Fighting Words: Black Women and the Search for Justice* (Minneapolis: University of Minnesota Press, 1998), 188.
6. Lorde, "Poetry Is Not a Luxury," 37, emphasis added.
7. In this sense, there is an overlap between Lorde's understanding of living and Simone de Beauvoir's insights in *The Second Sex*, trans. Constance Borde and Sheila Malovany-Chevallier (New York: Knopf, 2010).
8. Lorde, "Poetry Is Not a Luxury," 38.
9. Audre Lorde, "Uses of the Erotic: The Erotic as Power," in *Sister Outsider*, 59.
10. Lorde, "Poetry Is Not a Luxury," 37.
11. Lorde, "Uses of the Erotic," 55.
12. For Plato's discussion of eros and mania, see *Phaedrus*, trans. Alexander Nehemas and Paul Woodruff (Indianapolis, Ind.: Hackett, 1995), 244a–257b. See also Plato, *Symposium*, trans. Alexander Nehemas and Paul Woodruff (Indianapolis, Ind.: Hackett, 1989).
13. Audre Lorde, "Uses of the Erotic: The Erotic as Power," in *Sister Outsider*, 55.
14. Luce Irigaray, *This Sex Which Is Not One*, trans. Catherine Porter and Carolyn Burke (Ithaca, N.Y.: Cornell University Press, 1985.)
15. Audre Lorde, "Man Child: A Black Lesbian Feminist's Response," in *Sister Outsider*, 79.
16. Lorde, "Uses of the Erotic," 58.
17. Lorde, "Uses of the Erotic," 57.

18. Audre Lorde, “The Master’s Tools Will Never Dismantle the Master’s House,” in *Sister Outsider*, 111–12.

19. Lorde, “Uses of the Erotic,” 58.

20. Angela Y. Davis, *Freedom Is a Constant Struggle* (Chicago: Haymarket, 2016), 2.

21. Audre Lorde, “Uses of Anger: Women Responding to Racism,” in *Sister Outsider*, 127.

22. Lorde, “Uses of Anger,” 129.

23. Audre Lorde, *The Cancer Journals* (San Francisco: Aunt Lute Books, 1997).

24. Audre Lorde, *A Burst of Light* (Ithaca, N.Y.: Firebrand Books, 1988), 131.

25. Haunani-Kay Trask, *Eros and Power: The Promise of Feminist Theory* (Philadelphia: University of Pennsylvania Press, 1986), 94.

26. On extensions of Lorde’s eros to nonhuman lifeforces, see Cynthia Willett, *Interspecies Ethics* (New York: Columbia University Press, 2014), esp. “Introduction: New Ideals of Belonging and Africana Origins of Interspecies Living,” 1–28.

# 17 The Eternal Feminine

Debra Bergoffen

## In the Beginning

Though the phrase *the eternal feminine* is a belated addition to the philosophical lexicon, the idea that women possess an immutable nature that makes them fit for some things and unfit for others has been a part of the Western philosophical, religious, and intellectual traditions from the very beginning. By confining women to the roles of subservient wife, loving mother, and docile daughter, the idea of the eternal feminine marked sexual difference as the sign of an unbridgeable, irreconcilable otherness. Though most women accepted the idea that the mandates of the eternal feminine were inscribed in their nature and therefore obeyed them, others, the biblical Eve of (not after) the garden of Eden and the Greek Antigone, for example, finding their nature at odds with these mandates, breached them. Despite the fact that the inquisitive biblical woman was exiled and sentenced to a life of obedience to her husband punctuated with difficult childbirth, and the deviant Greek sister was condemned to death, the very fact of their existence suggests that the eternal feminine might be a disciplinary device rather than a description of women's inherent nature. The stories of Eve and Antigone trigger the suspicion that the "ought" of the norm represses the "is" of women.

In the biblical story of the Fall the first woman is the one who questions authority. The dictates of the eternal feminine are her punishment for being what she is naturally: curious. Questioning authority created the authority of the eternal feminine. Subordination to one's husband, compulsory motherhood, and confinement to the home is the recipe for foreclosing the possibility of another Eve coming on the scene and queering the order of things. The Greek Antigone shows that this fear is not unfounded. Though she was sealed in a cave for her trespass, her voice is not silenced. It continues to be heard in the continuous retelling of her resistance. Insofar as today's feminists may be seen as Eve's and Antigone's daughters, they may be read as either dumping the eternal feminine into the dustbin of history or as retrieving the other of the eternal feminine for an-other eternal feminine, one that recalls Eve's curiosity and Antigone's challenge.

## The Philosophers Take Up the Tale

Philosophers, who, Plato and Aristotle tell us, are drawn to philosophy by wonder, forgot to wonder about the inferior status of women. Taking the eternal feminine as the mark of sexual difference for granted, Socrates sent his wife away from his deathbed lest she spoil the last rational moments of his life. Aristotle insisted that men and women, given their essential inequality, could never be friends. Where these earlier thinkers found the matter of the eternal feminine either settled or irrelevant to the proper business of philosophy, Hegel thought otherwise. He wondered about it. Reflecting on Sophocles's *Antigone,* he famously called women the eternal irony of the community. Far from being a marginal matter, he found women's embodiment of this ironic principle essential to the dialectic of history. Freud's depiction of women in *Civilization and Its Discontents* echoes Hegel's, with this difference: where Hegel saw the laws of Reason successfully absorbing women's ironic contestation, Freud, identifying the eternal feminine with Eros, saw the antagonism of civilization to Eros unleashing the death instinct's fury.

Bringing the matter of women to the matter of philosophy, neither Hegel nor Freud questioned the veracity of the eternal feminine. Nietzsche was more astute. He called the eternal feminine a figment of men's imagination—a myth. Having no desire to puncture this object of men's desire, he taught men how to preserve it: keep women at a distance.[1] Beauvoir, drawing out the radical implications of seeing the eternal feminine as a myth, posed the question *Do women exist?* Identifying the idea of the eternal feminine as the ideology of a male-dominated social order that legitimated the oppression and exploitation of women, and having more allegiance to women's desire than men's, she dissected the pernicious effects of the myth of the eternal feminine and ordered it destroyed. Her orders have yet to take effect.

I think we need to pause before we execute them. The dominant image of the eternal feminine is, as the story of Eden makes clear, a reactionary image meant to contain a different principle of woman, the principle of the one who questions the authority of the rule/ruler. In evoking this principle, Antigone, like Eve, embodies the politics of resistance. As the eternal irony of the community, both articulate the principle of challenge and disruption. Before dumping the idea of the eternal feminine we might consider reading Hegel's image of woman as the eternal irony of the community as exposing the secret of the eternal feminine, that secret being that women's challenges to the unjust laws of the state can neither be dismissed nor ignored. As the irony of the community, their silenced, delegitimized voices disrupt the state's claims to legitimacy. The woman Hegel is thinking of when he calls woman the eternal irony of the community is Antigone. As an ironic figure she exposes the tragic flaw in a society that insists on the absolute authority of men's law. Hegel sees this flaw and its tragic consequences resolved in the dialectic of history, where women's and men's laws discover their interdependency. Taking up Hegel's insight without confining it to one figure, and noting that, contra Hegel, the patriarchal world represented by Creon has yet to be overcome by the dialectic, women's role as the eternal irony of the community remains essential to the pursuit of justice.

Following the thread of the secret of the eternal feminine we might turn the oppressive mantra of the eternal feminine, *Biology is destiny*, from a feminine irony of the community into a feminist irony, where the birthing body's promise of new life would confront the community with the eternal possibility of new beginnings and other ways of living. As a feminist irony it would not be silenced by the patriarchal laws of reason but would speak of the ongoing need to nurture the wonder and curiosity that imagines a world other than the one that currently imposes itself on us as immutable. From this perspective woman as the eternal feminine would be figured as a feminist question mark—a destabilizing force for justice rather than an argument for securing a questionable status quo.

## The Devil Is in the Details

For Hegel, the sexual difference is the material mark of an ethical difference. That men are thrust into the public life of the citizen and women are confined within the life of the family is neither an arbitrary nor a hierarchal sexual arrangement. As equal but different, men and women are the face of distinct and contesting ethical laws, the mandates of the city and the orders of the gods. Hegel, reading *Antigone* through the lens of this contestation, sees it as revealing the true meaning of the battle of the sexes and as exposing the consequences of taking this battle to extremes. The demands of the city and the directives of the divine must give each other their due. As the eternal irony of the community, Antigone reminds Creon of the consequences of forgetting the city's debt to the gods.[2]

From the perspective of the idea of the eternal feminine two things in Hegel's reading are significant. (1) Identifying women with the divine universal removes them from the transformative dialectic of history. Unlike men, who make and remake themselves as the laws of the city and citizenship change, women, as unhistorical beings, are sentenced to an inescapable, immutable existence. (2) Regarding women as the eternal irony of the community, human law sees women's disobedience as a transgression rather than as expressions of a legitimate moral demand. Though it cannot be said that Hegel endorses the subordination of women (the ethical demands of the divine) to men (the ethical mandates of the human), giving each moral law its due becomes a way of eternally confining women to their private roles as mothers, wives, and sisters and of reminding them that insofar as men regard them as a threat to public order they will be policed and silenced. Hegel does not question this policing. The Antigone who enters the public sphere is only justified in entering it as a mourning sister. She has no legitimate claims to citizenship or a public voice.

In commenting on Hegel's reading of *Antigone*, Luce Irigaray pays special attention to the fact that the ethical laws of the city are said to operate at the level of consciousness, whereas those of the divine are unconscious. Like Hegel, she aligns women with the unconscious forces that root and foster conscious life. Like Hegel, she finds that, as powerless on earth, "the forces of the world below become hostile because they have been denied the right to live in daylight. These forces rise up and threaten to lay waste to the community." Unlike Hegel, she insists that women have the right to "demand the right to pleasure, jouissance, even to effective action."[3] Here the threat women pose to public life, the threat of the return of the repressed, has nothing to do with an eternal feminine that, in the name of the gods and the rights/rites of the dead is hostile to politics, and everything to do with the failure of the political to give women the right to the living pleasures of "jouissance and effective action."

In resituating the source of women's threat to civic life Irigaray reinvigorates Freud's earlier warnings in *Civilization and Its Discontents*. Having no use for the idea of divine laws, ethical or otherwise, Freud retains an affinity for the idea of immutable forces and for the belief that the contest between these forces, the life drives of Eros and the death drives of aggression, tell the story of civilization. Here, as with Hegel, women are portrayed as the guardians of the bonds of family and at odds with men, who, driven by the demands of necessity (Ananke), withdraw from the family to become agents of the aggression that threaten the life of Eros. As the eternal irony of the community, women are now charged with being a "retarding and restraining influence."[4] This charge is not necessarily a condemnation. Watching the rise of Hitler, Freud indicates that women's restraining and retarding influence has become essential. Ending *Civilization and Its Discontents* with a call to Eros, the principle of the eternal feminine, to reassert herself, Freud asks whether absent such reassertion civilization is worth preserving. Unlike Irigaray, who is clear about what this reassertion means and how it would manifest, Freud provides no guidance as to how the principle of Eros would enter public life.

Simone de Beauvoir is not taken in by the idea of the eternal feminine. She is not seduced by the claim that as the embodiment of this idea woman can contest or redirect the course of history or civilization. She sees the idea of the eternal feminine as a ruse that keeps women out of the public domain, dependent on and subordinated to men, who have the power of politics and the purse. There is nothing equal about the public and private domains, especially since the public sets the rules of the private. As enacted in the idea of the eternal feminine, the sexual difference creates the difference between the sex that claims the rights of the absolute subject, the one who has the right to establish the moral and secular laws, and the sex that exists as the Other, the one destined to live according to his desire.

For Beauvoir, the idea of an eternal nature of woman is not just politically exploitative; it is an affront to the phenomenological-existential account of human beings as creators of the meaning of the world and themselves. As Hegel brought the matter of woman from the margins to the center of philosophy, Beauvoir makes the matter of woman a matter of the future of philosophy: Will it be attuned, attentive to, and relevant for human life and the demands of justice, or will it perpetuate ideas/ideals that, claiming to be absolute truths, denigrate the material realities of our existence?

The introduction to *The Second Sex* describes woman as the Other, the one alienated from her subjectivity and subjugated to the authority of Man, the Absolute Subject. At the end of volume 1 Beauvoir calls the idea of woman as the Other a product of Platonic thinking. What earlier philosophers called the battle of the sexes is, as she sees it, a contest between mythical Platonic Truth and the existential-phenomenological truths of the lifeworld. Like all myths, the Platonic idea of the eternal feminine is called upon to override the evidence of experience. It bars women from the possibility of validating their desires, becoming themselves through their actions, and of measuring themselves by their decisions.[5]

Calling the eternal feminine a myth and identifying it with the mythical thinking that characterizes Platonic thought, Beauvoir upends the story philosophy tells about itself. According to its biographers, philosophy marks the end of mythical thought and inaugurates the rule of reason. As rewritten by *The Second Sex,* the birth of philosophy marks a new form of mythical justification. Where earlier myths claimed the authority of the gods, philosophy's myths pass themselves off as authorized by reason. Finding that mythical thinking, however it is legitimated, has political implications, Beauvoir argues that few myths have been more advantageous to the ruling caste than the myth of the eternal feminine. Speaking the truth of experience to the power of the myth, Beauvoir pits the transformative power of time against the immobile eternity of the myth. She describes herself as living in a time of transition, when a new aesthetic of women is emerging. She asks to be read as a woman of her times, a philosopher participating in the work of reversing the relationship between the strictures of the myth of the eternal feminine and the truths of women's desires. Speaking in this way, she ties the future of philosophy to the fate of the eternal feminine: Will it abandon the mythical thinking that legitimates the ideal of the eternal feminine, or will it solidify patriarchal power in its name?

## Returning to Aristotle

Speaking for a philosophy that would contest the idea of the eternal feminine by fostering a new political aesthetic of women, Beauvoir calls on women and men to affirm their *fraternité.* This last line of *The Second Sex* has been criticized for being sexist and/or myopically French. Read through Aristotle's insistence on the impossibility of friendship between the sexes, however, it suggests that Beauvoir's appeal to *fraternité* strikes at the core of the subordinating power of the myth of the eternal feminine. Returning to Aristotle and the early days of philosophy, Beauvoir's reference to *fraternité* unmasks the relationship between the mythical thinking that idealizes woman as the eternal feminine and the political implications of insisting that the irreconcilable sexual difference makes the reciprocity of friendship between women and men unthinkable. The bodily and behavioral ideals of the eternal feminine are window dressing. However they may change with the times, whatever their cultural variation, they serve a single purpose: to preserve women's status as the dissonant other with whom friendship is foreclosed. Returning to Aristotle we understand that the matter of friendship is a political matter. It is not a question of who I like, but who I recognize as worthy of being recognized as an equal. Thus the importance of *fraternité.* To secure a place in the public realm women must be recognized as friends.

In looking toward a time when women and men affirm their *fraternité* Beauvoir directs us to a feminist version of what Derrida called a politics of friendship. In its feminist version the promise of this politics would entail aligning the call for *fraternité* with a call to embrace women as the eternal irony of the community. As the signature of the eternal feminine, women would imbue their friendship with men with the curiosity and wonder of the questions (philosophical and otherwise) that keep the present open and alive to the possibilities of the future.

## Notes

1. For an account of Nietzsche's complex account of the eternal feminine, see Frances Nesbitt Oppel, *Nietzsche on Gender: Beyond Man and Woman* (Charlottesville: University of Virginia Press, 2005).

2. Georg Wilhelm Friedrich Hegel, *The Phenomenology of Mind*, trans. J. B. Baillie (London: George Allen and Unwin, 1964), 496.

3. Luce Irigaray, *Speculum of the Other Woman*, trans. Gillian C. Gill (Ithaca, N.Y.: Cornell University Press, 1985), 225–26.

4. Sigmund Freud, *Civilization and Its Discontents*. trans. James Strachey (New York: Norton, 1961), 50.

5. Simone de Beauvoir, *The Second Sex*, trans. Constance Borde and Sheila Malovany-Chevallier (New York: Vintage Books, 2011), 266, 270.

# 18 Ethical Freedom

Shannon M. Mussett

The term *freedom*, viewed through the lenses of poststructuralism, deconstruction, or scientific determinism, can seem antiquated or even irrelevant. Given what we know about natural laws, the effects of power dynamics, language, and culture on the lives of human beings, freedom may appear as a kind of privilege rather than the expression of creative life and world formation. Simone de Beauvoir, however, maintains that freedom is a very real component of the human condition and one that must be fought for and won for ourselves and others through diligent introspection, life-affirming labor, and engaged political action. As such, freedom remains a vital and important concept in philosophical thought.

Beauvoir's understanding of freedom developed and deepened throughout her long and diverse writing career. Her earliest formulations were closely aligned with (though certainly not identical to) a Sartrean vision of freedom as transcendence—a rupturing of the givenness of the world through negation into an open future of possibilities. To be human is to be ontologically free. If human beings have any kind of essence, it is freedom as activity and willing, rather than freedom as stable nature or attribute. However, ontological freedom is not realized, expressed, or embodied in the same way across human differences. In fact, ontological freedom is always *situated*, such that transcendence can be more or less denied expression depending upon the situation (which itself is composed of myriad intersecting forces: time, place, history, culture, language, body, race, orientation, gender, ability, etc.) of the existent or group in question. As such, *authentic* or *ethical* freedom is freedom produced by and acting in a situation that is ambiguous and socially dependent.

*Pyrrhus and Cineas* (1943), Beauvoir's first serious philosophical essay, tackles the question of whether there is any reason to act when there exists no ultimate reason or terminus for action. There is no plateau for our various projects because once we stop, there is always something else to be done. In light of this, she observes that from the standpoint of reflection, "all human projects therefore seem absurd because they exist only by setting limits for themselves, and one can always overstep these limits, asking oneself derisively, 'Why as far as this? Why not further? What's the use?'"[1] Just as the king Pyrrhus argues to his advisor Cineas, there is no rational reason for action.[2] Why do this rather than that? There is no purpose except the one I give. Why continue to a new goal once I have completed the original project? Because there is no rest until we die. We act because we must, because we are human, engaged in numerous choices each moment of our conscious lives. However, in action lies freedom.

By her own admission, *Pyrrhus and Cineas* presents a provocative but ultimately thin version of freedom.[3] The ontological condition of freedom—I choose because I must—sounds less like a robust sense of the creation of self and situation characteristic of ethical freedom, and more like a forced life sentence. In addition, we are presented with the fundamental riddle of Beauvoir's existentialist freedom, namely, what does it mean to *will freedom*, and how is this an ethical choice? Put differently, how can I "will" what I already "am"?

We are born into a human world where our actions are shaped through interactions with the environment and others.[4] The world is not composed entirely of pregiven meanings to which we passively adapt ourselves but is rather a world in which we *belong*. To belong to the world means that we actively participate in it because "our relationship with the world is not decided from the onset; it is we who decide."[5] Action and choice involve a dynamic interplay of birth and death such that nothing is fixed—every ending is a new beginning; what was once vibrant can pass away; what is lost can be reincorporated into the present or projected into the future in novel ways since "the goal is a goal only at the end of the path. As soon as it is attained, it becomes a new starting point."[6] Freedom is an almost poetic movement between endings and beginnings, but this alone is insufficient to capture what concrete freedom is in any meaningful sense. For that, Beauvoir needs to elaborate the ambiguity of the human condition.

Ambiguity is no mere lack of clarity or definition; rather, it is central to authentic personhood. Rejecting identity in any kind of essential, permanent sense, Beauvoir argues that human beings are in constant flux due to the ecstatic and temporal nature of existence. Ethical freedom must necessarily reject an atemporal or absolute grounding for all action because such absolutism is the road to bad faith and tyranny. Ambiguity emphasizes movement between categories in the creation of meaning rather than the categories themselves. I am not a separate existent apart from the other but the movement of acting and willing between the poles of self and other. I am a consciousness as well as a body, but never fully pure transcendent thought and willing (as found in strains of Cartesian, Kantian, or Husserlian thought) nor purely a body (for to be merely a body would be to be a thing or a corpse). The poles are useful in understanding what dynamics are in play in ethical choice, and in that sense, they have a kind of reality, but their status is never absolute and is always changing. Ethics therefore requires a kind of fluidity of thinking and acting that is difficult to achieve, which is why "authenticity" (a problematic concept to be sure, in light of postexistential developments in philosophical thinking) is rare, perhaps even only ever momentarily achieved.

Thus, to engage in meaningful activity, what Beauvoir calls a "project," requires that one constantly place oneself in a temporal flux between past, present, and future, as well as between oneself and the environment and oneself and others that is *never fixed*.[7] Continuing this line of thought in *The Ethics of Ambiguity* (1947), Beauvoir shifts focus away from the condition of ontological freedom and toward the idea of ethical freedom as one that is in flux, thus lacking permanent foundations or goals. In what is one of the clearest explanations Beauvoir offers of this position, she writes:

> The good of an individual or a group of individuals requires that it be taken as an absolute end of our action; but we are not authorized to decide upon this end *a priori*. The fact is that no behavior is ever authorized to begin with, and one of the concrete consequences of existentialist ethics is the *rejection of all the previous justifications which might be drawn from the civilization, the age, and the culture; it is the rejection of every principle of authority*.[8]

Here, we find the heart of existentialist ethics. We must reject all previous rationalizations for past actions, meaning that earlier solutions can never justify choices in the present. To do so would be to live in the spirit of seriousness wherein absolutes are given, in advance, such that they determine present action and future goals. As difficult as it may be to grasp, to reject *every* principle of authority means that we must interrogate choice and action *moment to moment*. Such emphasis makes existentialist ethics truly exhausting and terrifying but also tremendously liberating. For although we cannot adopt earlier choices and cultural norms as absolute, we are also not bound by them. We can break with our discrete and cultural pasts in the creation of novel meaning, therefore preventing stagnation on the individual level and tyranny on the cultural.

The consequences of this position mean that there is very little that can be considered off the table in ethical freedom. Sometimes, for example, violence will be a required, if regrettable, option. A priori, violence is neither good nor evil.[9] However, the rejection of absolute authority opens us up to our connection with and responsibility to others: we treat the other "as a freedom that his end may be freedom; in using this conducting-wire one will have to incur the risk, in each case, of inventing an original solution."[10] Rejection of authority couples with a positive movement involving individual and collaborative creativity such that any goal projected into the future must be constantly and genuinely interrogated moment to moment: "The goal is not fixed once and for all; it is defined all along the road which leads to it. Vigilance alone can keep alive the validity of the goals and the genuine assertion of freedom. Moreover, ambiguity cannot fail to appear on the scene."[11] Ambiguity is the theater in which choice occurs, therefore the moral person must remain vigilant to the past, present, and future and remain open to the possibility that goals may have to be altered at any moment.

Action, however, does not occur in a vacuum. Even if I am physically alone, my very being is constituted by the existence and actions of others. The intersection of human projects is the counterpoint to ambiguity in Beauvoir's move from the fact of ontological freedom to the appeal of ethical freedom. It is a simple existential fact for Beauvoir that no aspect of my condition is not touched by other human beings. The ethical person realizes that choices are meaningless unless taken up by the projects of others: "Freedom wills itself genuinely only by willing itself as an indefinite movement through the freedom of others."[12] No mere platitude this, Beauvoir argues that actions are ethically meaningful only if others freely take them up in their own meaning-creating activities. Forcing my projects onto others, while always possible, is unethical, tyrannical, and fundamentally denies the interconnectedness of human existence.

Taking into consideration ontological freedom, the ambiguity of the situation, and our dependence on and responsibility to others, Beauvoir crystalizes ethical choice such that "the man of action, in order to make a decision, will not wait for a perfect knowledge to prove to him the necessity of a certain choice; he must first choose and thus help fashion history. A choice of this kind is no more arbitrary than a hypothesis; it excludes neither reflection nor even method; but it is also free, and it implies risks that must be assumed as such."[13] This extraordinary quote speaks to the riddle of how ethics requires that we will the freedom that we always already are. To act is to act in the space of incomplete knowledge. Embracing an ethics of ambiguity means accepting that our finitude grants us only partial perspective, but our freedom demands not only that we act but that we take responsibility for our actions. We cannot assume that there are "right" or "correct" choices that we more or less hit upon in our state of deficiency. Rather, as Beauvoir says, we *make* the choice right by our very choosing it. And even though authentic choice isn't arbitrary (it requires attention to temporality, to myself and others—some with whom I am connected and others I will never meet), it is never guaranteed to be right or good. Sometimes, despite our best intentions, we do violence to others and they to us because "one finds himself in the presence of the paradox that no action can be generated for man without its being immediately generated against men."[14] Thus, ethical freedom involves risk and failure. There is no escape from either, and yet we "must assume our actions in uncertainty and risk, and that is precisely the essence of freedom."[15] Assuming risk, failure, and uncertainty in the formation of a project that honors my own and others' freedom means to actively will the freedom that we always already are.

The idea that moral freedom emerges out of our finitude traverses Beauvoir's thought. When she turns to writing about marginalized and oppressed groups explicitly, she reaffirms the lack of a single solution promising liberation. Discussing in *The Second Sex* (1949) the production of women by forces that form them as auxiliary and secondary beings, she continues from the perspective of "existentialist morality."[16] True to her earlier development of moral freedom, she asserts, "Every subject posits itself as a transcendence concretely, through projects; it accomplishes its freedom only by perpetual surpassing toward other freedoms; there is no other justification for present existence than its expansion toward an indefinitely open future."[17] Transcendence can always fail to achieve positive expressions of freedom, languishing in more or less empty expenditures of complaint, resignation, mystification, or oppression. In fact, very few are fortunate enough to understand freedom and to be in a position to develop it in themselves and others (a position that opens Beauvoir up to criticisms of elitism and unchallenged class and racial privilege). However, to will one's freedom means precisely to acknowledge freedom in oneself (and the responsibility one therefore has for one's actions) and to work to create situations where other freedoms can do the same. In the case of women in *The Second Sex*, this means that diagnosing the problem of what it means to "become woman" is only the first step. One must then work to dismantle the scaffolding of patriarchal structures that both suppress the freedom of those deemed

Other and unjustly protect the freedom of those who occupy the subject position. In other words, one must act ethically and choose projects that encourage the expansion of freedom to the oppressed, even though there is no precise roadmap to success that elides risk and possible failure. Despite the potential pitfalls of ethical freedom, Beauvoir's writings champion various excluded and oppressed groups in the quest to build more just societies. Whether she speaks about the victims of the patriarchy in *The Second Sex*, French colonialism in Algeria,[18] the aged in advanced capitalist culture,[19] or victims of racism,[20] she maintains the central components of ambiguity, social interconnectedness, and human freedom as the ultimate sources and goals of all action.

To some, this conception of freedom will inevitably be unsatisfying because it resists absolutizing. But Beauvoir offers us a very real, concrete sense of freedom. We are creative, engaged, dynamic, intertwined individuals and collectivities making meaning in an otherwise meaningless world. Our lives and societies are aesthetic productions whose values are not predetermined and whose successes are never guaranteed. We are formed by history and society—inextricably bound up with norms of language, culture, identity, and power—but we are never fully determined by any of them. In this sense, freedom in Beauvoir is ultimately filled with hope and optimism. No matter how degraded and oppressed an existent is, there is always room for revolt and creation.[21]

In short, no one escapes time and place; freedom is always situated freedom. Factors conspire to keep many, if not most of humanity from exercising authentic moral choice—either because the arena of action is so limited as to prohibit meaningful projects, or because social and material forces mystify the oppressed into seeing their condition as natural rather than imposed. The difficulties of achieving authenticity have therefore been justifiably challenged by thinkers such as Michel Foucault, Jacques Derrida, and, more recently, K. Anthony Appiah and Amy Gutmann and Lewis Gordon.[22] Yet, many contemporary scholars champion authenticity, insofar as it remains socially oriented, avoiding relativism and self-centeredness.[23] Freedom—however thorny this concept has always been—remains central to who we are as human beings. And one of Beauvoir's greatest strengths can be found in the fact that her existentialism never allows for the total eclipse of freedom altogether. Even the most oppressed among us—the slave, the inmate suffering life imprisonment, the Jew in the camp, or the woman in the harem—remain ontologically free. So long as we live and are conscious, our humanity calls out and connects to others to liberate and be liberated. To do so is to live a life of genuine, ethical freedom, where we actively will what we in essence are.

## Notes

1. Simone de Beauvoir, *Pyrrhus and Cineas*, in *Simone de Beauvoir: Philosophical Writings*, ed. Margaret A. Simons with Marybeth Timmermann and Mary Beth Mader, trans. Marybeth Timmerman (Chicago: University of Illinois Press, 2004), 90.

2. It is helpful to understanding Beauvoir's position on the ultimate meaninglessness of action in this scenario to contrast it with a Hegelian understanding of rationality as the motive force driving human culture. Whereas Hegel's ultimate goal—absolute knowing—sets not only the destination but also the contours of the path of human development

throughout history, there simply is no ultimate goal or rational grounding for human action in Beauvoir's theory. All goals are made by the people and societies that choose them and will them into being.

3. Although in her memoir, *The Prime of Life*, Beauvoir says in hindsight that even in this early work she believed that "actual concrete possibilities vary from one person to the next. Some can attain to only a small part of those opportunities that are available to mankind at large." Simone de Beauvoir, *The Prime of Life*, trans. Peter Green (New York: Lancer Books, 1966), 661. In other words, Beauvoir claims that she was aware of the problems of transcendence denied, what constitutes a situation of forced immanence or oppression, from the very beginning of her philosophical and literary career.

4. Beauvoir states, "Relationships with things are not given, are not fixed; I create them minute by minute. Some die, some are born, and others are revived. They are constantly changing. Each new act of surpassing gives me anew the thing surpassed" (*Pyrrhus and Cineas*, 94).

5. Beauvoir, *Pyrrhus and Cineas*, 94.

6. Beauvoir, *Pyrrhus and Cineas*, 99.

7. Beauvoir explains that a "project is exactly what it decides to be. It has the meaning that it gives itself. One cannot define it from the outside. It is not contradictory; it is possible and coherent as soon as it exists, and it exists as soon as a man makes it exist" (*Pyrrhus and Cineas*, 100). By emphasizing that projects do not preexist our choosing of them, Beauvoir adheres to the centrality of human freedom in making the world meaningful.

8. Simone de Beauvoir, *The Ethics of Ambiguity*, trans. Bernard Frechtman (Secaucus, N.J.: Carol, 1997), 142, emphasis added.

9. Beauvoir, *Ethics of Ambiguity*, 147. As someone who lived through the Nazi Occupation of Paris as part of the Resistance, Beauvoir was aware that political choice may involve the violent ouster of murderous despots. However, such violence—even against the original perpetrators—is never justified in perpetuity, as her 1954 novel, *The Mandarins*, makes clear. Violence toward the occupiers and their collaborators was no longer ethical after the war was over, and the characters in the story who maintained that murdering collaborators after armistice was justified were shown to be as serious-minded as their original tyrants. See Simone de Beauvoir, *The Mandarins*, trans. Leonard M. Friedman (New York: Norton, 1999).

10. Beauvoir, *Ethics of Ambiguity*, 142.

11. Beauvoir, *Ethics of Ambiguity*, 153.

12. Beauvoir, *Ethics of Ambiguity*, 90.

13. Beauvoir, *Ethics of Ambiguity*, 123.

14. Beauvoir, *Ethics of Ambiguity*, 99.

15. Beauvoir, *Pyrrhus and Cineas*, 139.

16. Simone de Beauvoir, *The Second Sex*, trans. Constance Borde and Sheila Malovany-Chevallier (New York: Knopf, 2010), 16.

17. Beauvoir, *The Second Sex*, 16.

18. See Simone de Beauvoir, introduction to *Djamila Boupacha: The Story of the Torture of a Young Algerian Girl Which Shocked Liberal French Opinion*, trans. Peter Green (New York: Macmillan, 1962).

19. See Simone de Beauvoir, *The Coming of Age*, trans. Patrick O'Brian (New York: Norton, 1996).

20. See Simone de Beauvoir, *America Day by Day*, trans. Carol Cosman (Berkeley: University of California Press, 1990).

21. Yet Beauvoir's notion of freedom is not uncritically optimistic. Even as she maintains ontological freedom as the central aspect of human being, she becomes more attuned to the effects of enforced immanence, or oppression. Beauvoir, who writes early in her career, "The slave who obeys chooses to obey, and his choice must be renewed at every moment" (*Pyrrhus and Cineas*, 118), later notices that there are people, such as actual slaves and some women, "whose life slips by in an infantile world because, having been kept in a state of servitude and ignorance, they have no means of breaking the ceiling which is stretched over their heads. Like the child, they can exercise their freedom, but only within this universe which has been set up before them, without them" (*Ethics of Ambiguity*, 37), and finally comes to see that "when an individual or a group of individuals is kept in a situation of inferiority, the fact is that he or they *are* inferior" (*Second Sex*, 12).

22. See K. Anthony Appiah and Amy Gutmann, *Color Conscious: The Political Morality of Race* (Princeton, N.J.: Princeton University Press, 1996), and Lewis Gordon, *Existentia Africana* (New York: Routledge, 2000). Both works show suspicion about the notion of authenticity for its air of essentialism, in particular, racial essentialism.

23. Charles Taylor, for example, although a believer in the ethical benefits of authenticity, notes that one of the dangers in maintaining it as an ideal is that we can become myopically focused on self-improvement regardless of our social connections: "Self-determining freedom is in part the default solution of the culture of authenticity, while at the same time it is its bane, since it further intensifies anthropocentrism." Charles Taylor, *The Ethics of Authenticity* (Cambridge, Mass.: Harvard University Press, 1991), 69. See also Alessandro Ferrera, *Reflective Authenticity: Rethinking the Project of Modernity* (New York: Routledge, 1998); Charles Guignon, *On Being Authentic* (New York: Routledge, 2004); Somogy Varga, *Authenticity as an Ethical Ideal* (New York: Routledge, 2011); and Andrew J. Pierce, "Authentic Identities," *Social Theory and Practice* 41, no. 3 (July 2015): 435–57. All of these thinkers maintain a critical notion of authenticity, warning of the ways it can be co-opted by political and market demands, but refuse to reject outright the ethical benefits of maintaining a sense of the freedom possible in living an authentic life.

# 19 The Face

Diane Perpich

The *face*, as a philosophical term, is most closely associated with the writings of Emmanuel Levinas and especially with his first major work, *Totality and Infinity* (1961), whose opening lines raise the question of whether or not we are "duped by morality."[1] For Levinas, the question isn't primarily psychological or epistemological—it is not about why we believe what we do about our moral obligations. The question expresses, instead, a worry about the fragility of ethics. Written in the wake of the Second World War, *Totality and Infinity* begins with a reflection on the way the state of war divests moral norms of their customary weight. War is described as a "trial by force," and politics as the art of foreseeing war.[2] From this perspective, politically brokered peace belongs to the horizon of war, as does a technically conceived rationality put in the service of defeating one's opponent. Committed to winning "by every means" available, war challenges the idea of universal ethical imperatives and risks rendering the claims of morality "derisory."[3] What match is ethics, Levinas seems to wonder, against violent forces bent on destruction? The philosophical project that subsequently unfolds in the text is decidedly unlike that of traditional moral philosophy, both in its inventive terminology and in its distinctive style; however, the questions Levinas grapples with here at the outset of the book are familiar enough. What kind of force, *if any*, does ethics have to counter violence and technical rationality put at the disposal of violence? What kind of authority do moral or ethical claims wield, and how can such claims *compel* us to take up our responsibility for the other in the face of competing imperatives?

The *face* is Levinas's concretely determined answer to these questions, and while there is an intuitive appeal to the idea, what he means is also liable to be misunderstood. Philippe Nemo, for example, in a famous radio interview with Levinas, asks him in what the "phenomenology of the face" consists, and appears to think there is something special that "happens when I look at the Other face to face."[4] Later we get a sense of what Nemo thinks that might be when he comments, "War stories tell us in fact that it is difficult to kill someone who looks straight at you."[5] These kinds of statements suggest that the face is a direct prohibition on unethical action and that Levinas's project is to give a phenomenological description of why, in fact, the face appears to us in this way with this sort of message. Levinas's response is characteristic: he expresses skepticism about the idea of a *phenomenology* of the face, since phenomenology is the study of what appears and, again and again, he will insist that the face is not encountered as something perceived. This is the point, for example, of the oft-quoted line where Levinas says the best way to "see" the face is not even to notice the color of the other's eyes. His point is not that we should ignore particular features of how the other looks, but that when we are observing or perceiving another we are in relation to some*thing* as opposed to being face-to-face with some*one*. What makes Nemo's misreading understandable, however, is that Levinas also claims, again and again, that the relation to the face *is* immediately ethical. In fact, he says as much in the radio interview right after forestalling the question of how we perceive the face: "I think rather that access to the face is straightaway ethical."[6]

At least two fundamental ideas are thus braided together in Levinas's notion of the face: that of the face as defying perception or knowledge—the face "overflows"[7] any image or concept we might have of it—and that of the face as an immediately ethical encounter. One of the first essays to merge these ideas, which arise somewhat independently in Levinas's early writings,[8] is in a lesser known piece entitled "Freedom and Command," published in 1953. The first strand in the braid is present in Levinas's claim in that essay that "a face has meaning not by virtue of the relationships in which it is found, but out of itself."[9] The insistence on the face as signifying "out of itself" rather than as a result of a relation to other things or people has its origin in Levinas's challenge to Heideggerian fundamental ontology. For the latter, meaning is a function of the relation of a being to Being. This sounds rather obscure, but the easiest way to understand it may be to see it as a kind of practically inflected holism about meaning: meaning, for Heidegger, is largely a function of a relation between figure and ground or object and horizon. The idea goes back to Husserl's notion of a horizon of perception: when I attend to the book or the piece of paper on my desk, the other items on the desk, the lamp, other books and papers, the wood of the desk, and the whole of the surrounding room form a kind of horizon of potentiality to which I can turn in further acts of perception. Heidegger goes further and theorizes the items as belonging to an equipmental totality or whole, and the horizon as the contexture of practical assignments in light of which those equipmental wholes take on their meaning. Thus, a hammer and the night sky have meaning in virtue of a complex of practical human projects that render them intelligible. The sky, for example, can be equipment for navigating or an object of study within the larger project of scientific understanding, just as the hammer is a tool for nailing wood together within the larger project of building a shelter. The "world" on this view—and the term could refer to the "world of the ancient Mayans" or to the "world of contemporary physics"—is a totality of meanings that hang together in light of certain already given self-understandings.[10] Levinas's challenge to Heidegger is in his insistence that the face is the one exception to this in that it breaks with every horizon of meaning and every pregiven project.[11] The face of the Other has meaning out of or from itself: the face "*is* by itself and not by reference to a system."[12]

Levinas later acknowledges that insofar as we have a perception of the face in the ordinary sense, or knowledge of our friends, again in the ordinary sense, that particular perception or knowledge is produced in accord with the general manifestation of things and the world. For example, in "Meaning and Sense" (1972), Levinas writes, "The manifestation of the other is, to be sure, produced from the first in conformity with the way every meaning is produced. Another is present in a cultural whole and is illuminated by this whole, as a text by its context." *But*, he adds just a moment later, "the epiphany of the face involves a signifyingness of its own independent of this meaning received from the world. The other . . . signifies by himself."[13] In the interview with Nemo, he clarifies, "The relation with the face can surely be dominated by perception, but what is specifically the face is what cannot be reduced to that."[14] We will come back to this at the very end of this essay; its significance is crucial.

The second idea embedded in the notion of the face is the idea, already mentioned, of ethical immediacy: the face "straightaway" issues an irrevocable ethical command. Explaining this idea, Levinas says, "The first word of the face is 'Thou shalt not kill.' It is an order. There is a commandment in the appearance of the face, as if a master spoke to me."[15] The same idea is repeated in *Totality and Infinity*[16] in passages which speak of an "infinite resistance to murder, firm and insurmountable, which gleams in the face of the Other, in the total nudity of his defenseless eyes."[17] Levinas adds, "There is here a relation not with a very great resistance, but with something absolutely *other*: the resistance of what has no resistance—ethical resistance."[18] Ethical resistance to murder and annihilation, Levinas here makes clear, is not a physical or "real" sort of resistance. Indeed, elsewhere in the same passage Levinas speaks of the other's sovereign "no" being obliterated by the touch of a sword or a bullet to the heart. He notes, "If the resistance to murder were not ethical but real, we would have a *perception* of it, with all that reverts to the subjective in perception."[19] This implies not only that the resistance he terms "ethical" is not a direct counter force, but is of a different order than perceptible force—and perhaps somehow more or better than what might be seen or perceived, since perception always involves a certain subjective component. "Infinity presents itself as a face in the ethical resistance that paralyses my powers and from the depths of defenseless eyes rises firm and absolute in its nudity and destitution."[20] And in an earlier section of the same work: "The face resists possession, resists my powers," but does so "not . . . like the hardness of a rock against which the effort of the hand comes to naught."[21] Indeed, the face is the poor, the widow, and the orphan; the face commands absolutely but from a position of absolute destitution.

Both of the claims embedded in Levinas's account of the face—that the face is not primarily an object perceived and that access to the face is an immediately ethical encounter—merit greater scrutiny than they sometimes get in the secondary literature. Once again, the essay "Freedom and Command" is illuminating. In fact, it is one of the best essays to track the manner in which the two claims at issue here get woven together, without any claim of logical or conceptual entailment, but certainly with a suggestion that they are, at the least, two sides of a single coin. Having said that the face "has meaning not by virtue of the relationships in which it is found, but out of itself," Levinas adds, "That is what *expression* is."[22] *Expression* is a felicitous term for Levinas's purpose insofar as it connotes direct meaning-giving, that is, making one's thoughts or feelings known in speech or through one's countenance. In one sense, Levinas trades on our ordinary sense that a facial expression (perhaps *unlike* language) is unmediated or not as easily susceptible to dissimulation. We talk about someone's having "an honest face" or of being able to discern someone's feeling straightaway by his or her expression; some of us, famously, have no "poker face" and our moods or thoughts are too easily read from our faces. But in another sense, Levinas will be quick to say that this *is not* what he means by the face and that the kind of expression he is talking about is *speech*. But even then, what interests him about speech is not the content communicated but the way the one who communicates is present alongside whatever is said: "What is expressed is not just a thought. . . . It is also the other who is present in thought. Expression renders present what is communicated and the one who is communicating; they are both in the expression."[23] We are told that expression is thus an invitation to and already "social commerce" with the other.[24] And then, a line later, "The being that presents itself in expression already engages us in society, *commits us to enter into society with him*."[25]

The problem is that one could easily agree to the first idea or claim that Levinas embeds in the notion of the face (namely, that it overflows perception) and still not see one's way clear to the second (that is, that it makes an ethical demand to which I *must* respond). Suppose I agree that the relation to the other is categorically different from the relation to a thing, at least in the manner of the other's presentation; does that necessarily entail an ethical commitment of some kind? Levinas makes the jump by playing on multiple connotations of the term *expression*. He generates the idea on the one side of an unmediated access to the other in the face, that is, access that is not a function of context but is a presentation of the self *by itself* in its expressiveness; on the other side, he alludes to the idea of an ethical injunction to recognize the dignity of that self, that is, a right not to be killed, in the idea that the self expresses itself specifically as a plea or an injunction against murder. However, the bridge between the two ideas is more metaphorical than logical, to the point where Levinas's approach might be said to involve "metaphorical" rather than logical entailment. And lest one think that this strategy is used only once, or only in early essays, it is arguable that the strategy becomes *more* entrenched over time.

Rather than canvass the various ways scholars have responded, implicitly or explicitly, to the problem—e.g., the empirical reading of Levinas, the noncognitivist account, the transcendental reading, the theological reading, or the dismissal of his thought altogether as not, after all, an ethics—allow me instead to conclude with a suggestion about how the problem fits Levinas squarely into the terrain of contemporary ethical and moral philosophy. The authority to claim moral rights and address moral obligations to another is what is meant by *moral standing*. The term mirrors *legal standing*, which indicates having the right to make certain claims before the law and its representatives. Moral standing is often debated in particular terms where it is a question of holding *this* person accountable in *this* context, but it can also be understood as the broader question of who generally belongs to the moral community. In Levinasian terms, the latter question is "*Who* has a face?" Who has the authority or standing to bring moral claims or issue moral commands? We know already what sorts of answers Levinas's account will disallow: those that depend on the other having a particular discernible quality or characteristic. It is not because the other *looks* like me or *feels pain* like me or *reasons* like me or *speaks* like me that I am responsible to her. Nor is it because she has needs, or is destitute and vulnerable—despite Levinas's appeals to the nudity of a face and to the vulnerability of the widow and the orphan. Moral standing is misunderstood if it is reduced to something we can know or perceive about the other. Levinas could not be more explicit about this, and likely for the reasons that guide his reflections at the outset of *Totality and Infinity*: war is a matter of identifying those qualities—ethnicity often being first among them—that position one as belonging to or excluded from the community of those deemed to have moral standing. And, for Levinas, reason alone was not enough to protect those annihilated in the Second World War; it was insufficient to *prevent* the destruction of those reasoned to be *other*.

Again, while there may yet be important differences in how scholars interpret the face, the sort of inquiry or the horizon of inquiry to which this notion belongs should be clear. Why is the best way to see a face not even to notice the color of the other's eyes? Because there is a difference between looking *at* the other and being in a relation *to* the other. What is absolutely primary for understanding the locus of our ethical responsibility is not something we see or know from the standpoint of an isolated ego (an "I think") or a universal or God's-eye point of view (the "one knows"). It is only from inside the relation *to* the other, the relation face-to-face, that one is in a position to hear the other's demand *as* an ethical demand. While there is much that distinguishes Levinas's position from Buber's dialogical account of the I-Thou relationship or from Stephen Darwall's more recent account of the second-person standpoint, it is evident that his philosophy, like theirs, is addressed to this fundamental dimension of human experience.[26]

## Notes

1. Emmanuel Levinas, *Totality and Infinity*, trans. A. Lingis (Pittsburgh, Pa.: Duquesne University Press, 1969), 21.

2. Levinas, *Totality and Infinity*, 21.

3. Levinas, *Totality and Infinity*, 21.

4. Emmanuel Levinas, *Ethics and Infinity: Conversations with Philippe Nemo*, trans. R. Cohen (Pittsburgh, Pa.: Duquesne University Press, 1985), 85.

5. Levinas, *Ethics and Infinity*, 86.

6. Levinas, *Ethics and Infinity*, 86.

7. Levinas, *Totality and Infinity*, 51.

8. For a fuller account of the elements that Levinas brings together to form the notion of the face, see my essay "The Face of the Other," in *Oxford Handbook of Levinas*, ed. Michael Morgan (Oxford: Oxford University Press, 2018).

9. Emmanuel Levinas, "Freedom and Command," in *Collected Philosophical Papers*, trans. Alphonso Lingis (Dordrecht: Martinus Nijhoff, 1987), 20.

10. On this way of reading Heidegger, see John Haugeland, *Dasein Disclosed: John Haugeland's Heidegger*, ed. Joseph Rouse (Cambridge, Mass.: Harvard University Press, 2013).

11. See Emmanuel Levinas, "Is Ontology Fundamental?," in *Emmanuel Levinas: Basic Philosophical Writings*, ed. Adriaan T. Peperzak, Simon Critchley, and Robert Bernasconi (Bloomington: Indiana University Press, 1996), 5–6.

12. Levinas, *Totality and Infinity*, 75. See also the essay "The Ego and the Totality," where Levinas writes, "A face is the very identity of a being. There he manifests himself out of himself, and not on the basis of concepts" (in *Collected Philosophical Papers*, 41).

13. Emmanuel Levinas, "Meaning and Sense," in Peperzak et al., *Emmanuel Levinas*, 95.

14. Levinas, *Ethics and Infinity*, 85.

15. Levinas, *Ethics and Infinity*, 89.

16. This idea undergoes modification in Levinas's works after *Totality and Infinity*. In particular, from "The Trace of the Other" (1963) and "Phenomena and Enigma" (1965) onward, Levinas tends to speak less of the immediate or straightaway ethical encounter with the face and more often of the revelation of the other in a trace. I have argued elsewhere that the idea of the other's command as a "trace" is Levinas's response to the difficulty his thought finds itself in as it tries to navigate between the idea of the face as an imposition of ethics and the idea of ethics as a relationship without violence. See Diane Perpich, *The Ethics of Emmanuel Levinas* (Palo Alto, Calif.: Stanford University Press, 2008), 110–15.

17. Levinas, *Totality and Infinity*, 199.

18. Levinas, *Totality and Infinity*, 199.

19. Levinas, *Totality and Infinity*, 199.

20. Levinas, *Totality and Infinity*, 200.

21. Levinas, *Totality and Infinity*, 198.

22. Levinas, "Freedom and Command," 20.

23. Levinas, "Freedom and Command," 20–21.

24. Levinas, "Freedom and Command," 21.

25. Levinas, "Freedom and Command," 21, emphasis added.

26. See Martin Buber, *I and Thou*, trans. Walter Kaufmann (New York: Charles Scribner and Sons, 1970), and Stephen Darwall, *The Second-Person Standpoint: Morality, Respect and Accountability* (Cambridge, Mass.: Harvard University Press).

# 20 The Flesh of the World

Donald A. Landes

A nascent ontology plays tantalizingly across the pages of Maurice Merleau-Ponty's final and unfinished texts. These traces announce an ontology of intertwining, of spacing, and of reversibility, but above all they promise an ontology of the flesh (*chair*), a deceptively common word employed by the philosopher to name that which he boldly declares "has no name in any philosophy."[1] We find traces of a flesh of time and of the sensible, a flesh that has depths, secret folds, and that lines the visible with invisibility. But is there one flesh, or several? Is there a difference in kind between human flesh and the flesh of the world? Is flesh identical to Being, or is it an anthropological projection outward? Does the flesh of the world imply that everything is living flesh (hylozoism)?[2] Or does a primacy of *sentient* flesh ultimately leave Merleau-Ponty within the limits of transcendental phenomenology? Given his sudden death in 1961, Merleau-Ponty falls silent before resolving these tensions and hesitations.

Merleau-Ponty scholars have struggled to answer these questions, offering competing interpretations, critical responses, or new ways of extending this concept. Some emphasize what appears to be a difference in kind between human flesh (sentient-sensible) and the flesh of the world (sensible but not sentient), an interpretation often influenced by the Husserlian notion of *Leib* (animate flesh); others emphasize passages where the flesh seems to be a universal texture of Being, which leads to fusion or coinciding—an almost Bergsonian interpretation of Merleau-Ponty.[3] Although both interpretations justifiably claim textual evidence, they rarely consider the overall trajectory of Merleau-Ponty's thought as a clear rejection of either a projection outward or a fusion in indifference. In this essay, I examine the trajectory that culminates in Merleau-Ponty's thinking of the flesh of the world. The genesis of the "flesh (of the world)" concept reframes Merleau-Ponty's contribution not as a study of embodiment and being-*in*-the-world but as a radical thinking of the experience of belonging *from within*, a phenomenology of being-*of*-the-world. An unnamed "flesh (of the world)" haunts even Merleau-Ponty's early thinking, drawing his analysis to the limits of whatever philosophical method he had provisionally adopted. The "flesh (of the world)" reveals a looming crisis in the phenomenological project itself and leads Merleau-Ponty to rethink philosophical methodology as interrogation. The flesh—as the place of our being-*of*-the-world and as the principle of *reversibility* that is "the ultimate truth"[4] of existence—names both the object *of* and the ontological place *for* interrogation. This allows us to reject any difference in kind between my flesh and the flesh of the world, while simultaneously avoiding a fusion with universal flesh, into which I (and the Other) might dissolve without remainder. As Merleau-Ponty writes, "it is by the flesh of the world that . . . one can understand the lived body."[5]

## The Long Shadow of *Leib*

The term *flesh* recalls Husserl's study of *Leib* (in contrast to *Körper*) in *Ideas II*, a major influence on Merleau-Ponty's thinking.[6] Although both words translate as "body," *Leib* refers to *animate flesh*, whereas *Körper* generally names *inanimate* bodies.[7] Husserl thus emphasizes the difference between living and nonliving bodies, stressing doubled sensations, kinesthetic sensations, and the living body's spatial orientation.[8] Although *Leib* sometimes translates into French as *chair* (flesh),[9] Merleau-Ponty consistently uses *corps propre* (one's own body) or *corps phénoménal* (phenomenal body), placing the emphasis not on the living body but on the body *as lived*. Whenever Merleau-Ponty uses *chair* in his early work, it names *mere* flesh: living tissue as an object. The only occurrence of *Leib* in *Phenomenology of Perception* is translated by Merleau-Ponty as *corps vivant* (living body), not as *corps propre*.[10]

This subtle difference reveals Merleau-Ponty's key observation: our body is both an object in the world and *lived*. Moreover, that his analysis does not unfold under the banner of "animate flesh" already suggests that he senses a larger role for the lived body beyond the living/nonliving distinction. Consider the elusive conclusion of his analysis of the lived body: "Let us see clearly all that is implied by the rediscovery of one's own body [*le corps propre*]. It is not merely one object among all others that resists reflection and remains, so to speak, glued to the subject. Obscurity spreads to the perceived world in its entirety."[11] This announces a transition to the *ontological* significance of the lived body. As the site of an oscillation between activity and passivity, its obscurity "spreads," not as an anthropological projection but via the sudden realization that being-*of*-the-world is the ontological precondition for being-*in*-the-world. In other words, Merleau-Ponty discovers a crisis in the phenomenological project: "phenomenology's task was to reveal the mystery of the world," but what it discovers is that "the world is not what I think, but what I live; I am open to the world, I unquestionably communicate with it, but I do not possess it, it is inexhaustible."[12] Phenomenology will need a new theory of reflection, given the inexhaustible presence of the preexisting world beyond the constitutive activities of knowing that world that phenomenology was designed to enumerate. Reflection suddenly realizes it is constitutively haunted by that which resists reflection, an "originary field" or "pre-reflective fund . . . upon which it draws, and that constitutes for it, like an original past, a past that has never been present."[13] This "fund" has no name in any philosophy—it is the flesh of the world as the place of perception, intersubjectivity, and thought lingering at the limits of (Husserlian) phenomenology.

Merleau-Ponty's initial steps beyond this crisis remain tentative in *Phenomenology of Perception* and in the years immediately following. For instance, in 1951 he writes, "The twentieth century has restored and deepened the notion of flesh, that is, of animate body."[14] He now translates Husserl's *Leib* as "flesh," but this "flesh" remains the one trapped within the limitations of phenomenology as living tissue. He invokes the notion of "contingency" to characterize a certain "anonymous adversity" that—although not yet the "flesh (of the world)"—names the "astonishing junction between fact and meaning, between my body and my self, my self and others, my thought and my speech."[15]

This "anonymous" adversity does not receive a name until the late 1950s, when Merleau-Ponty demonstrates how the "flesh (of the world)" answers the crisis in the phenomenological project. He writes, "At the end of Husserl's life there is an *unthought*, which belongs for all that to him, but which nevertheless opens onto something else."[16] Consider Husserl's "phenomenological reduction," the suspension of our pretentions of accessing the world in itself so as to gain access to the constitutive acts (*noesis*) and their intentional objects (*noema*). In *Phenomenology of Perception*, Merleau-Ponty claimed, "The most important lesson of the reduction is the impossibility of a complete reduction."[17] Now he suggests that Husserl's obsessive returning to this question manifests an "unthought": that "to reflect is to unveil an unreflected" that nonetheless withdraws.[18] The "whole world of the natural attitude" haunts reflection, and thus "reflection does not enclose us in a closed, transparent milieu"; it unveils "a third dimension."[19] Reduction renders intelligible my being-*in*-the-world, but merely *reveals* indirectly my being-*of*-the-world. Moreover, my body is not just living flesh but a "network of implications," a "vinculum," a connecting tissue, a flesh.[20] As "I touch myself touching; my body accomplishes a 'sort of reflection.'"[21] This implies "an ontological rehabilitation of the sensible," since the thing and the world are "woven into the same intentional fabric as my body": "the flesh of what is perceived . . . reflects my own incarnation."[22] The long shadow of *Leib* now has a name: the "flesh (of the world)," the object and the place of all the modalities of reflection.

## Interrogation and Being-of-the-World

"Interrogation" is Merleau-Ponty's new philosophical method, articulated across the first three chapters of *The Visible and the Invisible*. The first chapter shows how "reflection" enacts a necessary stepping back to create a spacing (*écart*) for understanding the world. But reflection remains too far removed, resulting in skepticism and solipsism. Interrogation must develop a form of "hyper-reflection" that "plunges into the world" rather than attempting to survey it from above.[23] The second chapter considers dialectical thought. If reflection is too far removed, might we fare better with Sartre's *pure* nothingness? Interrogation reveals that we are rather an *operative* nothingness, since "even vision, even speech" are always "a carnal relation, with the flesh of the world."[24] Interrogation must establish a hyperdialectic that resists all synthesis and all radical opposition in order to think being-*of*-the-world as prerequisite for being-*in*-the-world:

"Openness upon the world implies that the world be and remain a horizon . . . because somehow he who sees it is *of* it and is *in* it."[25]

Chapter 3 extends Merleau-Ponty's critique of Husserl and distances "interrogation" from Bergsonism. Although Husserl attempted to further the phenomenological reduction by developing the eidetic reduction, Merleau-Ponty argues that he forgets how "my own experience interconnects within itself and connects with that of the others by opening upon one sole world, by inscribing itself in one sole Being."[26] The eidetic intuition of essences is secondary to my being-*of*-the world; I can see something only because I "do not see it from the depths of nothingness, but from the midst of itself; I the seer am also visible."[27] Is interrogation, then, a form of Bergsonian fusion, an intuitive *coinciding* with the flesh (of the world)? Merleau-Ponty is adamant in his rejection of a "return to the immediate, the coincidence, the effective fusion with the existent."[28] A "real fusion" would not *solve* the crisis of phenomenology; it would dissolve us into the flesh despite the evidence of experience: "My eyes which see, my hands which touch, can also be seen and touched, because . . . our flesh lines and even envelops all the visible and tangible things with which nevertheless it is surrounded, the world and I are within one another."[29] This reciprocal intertwining is not a fusion but an ongoing process of internal differentiation. The flesh (of the world) is the "metaphysical *principle*"[30] of reversibility, the *place* of our differentiation as spacing (*écart*), and the *object* of a properly constructed philosophical interrogation. Interrogation is not the search for an absolute rest in "fusion" but the absolute restlessness of having to forever begin anew.[31]

Thus Merleau-Ponty proposes to *interrogate* anew "seeing, speaking, even thinking," now from the perspective of being-*of*-the-world, from within flesh.[32] These experiences overflow our attempts to close a discourse around them and are always more than what we say of them; they indirectly present the inexhaustible of the flesh of the world. To see a visible thing, such as a red object, already implies a massive set of *invisible* temporal and spatial relations that structure the experience. The thing intertwines with other aspects (texture, light) and is "a sort of straights between exterior and interior horizons ever gaping open . . . a certain differentiation . . . a momentary crystallization."[33] On the other side, the "seer" is given the task of exploring things which, as other folds in the same flesh, are already familiar. Touching presupposes a shared kinship in being-*of* the tactile world. The seer could not see the visible unless he or she is "possessed by it, unless he [or she] *is of it*."[34] The perceiver's flesh, then, is his or her participation in the principle of folding or reversibility. The lived body is not the source of a projection outward, but rather "an *exemplar sensible*" that sustains a certain divergence: "When we speak of the flesh of the visible, we do not . . . describe a world covered over with all of our projections. . . . We mean that carnal being, as a being of depths . . . is a prototype of Being, of which our body, the sensible sentient, is a very remarkable variant, but whose constitutive paradox already lies in every visible."[35] The principle of carnal reflection, the flesh, "is indeed a paradox of Being, not a paradox of man."[36] Neither a projection nor a fusion, the oscillation between touching and touched reveals "quite unexpected relations between the two orders" that, although at first seemingly different in kind, turn out to reveal a connaturality in the flesh (of the world).

But what, then, is this flesh? Merleau-Ponty writes, "The flesh is not matter, is not mind, is not substance. To designate it, we should need the old term 'element,' in the sense . . . of a general thing . . . a sort of embodied principle that brings a style of being wherever there is a fragment of being. The flesh is in this sense an 'element' of Being."[37] The flesh is an embodied principle of reversibility and the place and general style of Being revealed by the interrogation of being-*of*-the-world. The flesh is thus also the place for the more agile foldings of intersubjectivity, language, and thought. This does not amount to a fusion and a loss of difference, since Merleau-Ponty means "a reversibility always imminent and never realized."[38] The flesh is forever "incessantly escaping" its own folding back, forever failing to encompass itself, and thus maintaining itself forever open as the restless place of "the reversibility which is the ultimate truth" revealed in our being-*of*-the-world.[39]

## Criticisms and Developments

Significant criticisms and developments of this concept are to be found in feminist philosophy. One concern is that the "flesh (of the world)" effaces difference in the self-Other relation. According to Beata Stawarska, Merleau-Ponty universalizes categories from male experience by not recognizing a difference between self-touching and touching another person, thereby reducing the other to the same.[40] Or again, Luce Irigaray contends that the "flesh of each one" in the relation of sexual difference is not "substitutable."[41] Merleau-Ponty's position, she argues, is a "labyrinthine solipsism," a fundamental narcissism in the presumption of reversibility of seer and seen.[42]

In response, Judith Butler reveals that Irigaray's critique involves presuppositions that lead to an unfair condemnation of Merleau-Ponty's elemental logic.[43] Moreover, she suggests that Irigaray's dialogical style demonstrates a relation with the Other that is neither simply "substitutability" nor "radical opposition," but enacts precisely the "intertwining" and "dynamic differentiation in proximity" the flesh implies.[44] For Butler, the ethical questions of co-implication in the flesh are perhaps more difficult than those of an ethics of radical alterity.[45] This urgent ethical role for the flesh is described by Gail Weiss as follows: "How the flesh stylizes being suggests an ongoing process of differentiation that cannot be reduced to sameness. And yet, insofar as it stylizes, the flesh also unifies, weaving together disparate gestures, movements, bodies, and situations into a dynamic fabric of meaning that must be continually reworked, made, and unmade."[46]

In this essay, I have located the flesh of the world as the principle and the place of ongoing differentiation as revealed through the analysis of our being-*of*-the-world. This avoids not only the simple projection of the "I can"[47] of the *corps propre*, but also the dissolving of difference into an undifferentiated mass. Moreover, the flesh allows us to emphasize both vulnerability and a possible (though forever incomplete) communication across difference. The assumption of *substantial* fleshly difference—certain flesh seen as "innately and therefore irremediably inferior to the bodies of others"[48]—has created an inexcusable burden of violence borne by feminine embodiment and other foldings of the flesh. Thinking the ontological possibilities and dangers of the flesh of the world—as a restless and interiorly differentiating mass that now has a name in at least one philosophy—seems a promising place to begin the search for an *ethical* response.

## Notes

1. Maurice Merleau-Ponty, *The Visible and the Invisible*, trans. Alphonso Lingis (Evanston, Ill.: Northwestern University Press, 1968), 147.

2. David Abram, *The Spell of the Sensuous* (New York: Vintage, 1996). For a Merleau-Pontian philosophy of nature, see Ted Toadvine, *Merleau-Ponty's Philosophy of Nature* (Evanston, Ill.: Northwestern University Press, 2009).

3. See Renaud Barbaras, *The Being of the Phenomenon*, trans. Ted Toadvine and Leonard Lawlor (Bloomington: Indiana University Press, 2004), chapter 10; Françoise Dastur, *Chair et langage* (Fougères: Encre Marine, 2001), 86–87; M. C. Dillon, *Merleau-Ponty's Ontology*, 2nd edition (Evanston, Ill.: Northwestern University Press, 1997), 164–67; Fred Evans and Leonard Lawlor, "The Value of Flesh," in *Chiasms: Merleau-Ponty's Notion of the Flesh*, ed. Fred Evans and Leonard Lawlor (Albany, N.Y.: SUNY Press, 2000), 10.

4. Merleau-Ponty, *The Visible and the Invisible*, 155.

5. Merleau-Ponty, *The Visible and the Invisible*, 250.

6. Edmund Husserl, *Ideas Pertaining to a Pure Phenomenology and to a Phenomenological Philosophy*, book 2, trans. Richard Rojcewicz and André Schuwer (Dordrecht: Kluwer, 1989).

7. Husserl, *Ideas Pertaining to a Pure Phenomenology*, xiv. See also Jenny Slatman, "The Körper/Leib Distinction," in this volume.

8. Slatman, "The Körper/Leib Distinction." See Maurice Merleau-Ponty, *Phenomenology of Perception*, trans. Donald A. Landes (London: Routledge, 2013), part 1.

9. Pascal Dupond, *Dictionnaire Merleau-Ponty* (Paris: Ellipses, 2008), 17.

10. Merleau-Ponty, *Phenomenology of Perception*, 295.

11. Merleau-Ponty, *Phenomenology of Perception*, 205.

12. Merleau-Ponty, *Phenomenology of Perception*, lxxxv, lxxx–lxxxi.

13. Merleau-Ponty, *Phenomenology of Perception*, 252.

14. Maurice Merleau-Ponty, *Signs*, trans. Richard C. McCleary (Evanston, Ill.: Northwestern University Press, 1964), 227.

15. Merleau-Ponty, *Signs*, 239.

16. Merleau-Ponty, *Signs*, 160.

17. Merleau-Ponty, *Phenomenology of Perception*, lxxvii.

18. Merleau-Ponty, *Signs*, 161.

19. Merleau-Ponty, *Signs*, 162.

20. Merleau-Ponty, *Signs*, 166.

21. Merleau-Ponty, *Signs*, 166.

22. Merleau-Ponty, *Signs*, 167.

23. Merleau-Ponty, *The Visible and the Invisible*, 39.

24. Merleau-Ponty, *The Visible and the Invisible*, 83–84.

25. Merleau-Ponty, *The Visible and the Invisible*, 100, emphasis added.

26. Merleau-Ponty, *The Visible and the Invisible*, 110.

27. Merleau-Ponty, *The Visible and the Invisible*, 113.

28. Merleau-Ponty, *The Visible and the Invisible*, 122–23.

29. Merleau-Ponty, *The Visible and the Invisible*, 123.

30. Gail Weiss, "Écart: The Space of Corporeal Difference," in Evans and Lawlor, *Chiasms*, 204.

31. Merleau-Ponty, *The Visible and the Invisible*, 125.

32. Merleau-Ponty, *The Visible and the Invisible*, 130.

33. Merleau-Ponty, *The Visible and the Invisible*, 132–33.

34. Merleau-Ponty, *The Visible and the Invisible*, 135.

35. Merleau-Ponty, *The Visible and the Invisible*, 136.

36. Merleau-Ponty, *The Visible and the Invisible*, 136.

37. Merleau-Ponty, *The Visible and the Invisible*, 139, translation modified.

38. Merleau-Ponty, *The Visible and the Invisible*, 147.

39. Merleau-Ponty, *The Visible and the Invisible*, 155.

40. Beata Stawarska, "From the Body Proper to Flesh: Merleau-Ponty on Intersubjectivity," in *Feminist Interpretations of Maurice Merleau-Ponty*, ed. Dorothea Olkowski and Gail Weiss (University Park: Pennsylvania State University Press, 2006), 92.

41. Luce Irigaray, *An Ethics of Sexual Difference*, trans. Carolyn Burke and Gillian C. Gill (Ithaca, N.Y.: Cornell University Press, 1993), 167.

42. Irigaray, *An Ethics of Sexual Difference*, 157. Tina Chanter suggests that although Irigaray is nonetheless "right to criticize [Merleau-Ponty] for not going far enough," the flesh might still offer feminist philosophy a "genuinely radical alternative." Tina Chanter, "Wild Meaning: Luce Irigaray's Reading of Merleau-Ponty," in Evans and Lawlor, *Chiasms*, 220.

43. Judith Butler, "Sexual Difference as a Question of Ethics: Alterities in the Flesh in Irigaray and Merleau-Ponty," in Olkowski and Weiss, *Feminist Interpretations of Merleau-Ponty*, 92.

44. Butler, "Sexual Difference as a Question of Ethics," 112, 115.

45. Butler, "Sexual Difference as a Question of Ethics," 116.

46. Gail Weiss, "Urban Flesh," in Olkowski and Weiss, *Feminist Interpretations of Merleau-Ponty*, 148.

47. See Iris Marion Young, "Throwing Like a Girl," in *On Female Body Experience* (Oxford: Oxford University Press, 2005), 27–45; Gail Weiss, "The Perils and Pleasures of the 'I Can' Body," *Symposium* 21, no. 2 (2017): 63–80.

48. Gail Weiss, "Pride and Prejudice: Ambiguous Racial, Religious, and Ethnic Identities of Jewish Bodies," in *Living Alterities: Phenomenology, Embodiment, and Race*, ed. Emily S. Lee (Albany, N.Y.: SUNY Press, 2014), 215.

# 21 Geomateriality

Ted Toadvine

The elemental materials of our surroundings, both solid and fluid, are the literal and metaphorical foundation of our earthly existence. Rocks and their sediments provide the ground on which we walk, the soil in which we plant, materials for our tools and constructions, and places to bury our wastes. The air we breathe and water we drink rejoin larger cycles in the skies and oceans. The world as we know and inhabit it, with its places, biota, and weather patterns, is framed spatially and temporally by myriad geological and atmospheric processes of local, regional, and global scale. Geomateriality serves, then, as a basic ontological substratum for the natural and built environments of our daily lives, our lifeworlds, insofar as it furnishes the constitutive elements for every physical reality, our bodies included, and therefore conditions all life and thought. Advances in our scientific understanding of these geomaterial elements and processes increasingly inform our everyday lives and culture, inspiring, in the words of Elizabeth Ellsworth and Jamie Kruse, "a growing recognition that the geologic, both as a material dynamic and as a cultural preoccupation, shapes the 'now' in ever more direct and urgent ways."[1] One important symptom of this urgency is our belated recognition of the human influence over processes of planetary scale and geological duration, succinctly expressed in the proposal to name our current geological epoch "the Anthropocene,"[2] which sharpens our appreciation of the ethical dimensions of our inescapable entanglements in elemental relationships. Phenomenology's long tradition of investigating the earth and elements in ontological terms, often in dialogue with such theorists of materiality as Henri Bergson, Alfred North Whitehead, and Gaston Bachelard, makes a major contribution to appreciating the stakes of these elemental relationships for our conceptions of world, embodiment, and time. Geomaterial phenomenology therefore anticipates and informs the recent geological turn in the arts and humanities, which emphasizes our reciprocal implication in geological processes, the active agency of elemental forces in our daily lives, and an appreciation of "deep" temporal horizons.[3]

Phenomenology's approach to materiality is distinctive because of its critical distance from metaphysical naturalism, the view that what exists is limited to physical reality as described by the natural sciences. As Husserl demonstrates in *Ideas II*, the naturalistic view of material objects as "pure things" involves an unacknowledged reference to a perceiver whose senses, movements, and perceptual norms contribute to the constitution of objectivity.[4] More generally, the sciences necessarily depend on the historical and cultural lifeworld, our shared everyday practical and pretheoretical environment, for their evidential and contextual background and their ultimate justification. From a transcendental perspective, the lifeworld is both the ultimate world-horizon for the emergence of meaning and the unique, pregiven "earth-ground" generative of all physical and living bodies in space-time.[5] A return to the lifeworld as the ontological foundation of experiential meaning opens the prospects for richer descriptions of the expressive, aesthetic, and ethical dimensions of geomateriality than naturalism can provide.

The rediscovery of the lifeworld shows that material nature is essentially historical and irreducible to the objective matter described by the sciences, opening paths for more originary descriptions of materiality. Taking their cue from Husserl's nonnaturalistic approach, subsequent phenomenologists have pursued investigations in two primary directions: the relation of earth and the elements to world, and the embodied experience of materiality. Along the first path, Heidegger calls attention to the originary sense of nature, termed *phusis* by the ancient Greeks, that is characterized by self-unfolding emergence, such as the sprouting of a plant. The self-emergence of *phusis* is inseparable from its withdrawal or self-concealment, which is not a hiddenness but rather a source of sheltering and reserve: to emerge and extend itself into the air, the plant must be rooted in the dense opacity of the soil. *Earth* is Heidegger's term for this sheltering and self-concealing aspect of *phusis*, manifest not only in the literal soil but also in the canvas and pigments of a painting, the sound of a spoken word, and the flesh of the human body. *Earth* names the phenomenological experience of materiality as what grounds, supports, and shelters the emergence of meaning while simultaneously receding from its own disclosure.[6] This description of earth captures the dynamic strife between the opening of a world of referential meanings and the grounding of this world in an obdurate thingliness. The scientific understanding of matter as objectivity and the technological reduction of earth to raw materials violate earth's mystery by forcing it into simple presence, whereas poetic dwelling preserves and safeguards the earth and sky, gods and mortals.[7]

Rejecting Heidegger's fascination with the mystery of the earth, Levinas describes our originary relation with the elements as one of corporeal immersion in sensible enjoyment, a "living from" that is paradigmatically alimentary.[8] In sensible enjoyment the self is first established as self, while the exteriority that one lives from is affirmed prior to all thought or representation, and this independence within dependence is the very meaning of embodiment. The elemental in Levinas's sense is prior to all discrete things; it is content without form that recedes into the anonymous and boundless depths of earth or sky, sea or forest. Immersion in the elements first teaches the meaning of the empirical, of the materiality and substantial plenitude of being. Although the body enjoys a fundamental "agreement" with the elements that nourish it, this agreement is marred by insecurity: the elements, in their immemorial indefiniteness, cannot be possessed, leaving the self vulnerable to an uncertain future. The fathomless depths of the elements open onto the "there is," the nocturnal nothingness that remains after the world disappears, home to faceless mythical gods. Avoiding the paganism that tempted Heidegger requires a turn away from the elements, away from fascination with the earth, toward the social relation and genuinely ethical transcendence in the face of the other. For Levinas, then, the resistance of geomateriality is to be mastered through labor and technology, ultimately in the service of approaching the other without empty hands.[9]

Joining insights from Heidegger and Levinas, John Sallis suggests that a return to the sensible elements offers an encounter with nature's resistance and vulnerability that avoids the difficulties of classical materialism. Rather than approaching the elements as materials from which nature is composed, Sallis shifts our attention to the manifestive role of "elementals"—e.g., wind, sea, earth, sky—insofar as they bound and articulate the horizon within which all things show themselves. Unlike particular sensible things, which can in principle be experienced from any side, elementals may be encountered only from a single edge that opens onto an encompassing expanse: sea, sky, and earth recede from us toward an open horizon. Elementals thereby sensibly frame our experience of things without themselves being experienced as things. Every experience is framed by an elemental context: at this specific place on earth, at this time of day marked by the sun's passage through the sky, within the atmosphere of this particular season and climate, and so on. The manifestive character of elementals may, on Sallis's view, provide the basis for a renewed encounter with nature and a responsiveness to its alterity.[10] Sallis's attention to the framing role that elementals play in the manifestation of the world, echoing Husserl's description of the lifeworld as earth-ground, is a welcome reminder that geomateriality operates along multiple registers and is not reducible to the sensible constituents, the "matter," of things.

Husserl's early investigation in *Ideas II* opens another register for geomaterial exploration precisely through the body's own entanglement in material nature, as recognized by Landgrebe and Merleau-Ponty.[11] Sensibility entails that the body share the materiality of what it senses, such that the experience of one's own corporeality can illuminate the materiality of the world—a materiality distinct in this case from that of "pure things" naturalistically described. For Levinas, as noted above, the body's enjoyment of the elements within which it bathes and by which it is nourished nevertheless remains a relation with exteriority; the body does not participate in the elemental as such but establishes a separation from it within its very dependence. For Husserl, by contrast, the constitution of corporeality and of material nature are indivisible, and the body is consequently a Janus-faced "double reality," with one face turned toward sensible nature while the other faces the life of spirit.[12] Landgrebe draws radical conclusions from this "natural side" of subjectivity: insofar as corporeality and material nature "constitute themselves in one another," their relation "*shatters the traditional separation of inner and outer*, of an *immanence* as the range of the subjective from a *transcendence* of objects which stands in opposition to it."[13] It is Merleau-Ponty, however, who pushes these analyses further, extending Husserl's own example of the double-constitution of the body through touch: as touched, the body is a material, physical thing, while as touching it is a sensing flesh.[14] On Merleau-Ponty's account, this intertwining of sentient and sensed results in an "ontological rehabilitation of the sensible," according to which the blurring of the subject-object distinction in the body must also be extended to the perceived world and accord to all material things the status of "flesh."[15] The "other side of things," their resistant materiality, can therefore be encountered as a variant of our own flesh and as echoing the body's sensible-sentient dehiscence. It follows that every sensible being incorporates visible (sensible, material) as well as invisible (expressive, latent) dimensions.[16] Furthermore, as Jane Bennett and Jean-Luc Nancy each point out, the materiality of our bodies necessarily encompasses even the quasi-minerality of bone.[17]

Bone outlasts the living body, and, more generally, the geomaterial unfolds in a temporality scarcely conceivable from the perspective of lived time. Commenting on the way that gravestones evoke the "peculiar temporality" of stone, Sallis remarks, "Stone comes from a past that has never been present, a past unassimilable to the order of time in which things come and go in the human world."[18] Levinas also notes the "unrepresentable antiquity" of the elements, their withdrawal into an immemorial past whose insecurity first opens one's relation to the future.[19] For Merleau-Ponty, on the other hand, it is the body's prereflective unity with nature that is best characterized as an "absolute past," a "pre-history," or a "past that has never been present."[20] This absolute past conditions and makes possible lived, personal time, just as the prereflective life of the body conditions but exceeds our reflective capacity to equal it. Insofar as the absolute past is associated with the body's thingly materiality, this past is precisely the immemorial dimension of our own liability to the geomaterial. The deep or geological past is therefore the repressed heart of lived time, an unassimilable past that outstrips any integration with the organic and historical temporality of our lives. The abyssal character of deep time, whether the prehistorical span of the geological or the earth's far future, is our experience of its anachronous interruption of lived temporality from within.[21] Quentin Meillassoux has criticized the incapacity of "correlationist" philosophies such as phenomenology to account for the "ancestral" past that preceded all life on earth.[22] Yet geomaterial phenomenology opens us to deep time's distinctive stratigraphic rhythms—cosmic, geological, evolutionary, prehistoric—and the differential ways that these involve us affectively and corporeally.

As we take stock of our own ineffaceable traces within geological history and orient ourselves toward the earth's unimaginably distant futures, geomaterial phenomenology opens us to the relation between the world and its elemental conditions, the body's essential materiality, and the plexity of deep time at the edges of our experience and of the world as we know it. While constitutive of our bodies and our world, the elements are indestructible and immemorial world travelers, bridging the passage from each age of the earth to the next. Their lesson is that, while all human worlds are precarious, the ultimate sense of existence exceeds human meaning and control.

## Notes

1. See Elizabeth Ellsworth and Jamie Kruse, eds., *Making the Geologic Now: Responses to Material Conditions of Contemporary Life* (Brooklyn, N.Y.: Punctum Books, 2012), 7.

2. The proposal to make the Anthropocene a formal unit of geological epoch divisions in the International Geological Time Scale, under consideration by the

International Commission on Stratigraphy, has received widespread attention and debate among scholars across disciplines. The term was first proposed by Paul Crutzen and Eugene Stoermer in "The 'Anthropocene,'" *Global Change Newsletter* 41 (2000): 17–18, reprinted at IGBP, www.igbp.net/news/opinion/opinion/haveweenteredtheanthropocene.5.d8b4c3c12bf3be638a8000578.html.

3. In addition to Ellsworth and Kruse, *Making the Geologic Now*, see also Jeffrey Cohen, *Stone: An Ecology of the Inhuman* (Minnesota: University of Minnesota Press, 2015); Heather Davis and Etienne Turpin, eds., *Art in the Anthropocene: Encounters among Aesthetics, Politics, Environments and Epistemologies* (London: Open Humanities, 2015).

4. Edmund Husserl, *Ideas II*, trans. Richard Rojcewicz and André Schuwer (Dordrecht: Kluwer Academic, 1989).

5. On the transcendental role of the lifeworld as earth-ground, see Anthony Steinbock, *Home and Beyond: Generative Phenomenology after Husserl* (Evanston, Ill.: Northwestern University Press, 1995), 97–122.

6. See Martin Heidegger, "The Origin of the Work of Art," in *Basic Writings*, ed. David Farrell Krell (San Francisco: HarperCollins, 1993). For a more complete account of the relation between *phusis* and earth in Heidegger's thought, see Bruce Foltz, *Inhabiting the Earth* (Atlantic Highlands, N.J.: Humanities Press, 1995), especially 123–53.

7. See Heidegger, "Building Dwelling Thinking," in Krell, *Basic Writings*, 347–63. See also Andrew Mitchell, *The Fourfold: Reading the Late Heidegger* (Evanston, Ill.: Northwestern University Press, 2015).

8. See Emmanuel Levinas, *Totality and Infinity*, trans. Alphonso Lingis (Pittsburgh, Pa.: Duquesne University Press, 1969), especially 109–74.

9. See Levinas, "Heidegger, Gagarin and Us," in *Difficult Freedom*, trans. Seán Hand (Baltimore, Md.: Johns Hopkins University Press, 1990), 231–34.

10. See John Sallis, *Force of Imagination: The Sense of the Elemental* (Bloomington: Indiana University Press, 2000); "The Elemental Earth," in *Rethinking Nature: Essays in Environmental Philosophy*, ed. Brucy Foltz and Robert Frodeman (Bloomington: Indiana University Press, 2004), 135–46.

11. Ludwig Landgrebe, "The Phenomenology of Corporeality and the Problem of Matter," in *The Phenomenology of Edmund Husserl*, ed. Donn Welton (Ithaca, N.Y.: Cornell University Press, 1981), 33–49; Maurice Merleau-Ponty, "The Philosopher and His Shadow," in *Signs*, trans. Richard McCleary (Evanston, Ill.: Northwestern University Press, 1964), 159–81.

12. Husserl, *Ideas II*, 297.

13. Landgrebe, "The Phenomenology of Corporeality and the Problem of Matter," 25 (emphasis in original).

14. Husserl, *Ideas II*, 153.

15. Merleau-Ponty, "The Philosopher and His Shadow," 166–67.

16. See Merleau-Ponty, *The Visible and the Invisible*, trans. Alphonso Lingis (Evanston, Ill.: Northwestern University Press, 1968), especially 130–55.

17. See Jane Bennett, *Vibrant Matter: A Political Ecology of Things* (Durham, N.C.: Duke University Press, 2010), especially 10–11; Jean-Luc Nancy, *Being Singular Plural*, trans. Robert Richardson and Anne O'Byrne (Stanford, Calif.: Stanford University Press, 2000), 18.

18. John Sallis, *Stone* (Bloomington: Indiana University Press, 1994), 26.

19. Levinas, *Totality and Infinity*, 137ff.

20. Merleau-Ponty, *Phenomenology of Perception*, trans. Don Landes (London: Routledge, 2012), 139, 252, 265, 366.

21. See Ted Toadvine, "The Elemental Past," *Research in Phenomenology* 44, no. 2 (2014): 262–79.

22. Quentin Meillassoux, *After Finitude*, trans. Ray Brassier (New York: Continuum, 2008), 10.

# 22 The Habit Body

Helen A. Fielding

The habit body is at the heart of Maurice Merleau-Ponty's phenomenological approach to embodied perception.[1] Although the body has an object side, or a material existence, for Merleau-Ponty the habit body provides our means of having a world. Habit is not an automatic reflex, but is rather the incorporation of a motor signification or meaning that becomes the body's own.[2] This signification does not first go through the intellect as a representation that is then communicated to the body; instead the moving body engages a motor signification. For example, one is able to type proficiently on a keyboard once one moves beyond cognitively identifying where the letters are. In fact, the body has incorporated the keyboard when the fingers know where the letters are, when this knowledge becomes a questioning that is a motor effort answered by the keyboard, or more broadly by the world one inhabits.[3]

Accordingly, habits are both motor and perceptual because they inhabit the world between "explicit perception and actual movement."[4] Once a habit is formed we do not have to cognitively interpret what we perceive in order to adjust our movements appropriately. Habit is in fact what "relieves us" of this task because our bodies know how to engage in the world without explicit instruction.[5] The keyboard becomes an extension of my body. My fingers don't type letters; they engage with the essence of the visual word that is "endowed with a typical or familiar physiognomy."[6] As Merleau-Ponty describes it, the keyboard opens up a "motor space [that] stretches beneath [his] hands." Each word read is "a modulation of visual space," each movement is a "modulation of manual space."[7] This means that each "visual structure" has a "motor essence, without our having to spell out the word or to spell out the movement in order to translate the word into movement."[8] The corporeal schema structured through habit is the "experience of my body in the world," and perceptual habit is in turn the "acquisition of a world."[9]

Perception and motility are inextricably intertwined. To caress someone's arm, my hand must move along its surface with precisely the right pressure and speed to have a sense of its texture, to connect flesh to flesh. The other's body teaches me how to touch. This knowing is not innate; it is learned and sedimented in the habit body. The gaze perceives to the extent it learns to interrogate the things, and the way in which it does so, "in which it glances over them or rests upon them" determines in what way the thing is perceived and how much.[10] Perception as a questioning of the world is then always already imbued with sense that belongs to the situation.

Derived as it is from the interpenetration of embodied subject and world, the corporeal schema is a "certain structure of the perceived world."[11] We learn to perceive the world, which in turn teaches us how to perceive—there is no world simply laid out before our senses. Habit, then, is the body's understanding of itself in the world. It is the "experience of the accord between what we aim at and what is given, between the intention and the realization."[12] Our bodies sediment ways of understanding that become habits that anchor us in the world. I pick up my water glass because I am thirsty, and my living body engages itself in a world it understands. Because the corporeal schema is behind my actions and structures them, it is never in itself perceptible.

Ways of perceiving are also habits at a cultural and historical level—new ways of perceiving are instituted, and these institutions found new ways of moving and hence understanding, becoming part of the background against which things, people, and relations appear. Analyzing racialization as just such a cultural habit of perception, for example, allows us to understand why its structure recedes into the background, making it appear natural, but nonetheless shapes the ways in which we respond to one another. Linda Martín Alcoff points out that "race works through the domain of the visible," and since we learn how to perceive, "the perceptual practices involved in racializations are then tacit, almost hidden from view, and thus almost immune from critical reflection."[13]

Because we cannot perceive our own corporeal schema that structures how we perceive and that emerges through our interaction with a world, racialization tends to fall into the background. In fact, racialization can become the world, or level, in particular for non-racialized people, against which habitual relations appear. Merleau-Ponty describes how phenomenal bodies lend themselves to this process since they have this extraordinary power to move into levels and take them up. For example, when a light is first turned on at the end of the day, the yellow light might be jarring and appear almost as an object itself. But as one's eyes adjust to the new lighting level and take it up, it recedes into the background, becoming instead that which "directs [the] gaze and leads [one] to see the object." As Merleau-Ponty explains, "lighting is not on the side of the object, it is what we take up, what we adopt as a norm, whereas the illuminated thing stands in front of us and confronts us." In fact, "in one sense [light] *knows* and *sees* the object." Lighting operates as a "norm" and seems "neutral" because we don't perceive light itself; we "perceive according to light."[14] Whiteness similarly tends to function as a neutral level, which becomes apparent if we insert "whiteness" into Merleau-Ponty's text: "We must say that [whiteness], by taking on the function of lighting, tends to situate itself as prior to every color, tends toward the absence of color, and that correlatively objects distribute the colors of the spectrum according to the degree and to the mode of their resistance to this new atmosphere."[15] Whiteness does not in itself appear but nonetheless provides both a background norm and a spotlight that seems to know in advance what it illuminates.[16] What is important here is that "settling" into levels like lighting or whiteness is a "bodily operation" that draws upon a "world whose fundamental structures we carry with ourselves."[17] As Alia Al-Saji points out, the habit of objectifying vision works because in order to see an object, the shadows and light that allow the object to come into relief within a world are overlooked. The object is seen because the habitual, historical, and cultural contexts that allow the object to appear as an object disappear. Similarly, with racializing vision, the objectifying habits of perception recede into the background and their "premises" are forgotten.[18] Breaking open this cultural habitus or level is challenging precisely because it remains in the background.

For those who live in between worlds, and who are never at home in one world, the cultural habitus does not recede from view. We are said to have a habit when our body understands and incorporates a new gesture. But as Mariana Ortega points out, those who live on the margins and "in-between-worlds" are denied such ease of movement.[19] In Heidegger's description of habit, the everyday world is ready to hand. He notices his hammer, which is equipment that belongs to a totality of involvements, only when it breaks down. Things are incorporated into an everyday habitual world that our bodies know and take up unthinkingly. Reflection is demanded only when there is a rupture in that everyday world.[20] Ortega describes how, for those who live on the margins, there is a greater possibility for the critical reflection that belongs to the phenomenological method since there is no one apparently fixed background level against which all things, people, and relations appear. Instead, those who live in-between-worlds experience a level as constantly shifting, so it remains in the foreground like a newly turned-on light.

This was the case for Frantz Fanon, who could not escape the contingency, which Merleau-Ponty describes as the "living experience of vertigo and nausea" that fills him with "horror."[21] Fanon's experience of being racialized by the French before, during, and after the Second World War institutes a shift in his experience of his corporeal schema from the seat of his "I can" to that of an "I cannot."[22] The possibilities of what he can do within a given situation, the ways he can expand into and take up space are collapsed into an objectifying "racial epidermal schema," whereby his actions are circumscribed by the reductive myths that are projected onto the surface of his skin.[23] Iris Marion Young similarly observes in her pivotal essay that girls' bodies become split between being a subject as the seat of their capacities and becoming an object to be looked at. This split inhibits and interrupts what girls are able to do.[24] In his discussion of the phantom limb, Merleau-Ponty describes how the habitual body guarantees the actual one. As the seat of my possibilities, the world opens up as an extension of my body. In the case of amputation, he reflects, "How can I perceive objects as manipulable when I can no longer manipulate them?"[25] They become manipulable in a general sense but not for the person missing the limb. A world can disable certain bodies that are not accommodated in their alternative ways of inhabiting it. A lecture hall entered by stairs appears as a place of learning only in a general sense to a student who moves by wheelchair, but not in a concrete one.[26] Similarly, when objectified bodies cannot extend into space, when the world is not manipulable for them, their habitual bodies guarantee a body that is experienced as less capable, as the "I cannot."

As Helen Ngo explains, the "I can" of the habitual body is our hold upon the world that allows us to take up, inhabit, and engage with it. It is, in Merleau-Ponty's words, a chiasmic and "simultaneous experience of the holding and the held in all orders."[27] Ngo reminds us that "the Latin root for habit, *habēre*, can also mean 'to hold,'" and the German word *halten* is the root of *Haltung* or "posture."[28] I would add to this list the French word for "behavior," *comportement*, which also has the root of *porter*, or "to carry oneself in relation to the world." As Ngo describes, "holding is not only active, it also enables and prepares us for action and movement. Habitual movements and orientations, insofar as they continue to participate in the body schema, are held in the body in a continuous and ongoing way."[29] The racializing habits of white bodies are not thus simply repeated actions; they are more substantially an attitude and a way of expanding into space and engaging with others and the world.

Nonetheless, the ways in which we hold ourselves and orient ourselves in relation to others can shift, providing, as Ngo argues, a possibility for change. Because the body is not an automaton, it is also capable of learning new significations and shifting the ones that exist. As Merleau-Ponty describes it, "occasionally a new knot of significations is formed."[30] For example, "learning to see colors is the acquisition of a certain style of vision, a new use of one's own body; it is to enrich and to reorganize the body schema." The body as a habit body is "a system of motor powers or perceptual powers." It is not an "I think" but is rather a "totality of lived significations that moves towards its equilibrium." Previously sedimented movements are "integrated" into a new way of moving, ways of perceiving are "integrated into a new sensorial entity." Our given corporeal capacities are taken up in "a richer signification that was, up until that point, merely implied in our perceptual or practical field." Our equilibrium can thus be "reorganized" since shifting one aspect of the structure shifts the whole.[31]

While the habit body can be oppressive, it can also provide the "potential for good living," which, as Elena Cuffari points out, can be achieved through the "cultivation of certain kinds of habits."[32] The word *habit* also has roots in the ancient Greek word *hexis*, which we know from Aristotle refers to actions and emotional reactions cultivated over time.[33] For the elderly in particular, habits reveal the two possibilities Beauvoir discusses in her treatise on aging: either habits become entrenched and rigid, or they allow for the spontaneity in the present moment she refers to as a "kind of poetry."[34] She draws on this distinction from her engagement with Henri Bergson, for whom habit as action learned by the body is connected to usefulness, which is distinct from memory-images that belong to thought and imagination.[35] For Beauvoir this means that habits in the elderly can become rigid, as with the old man who is grumpy when the table he sits at each day has been taken, or they can open up creative possibilities for disclosing existence, as in her example of taking afternoon tea with friends that allows for living the moment more intensely and with joy.[36] Attention and disclosure allow one to remain engaged with the world, continuing to embrace the "passion" that inheres in the "human condition."[37] Key for Beauvoir is that we are allowed to choose our habits freely, and cultivate them further, which is not possible if the elderly experience anxiety over their daily existence.

Exile, like aging, can lead to a loss of identity tied to embodied habit. If habit is a kind of holding and being held, then the loss of habits can become a losing of one's grip, as the world in turn gives up its hold. Gilles Deleuze, following Bergson, is critical of the habit body given to us by others.[38] With Félix Guattari he calls for relinquishing the stratified, organized, and sedimented body in order to achieve the Body without Organs.[39] But, as we have seen, the organized body given to us by others is not necessarily oppressive. Incorporating certain shared and living structures necessary for existence allows for the ongoing enactment of identity. Reflecting upon his family and friends fleeing Syria over the six years of civil war, the novelist Khaled Khalifa, who chose to stay, observes how they "lose their identity": "Abandoning a small set of habits that constitute personal contentment would be intolerable to me. I'm thinking of my morning coffee at home, or coffee with my friends before going to work, chatting, of the city's smells, dinners, the smell of rain in autumn."[40] Habits open up the worlds to which they belong, and which structure our identities over time. To give up these habits for those in exile is, as for the aged, akin to giving up a part of the self. In short, since the habit body is our means of having a world, it provides a nexus for critical ethical concerns. The habit body structures the ways we live, engage with the world and with others. Phenomenology allows us to bring the habit body into view so that we can shift some habits, preserve others, and cultivate new ways of engaging the world.

## Notes

1. Dermot Moran maintains Merleau-Ponty drew many of his ideas on habit from Husserl. Moran provides an important elaboration of Husserl on habit, a theme I do not address here. See Moran, "Edmund Husserl's Phenomenology of Habituality and Habitus," *Journal of the British Society for Phenomenology* 42, no. 1 (2011): 53–77.

2. Maurice Merleau-Ponty, *Phenomenology of Perception*, trans. Donald A. Landes (New York: Routledge, 2012), 144.

3. Merleau-Ponty, *Phenomenology of Perception*, 145.

4. Merleau-Ponty, *Phenomenology of Perception*, 153.

5. Merleau-Ponty, *Phenomenology of Perception*, 154.

6. Merleau-Ponty, *Phenomenology of Perception*, 145.

7. Merleau-Ponty, *Phenomenology of Perception*, 145.

8. Merleau-Ponty, *Phenomenology of Perception*, 145.

9. Merleau-Ponty, *Phenomenology of Perception*, 142, 154.

10. Merleau-Ponty, *Phenomenology of Perception*, 154.

11. Maurice Merleau-Ponty, *Le monde sensible et le monde de l'expression: Cours au Collège de France Notes, 1953*, ed. Emmanuel de Saint Aubert and Stefan Kristensen (Geneva: Mëtis Presses, 2011), 144, my translation.

12. Merleau-Ponty, *Phenomenology of Perception*, 146.

13. Linda Martín Alcoff, "The Phenomenology of Racial Embodiment," in *Visible Identities: Race, Gender and the Self* (Oxford: Oxford University Press, 2006), 187–88.

14. Merleau-Ponty, *Phenomenology of Perception*, 323–24.

15. Merleau-Ponty, *Phenomenology of Perception*, 324.

16. For further discussion, see Helen Fielding, "White Logic and the Constancy of Color," in *Feminist Interpretations of Maurice Merleau-Ponty*, ed. Dorothea Olkowski and Gail Weiss (University Park: Pennsylvania State University Press), 73–89.

17. Fielding, "White Logic and the Constancy of Color," 325, 341.

18. Alia Al-Saji, "A Phenomenology of Critical-Ethical Vision: Merleau-Ponty, Bergson and the Question of Seeing Differently," *Chiasmi International* 11 (2009): 379.

19. Mariana Ortega, *In-Between: Latina Feminist Phenomenology, Multiplicity, and the Self* (Albany, N.Y.: SUNY Press), 60.

20. Martin Heidegger, *Being and Time*, trans. John Macquarrie and Edward Robinson (Oxford: Blackwell, 1962), 102–7.

21. Merleau-Ponty, *Phenomenology of Perception*, 265.

22. Frantz Fanon, *Black Skin, White Masks*, trans. C. L. Markmann (New York: Grove Press, 1967). Al-Saji too addresses this phenomenon in "Phenomenology of Critical-Ethical Vision."

23. Fanon, *Black Skin, White Masks*, 112.

24. Iris Marion Young, "Throwing Like a Girl," *Human Studies* 3, no. 2 (1980): 137–56.

25. Merleau-Ponty, *Phenomenology of Perception*, 84.

26. See, for example, Tanya Titchkosky, *Disability, Self and Society* (Toronto: University of Toronto Press, 2003), and Rosemarie Garland-Thomson, "Misfits: A Feminist Materialist Disability Concept," *Hypatia* 26, no. 3 (2011): 591–609.

27. Maurice Merleau-Ponty, *The Visible and the Invisible*, trans. Alphonso Lingis (Evanston, Ill.: Northwestern University Press, 1968), 266.

28. Helen Ngo, "Racist Habits: A Phenomenological Analysis of Racism and the Habitual Body," *Philosophy and Social Criticism* 42, no. 9 (2016): 863–64.

29. Ngo, "Racist Habits," 864.

30. Merleau-Ponty, *Phenomenology of Perception*, 155.

31. Merleau-Ponty, *Phenomenology of Perception*, 154–55.

32. Elena Cuffari, "Habits of Transformation," *Hypatia* 26, no. 3 (2011): 535.

33. Bonnie Bent, "Habits and Virtues," in *Aquinas's Summa Theologiae: Critical Essays*, ed. Brian Davies (Lanham, Md.: Rowman & Littlefield, 2005), 224.

34. Simone de Beauvoir, *The Coming of Age*, trans. Patrick O'Brian (New York: Norton, 1996), 468.

35. Henri Bergson, *Matter and Memory*, trans. N. M. Paul and W. S. Palmer (New York: Zone Books, 1991), 80–88.

36. For further discussion see my article "The Poetry of Habit: Beauvoir and Merleau-Ponty on Aging Embodiment," in *Simone de Beauvoir's Philosophy of Age*, ed. Silvia Stoller (Berlin: de Gruyter, 2014), 69–81.

37. Beauvoir, *The Coming of Age*, 42.

38. See Gilles Deleuze, *The Logic of Sense*, trans. Mark Lester with Charles Stivale, ed. Constantin V. Boundas (New York: Columbia University Press, 1990), 319–20.

39. Gilles Deleuze and Félix Guattari, *A Thousand Plateaus*, trans. Brian Massumi (Minneapolis: University of Minnesota Press, 1987), 159–62.

40. Khaled Khalifa, "Living in a Void: Life in Damascus after the Exodus," *Guardian*, August 22, 2017, https://www.theguardian.com/world/2017/aug/22/living-in-a-void-life-in-damascus-after-the-exodus.

# 23 Heteronormativity

Megan Burke

Heteronormativity is a central concept in feminist philosophy and queer theory that names and describes heterosexuality as a compulsory system of power enforced through masculinist and naturalized binary gender norms and sexual aesthetics. More specifically, heteronormativity is used to name a constitutive structure of subjectivity with particular historical conditions that materializes through a constellation of social and interpersonal relations and practices. Such relations and practices include the naturalization of heterosexual desire, the compulsory social character of heterosexuality, the subordination of women through masculinist heterosexuality, the co-constitution of the binary gender categories "man" and "woman" and heterosexuality, the designation and valorization of certain sex acts and forms of pleasure as normal and desirable, and the sexualized stigmatization and violence committed against people of color and individuals who do not conform to dominant norms of gender and/or sexuality. Although first popularized through the notions of "obligatory heterosexuality," "compulsory heterosexuality," and "the heterosexual matrix" in the context of feminist thought, phenomenological description of heteronormativity precedes the term. In fact, a phenomenological reading of Simone de Beauvoir's *The Second Sex* offers a robust descriptive account of the relation between heteronormativity, gender subjectivity, and women's experience and subordination.[1] Indeed, as will be detailed in what follows, Beauvoir's work can be considered the catalyst for many contemporary phenomenological considerations of heteronormativity. But however important Beauvoir may be to the phenomenological treatment of heteronormativity, there are two main ways to trace the term and the reality it names in the context of phenomenology. First, heteronormativity can be understood as an ideology that structures the classical phenomenological tradition, and second, it names an experience that is intelligible through phenomenological description. Although it is possible to trace heteronormativity within phenomenology, it is important to keep in mind that investigations and considerations of heteronormativity have been and remain marginal.

## As a Normative Structure

Despite positive engagements with phenomenology, feminist and queer thinkers have long argued that heterosexuality and a masculinist economy of heterosexualized power are tacit and problematic assumptions in key phenomenological texts. More specifically, the base premise of these criticisms is that canonical texts and thinkers often presuppose heterosexuality and heterosexualized notions of gender rather than directly confront or challenge deep-rooted ideas and expectations about gendered sexuality and sexualized genders. The presumption of a heteromasculinist subject, that is, a subject who commits to the sexual domination of women, and views of the female body as the passive receptacle for and object of male eroticism are key manifestations of these assumptions regarding heterosexuality and gender. Ultimately, feminist and queer criticisms, although not uniform, share the perspective that a normative sexual ideology structures the tradition. Many of these criticisms emphasize phenomenology's reliance on the natural attitude, particularly with regard to a heterosexist ideology of gender and sexuality, and articulate the existential and political implications of the perpetuation of such ideology. Insofar as the literature in this area is abundant, this entry will focus on foundational and novel contemporary criticisms.

Judith Butler's account of the constitutive relationship between gendered subjectivity and compulsory heterosexuality in *Gender Trouble* is arguably the most formative critique of heterosexuality as a normative sexual ideology.[2] For Butler, a socially enforced, obligatory heterosexuality is a key regulatory system and disciplinary mechanism that produces a normative schema of binary gender, namely the production of the "complementary" "masculine man" and "feminine woman" dyad. As will be discussed further in the following section, the social repetition of these fabricated heterogender categories through compulsory heterosexuality renders such binary genders as "real" and, in turn, excludes and subjects those who exceed or transgress this normative schema of gender to physical and existential punishment. With regard to the normative critique in particular, however, Butler argues that the assumption of heterosexuality in accounts of subjectivity and gender is central to the construction and reification of compulsory heterosexuality as a paradigm of social life and philosophical thought. For Butler, views of heterosexuality as natural and thus normal constitute a normative logic that precludes recognition of and eliminates queer existence and possibility. Consequently, as Butler sees it, heterosexuality operates as a normative condition and constraint that, when left unquestioned, operates as a violent and exclusionary epistemological and ontological foundation.

Although not always motivated by *Gender Trouble*, work that criticizes the tradition in particular uncovers heterosexuality as a tacit norm in phenomenology. Perhaps because, aside from Beauvoir, Maurice Merleau-Ponty offers the most explicit phenomenological theory of sexuality, negative readings of his work are central to exposing how heteronormativity structures phenomenological inquiry. For instance, Luce Irigaray and Butler, among others, argue that Merleau-Ponty's work is an expression of heterosexual ideology.[3] In particular, Irigaray suggests Merleau-Ponty's work is founded upon a sexual logic structured by the masculine gesture of the sexual appropriation of women. Butler argues that his work is founded upon an unspoken commitment to a masculine subject whose "normal" erotic experience is demarcated by an objectification of the female body. Taken together, Irigaray and Butler suggest that Merleau-Ponty conceives of subjectivity and sexuality through a relation of heterosexualized gender subordination.

This critique of Merleau-Ponty shares much in common with the critiques of Martin Heidegger advanced by thinkers like Irigaray and Tina Chanter. Irigaray argues that Heidegger's conception of home and his claim that subjectivity is affirmed through the project of building a dwelling place is anchored in a patriarchal gender system wherein the feminine and woman are the materials used to build a home. This material and thus existential use of woman is an expression of sexualized domination rather than just patriarchal oppression because woman is positioned as the container for male desire. In her reading of Heidegger's ontology, Chanter is not explicitly concerned with its heteronormative dimensions, but suggests that the alleged neutrality of Dasein presumes a heteromasculinist subject who can extract himself from the concrete world.[4]

Contemporary developments in feminist and queer criticism tend to suggest that some ways of doing phenomenology are heteronormative. In her groundbreaking text, *Queer Phenomenology*, Sara Ahmed argues that phenomenology is often founded upon a "straight" or heteronormative orientation toward the world.[5] She suggests that Husserl's phenomenological practice is made possible by setting aside or bracketing the gendered and sexualized sphere of domesticity. Ahmed reads Husserl's famous epoché as a straightening device, an orientation to thinking that relies on tending to "straight" objects or those objects that appear through sedimented histories of gendered heterosexuality. The effect of such a straight phenomenology is, for Ahmed, that queer objects disappear. The work of Iris Marion Young and Bonnie Mann offers a different way to consider phenomenology as a heteronormative practice by centering their analyses on the perspectives and experiences of girls and women.[6] Mann's work, for instance, shows that phenomenological examples and concerns, like Sartre's famous example of bad faith or contemporary accounts of shame, situate women in ways that are deeply heterosexist, but also neutered of their heterosexism. On this reading, phenomenology becomes a practice that regularly fails to account for its own heteronormativity and thus obfuscates the phenomena it sets out to describe or offers conceptual frameworks that operate as apparatuses of an oppressive sexualized gender system.

Ultimately, from feminist and queer perspectives, heteronormative ontological, epistemological, and ethical commitments realize and sustain legacies of heterosexist domination. Insofar as such commitments are said to underlie phenomenological projects, the criticisms elucidate a prescriptive project at the heart of the phenomenological canon. Interestingly, however, some scholars have argued that certain feminist phenomenological projects reify heteronormativity, even as they seek to undermine it. For example, Irigaray has been criticized for reducing difference to heterosexuality, for privileging heterosexuality as the primary ethical relation, and for maintaining heterosexuality as an ahistorical logic of sexual difference. It has also been argued that Beauvoir fails to challenge heterosexuality as an oppressive social institution in her account of women's experience. Although there is significant resistance to these readings of Irigaray and Beauvoir and to the aforementioned criticisms of canonical thinkers, the charge of heteronormativity is an invitation to take seriously how normative heterosexuality is structured by a hierarchical and binary gender system that grounds phenomenological inquiry.

## The Descriptive Task

Beauvoir is a key, but marginalized, thinker in the phenomenological tradition who attends to heteronormativity as a lived experience and as a structure of possibility and legibility. Arguably, it is the attention she pays to structures of experience presupposed in canonical texts, like heteronormativity, that marginalizes her work within phenomenology more generally. In *The Second Sex*, the first phenomenological investigation of sexed embodiment, Beauvoir offers a compelling account of the relation between women's oppression and compulsory heterosexuality that is not only novel in its own right but is also the basis for many of the contemporary descriptions of heteronormativity. Consequently, in what follows, attention will first be drawn to Beauvoir and her legacy and then to developments that exceed her work.

As a feminist phenomenologist, Beauvoir sets out to examine women's experience and, in particular, the conditions that produce their subordination. Throughout *The Second Sex* she explores the ways one becomes a woman by making herself a passive and relative existence—a feminine existence—a becoming that is constituted primarily in and through real or imaginary sexualized relations with men. Beauvoir discloses how heterosexist aesthetics, social relations, epistemologies, and alienating experiences of heterosexual eroticism are formative to the process of becoming a woman in a patriarchal society. Although Beauvoir herself does not name the social enforcement of heterosexuality as a normative condition for becoming a woman in a patriarchal society, her phenomenological description shows a constitutive and binding relation between the realization of oneself as a woman, as a passive body-subject in the world, and hetero-eroticism. Consequently, it makes sense to read Beauvoir's phenomenology of feminine existence as a description of the operation of a heteronorm of intelligibility.

Feminist scholars working in phenomenology turn to Beauvoir's project to elucidate the heterosexualized structures of feminine existence. Young's groundbreaking essay "Throwing Like a Girl" is perhaps the best and originating example of this turn to Beauvoir. In her essay, Young accounts for the way feminine bodily existence as inhibited, timid, and anchored in immanence is a lived effect of sexual objectification produced in a patriarchal society. Young thus shows that female body comportment is structured by heteromasculinist eroticism. Building on Beauvoir and Young, Sandra Lee Bartky's phenomenology of domination discloses how women's psychic and corporeal experiences are regulated by heterosexist structures and practices that impoverish women's agency and emotional and physical well-being.[7] Other feminist phenomenologists, like Ann Cahill[8] and Mann, extend this work by considering how rape and sexual harassment against women by men are normative threats in a culture where sexual violence against women is prevalent. More recent scholarship considers how Beauvoir offers an explicit account of the way heterosexual domination is central to women's sexual subjectification.[9]

Instead of a focus on structures of existence and constitutive experiences of feminine existence, the second strand of literature with Beauvoirian roots underscores her notion of becoming in order to account for the heteronormative construction of "woman" as a social category of intelligibility. Monique Wittig's well-known claim "Lesbians are not women" is central to this body of literature.[10] Wittig reads Beauvoir's claim that one is not born a woman through a materialist feminist lens in order to claim becoming a woman necessarily means that one becomes heterosexual. Central to Wittig's position is that "woman" is a heterosexual category such that "woman" is the sexual property of "man." More specifically, Wittig suggests that "women" is a class category produced through an oppressive and naturalized economic system of heterosexual reproduction wherein "men" are the ruling class who exploit "women." For Wittig, there is thus a constitutive relation between "woman" and heterosexuality, leading her to suggest that lesbianism is a flight from the subject position of "woman."

Butler's work in *Gender Trouble* is also anchored in Beauvoir's notion of becoming. However, Butler's project is, like Wittig's, to account for the sexualized construction of the category "woman." While Beauvoir shows how heterosexual marriage is central to becoming a woman in the patriarchal sense, it is Butler who explicitly accounts for the way the enforcement of heterosexuality produces "woman" as a legible subject position. In doing so, Butler advances an account of gender intelligibility as it is constituted through a socially produced and regulatory schema of heterosexuality, or what she names the heterosexual matrix. From Butler's view, "feminine woman" and "masculine man," although taken to be natural and real, are actually performative effects of the repetition of heterosexual norms that govern social life. The repetition of these normative genders, requisite for survival and social recognition, sediments heterosexuality into the life of the gendered subject. Butler develops the relation between the heterosexual matrix and gender intelligibility in her later work, *Bodies That Matter*, to further account for how the matrix works through systematic ontological and physical violence against persons who do not conform to normative schemas of gender or sexuality.[11] Although Butler maintains an ambiguous relationship to phenomenology throughout her work on gender, her account of the way normative genders are constituted through normative heterosexuality is undoubtedly influential to phenomenological accounts of heteronormativity.

Drawing on key Butlerian insights about gender and sexual normativity, Ahmed offers the most explicit phenomenology of heteronormativity. Ahmed's queer phenomenology merges queer theory with phenomenology, including but not limited to Beauvoir's work. In this queering of phenomenology, Ahmed gives an account of the way subjective existence gets straightened out (i.e., becomes heteronormative) or becomes queer. In a departure from Beauvoir's influence, however, Ahmed's work brings a critical discussion of the relationship between processes of colonial racialization and heteronormativity into contemporary discussions. For Ahmed, assuming an existence that is normatively oriented—a straight existence—requires a racialized orientation of whiteness that creates and sustains white supremacist habits of desire and belonging.

Importantly, Ahmed stages her investigation of racialized heteronormativity through Frantz Fanon's phenomenology of colonial racism in *Black Skin, White Masks*. Ahmed's critical appropriation of Fanon, whose own phenomenological work is structured by normative heterosexuality, misogyny, and homophobia, shows how racial identity, belonging, and hierarchies are realized through heterosexual processes and aesthetics. The confluence of whiteness and normative heterosexuality thus underscores the way colonial power works through sexualized existence and sexual orientation.

Given that Beauvoir fails to discuss the way racial, ethnic, and geopolitical differences shape women's experience, Ahmed's work opens up an important development in feminist and queer accounts of heteronormativity. Whereas women of color feminist scholars have long insisted on the necessity of intersectional thinking, Ahmed's phenomenological account draws attention to the way subjectivity and experience are co-constituted by normative racial and sexual horizons and modes of perception. Work that further investigates and complicates the relation between and the normative constitution and experience of gender, sexuality, and race could prove to be important for the descriptive task of a phenomenology of heteronormativity.

## Future Directions

Insofar as there have long been thinkers, especially in marginalized traditions like feminist philosophy and critical race theory, who neither take up phenomenology nor consider themselves phenomenologists, but nonetheless account for the way histories and realities of oppression are shaped by, structure, and disclose heteronormativity, it is important to consider not only how but also why phenomenologists might want to take seriously work outside of the tradition. For instance, women of color feminists have long examined the lived experience of the relation between normative sexuality, heterosexism, white supremacy, and colonial ways of being. Additionally, Talia Mae Bettcher's account of transphobia in "Evil Deceivers and Make Believers" shows how a violent heterosexual framework produces transphobic violence.[12] Queer crip theorists and scholars in feminist disability studies also offer critical accounts of how normative heterosexuality and heterogenders are realized through and structured by ableist ideologies. These discussions of the constitution of heteronormativity through and as the means of creating and maintaining social hierarchies and legacies open up new possibilities for phenomenological considerations of heteronormativity. At the same time, because of the marginal treatment of heteronormativity in phenomenology, there remains a need for phenomenological inquiries to take seriously the operation of heteronormativity as a structure of thinking and existence and for phenomenological accounts of heteronormativity to critically take up the phenomenological tradition.

## Notes

1. Simone de Beauvoir, *The Second Sex*, trans. Constance Borde and Sheila Malovany-Chevallier (1949; New York: Knopf, 2010).

2. Judith Butler, *Gender Trouble: Feminism and the Subversion of Identity* (New York: Routledge, 1990).

3. Luce Irigaray, *An Ethics of Sexual Difference*, trans. Carolyn Burke and Gillian C. Gill (1984; Ithaca, N.Y.: Cornell University Press, 1993); Judith Butler, "Sexual Ideology and Phenomenological Description: A Feminist Critique of Merleau-Ponty's *Phenomenology of Perception*," in *The Thinking Muse: Feminism and Modern French Philosophy*, ed. Jeffner Allen and Iris Marion Young (Bloomington: Indiana University Press, 1989).

4. Tina Chanter, "The Problematic Normative Assumptions of Heidegger's Ontology," in *Feminist Interpretations of Heidegger*, ed. Nancy J. Holland and Patricia Huntington (University Park: Pennsylvania State University Press, 2001), 73–108 .

5. Sara Ahmed, *Queer Phenomenology: Orientations, Objects, Others* (Durham, N.C.: Duke University Press, 2006).

6. Iris Marion Young, *On Female Body Experience: "Throwing Like a Girl" and Other Essays* (Oxford: Oxford University Press, 2005); Bonnie Mann, "Creepers, Flirts, Heroes and Allies: Four Theses on Men and Sexual Harassment," *APA Newsletter on Feminism and Philosophy* 11, no. 2 (Spring 2012): 24–31.

7. Sandra Lee Bartky, *Femininity and Domination: Studies in the Phenomenology of Oppression* (New York: Routledge, 1990).

8. Ann Cahill, *Rethinking Rape* (Ithaca, N.Y.: Cornell University Press, 2001).

9. Jennifer McWeeny, "The Second Sex of Consciousness: A New Temporality and Ontology for Beauvoir's 'Becoming a Woman,'" in *On ne naît pas femme: On le devient: The Life of a Sentence*, ed. Bonnie Mann and Martina Ferrari (Oxford: Oxford University Press, 2017), 231–74.

10. Monique Wittig, *The Straight Mind and Other Essays* (Boston: Beacon Press, 1992), 32.

11. Judith Butler, *Bodies That Matter: On the Discursive Limits of "Sex"* (New York: Routledge, 1993).

12. Talia Mae Bettcher, "Evil Deceivers and Make Believers: On Transphobic Violence and the Politics of Illusion," *Hypatia* 22, no. 3 (Summer 2007): 43–65.

# 24 Hometactics

Mariana Ortega

The notion of home is both deeply familiar and remarkably foreign: familiar because it can be summoned by a smell, an old photograph, a worn-out couch, a simple memory of rooms that we considered safe; foreign because so many have not had the pleasure of a stable space of nurturing and love that "home" is supposed to provide. Already we get a sense that "home" is not always what it is supposed to be, that it is a trope, a myth, but one that is especially powerful as it pulls us both forcefully and tenderly to dream of it, to long for it, even when we know better. "Tactics," on the other hand are commonly referred to in the context of battles and wars. They are typically understood as attempts at winning or situating ourselves in a position that will be to our advantage, but they can also be understood in a less agonistic way. Michel de Certeau understands them as the "art of the weak," or ingenious, improvised resistant practices performed by those who do not have power.[1] Here "home" and "tactics" come together. Through the notion of *hometactics* I illustrate an important aspect of our lived experience, namely the fact that in the absence of a home of the type that appears in movies, books, and myths—one that is nurturing and in which we find ourselves at ease—we engage in practices that allow us to feel comfortable and to get a sense of belonging in various spaces, including ones that are not welcoming or that highlight membership in communities with whom we don't share identity markers. Ultimately hometactics are practices of home-making that do not reify the mythology of home as a nurturing, familiar space—the space where I can be me in any way I want—but that allow us to attain a sense of comfort, even a sort of familiarity and belonging in spaces that are not welcoming, safe, or familiar or that are in worlds that "undo" us.

I am acknowledging and writing from a tension between knowing that the notion of home has a mythic stature that is deceitful but also feeling the need to have a home or, rather, to have the sense of warmth, coziness, familiarity, enjoyment, and belonging that the mythic home is alleged to have. When considering the notion of hometactics we need to begin with the recognition of this tension so as to not be taken away in the flights of fancy regarding spaces of pure and authentic belonging. For me, then, to think about home is to think about a belonging that is tenuous, complex, and *forged* by our practices rather than simply given. To connect this kind of belonging to tactics is to describe an *embodied* praxis rather than a theoretical exercise. It is a praxis that we are already engaged in as we navigate our various ways of being in the various worlds that we inhabit. This praxis discloses a layer of lived experience that is already at work, irrespective of whether or not it is made explicit by phenomenological accounts. Hometactics are thus *micro*techniques of lived experience—everyday ways in which we attempt to forge a sense of ease, familiarity, and belonging in our everyday spaces. The aim, then, is not to offer a politics of location or a politics of relation, as can be found in the literature,[2] but to provide a phenomenological description of the ways in which, like the so-called weak that de Certeau describes, we "make do"—or rather, "make" home(s).[3]

Importantly, the home-making associated with hometactics has been discussed differently in the context of phenomenology as this tradition has provided a description of being at ease in the world as well as of the *unheimlich* (not-being at home, not-dwelling, uncanniness, strangeness, alienation), both of which fail to provide a more comprehensive and complex account of selfhood. We can read the Heideggerian account as providing a sense of home-ness insofar as human beings are being-in-the-world by way of a familiarity and ease in everyday life through participation in a practical orientation with equipment, or what Heidegger calls the "ready-to-hand."[4] Moreover, in the Heideggerian account, the everyday self or the self under the mode of "the They" acquires familiarity with the world by blindly following norms and practices. Nevertheless, this familiarity acquired by way of a practical orientation through equipment or by blind following of norms and practices ruptures as equipment breaks down and anxiety prompts the self to question prescribed norms and practices, thus leading to existential crises and a sense of not belonging in the world or not-being-at-home.[5]

Yet these ruptures of norms and practices, as well as ruptures of existence that Heidegger's account describes, do not tell the entire story. We need to move beyond traditional phenomenological accounts given that they make presuppositions about subjectivity and selfhood as well as about the manner in which the self is in the world. For example, this influential Heideggerian account of being-in-the-world describes the everydayness of *Dasein* as connected to a practical orientation in the world via equipment that allows for ease and comfort in daily existence. This normative ease is taken for granted until there is a breakdown in equipment or an existential crisis that reveals the uncanniness of existence. A more complex notion of selfhood needs to be articulated in order to reveal the complexity of the notion of belonging as well. It is thus necessary to analyze hometactics as practices of home-making in light of the experience of what I refer to as multiplicitous selfhood.

To be a multiplicitous self means to be a self that occupies multiple positionalities in terms of social identities, be it race, class, sex, gender, ability, nationality, etc., and thus lives in various worlds; it is being-in-worlds as well as being-between-worlds.[6] The self is thus constantly negotiating different aspects of her identity that in many cases lead to difficulties and contradictions. For multiplicitous selves that are marginalized and/or bi/multicultural, the lived experience of being-in-and-between worlds is one in which there are constant ruptures of precisely the everyday practical orientation in the world that phenomenologists such as Heidegger, Sartre, and Merleau-Ponty see as the mark of being-in-the-world. The end result is this self's constant awareness of not-being-at-home, not-dwelling, a marked sense of not feeling at ease or having a sense of familiarity in many of the worlds she inhabits (both thin and thick senses of not-being-at-ease.[7] Gloria Anzaldúa captures it best in her key work, *Borderlands/La Frontera* in which she paints a powerful portrait of what it means to live as a multiplicitous self that doesn't quite fit in any of the worlds that are connected to her various social identities.[8] She vividly describes the anguish, fear, and anxiety of the multiplicitous self's body that walks the paths of various crisscrossing worlds. She thus doesn't experience being-in-the-world as classical phenomenologists describe it.

Taking into consideration the lived experience of the multiplicitous self in general, and the marginalized or multicultural multiplicitous self in particular, discloses a sense of not-being-at ease in both thin and thick senses. Yet here a door also opens. While multiplicitous selves whose social locations are not dominant experience a deep sense of not being at home, there are moments in which they attempt to find familiarity and ease, but not the ease that comes from mindlessly following everyday norms and practices. There is also the comfort that arises from practices that multiplicitous selves engage in so as to navigate spaces in which they do not fit or belong—hence the need for hometactics.

Hometactics are to be understood as *micropractices* of lived experience, as they have to do with everyday practices rather than with actions associated with larger structures. They are "tactics" in the sense provided by de Certeau when he distinguishes between strategies and practices and defines strategies as connected to larger, normative, limiting dominant structures, and tactics as associated with creativity, inventiveness, and diverting spaces. Tactics are, according to de Certeau, practices by those who lack power and have to "make do"—hence tactics are the "art of the weak." De Certeau provides examples of tactics in the figure of the immigrant who "makes do" in her new city by being creative, the cook who improvises recipes, the streetwalker that makes the city hers precisely by walking it. Yet the so-called weak in de Certeau's discussion end up demonstrating a strength, creativity, and adaptability that the strategist may not achieve. In the midst of being-in-worlds and being-between-worlds that are not only contradictory but may also be unwelcoming and even hostile, multiplicitous selves engage (are already engaging) in practices that yield a sense of much needed familiarity and ease.

While de Certeau understands tactics in terms of the manner in which they engage and disrupt the temporal, I understand them as engaging both the temporal and the spatial. That is, they enhance the possibility of the multiplicitous self being-at-ease, feeling comfort, and even a sense of belonging in particular spaces (or groups). This sense of belonging, of course, should not be understood as normatively belonging (feeling completely at ease with norms and practices as well as intelligibility), what we may call authentic belonging (feeling that one fully belongs due to one's identity, a type of a politics of location in which the belonging is a given rather than forged through practices) or a "pure" belonging (a sense of uncontroversial belonging not only normatively and authentically but also without the possibility of rupture).

The belonging associated with hometactics is one that "makes do" and is creatively constructed in our everyday dealings in worlds. It is forged through opportunities that the multiplicitous self discovers or improvises in order to find ease and make life more livable. Examples vary and are connected to individual needs and desires of the particular selves (or groups) engaging in them as well as worlds inhabited (hence the unmappable character of these practices, as de Certeau acknowledges). Examples of hometactics include modification of spaces to remind us of particular environments that are familiar or welcoming to us, such as having particular plants in the home, painting walls in colors that are associated with one's past, and arranging furniture in ways that will make it easier for one to interact with others. There are other, more elaborate hometactics that "open" spaces for us so that we can feel comfortable in them and can better engage with others who might also be occupying those spaces, for example, writing a philosophy text that includes issues that matter to the person rather than reproducing the expected intellectual, philosophical discussion (my own hometactic to survive in the world of philosophy), speaking a language that makes one feel more "at home" (a linguistic hometactic), preparing foods that provide a sense of comfort, and forging relationships with people such that they become like "family" when one's family members are far away. Importantly, hometactics also include using creative outlets to make life more manageable when expectations of productivity do not allow for leisure time—in these moments even reading one short poem as one starts a long day of work becomes a hometactic. These "everyday practices" have the possibility to become hometactics when they literally help us make home(s), home-making understood in the sense of creating an environment that allows for a sense of ease, comfort, and even belonging. These may perhaps be practices that multiplicitous selves that have dominant identities might engage on a daily basis as well, but the meaning of these practices as "home-making" might not register or be an issue at all for them, since these selves might find themselves feeling at home, at ease, or feeling a sense of comfort and familiarity as a matter of fact (a privilege of always feeling as if one has a home). That is precisely what the multiplicitous self at the margins due to her culture, sexuality, or other social location cannot enjoy. Their everydayness is one of ruptures and a life of not being-at-ease. There is no specific aspect of hometactics that makes them practices of home-making due to the various ways in which multiplicitous selves might find comfort and a sense of belonging. Hometactics are thus decentered and unmappable in this sense. That is, there is no way to pinpoint the particular element that makes them hometactics. This makes hometactics as multiplicitous as the different multiplicitous selves that deploy them. These tactics, which are multifaceted, decentered, unmappable, and personal, as well as relational, and spatiotemporally engaged by embodied, multiplicitous selves, do not displace systems of power guarded by strategies and other tricks of power—yet their power resides in the possibilities that they open for the multiplicitous self's existential well-being insofar as they allow for glimpses and more sustained moments of comfort and ease where these selves had little possibility of belonging.

Understandably, there may be concerns that hometactics are a way of depoliticizing spaces given that a feeling of uneasiness may in fact serve as a wake-up call for resistant or critical engagement, as various Latina feminist phenomenologists point out.[9] Consequently, they could be seen as either connected to (a) fomenting assimilation or the deployment of hometactics for the purposes of fitting in within dominant schemas or (b) colonization, the practicing of hometactics on the part of dominant selves to forge a particular imperial vision upon a space, both of which would also contribute to the personal well-being and sense of comfort for those engaging in the tactics. Nonetheless, let us remember that even though there are risks involved with hometactics—after all, multiplicitous selves cannot be sure of how effective such practices will be, how they can be co-opted, misunderstood, or undermined by others—their principal aim rests in the possibility of alleviating the not-being-at-ease that is part of being-in-worlds, especially for those multiplicitous selves that do not occupy dominant social locations. Their importance rests in this possibility. Tactics that are intentionally used for the purposes of assimilation and colonization or other undermining projects would no longer constitute hometactics in the sense being described here. As micropractices of the lived experience of multiplicitous selves who feel the uncanniness and the not-being-at home that is part and parcel of human existence, especially for those whose social location or identities are undermined, marginalized, and demeaned, hometactics allow for the possibility of a sense of ease, comfort, and belonging—a breath of fresh air in the midst of confining, suffocating worlds.

## Notes

1. Michel de Certeau, *The Practice of Everyday Life* (Berkeley: University of California Press, 1984), 37.

2. Aimee Carrillo-Rowe, *Power Lines: On the Subject of Feminist Alliances* (Durham, N.C.: Duke University Press, 2008). Also see Chandra Talpade Mohanty, *Feminism without Borders, Decolonizing Theory, Practicing Solidarity* (Durham, N.C.: Duke University Press, 2003).

3. For de Certeau those that lack power are constantly "making do" or improvising so as to take advantage of the environment set up by dominant structures. By doing so, they are also making their lives more livable. In the same manner, hometactics can help us create more home-like environments. de Certeau, *The Practice of Everyday Life.*

4. Martin Heidegger, *Being and Time*, trans. John Macquarrie and Edward Robinson (New York: Harper and Row, 1962).

5. For an interesting analysis of the centrality of the uncanny in Heidegger's phenomenology see Katherine Withy, *Heidegger on Being Uncanny* (Cambridge, Mass.: Harvard University Press, 2015).

6. Mariana Ortega, *In-Between: Latina Feminist Phenomenology, Multiplicity, and the Self* (Albany: State University of New York Press, 2016), chapter 2.

7. It is important to differentiate various senses of not-being-at-ease. A thin sense of not-being-at-ease is, in my view, the sense of uneasiness that arises from ruptures or breakdowns in normative structures that provide a daily sense of practicality and intelligibility. A thick sense of not-being-at-ease, on the other hand, involves ruptures that lead to existential crises connected to self-understanding. Ortega, *In-Between*, 58–63.

8. Gloria Anzaldúa, *Borderlands/La Frontera: The New Mestiza* (San Francisco: Aunt Lute Press, 1987).

9. Consider Anzaldúa's claims about the creative and resistant power that arises out of existence in the borderlands that is fraught with ruptures and the feeling of not being at home. Anzaldúa is thus providing a phenomenological account of the lived experience of the borderlands as sites of creative resistance and personal transformation.

# 25 Horizons

David Morris

> External perception is a constant pretension to accomplish something that, by its very nature, it is not in a position to accomplish.
> —EDMUND HUSSERL, *Analyses Concerning Passive and Active Synthesis*, PART 2, §1

With this insight as his guiding star and the concept of horizons into which it leads, Husserl reveals perception, cognition, and reflection as conditioned, oriented, delimited, and buoyed by never-yet-determinate background horizons that continually billow and flow beyond our grasp. The transcendental subject, who bent its sails to the inner currents of its own mind, so as to steer thinking beyond divinely ordered foundations, is brought back down to earth—but a new sort of earth borne by the contingent winds of what we might call *intersectional being*.

Horizons thus reveal phenomenology itself as an intersectional operation of ourselves and being—suggesting that horizons manifest a "foundational" clue to an intersectional phenomenology. To show this, the first section briefly charts Husserl's concept of horizons; the second tacks through Heidegger and Merleau-Ponty to show how they deepen the horizon-concept in their work on body and world; the third reaches through Beauvoir, Young, Fanon, and Ahmed to show how they figure intersectional identities through this body-world horizon; and the final section shadows recent work by Weiss to venture deeper implications for the horizon of phenomenology itself.

## Husserl's Opening of Horizons: Inner, Outer, and Empathic

Our word *horizon* goes back to the Greek *horismos*, "a boundary," but also what delimits or defines things. The earth's horizon is a peculiarly visible boundary that delimits earth from sky but also serves as a background against which visible things stand out. When things show up as salient in rising above the horizon, they also reveal that there is more that might be seen, beyond the horizon. Yet the horizon's very operation as this sort of background for the appearance of things precisely precludes stepping over or beyond it to catalogue this "more" it might offer up. We can neither catch up to visible horizons nor exhaust their "more": they recede beyond and exceed us even as they orient vision.

This peculiar dynamic manifest in visible horizons is crucial to Husserl's philosophical appropriation of the horizon. Previous Western philosophers, e.g., Neo-Platonist and medieval philosophers, but also Leibniz, and most of all Kant, referred to horizons in studying the ways that knowledge, being, and our identities are inherently delimited and rendered intelligible by backgrounds that transcend us. Husserl's phenomenological effort, though, is to *describe* how such delimiting backgrounds actually operate as conditions of intelligibility. And he does this by attending to the way horizons *appear*, versus, say, deducing such conditions as a nonappearing a priori. Let us see how this reveals dynamical, open-ended horizons.[1]

One of Husserl's favorite examples is a die. Seek one out; perhaps one lingers in a game box in your cupboard. Suppose one is really there. What does this mean? How do you encounter it as real versus an illusion, a dream, or something remembered that turned out to be missing? Husserl shows how even a real, actual die is never given as fully grasped at once. Encountering it as real means *intending toward it* such that you see its 2-face as inviting turning it (or moving yourself around) so as to reveal an adjoining 1-face, or 4-face, or opposite 5-face; and you can *fulfill* that intention.[2] But when you do, this *horizon* of further, adjoining faces itself transforms: when you turn the 4-face toward you, the die's horizon alters, for now the opposite face would be the 3-face. Husserl's point is that this dynamically changing horizon is intended and meant along with the identity of the die. This is what Husserl calls its *inner* horizon: a horizon implied right within our sense of something as being such and such. The inner horizon, though, opens to an *outer* horizon: something beyond what is now meant, that can clash with it, or alter or generate new senses, or even new sorts of horizons. We first had to learn the horizon-sense of a die, by gathering its meaning out of open horizons that offer possibilities of turning things this way or that. But this means being open to new things too, or finding we were wrong, and so on. Indeed it is precisely because our sense of things can be overturned, beyond inner horizons we ourselves project, that there can be a difference between a real, imagined, remembered, missing, or fake die.

Each apparent thing has its sense against its own inner background horizon but also by the way its appearing verges into an open outer horizon that can transform it. And this is the case not just for perceived but ideal things: a geometrical cube, e.g., is meant by thinking about the characteristic way its meant surfaces, or meant claims about it, lead, via an inner horizon, into each other, and open to an outer horizon, e.g., the cube leading into a thought of a rhombohedron, a hypercube, or geometry itself. Further, perceived and ideal things ultimately have solid, verifiable meanings only because we can share encounters with them with others, via what Husserl calls *empathic horizons*.

Husserl's revelation of horizons as integral with the meant sense of perceived or ideal things deflates any claim that we can ever fully accomplish an act of perception or ideation within ourselves. Philosophy is fundamentally opened to something more that exceeds us spatially, temporally, and also cognitively, since each thought has its sense in there being more to think.

## Deepening Horizons: Heidegger and Merleau-Ponty on Body-World Horizons

Let us now turn from Husserl's die to a more earthy example. You are visiting and wandering a city. Seeing, down the block, a wide, paved opening between buildings, you find yourself veering toward it as a new street to explore. This very movement of your body intends this opening as "street," via horizons implicit in what you take as ready-to-hand (in Heidegger's terminology): the opening means "street" in referring to further things to be done with it. In Montreal, though, this opening might turn out to be not a street but a *ruelle*, an alleyway. These are usually inhabited as neighborhood enclaves for kids to play, and if you are lucky you might find a *ruelle* turned into a garden by the community, or into an arts venue, maybe with an opening party going on. Your inner horizon, as never fully self-enclosed, is thus transformed by outer horizons always implied in it, and by empathic horizons—other people doing things that change your sense of cities and streets.

In the terminology of Heidegger's *Being and Time*, you encounter building openings in cities as streets, roads, alleys, etc., in their being part of a *world*—a totality of meant things that refer to one another as letting us do various things with them. We encounter this world by being in and toward it, by being-in-the-world. And we do this by being a being that is here or there, bodily in some sense. In other words, *Being and Time* effectively turns Husserl's horizon-concept into another key phenomenological concept: *world*.[3] Our being-in-the-world, as being-with one another, is the horizon against which we make sense of being. This opens us and our philosophy to a being that always exceeds us. While Heidegger's explicit use of the term *horizon* is more or less confined to *Being and Time*, the issue at stake here proliferates across his philosophy: his concepts of the clearing, the fourfold (in which possibilities of delimitable things on earth stand out against the open sky), *Spielraum*, even of *Ereignis*, the event, clearly offer new ways of thinking about ourselves and being as horizonally open.

Merleau-Ponty, in contrast, continually uses the word *horizon*. It pervades the *Phenomenology of Perception*, which effectively incorporates horizons into the dynamics of the body-world relation: inner horizons turn into habitual comportments of our body-schema (see the chapter on habit), which play out against the outer horizon of the world in which we move and develop, in and through our relations to others. But Merleau-Ponty also seeks to grasp how horizons of meaning and sense are at one with nature and being, and to do so he must trace the horizonal structure of body, world, and others down to shared roots in being. This leads to a further transposition of horizons: into being itself. In a nutshell, Merleau-Ponty's effort to resolve the above problem about meaning leads him to see that, e.g., being is structured by lateral or diacritical relations between things that are transtemporal and transspatial. Spelling this out would take another work, but his effort to understand how meaning emerges within horizons of being itself and without being ideally delimited in advance (as in Kantian horizons) leads him to grasp that being is itself horizonal.

The phenomenological concept of horizons can thus lead to the thought that *being and beings are themselves intersectional*: far from Bishop Butler's dissectional claim that "every thing is what it is and not another thing," things bear their sense only in and through their being intersectionally with and open to other things—and to place and temporality.

## Intersectional Horizons: Beauvoir, Young, Fanon, and Ahmed

This ontological intersectionality implied in the horizon-concept is complemented by an intersectionality of identity also implied therein. Let us return to the *ruelles* of Montreal. If you move around using a wheelchair, a *ruelle* without a sidewalk ramp impedes your accessing it; a *ruelle* occupied by people who look at your skin, body, *sheitl*, *hijab*, or habits in ways that render you alien or abject may exclude your being in it; for a woman or trans person, an unlit *ruelle* at night might appear as a place of trauma or possible violence, not a *ruelle*-as-place-I-can-go.

Taking up horizons via body-world relations, and taking body and worlds concretely, lets us see how empathic outer and inner horizons are co-implicated. In our world, empathic, shared relations with others also open possibilities of violence and transgression, of ingressions of outer horizons into inner-borne bodily horizons, via gender, orientation, race, other identities. Such ingressions, though, can also prove welcoming, as in a *ruelle* opened up for Montreal's *Divercité* and pride celebrations.

Points such as these are developed in early and ongoing work that takes up the horizon-concept in feminist philosophy and philosophy of race. For example, while the word *horizon* appears only a handful of times in Beauvoir's *The Second Sex*, her sustained focus is the way that the body-world horizon of women is distorted by impositions and prejudices of discriminatory "anti-empathic" horizons. So too with the work of Young. Fanon traces racialized dimensions of these horizons, and in his works on colonization and revolution reveals ways that colonial oppression undermines horizons and complicates liberatory efforts. And Beauvoir's *The Coming of Age* gives an early study of the ways that issues of ability and disability are implied in and modulated by these horizons—her point is that the inner salience of ageing is never ourselves inborn; it is wrought by empathic and outer horizons. Ahmed's *Queer Phenomenology* shows how issues of orienting horizons can sustain or undermine sexual orientations.

To the extent that Beauvoir, Fanon, Young, Ahmed, and others find (or fail to find) cross-links between various horizons of identity, their developments of the phenomenological horizon-concept offer openings to intersectional identities. And to the extent that the identities they explore appear within and against a shared world-horizon, these identities would seem to have to be, at least in principle, intersectional. Indeed, approaching intersectional identities through the phenomenological horizon-concept potentially seems to entail an in-principle openness of identities to one another, via the deeper horizonal openness broached by ontological intersectionality. There is not quite any way of having a non-intersectional identity—except through the sort of pretense that Husserlian horizons dismantle. Identities inherently open the potential for what Lugones calls "world-traveling" (see her chapter 28): we could always stumble into that *ruelle* that opens a new world already implied in our own. But that might never happen: we might succumb to the closed security-state of our own pretenses.

## The Horizon of Horizons: Intersectional Being and the Open Future of Phenomenology

While phenomenological approaches to feminist philosophy implicitly engage the horizon-concept, the term *horizon* seldom appears as such in books, articles, or indices in this area. In striking contrast, *horizon* is the central topic and term of Gail Weiss's book *Refiguring the Ordinary*,[4] which helps us see how the horizon-concept opens up new possibilities for philosophy. To extract and condense a highly nuanced point (that Weiss develops via critical analysis of studies of concrete cases, e.g., the upheavals around the beating of Rodney King), Weiss's effort is to show how the horizonal dynamic and structure of shared human situations allows the emergence of seemingly closed inner horizons, that intend prejudiced and isolated identities—yet the reality is that this pretense of closure is always contrived out of horizons that are still open, that afford possible refiguring. Shifts in the ways our horizons are figured are thus not achieved by imposing outside norms from above or in advance, but by inner fermentation of openings always possibly portended in the very being of horizons.

Overall, the suggestion here is that phenomenology's discovery of horizons would in effect permanently and always undermine any pretense of phenomenology or philosophy to claim it is a closed book. Thinking and reflection are figured out of an intersectional being that opens beyond us, with which we intersect. As Merleau-Ponty puts it in *The Visible and the Invisible*, in a quote that stands epigraph to a key chapter in Weiss, "No more than the sky or the earth is the horizon a collection of things held together, or a class name, or a logical possibility of conception, or a system of 'potentiality of consciousness': it is a new type of being, a being by porosity, or by generality, and the one before whom the horizon opens is caught up, englobed, within it."[5]

## Notes

1. The most extensive study of horizons in Husserl is Saulias Genusias, *The Origins of the Horizon in Husserl's Phenomenology* (Dordrecht: Springer, 2012). For the horizon in Husserl, see §§1–4 of Edmund Husserl, *Analyses concerning Passive and Active Synthesis: Lectures on Transcendental Logic*, trans. A. J. Steinbock (Dordrecht: Kluwer, 2001); or Husserl, *Cartesian Meditations*, trans. D. Cairns (1931; Dordrecht: Kluwer, 1991), §19. The most beautiful statement is Husserl, *Experience and Judgment: Investigations in a Genealogy of Logic*, trans. J. S. Churchill and K. Ameriks (Evanston, Ill.: Northwestern University Press, 1973), §8, but the writer in fact is his assistant Landgrebe.

2. See Jennifer McWeeny's entry in this volume, "Operative Intentionality," for further discussion of this point.

3. See H. Pietersma, "Husserl and Heidegger," *Philosophy and Phenomenological Research* 40, no. 2 (1979): 194–211, for this point.

4. Gail Weiss, *Refiguring the Ordinary* (Bloomington: Indiana University Press, 2008).

5. Maurice Merleau-Ponty, *The Visible and the Invisible*, trans. A. Lingis (1964; Evanston, Ill.: Northwestern University Press, 1968), 148–49, translation modified.

# 26 Imaginaries

Moira Gatens

The concept of the imaginary has a checkered genealogy, and it is wise to resist the inclination to provide a singular definition. It is a term deployed in disciplines as diverse as psychoanalysis, sociology, philosophy, feminist theory, cultural and literary studies, political theory, and anthropology. This brief expository essay will offer one approach to understanding the meaning and scope of the idea of the imaginary.[1] First, consideration will be given to the *body image* and *imaginary bodies*. The idea of a body image, or *Gestalt*, is not strictly confined to psychoanalysis, but for present purposes it makes sense to track it to the pioneering work of Sigmund Freud and Jacques Lacan.[2] The pluralization of the concept of the imaginary characterizes critical feminist attempts to theorize the cultural meanings of sexual difference, along with other embodied differences (e.g., race, ability, sexuality). The research of Luce Irigaray and Linda Alcoff are relevant here.[3] Second, an account of *social imaginaries* will be offered. The idea of a social imaginary figures in the work of Cornelius Castoriadis and Charles Taylor. Third, connections will be drawn between social imaginaries and the *power-knowledge* nexus. The work of Miranda Fricker and José Medina around notions of epistemic injustice and epistemic resistance bring together power, knowledge, and the social imagination to show how imaginaries can be deeply damaging to denigrated social identities. In this sense, individuals are vulnerable insofar as they are treated in stereotyped ways that drastically limit their capacity to speak or act in a way that defies powerful prejudicial expectations. The essay will close with a sketch of the liberatory potential of politically resistant *counterimaginaries* as these have been realized in the work of Medina and Charles Mills and through artistic endeavor.

## The Body Image and Imaginary Bodies

The mind-body distinction is part of the philosophical legacy of the West. It is reflected in traditional approaches to reason-passion and culture-nature and the discriminatory associations commonly drawn between these sets of dichotomies on the one hand and sex and race differences on the other.[4] Freud challenged mind-body dualism with the claim "The ego is first and foremost a bodily ego; it is not merely a surface entity, but is itself the projection of a surface." Put differently, the conscious ego, or "self," "is first and foremost a body-ego."[5] Following on from this embodied approach to consciousness, Lacan posited "the mirror stage" as crucial to the newborn's development into a subject, capable of uttering "I."[6] He claims that humans are born premature and our abilities develop unevenly. A child around twelve to eighteen months can perceptually and cognitively grasp that it is a whole before it *feels* itself to be a unity. It sees its integrity in the mirror, or reflected in an other, and so its ego, or self, is fundamentally yoked to an experience of (mis)recognition. The moment is joyfully recognitive because it anticipates bodily integrity, yet it also involves an alienating misrecognition because the mirror reflection (or other) is over there and not here, where the body is lived in fragments. Lacan's notion of the body image is important because it signals the child's entry into the Imaginary order—one of the three orders that structure human experience, the other two being the Symbolic and the Real.[7] The trope of the mirror captures the specular dimension of human reality insofar as it reveals the tension between the *felt* "body in bits and pieces" and the *seen* image of completeness. The human fascination with images, and the great pleasure and anxiety invested in images, is understood not only in terms of creativity but, more profoundly, in the irresistible appeal of beguiling imaginaries.

The notion of the body image came to play an important role in some feminist approaches to sexual difference not least because of Lacan's provocative claim that the male child's body image more closely satisfies the fantasy of wholeness insofar as he has a penis.[8] In a manner reminiscent of Freud, Lacan problematically treats sexual difference as grounded in anatomy as well as culture. Irigaray challenged the authority of psychoanalysis to dictate the psychological consequences of anatomical difference along with Lacan's division between the Imaginary, the Symbolic, and the Real. Her playful and evocative interventions into psychoanalytic theory include her image of the sex "which is not one" but rather "at least two," an embrace of lips, which she counterposes to the imaginary of the "wound" or "hole" of the female sex.[9] In this way she disrupts the Symbolic quite as much as the Imaginary order. Other theorists developed critical accounts concerning how race, sexuality, and ability figure in the imaginary. For example, Alcoff argued that racialization can "block the development of coherent body images" in those whose identities have been alienated by an oppressive white imaginary.[10] Ultimately, such invaluable contributions demonstrate that the revaluation of difference demands theories of imaginaries, in the plural, along with specific critiques of their power to determine the valence of social and political identities.

## Social Imaginaries

Theorists of race, sex, and ability broadened the individualistic psychoanalytic approach to the body image to include collective bodies. However, the notion of the social imaginary has labyrinthine lines of descent. In addition to the theorists already discussed, Castoriadis presented what he terms "the radical imaginary": the phenomenon by which human cultures come to posit a thing as standing in for something that it is not, for example, a sword as symbol of sovereign power. It is misleading to explain the imaginary in terms of the creative subjective imagination because without the instituting social imaginary there would be no subjects. Any given society is self-creating and inaugurates a new *eidos* that cannot be reduced to prior determinations.[11] Rather, the institution of human societies involves creativity and novelty. For him, the social imaginary structures human reality. It is the background or framework through which human reality is mediated. Castoriadis's influences include Aristotle, Immanuel Kant, and Karl Marx as well as psychoanalytic theories. Castoriadis insists on the ontological primacy of the imaginary to human historical and political life. As Susan James explains, on this view we are all "walking and complementary fragments of the imaginary institution of society, produced in conformity with its significations."[12] An important aspect of the doubled instituting and instituted social imaginary is the human capacity to modify and reinterpret the symbols, myths, and legends through which societies are formed and thus to alter the social realities that we inhabit. Despite the creativity and openness of Castoriadis's account of the imaginary, some have maintained that the privilege he accords Western forms of life and thought amount to a "staggering Eurocentrism."[13] His imaginary fails to acknowledge modernity as plural and so is unable to accommodate the creative reimaginings of a variety of culturally distinct ways of living with and in modernity.

Taylor acknowledges that agency is embodied and embedded in culturally specific ways and that the historical present is characterized by multiple modernities. He defines the social imaginary of a given people at a given time as a kind of "repertory of collective actions," an "ensemble of imaginings that enable [certain social] practices by making sense of them."[14] Moreover, because such imaginings are widely shared they enjoy "a sense of legitimacy."[15] Modern Western democratic polities are distinguished from the premodern period by a social imaginary where society is understood as a moral order based on mutually beneficial exchange between equals. Three major formations characterize modernity: the market economy, the public sphere, and a self-governing people. Although Taylor notes the divergent ways in which different nation-states inhabit modernity, he is less attentive to the different ways in which sexed and raced bodies are differently enabled within any given nation-state. Consider his description of the public sphere. He describes this sphere as "extrapolitical" because "public opinion is not an exercise of power, it can be ideally disengaged from partisan spirit and rational." The new public sphere may be understood "as a discourse of reason *on* and *to* power rather than *by* power." It expresses "a discourse of reason outside power, which nevertheless is normative for power."[16] Arguably Taylor perpetuates a masculinist, "white" social imaginary that is blind to the way in which the poor, women, and people of color typically lack adequate access to the public sphere because of embodied and embedded unequal power relations.[17] Even though Taylor sees that phenomenology and hermeneutics are interlaced, he fails to note that the lived reality of oppressed groups puts them at a severe hermeneutic disadvantage. If human subjects are constituted as such through power relations, then there is no discourse, rational or otherwise, outside of power.[18]

## Power, Knowledge, and Injustice

Fricker brings together discourse, power relations, and social identity in order to describe two kinds of epistemic injustice: testimonial and hermeneutic. The former involves a speaker receiving less credibility than he deserves because of the hearer's prejudice; the latter involves a more profound injustice, where a society lacks the collective resources to interpret the way people from marginalized groups experience a specific act, acts, or type of behavior. An example of the first kind of injustice is the low credibility that people of color may experience when speaking to police. An example of the latter is the hermeneutical gap that used to exist in the interpretation of predation as sexual harassment before feminists coined that term.[19] Fricker shows that power relations are intrinsic to the way our identities are constituted, and so even where formal access to the public sphere exists it does not necessarily guarantee substantive participation in the exchange of views or in the formation of public opinion. However, her division of epistemic injustice into two kinds may well be an abstraction because, as she notes, "hermeneutical injustice most typically manifests itself in the speaker struggling to make herself intelligible in a testimonial exchange [and this] raises a grim possibility: that hermeneutical injustice might often be compounded by testimonial injustice."[20] Although Fricker uses the term *social imagination* rather than *social imaginary*, it is difficult to see what is the difference. Like other conceptions of the imaginary treated here, her account of social imagination involves a background hermeneutic that includes images, pictures, narratives, and stereotypes. This background hermeneutic enables social coordination and may "condition our judgments without our awareness," even against our consciously held beliefs.

Like Castoriadis and Taylor, Fricker sees the social imagination as "a mighty resource for social change" as well as "an ethical and epistemic liability."[21] The ubiquity and relative automaticity of the operations of the social imaginary give it this oddly ambiguous power. As James states, although "coming to understand the workings of social imaginaries is a vital condition of change, there is no recipe for success, no procedure for undermining or replacing particular images or their effects. In many cases, the task of modifying the way we understand ourselves and others, together with the way we feel, will be long and unpredictable, and will be achieved by imaginative techniques over which we have at best imperfect control."[22] Like James, Medina asserts that the social imaginary is "extremely hard to change." However, in a departure from Fricker's approach, Medina posits solidarity, plural forms of imagining, and counterpublics as crucial to epistemic resistance.[23] Where Fricker sees hermeneutic injustice as largely beyond the scope of an individual's ethical responsibility, Medina asks, "When and in what sense is thinking or acting on the basis of a biased social imaginary blameworthy?"[24]

Rejecting a hard and fast distinction between the individual and the collective, and between the epistemic, the ethical, and the political, he argues for a robust epistemic responsibility and an insurrectionist imagination.[25] On his account, the problem is not only blindness or insensitivity to oppression but also an active ignorance, a metablind "needing not to know" on the part of the privileged. Changing present ways of relating to each other, then, requires the cultivation of a new kaleidoscopic social sensibility that is open-minded, pluralistic, and experimental.

## Counterimaginaries

"Imagination is not a luxury or a privilege, but a necessity."[26] Far from being false or illusory, the symbols, metaphors, and narratives that characterize a given people at a particular place and time shape the fundamental social realities through which they become who they are. Indeed, the capacity to imagine things otherwise is an admirable feat of resistance that dwells at the core of every movement for liberation. Part of what is involved in resistant epistemologies is the challenge to cherished dominant narratives, for example, those of national origins or the "just so" stories of the creation of civil society. An example of the former is indigenous peoples' assertion of the invasion of their lands as a counterpoint to the image of the brave frontier settler, and of the latter, the challenge presented by accounts of the sexual and racial contracts as against the "neutral" individual of classic social contract theory. As Mills argues in *The Racial Contract*, traditional political theory is dominated by a kind of inverted knowing about our white supremist past and the bloodied grounds on which contemporary societies rest. What he calls "an epistemology of ignorance," that is, "a particular pattern of localized and global cognitive dysfunctions [produces] the ironic outcome that whites will in general be unable to understand the world they themselves have made."[27]

Along with Mills, Medina considers "the battle of the imaginations" that characterizes social conflict to constitute a kind of political activism.[28] He introduces Foucauldian-inspired notions of countermemory, counterimagination, and insurrectionist epistemologies that aim to bring into view that which has been silenced or obscured by epistemic arrogance and destructive imaginaries. "Genealogies are insurrections against monopolizations of the social imagination; they provide new venues for imaginative appropriations of a heterogeneous past, which in turn open new paths for projections into the future."[29] This approach promises to make patent suppressed events and silenced and excluded voices. For Medina and others, these insurrectionist practices do not have to be invented ex nihilo: elements of the counterimagination are already present but require support and social solidarity to grow stronger.[30] In addition to the significant challenges to mainstream theory that have been the focus of this essay, literary, filmic, and other artistic creations have long inspired liberatory movements with their strong visions of alternate imaginaries, realities, and sensibilities. The artistic works of Ken Gonzales-Day, bell hooks, Judy Chicago, and Rachel Perkins, just to name a few, have contributed to creating counterimaginaries which have challenged, perhaps emboldened, the way their audiences experience themselves and others.[31]

## Notes

1. For a critical summary of notions of the imaginary, see Susan James, "Freedom and the Imaginary," in *Visible Women: Essays on Feminist Legal Theory and Political Philosophy* (Portland Ore.: Hart, 2002), 175–95.

2. Kathleen Lennon offers a different genealogy that includes Kant, Sartre, Merleau-Ponty, and Irigaray. See *Imagination and the Imaginary* (London: Routledge, 2015). Lennon also mentions a marginal genealogy derived from Spinoza's conception of the imagination, deployed by Moira Gatens in *Imaginary Bodies: Ethics, Power and Corporeality* (London: Routledge, 1996). For a different but compelling approach, see Chiara Bottici, *Imaginal Politics: Images beyond Imagination and the Imaginary* (New York: Columbia University Press, 2014).

3. Luce Irigaray, *This Sex Which Is Not One* (Ithaca, N.Y.: Cornell University Press, 1985); Linda Martín Alcoff, *Visible Identities: Race, Gender, and the Self* (New York: Oxford University Press, 2006). See also Drucilla Cornell, *The Imaginary Domain: Abortion, Pornography, and Sexual Harassment* (New York: Routledge, 1995); Gail Weiss, *Body Images: Embodiment as Intercorporeality* (New York: Routledge, 1999); Rosalyn Diprose, *The Bodies of Women: Ethics, Embodiment and Sexual Differences* (London: Routledge, 2005); Susan Wendell, *The Rejected Body: Feminist Philosophical Reflections on Disability* (London: Routledge, 1996); Elizabeth Grosz, *Volatile Bodies: Toward a Corporeal Feminism* (Bloomington: Indiana University Press, 1994).

4. Feminists have criticized the way women and people of color have been associated with the body, nature, and passion, and so deemed "naturally" subject to white men, who are associated with the mind, reason, and culture. See Diana Fuss, *Essentially Speaking: Feminism, Nature and Difference* (New York: Routledge, 1989).

5. Sigmund Freud, "The Ego and the Id," in *The Standard Edition of the Complete Psychological Works* (London: Hogarth Press, 1978), 19: 26, 27. Note the resonance with Benedict Spinoza's refutation of mind-body dualism: "The object of the idea constituting the human Mind is the Body, or a certain mode of Extension which actually exists, and nothing else." *The Collected Works of Spinoza*, vol. 1: *Ethics* (Princeton, N.J.: Princeton University Press, 1985), part 2, proposition 13.

6. Jacques Lacan, "The Mirror Stage as Formative of the Function of the I as Revealed in Psychoanalytic Experience," in *Écrits* (London: Tavistock, 1977), 1–7.

7. See Lacan, *Écrits*, ix–x.

8. Jacques Lacan, "Some Reflections on the Ego," *International Journal of Psychoanalysis* 34 (1953): 13. I merely note here the complex question of the distinction between the penis and the phallus.

9. Irigaray, *This Sex*, 23–33.

10. Alcoff, *Visible Identities*, chapter 11.

11. Cornelius Castoriadis, *The Imaginary Institution of Society* (London: Polity, 1987).

12. James, "Freedom and the Imaginary," 181.

13. Dilip Parameshwar Gaonkar, "Toward New Imaginaries: An Introduction," *Public Culture* 14, no. 1 (Winter 2002): 9.

14. Charles Taylor, *Modern Social Imaginaries* (Durham, N.C.: Duke University Press, 2004), 25, 165.

15. Taylor, *Modern Social Imaginaries*, 23.

16. Taylor, *Modern Social Imaginaries*, 90–91.

17. For example, in *The Sexual Contract* (London: Polity, 1988), Carole Pateman argues that women do not make the transition into modernity on the same terms as men. They are not genuine parties to the "social contract," conceived in terms of the imaginary of "exchange for mutual benefit." Rather, they remain stuck with a premodern "status" mode of being ("woman"), not a modern "contract" abstract individual. See also Charles Mills, *The Racial Contract* (Ithaca, N.Y.: Cornell University Press, 1997).

18. This view is artfully defended by Amy Allen in *The Politics of Our Selves* (New York: Columbia University Press, 2008).

19. In case one may be tempted to think of epistemic injustice as less serious than other kinds of social injustice, consider the following empirical examples: the low credibility attributed to the testimony of Duwayne Brooks, a black English youth who witnessed the murder of his friend, Stephen Lawrence, at the hands of neo-Nazis; and Carmita Woods, who lost her job and was refused government assistance because she lacked the hermeneutic resources to describe her boss's unwanted sexual aggression in terms that would have justified her resignation to the relevant authorities.

20. Fricker, *Epistemic Injustice*, 159.

21. Fricker, *Epistemic Injustice*, 37–38.

22. James, "Freedom and the Imaginary," 187.

23. José Medina, *The Epistemology of Resistance: Gender and Racial Oppression, Epistemic Injustice, and Resistant Imaginations* (New York: Oxford University Press, 2013).

24. Medina, *Epistemology of Resistance*, 133.

25. Medina, *Epistemology of Resistance*, 82, chapter 6.

26. Medina, *Epistemology of Resistance*, 268.

27. Mills, *Racial Contract*, 18.

28. Medina, *Epistemology of Resistance*, 252.

29. Medina, *Epistemology of Resistance*, 292.

30. Along with Medina, both Kristie Dotson, "A Cautionary Tale, on Limiting Epistemic Oppression," *Frontiers: A Journal of Women Studies* 33, no. 1 (2012) and Mariana Ortega, *In-Between: Latina Feminist Phenomenology, Multiplicity, and the Self* (Albany, N.Y.: SUNY Press, 2016) disagree with Fricker's characterization of the hermeneutic horizon as monolithic or singular. Rather, marginalized groups often enjoy (marginalized) imaginaries that include hermeneutic resources that are invisible to dominant social identities. In this context, the notion of "double-consciousness" developed by W. E. B. Du Bois in *The Souls of Black Folk* (New York: Penguin Classic, 1996), is important.

31. For Gonzales's "Erased Lynchings Series," see https://kengonzalesday.com/erased-lynchings/; for Judy Chicago's *Dinner Party*, see https://www.brooklynmuseum.org/exhibitions/dinner_party; bell hooks is an author of fiction and theory; Rachel Perkins is an indigenous Australian filmmaker.

# 27 Immanence and Transcendence

Shiloh Whitney

While immanence and transcendence are positioned in existentialism and phenomenology as key concepts for describing the structure of experience, problematizing this distinction also emerges as a theme, especially in the work of Maurice Merleau-Ponty, Simone de Beauvoir, and Frantz Fanon. These three thinkers offer phenomenological accounts that rethink the immanence-transcendence distinction such that their relationship is not oppositional. Each reacts against the Sartrean treatment of the immanence-transcendence distinction as an agonism, a *struggle* for transcendence. Merleau-Ponty's work demonstrates that problematizing the immanence-transcendence distinction, especially in its agonistic Sartrean form, is necessary for a phenomenology of experience as embodied. Beauvoir's and Fanon's work demonstrates that problematizing this distinction is necessary for a phenomenology of gendered and racialized oppression.

## The Struggle for Transcendence, from Hegel and Husserl to Sartre

The sense of *transcendence* that opposes *immanence* has a Hegelian heritage: transcendence is the movement of self-relating negativity that characterizes subjectivity, while immanence is the static unity of (mere) objects. Husserlian phenomenology shows the influence of this Hegelian notion of transcendence in the concept of the transcendental ego, the essence of consciousness as a temporal flow that always transcends its objectification in any particular "intentional act" or conscious grasp. For Husserl, the movement of transcendence is identified with the flow of time: the being of consciousness from one moment to the next, which is self-relating but noncoincident. For Husserl, this movement of transcendence can be an *operative* intentionality and is not necessarily the objectifying gesture of an *act* intentionality.[1]

The Sartrean notions of being-for-itself and being-in-itself are adaptations of this Hegelian and Husserlian tradition of defining human subjectivity in terms of a transcendence. In Sartre's treatment of these concepts, human transcendence is the key discovery of existentialism: our essence is to not have an objectifiable or fixed essence, but rather to be caught up in a transcendent relation to our immanent and factual situation. The Sartrean theorization of the relation between transcendence and immanence posits the negativity that characterizes transcendence's relation to immanence as agonism: not only noncoincidence but an active opposing or "nihilation."[2] Subjectivity for Sartre is an existential struggle for transcendence, an active overcoming of immanence.[3]

This agonism in Sartre's understanding of subjectivity extends to his account of relations between subjects.[4] Insofar as subjectivity is attained in the gesture of opposing oneself to objects, nihilating one's intentional object, there is no possibility of simultaneous mutual recognition: to assert myself as a subject is to objectify you, and likewise to recognize you as a subject is to be complicit in your objectification of me.[5] This is influenced by Hegel's account of the conflicts that necessarily arise in relations between consciousnesses, exemplified in the unhappy consciousness of the master-slave dialectic, where the struggle for transcendence is played out as a struggle for mastery over another.[6]

## Merleau-Ponty and the Ambiguous Transcendence of Embodied Experience

Merleau-Ponty's work does not explicitly engage with critical theories of gender and race, yet it has yielded crucial resources for thinkers who do. In her landmark essay "Throwing Like a Girl," Young argues that Merleau-Ponty's work is radical in the phenomenological tradition and crucial for feminist theory insofar as he "locat[es] subjectivity" and "the status of transcendence" "not in the mind or consciousness, but in the *body*."[7] Weiss has recently expanded this claim, arguing for the particular usefulness of Merleau-Ponty's work for critical theories of race, gender, and disability.[8]

In Young's initial formulation of the "ambiguous transcendence" of the body, she locates a gendered oppression in a "'bad' or self-limiting ambiguity that interrupts our fluid engagement with the world."[9] Is this ambiguous transcendence to be overcome, or embraced? Weiss suggests that we can find in Merleau-Ponty a "'good' or productive ambiguity" of transcendence, one "that opens up new possibilities of movement and meaning."[10] In her reconsideration of the "Throwing Like a Girl" essay twenty years after its initial publication, Young herself affirms that a *revalued* ambiguous transcendence is crucial for feminist theories of the body.[11]

Because for Merleau-Ponty our movements and all our sensorimotor behavior is itself "a reference to the object,"[12] intentionality is located, not in consciousness as a transcendence of things (including the body), but rather in the body proper: intentionality is not an act of consciousness but an operation of the body as a network of sensorimotor and affective relations to the world and others as well as to itself. Thus it is the body becoming oriented toward and moving within its surroundings that is "the elementary power of sense-giving."[13] When we begin our phenomenological investigation from everyday perceptual experience, we find that the fundamental self-relating movement of experience is not the self-relating negativity of consciousness-raising itself up out of immersion in the unreflective flow of living. It is rather the persistently prereflective sensorimotor and affective body becoming oriented in the world with others. Merleau-Ponty calls this bodily intentionality the "body schema."[14]

If intentionality is embodied, then it cannot be defined as transcendence in opposition to immanence. It is not an intentional *act* at all: it is as much a passion as an action.[15] Embodied intentionality is our inherence in things as much as it is our grasp of them.[16] While Sartre locates transcendence in the intentional acts of consciousness, for Merleau-Ponty it is a feature of phenomenalization itself, occurring operatively through the body rather than as an act of consciousness: an "unmotivated springing forth of the world" through our body.[17]

This is not merely a principled theoretical refusal of the opposition of transcendence and immanence. It is the phenomenological discovery that insofar as experience is embodied, the phenomenological evidence offered up in experience is fundamentally resistant to description in terms of an opposition of transcendence and immanence. As Young glosses this result, "all transcendence is ambiguous."[18] The relationship of the body and world in perceptual experience is not a relation of transcendence overcoming immanence, mastering it. The relation between transcendence and immanence is *ambiguous*, a reciprocal genesis or development rather than a struggle for mastery.

Thus the transcendence of the body schema is ambiguous because it is immanent in two senses. First, it is immanent in the sense that *it is a set of organic capacities* (sensing, moving, feeling) *that persist as actual flesh*, a power not merely to be conscious of the world, but to sense, move, and feel with organs, muscles, and visceral systems. As such it is not a power seated in consciousness and hidden away from the material world and others, but rather a carnal connection between a body and an environment. Since it is material and fleshy rather than abstract and psychical, it is not an inalienable power. It develops and ages, is vulnerable to carnal damage and deterioration—indeed, this variability and exposure is fundamental rather than accidental to it.

This entails that transcendence of the body schema is ambiguous because it is immanent in a second sense: as a power to sense, move, and feel rather than merely to be conscious of the world from afar, embodied transcendence *is itself sensed, moving, and affecting*. The body's self-relation to the world and others is itself embodied and experienceable for others. The bodily intentionality of others makes itself *felt* in our own embodied orientation, and ours in theirs. Merleau-Ponty observes that our experiences of others routinely include experiences of seeing others seeing, feeling others being moved. He writes that when his "interlocutor gets angry," this anger is not "in some otherworldly realm, in some shrine located beyond the body of the angry man."[19] Rather "it really is here, in this room and in this part of the room, that the anger breaks forth. It is in in the space between him and me that it unfolds. . . . My opponent's anger is on his face."[20] *Our intentional relation to the world and to others is visible, moving, and affecting* rather than spirited away in unassailable and unambiguous transcendence. Even our "secret affective movements"[21] are incarnated here in our bodies and this space between us, rather than merely being indicated here while their true home is elsewhere in some definitively psychical and private domain.

Thus Merleau-Ponty's account of relations with others reflects this fundamental ambiguity of transcendence and immanence. This is of course no guarantee that we will always understand each other, any more than perception guarantees we will never misperceive. And it is no guarantee that we will not do violence to each other's capacities for ambiguous transcendence. On the contrary: it allows us to account for those situations.

## Oppression and the Struggle for Transcendence

Insofar as transcendence is a bodily transcendence, it cannot be singled out from immanence and valorized as an inalienable condition that elevates the human subject from nature and animality: a valorized freedom of consciousness from bodily materiality and social interdependence. Any such valorization of transcendence would itself be bad faith, a sleight of hand that can be sustained only by obscuring part of the phenomenon at issue.

This makes possible the *reversal of the significance of the Sartrean struggle for transcendence* that we see in Beauvoir's and Fanon's phenomenologies of gendered and racialized oppression. The overcoming of immanence is there no longer positioned as a noble struggle for existential achievement. Instead that achievement is itself problematized. Its false universality and existential weakness are exposed.[22] Instead of being definitively human, overcoming immanence is a particular mode of subjectivity enjoyed by a privileged few. Instead of being the definitive exercise of existential freedom, it is implicated in the subjugation and bondage of marginalized social groups.

Thus the notion of a struggle for transcendence is put to use in Beauvoir's and Fanon's phenomenologies to theorize the structure of gendered and racialized oppressions. The agonism emphasized in Sartre's account of consciousness and relations with others informs Beauvoir's concept of "otherness" as the central feature of women's oppression: "What singularly defines the situation of woman is that . . . an attempt is made to freeze her as an object and doom her to immanence."[23] An experience of sovereignty and transcendence for masculine subjects is purchased through the denigration of women to the status of Other, inessential. This revalued agonism also informs Fanon's analysis of "negrophobia": the attempt to project onto black bodies "the darkness inherent in every ego," "primitive mentality" and "animal eroticism,"[24] thus quarantining ambiguity and immanence in black bodies and expelling it from white bodies and spaces.

The scholarship on Beauvoir and Fanon tends to agree that this critical reappropriation of the struggle for transcendence in the phenomenology of oppression is at its best when it acknowledges that the very notion of transcendence as a definitively human triumph over immanence is itself a product of hierarchical practices of sexism, colonial racism, and ableism, and is implicated in suspect hierarchies of nature and culture, humans and animals, minds and bodies.[25] Thus phenomenologies of oppression would concede too much when they describe the injustice of oppression in terms of inhibited transcendence.

## Oppression as the Inhibition of Ambiguous Transcendence

Repositioning the struggle for transcendence as part of oppressive relationships among social groups does not make it political *rather than* ontological. The oppression Beauvoir and Fanon describe affects the oppressed person in her being, diminishing her existential capacities. Fanon describes the racializing gaze of whites influencing his own self-relation as an embodied intentionality: "The body schema, attacked in several places, collapsed, giving way to an epidermal racial schema."[26] The body schema that is harmed by racism is materially inhibited by this misrecognition, infecting even proprioceptive experience with a persona woven by colonial racism.[27] Thus when Fanon writes that "ontology is made impossible in a colonized and acculturated society," this means that there is not one structure of human being, but also the unmaking of that being through oppression.[28]

This is another implication of acknowledging the ambiguity of transcendence. If our precise capacities for transcendence are embodied and intimately linked to our immanent being, then these capacities are cultivated in our concrete situations, including our membership in social groups with concrete histories and hierarchies. Fanon's account of the collapse of the body schema is not an inhibition of transcendence simpliciter, but an inhibition of *embodied* transcendence: a persistent and intrusive objectification that does not simply reduce the subject to her body, but that denies the black body any role in transcendence. As Gordon writes, "what antiblack racism demands of the black body is for it to live as . . . a body without a perspective."[29] This oppression is not a reduction to immanence, but rather an inhibition of *the ambiguous transcendence of the body schema*. Antiblack racism as Fanon describes it makes the subject status of black people contingent on achieving an impossible alienation from their bodies. Beauvoir describes gendered oppression similarly when she writes that "woman *is* her body as man *is* his," yet "her body is something other than her."[30]

Thus the violation of our being in oppression cannot be understood through the opposition of transcendence and immanence. It is not "merely" our bodies, our immanence, that are affected by oppression, as if oppression is a bondage of the flesh alone. Nor is oppression indifferent to our bodies, targeting only our possibilities for pure transcendence. Oppression diminishes our existential capacities insofar as *it is the denial of our ambiguous transcendence*, the demand that we negate our embodiment in order to realize our being. It marks the bodies of marginalized people as exemplars of immanence and limits our possibilities for transcendence to those that can be had at the expense of being at home in our flesh.[31] With the ambiguous transcendence of the body schema "collapsed" or "amputated," our being is denied a place, a body of one's own.[32]

The politics that affirm marginalized identities have sometimes re-created the refusal of ambiguous transcendence insofar as they have demanded that we make claims to redress injustice on the basis of too simple notions of identity that abstract from our concrete situations, immersed not in one world, but many.[33] A more critical and intersectional phenomenology calls for research that invents the critical categories we need to make political claims from a position of embodying and assuming this intersectional ambiguity, rather than obliging us to make political claims from a position of having transcended it.

## Notes

1. Unlike the oppositional or objectifying character of the act intentionality of judgments and volitions, an operative intentionality expresses a pre-predicative unity of the subject and object of an intentional relation.

2. See Jean-Paul Sartre, *The Philosophy of Jean-Paul Sartre*, ed. Robert Denoon Cumming (New York: Random House, 1965), especially "The Encounter with Nothingness."

3. This shows Hegel's influence: transcendence is for Hegel an *achievement*, the achievement of raising ourselves up out of immersion in unreflective consciousness. See Genevieve Lloyd, *The Man of Reason: "Male" and "Female" in Western Philosophy* (Minneapolis: University of Minnesota Press, 1984) for a discussion.

4. See Kris Sealey's entry in this volume, "Being-in-Itself, Being-for-Itself, and Being-for-Others."

5. See Sartre, *The Philosophy of Jean-Paul Sartre*, especially "The Encounter with the Other."

6. Some credit for this agonism in Sartre's phenomenology is usually attributed to the influence of Kojève, who taught Hegel to Sartre's generation of French philosophers and who emphasized Hegel's account of self-consciousness in the master-slave dialectic over later, more reconciled moments in Hegel's account of the phenomenological development of spirit.

7. Iris Marion Young, "Throwing Like a Girl: A Phenomenology of Feminine Body Comportment, Motility, and Spatiality" (1980), in *On Female Body Experience: "Throwing Like a Girl" and Other Essays* (New York: Oxford University Press, 2005), 35. For further scholarship on the importance of a phenomenology of the body for critical theories of race, gender, and disability, see Sara Heinämaa, "What Is a Woman? Butler and Beauvoir on the Foundations of the Sexual Difference," *Hypatia* 12, no. 1 (1997): 20–39, and Sara Heinämaa, "Simone de Beauvoir's Phenomenology of Sexual Difference," *Hypatia* 14, no. 4 (1999): 114–32; Elizabeth Grosz, *Volatile Bodies: Toward a Corporeal Feminism* (Indianapolis: Indiana University Press, 1994); Gail Weiss, "The Normal, the Natural, and the Normative: A Merleau-Pontian Legacy to Feminist Theory, Critical Race Theory, and Disability Studies," *Continental Philosophy Review* 48 (2015): 77–93, and Gail Weiss, *Body Images: Embodiment as Intercorporeality* (New York: Routledge, 1999); Gayle Salamon, "The Phenomenology of Rheumatology: Disability, Merleau-Ponty, and the Fallacy of Maximal Grip," *Hypatia* 27, no. 2 (2012): 243–60, Gayle Salamon, *Assuming a Body: Transgender and Rhetorics of Materiality* (New York: Columbia University Press, 2010), and Gayle Salamon, "The Place Where Life Hides Away: Merleau-Ponty, Fanon, and the Location of Bodily Being," *Differences* 17, no. 2 (2006): 96–112; Alia Al-Saji, "Bodies and Sensings: On the Uses of Husserlian Phenomenology for Feminist Theory," *Continental Philosophy Review* 43 (2010): 13–37.

8. Weiss goes further than Young in her reading of Merleau-Ponty's revision of the immanence-transcendence distinction, writing, "I believe he is rejecting the notion of bodily immanence and therefore the traditional transcendence/immanence distinction altogether." Weiss, "The Normal, the Natural, and the Normative," 80.

9. Weiss, "The Normal, the Natural, and the Normative," 80.

10. Weiss, "The Normal, the Natural, and the Normative," 80.

11. Iris Marion Young, "'Throwing Like a Girl': Twenty Years Later," in *Body and Flesh: A Philosophical Reader* ed. Donn Welton (Malden, Mass.: Blackwell, 1998).

12. Maurice Merleau-Ponty, *Phenomenology of Perception*, trans. Donald A. Landes (1954; New York: Routledge, 2012), 171.

13. Merleau-Ponty, *Phenomenology of Perception*, 177.

14. Merleau-Ponty, *Phenomenology of Perception*, 127.

15. See Merleau-Ponty's emphasis on Husserl's notion of "operative intentionality" as prior to "act intentionality" (*Phenomenology of Perception*, lxxxii, 18), and Sara Heinämaa, "From Decisions to Passions: Merleau-Ponty's Interpretation of Husserl's Reduction," in *Merleau-Ponty's Reading of Husserl*, ed. Ted Toadvine (Boston: Kluwer Academic, 2002), on the role of passions in Merleau-Ponty's adaptation of phenomenological method.

16. See Salamon's "The Phenomenology of Rheumatology," a critique of gripping or grasping as a model for embodied intentionality in Merleau-Ponty's phenomenology, and its implications for the uses of Merleau-Ponty for a critical phenomenology of ability and disability.

17. This has methodological significance for Merleau-Ponty; it is why he claims the reduction cannot be completed, and why he insists that "Husserl's transcendental is not Kant's." Merleau-Ponty, *Phenomenology of Perception*, 14. See Heinämaa's reading of Merleau-Ponty's modification of the method of the reduction, "From Decisions to Passions."

18. Young, "Throwing Like a Girl" (1980), 36.

19. Maurice Merleau-Ponty, *The World of Perception*, trans. Oliver Davis (1948; New York: Routledge, 2009), 63.

20. Merleau-Ponty, *The World of Perception*, 63.

21. Maurice Merleau-Ponty, "An Unpublished Text by Maurice Merleau-Ponty: A Prospectus of His Work," trans. Arleen B. Dallery, in *The Primacy of Perception* (Evanston, Ill.: Northwestern University Press, 1964), 5.

22. See Lloyd's discussion of Hegel, Sartre, and Beauvoir: "'Transcendence,' in its origins, is a transcendence *of* the feminine" (*The Man of Reason*, 101); also Young, "'Throwing Like a Girl': Twenty Years Later"; Weiss, "The Normal, the Natural, and the Normative"; and Jennifer McWeeny, "Varieties of Consciousness under Oppression: False Consciousness, Bad Faith, Double Consciousness, and *Se faire objet*," in *Phenomenology and the Political*, ed. S. West Gurley and Geoff Pfeifer (New York: Rowman and Littlefield, 2016).

23. Simone de Beauvoir, *The Second Sex*, trans. Constance Borde and Sheila Malovany Chevallier (New York: Vintage, 2011), 17.

24. Frantz Fanon, *Black Skin, White Masks*, trans. Richard Philcox (1952; New York: Grove Press, 2008), 164, 105.

25. There is some dispute in Beauvoir scholarship about the extent to which she affirms the Sartrean view that transcendence and freedom must be achieved in an agonistic relation with immanence. See Lloyd, *The Man of Reason*; Iris Marion Young, "Humanism, Gynocentrism and Feminist Politics," *Women's Studies International Forum* 8, no. 3 (1985): 173–83; and Heinämaa, "What Is a Woman?" and "Simone de Beauvoir's Phenomenology of Sexual Difference."

26. Fanon, *Black Skin, White Masks*, 92.

27. Fanon, *Black Skin, White Masks*, 91.

28. Fanon, *Black Skin, White Masks*, 89. See McWeeny, "Varieties of Consciousness under Oppression"; Lisa Guenther, "Epistemic Injustice and Phenomenology," in *The Routledge Handbook of Epistemic Injustice*, ed. Ian James Kidd, José Medina, and Gaile Pohlhaus Jr.

(New York: Routledge, 2017), on the uses of phenomenology for social and political philosophy and their ontological and methodological implications.

29. Lewis Gordon, *Bad Faith and Antiblack Racism* (1995; New York: Humanity Books, 1999), 102.

30. Beauvoir, *The Second Sex*, 41.

31. This offers an important alternative to readings of Beauvoir as accepting the Sartrean struggle for transcendence (see Lloyd, *The Man of Reason*, and Young, "Humanism, Gynocentrism and Feminist Politics"). When Beauvoir's descriptions of feminine experience suggest that "women must struggle with their own bodies, if they are to achieve true selfhood and freedom" (Lloyd, *The Man of Reason*, 101), this may not be because Beauvoir accepts that women "can achieve transcendence only at the expense of alienation from their bodily being" (101). Rather, she recognizes that our oppression cuts us off not from pure transcendence but from ambiguous transcendence, obliging us to experience our bodies as burdens and to enjoy transcendence only at the expense of being at home in our own flesh. Note that in *The Ethics of Ambiguity*, it is the struggle "to assume our fundamental ambiguity" rather than the struggle to overcome immanence that is valorized as the site of existential freedom. See Simone de Beauvoir, *The Ethics of Ambiguity*, trans. Bernard Frechtman (1948; Secaucus, N.J.: Citadel Press, 1997).

32. Fanon, *Black Skin, White Masks*, 92, 119. Thus Fanon writes that the experience of oppression is an experience of *nonbeing*: "A feeling of inferiority? No, a feeling of not existing" (118). See Lewis Gordon, *What Fanon Said: A Philosophical Introduction to His Life and Thought* (New York: Fordham University Press, 2015), on Fanon's notion of nonbeing.

33. For phenomenological accounts of belonging to multiple worlds, see Maria Lugones, "Playfulness, 'World'-Traveling, and Loving Perception," *Hypatia* 2, no. 2 (1987): 3–19; Audre Lorde, *Sister Outsider* (1984; Berkeley, Calif.: Crossing Press, 2007).

# 28 Intercorporeality

Scott Marratto

The term *intercorporeality* translates the French neologism *l'intercorporéité*, which first appears in the writings of Maurice Merleau-Ponty in the 1950s. It exemplifies phenomenology's distinctive approach to the problem of intersubjectivity, an approach predicated on the insight that our relations with others are established first of all on the basis of our shared embodiment.[1] The phenomenological approach thus displaces the traditional Cartesian "problem of other minds." For the Cartesian, the existence of other minds is a problem insofar as Cartesian subjectivity is defined by a direct and transparent access to one's own mind; it would follow, ex hypothesi, that since I have no such access to the mind of another, I can never be sure that others are not robots or "zombies," and my discovery that others have minds must result from inference or analogical reasoning. According to the thesis of intercorporeality, on the other hand, we understand that others are subjects, that they have minds, on the basis of an "intentional encroachment" between our bodies.[2] As intercorporeal, my body responds directly to the immanent significance of the behaviors of others; my own gestures are prolongations, responses, or pretheoretical motor "interpretations" of those behaviors.[3]

There are at least two antecedents for this concept as it emerges in phenomenology. First, according to Husserl's account of intersubjectivity, there is a decisive moment of "passive synthesis" involved in our perception of others for which he uses the term *pairing* (*Paarung*).[4] Pairing happens when I perceive the behavior of another living body as reflective of my own body's motor capacities.[5] It thus facilitates what Husserl calls an "analogical transfer" of sense between my own body and that of the other person. We must note, though, that, as a form of *passive* synthesis, this transfer of sense is not an explicit cognitive operation; it is, rather, as Merleau-Ponty understands it, an echoing, in my own body, of motor intentions at play in the bodily behavior of the other.[6] The second antecedent is the psychologist Henri Wallon's concept of "syncretic sociability," or "transitivism," to which, in his 1950–51 Sorbonne lecture course, The Child's Relations with Others, Merleau-Ponty connects the Husserlian concept of pairing. According to Wallon's account of child development, there is a primary stage of indistinction in the child's sense of her own identity relative to others. This indistinction, or confusion, may be said to have been overcome developmentally insofar as the child eventually develops a sense of her own boundedness, but, ontologically, a certain porousness, or indeterminacy, of the lived-body continues to subtend the adult's developed capacities for intersubjective life, including sympathy, expression, eroticism, and language.[7] There is for each of us a captivating eloquence to the movements of others' bodies because, as Merleau-Ponty says, the perception of the other's behavior is such as to arouse in me "the preparation of a motor activity related to it."[8]

The constitutive porousness of the intercorporeal lived-body, indicated in the concepts of pairing and syncretic sociability, is particularly well-illustrated in Merleau-Ponty's rereading of Husserl's account of "double-touch," the experience of touching my left hand with my right. Merleau-Ponty's account of this experience differs significantly from that of Husserl.[9] Husserl notes a crucial phenomenological distinction between touching my own body and merely seeing it: my view of myself as a visible object is never so direct as my experience of myself as a tactile object, and my ability to recognize the specular image of my own body relies upon this immediate sense of my own body as, at once, touching and touched.[10] According to Husserl, my experience of the other, like my experience of my own visible body, is always indirect. In his own discussions of this phenomenon, however, Merleau-Ponty points to an element of *discontinuity* between the touching and the tactile body that one does not find in Husserl's account: "The right hand, as an object, is not the right hand that does the touching."[11] Thus, the distinction between the tactual body and the visible body, so central in Husserl's analysis of the constitution of the lived-body, is notably downplayed in Merleau-Ponty's account.[12] Rather than continuity, the body, according to Merleau-Ponty, is characterized by an "ambiguous organization" in which subjectivity and objectivity trade places, as it were, without ever quite coinciding.[13]

In the 1960 essay, "The Philosopher and His Shadow," Merleau-Ponty draws the conclusion that it is precisely this discontinuity between the body and itself that opens us to the experience of other selves. He writes, "My right hand was present at the advent of my left's active sense of touch. It is in no different fashion that the other's body becomes animate before me when I shake another man's hand or just look at him."[14] There is, according to Merleau-Ponty, a kind of spatially dispersed coexistence or "compresence" between my body as touching and my body as touched into which the body of the other inserts itself: "The other person appears though an extension of that compresence; he and I are like organs of one single intercorporeality."[15] Merleau-Ponty speaks of the way in which the hand of the other and my own hand "substitute" for each other, or the way our bodies "annex" one another. The concept of intercorporeality is thus deeply ambiguous: on the one hand, it suggests a *continuity* between myself and the other, an absence of definite boundaries, but this continuity is made possible only because of a sense of *discontinuity*, estrangement, anonymity, even dispossession, that prevents my body from ever being unambiguously my own. A sense of the anonymity of my own body is a condition of the possibility of experiencing another body as that of a *person*.

Though it affirms a certain anonymity of the body, and a confusion of self and other, intercorporeality entails neither that my experiences initially occur as the experiences of no one in particular,[16] nor that my own experience vouchsafes some direct access to another's field of lived experience.[17] Rather, it entails an understanding of the body as inscribed within a living nexus of significance in the context of which I am able to grasp, in my own body's capacities, the sense of the capacities and intentions evident in the behavior of others, and, further, that the dense materiality and opacity of my own body is an opening onto an anonymous life enabling me to experience, in my own sensation, a presentiment of the other's sentience. Rather than closing the gap between me and the other, intercorporeality opens the gap between me and myself such that I encounter a spectral otherness in the interpretive responsivity of my own body's behavior.

This metaphysical porousness and lability of the intercorporeal body is emphasized in recent phenomenological accounts of the subject's inscription in political contexts. Elizabeth Grosz, for example, has discussed the tension (or "contradiction") between the conception of the body as "the locus of lived experience" (thematized by classical phenomenology) and the body as "a surface of inscription" (thematized, for example, in Foucault's account of carceral power). According to Grosz, feminist theories of embodiment must account for the way in which the body as a surface of inscription gets taken up into the lived body such that my own body (as I live it) reflects the processes of its own social and discursive constitution.[18] This intertwining of the lived body and the socially mediated objective body, entailed by the thesis of intercorporeality, is exemplified in Iris Marion Young's famous account of the way in which the "I can" of the sensorimotor body, its powers of movement and behavior, reflect the gender norms of the cultural context within which the body is inscribed.[19] A similar insight is implicit in Frantz Fanon's concept of a "racial epidermal schema" that, in the context of racism in a colonial context, reshapes the black subject's experience of his or her own body and its possibilities.[20] Each of these accounts builds upon the concept of intercorporeality insofar as they show how the body is constituted, in part, through the sedimentation of its responses to the immanent significance of the behaviors of others. Through my own behavior, I take up into my own lived body the sense of the behavior of others toward me; we thus cannot rigidly distinguish a proprioceptive "body schema" from a socially constituted "body image."[21]

These elaborations of the Merleau-Pontian concept of intercorporeality into a distinctively political register entail a fundamental challenge to reductively naturalistic or biological accounts of the body or bodily differences (based, for example, on race, sexuality, sexual difference, disability). Judith Butler's account of sexual difference as constituted through performative acts is illustrative of this challenge. Butler's account of the performative constitution of sexual difference stresses the way in which the identities of bodies are enacted via iterations of ritualized conduct. On the one hand, according to this account, sexual difference is something we *do*, or enact, through the expressivity of our behavior; on the other hand, the iterative performances that constitute sexual differences at least partly precede our own initiative or reflective awareness—they are, so to speak, enacted *through* our behavior.[22] The body, understood as the bearer of performatively constituted identities, is necessarily an intercorporeal body, which means that its constitutive features cannot be understood as manifestations of an underlying biological nature or essence. This approach to thinking about sexuality and sexual difference on the basis of intercorporeality has also been fruitful for thinking about transgendered identities. Gayle Salamon, for example, has developed the Merleau-Pontian concepts of "body schema" and "sexual schema" to reflect the intercorporeal constitution of sexual difference.[23] In doing so she, like Butler, challenges the idea that the body is a fixed material substrate for socially constituted gender differences.

Finally, the notion of intercorporeality, as it is taken up by recent scholars, arguably entails a posthumanist conception of the body, one that challenges traditional distinctions between the organic and the technical. In *Phenomenology of Perception*, Merleau-Ponty famously suggested that the white cane of the blind person is not simply an intermediary between the perceiving body and the world, but comes to be included within the organization of the lived body itself. Grosz expands upon this idea when she speaks of "the human body's capacity to open itself up to prosthetic synthesis, to transform or rewrite its environment, to continually augment its powers and capacities through the incorporation into the body's own spaces and modalities of objects that, while external, are internalized, added to, supplementing and supplemented by the 'organic body.'"[24] Thus, we might even say that the notion of intercorporeality anticipates Donna Haraway's notion of the cyborg condition of the posthumanist body.

Though some of these developments may seem to challenge Merleau-Ponty's account of embodiment—insofar as he is accused of not having sufficiently accounted for differences in sex and sexuality, race, and class[25]—it must also be noted that his concept of intercorporeality anticipates these recent developments in theorizing the body insofar as it affirms, in an ontological register, the non-self-identity of the body, the porousness of its boundaries. The body, as Merleau-Ponty understands it, is constitutively inscribed in a history, a language, a culture, a material context. As intercorporeal, the body "cannot be compared to the physical object, but rather to the work of art."[26]

## Notes

1. See, for example, Maurice Merleau-Ponty, *Cartesian Meditations: An Introduction to Phenomenology*, trans. Dorion Cairns (The Hague: Martinus Nijhoff, 1960), esp. §§ 50–54.

2. Maurice Merleau-Ponty, *Signs*, trans. Richard McLeary (Evanston, Ill.: Northwestern University Press, 1964), 169. Merleau-Ponty takes the term from Husserl's "Intentionale überschreiten," which appears in the *Cartesian Meditations*.

3. Maurice Merleau-Ponty, *The Primacy of Perception*, trans. James Edie (Evanston, Ill.: Northwestern University Press, 1964), 118.

4. See *Cartesian Meditations*, §51.

5. For an excellent treatment of this concept and its import for phenomenology, see Peter Costello, *Layers in Husserl's Phenomenology: On Meaning and Intersubjectivity* (Toronto: University of Toronto Press, 2012).

6. It is useful to contrast this approach with so-called theory-of-mind accounts of intersubjectivity; see Dan Zahavi, "The Embodied Self-Awareness of the Infant: A Challenge to the Theory of Mind," in *The Structure and Development of Self-Consciousness*, ed. Dan Zahavi, T. Grunbaum, and Josef Parnas (Amsterdam: John Benjamins, 2004).

7. Merleau-Ponty, *Primacy of Perception*, 145–46.

8. Merleau-Ponty, *Primacy of Perception*, 146.

9. Husserl's account appears in *Ideas Pertaining to a Pure Phenomenology and to a Phenomenological Philosophy (Ideas II)*, trans. Richard Rojcewicz and André Schuwer (Dordrecht: Kluwer, 1989), §§ 36–37. Merleau-Ponty considers the phenomenon in several places, including *Phenomenology of Perception*, trans. Donald Landes (London: Routledge, 2012), and in *Signs*, 168.

10. "What I call the seen Body is not something seeing which is seen, the way my Body as touched body is something touching which is touched" (Husserl, *Ideas II*, 155).

11. Merleau-Ponty, *Phenomenology of Perception*, 94.

12. Merleau-Ponty, *Phenomenology of Perception*, 94.

13. Merleau-Ponty, *Phenomenology of Perception*, 95.

14. Merleau-Ponty, *Signs*, 168.

15. Merleau-Ponty, *Signs*, 168.

16. There have been some criticisms of the idea of intercorporeality along these lines. See, for example, Dan Zahavi, *Self-Awareness and Alterity: A Phenomenological Investigation* (Evanston, Ill.: Northwestern University Press, 1999). For criticism targeting the notion of "syncretic sociability," see Shaun Gallagher, "The Earliest Sense of Self and Others: Merleau-Ponty and Recent Developmental Studies," *Philosophical Psychology* 9, no. 2 (1996): 211–33. For a response to these criticisms, see Kym Maclaren, "Embodied Perceptions of Others as a Condition of Selfhood? Empirical and Phenomenological Considerations," *Journal of Consciousness Studies* 15, no. 8 (2008): 63–93.

17. For an example of this criticism of intercorporeality, see Jacques Derrida, *On Touching—Jean-Luc Nancy*, trans. Christine Irizarry (Stanford, Calif.: Stanford University Press, 2005), 190. For a response to this criticism, see my *The Intercorporeal Self: Merleau-Ponty on Subjectivity* (Albany: State University of New York Press, 2012), esp. 128–47.

18. Elizabeth Grosz, "Bodies and Knowledges: Feminism and the Crisis of Reason," in *Feminist Epistemologies*, ed. Linda Alcoff and Elizabeth Potter (London: Routledge, 1993), 187–216. See also Elizabeth Grosz, *Volatile Bodies: Toward a Corporeal Feminism* (Bloomington: Indiana University Press, 1994).

19. Iris Marion Young, *On Female Body Experience: "Throwing Like a Girl" and Other Essays* (Oxford: Oxford University Press, 2005), 27–45.

20. Frantz Fanon, *Black Skin, White Masks*, trans. Richard Philcox (New York: Grove Press, 2008), 90.

21. Shaun Gallagher, among others, has insisted on the distinction between these; see his "Body Schema and Intentionality," in *The Body and The Self*, ed. Jose Luis Bermudez, Anthony Marcel, and Naiomi Eilan (Boston: MIT Press, 1995). But Gail Weiss has argued against this position; invoking and extending Paul Schilder's account of the body image she insists instead that a layering of multiple, socially constituted "body images" is co-constitutive of the "body schema." See Gail Weiss, *Body Images: Embodiment as Intercorporeality* (New York: Routledge, 1999), esp. chapter 1.

22. Judith Butler, "Performative Acts and Gender Constitution: An Essay in Phenomenology and Feminist Theory," *Theatre Journal* 40, no. 4 (December 1988): 519–31.

23. Gayle Salamon, *Assuming a Body: Transgender and Rhetorics of Materiality* (New York: Columbia University Press, 2010).

24. Grosz, *Volatile Bodies*, 188.

25. A well-known example of this criticism is Luce Irigaray's reading of Merleau-Ponty's *Visible and the Invisible* in *An Ethics of Sexual Difference*, trans. Carolyn Burke and Gillian Gill (Ithaca, N.Y.: Cornell University Press, 1984), 151–84.

26. Merleau-Ponty, *Phenomenology of Perception*, 152.

# 29 The *Körper-Leib* Distinction

Jenny Slatman

## History, Semantics, and Translation

Most contemporary phenomenologists who work on the theme of the body or on embodiment draw on the distinction between *Körper* and *Leib*. From a phenomenological perspective, the two concepts refer to two different ways in which a person's body can appear (*erscheinen*). Because in phenomenology the "way of appearance" (*Erscheinungsweise*) is directly related to meaning or sense (*Sinn*), we can also say that the *Körper-Leib* distinction refers to the fact that the body can have different meanings. *Körper* refers to the body as an object, something to which physical qualities can be attributed. *Leib*, by contrast, implies the body as a subject, a zero point for perception and action. In this entry, I will first show why the articulation of this distinction in the beginning of the twentieth century has been so important for the development of phenomenology of the body. Subsequently, and seemingly paradoxically, I will explain why a careful interpretation of the phenomenon of *Leib* may lead to the obliteration of the distinction.

In contemporary German, both *Körper* and *Leib* are used to refer to the body, and in their everyday usage they are virtually interchangeable. It was observed, however, that in everyday language the usage of *Körper* is increasingly preferred, in particular because its connotation of being instrumental is more in line with the contemporary worldview according to which bodies can be manipulated, repaired, and used.[1] Still, everyday German preserves some interesting uses of the term *Leib*, such as in the distinction between *Unterleib* (lower part of the body) and *Obenkörper* (upper part of the body) and in the sayings *mit Leib und Seele* (passionately), *Leib und Leben darstellen* (taking high risks, perilous), and *auf den Leib geschnitten sein* (fitting like a glove).

In philosophy, the conceptual distinction between *Körper* and *Leib* has been developed notably in the beginning of the twentieth century by German philosophers such as Edmund Husserl (1859–1938), Max Scheler (1874–1928), and Helmuth Plessner (1892–1985). Husserl's interpretation is most well-known. The reason for this is that Husserl's analysis—his then still unpublished *Ideas II* in particular—has been invigorated by Merleau-Ponty (1908–1961), and it is exactly the work of this French philosopher that has been, and still is, of vast importance for contemporary studies on the body and embodiment in philosophy, anthropology, and sociology; in gender, queer and race studies; in disability studies; and even in the more practical field of health and nursing studies.

Before diving into the philosophical analysis of the *Körper-Leib* distinction, we first need to look briefly into the etymology and semantics of both German words. *Körper* stems from the Latin *corpus* and refers to bodies as physical entities, including celestial bodies, geometrical entities, and dead bodies, corpses. *Leib*, by contrast, is related to the verbs *leben* (to live) and *erleben* (to experience, to go through) and the adjectives *lebendig* (animated, lively) and *leibhaft* (in person, in the flesh). As such, *Leib* refers to the body as it is experienced or lived instead of the body as it can be measured or quantified. Unfortunately, the English language, like the French, has only one word to denote the physical existence of human beings: "body." To preserve the phenomenological nuance that comes with the *Körper-Leib* distinction, various translations have been proposed. The translator of Husserl's *Ideas II*, for example, translates *Körper* and *Leib* as "body" and "Body." To define *Leib*, Merleau-Ponty in *Phenomenology of Perception* uses the French terms *corps vécu* (lived body), *corps propre* (one's own body), and *corps sujet* (body as subject or subjective body).[2] Current English translations of the *Körper-Leib* distinction therefore include the following twin concepts: "physical/material body" versus "lived/animated body" or "objective body" versus "subjective body." As we will see, *Leib* is more a pre-intentional, pre-objective, or nonintentional object, or even a "non-thing,"[3] than an intentional object.

## The *Leib* as a Conditioned Condition

The *Körper-Leib* distinction comes to the fore for the first time in Husserl's analysis of the different ways in which transcendental consciousness gives meaning to what appears. In *Ideas II*, which was written in 1912 but first published posthumously in 1952, Husserl describes how the constitution of *Leib* (which belongs to animated animal [*Animalische*] nature) differs from the constitution of *Körper* (which belongs to material nature). It is clear here already that, according to Husserl, neither *Leib* nor *Körper* is given as such. They are both constituted by consciousness. Or, to put it differently, they involve two different ways in which the body appears to consciousness. The difference between the two becomes clear if we concentrate on the experience of one's own body. Husserl takes the example of one's hands touching one another to explain the difference. If one touches one's left hand with one's right hand, the left hand can be experienced in two different ways. First, it can be experienced as a thing with a certain extension and with certain properties. In this case, the left hand is the "physical thing left hand," or a *Körper*. It is the intentional correlate of the right hand's touching. But second, the left hand is also experienced as the localization of sensations (*Empfindungen*). The moment of touching one's left hand is accompanied by a series of touch sensations (*Tastempfindungen*) in this hand, and since these sensations do not constitute physical properties such as smoothness or roughness, they do not constitute the physical thing "left hand." Rather, they constitute the experience that I feel in my left hand, that it is touched. This experience, which affirms the "me-ness" of one's body (I feel at once that the touched body is undeniably mine), constitutes the *Leib*.

The *Leib* is thus constituted through sensations that are localized in the organ of perception; i.e., touch sensations are localized in the touching "organ." Husserl coins the term *Empfindnisse* ("sensings") to indicate these localized sensations. Other examples of "sensings" include sensations of warmth and cold, proprioceptive and kinesthetic sensations, and pain. Visual sensations, by contrast, are not localized in the organ of perception, i.e., in the eye. Nonlocalized sensations, such as those provided by visual perception, constitute the body as extended thing, or *Körper*. As is well-known, the idea of adumbrations (*Abschattungen*) lies at the heart of the phenomenological theory of appearance. Phenomenal reality appears as a reality with real properties. It is not given at once; rather, it is always given through manifold adumbrations and sensuous schemes. This means that one and the same thing is presented in different horizons and perspectives, and that no single perspective can exhaust the possibilities of appearing. If we perceive a table, for example, there is always one of its sides that we cannot actually perceive, and yet we still perceive one and the same table. The perceived table is never fully present to consciousness: its rear sides are only co-present (or "appresent"). The same holds for one's hand. If one's left hand appears as the thing "left hand," it appears through the constantly changing, manifold adumbrations. The "sensings" (*Empfindnisse*) of one's left hand, however, are, according to Husserl, not given through adumbrations or schematization. One's body as one's own, as *Leib*, is given without any perspective and is thus entirely present. Consequently, Husserl argues that the *Leib* comprises the "zero point" of all orientations, its spatiality being characterized as an "absolute here."

Here we see that Husserl's description of *Leib* involves some ambiguity. Whereas he understands *Leib* as something constituted by transcendental consciousness, it simultaneously constitutes a "zero point." Elsewhere he writes that the *Leib* is, "in the first place, the medium of all perception; it is the organ of perception [*Wahrnemungsorgan*] and is necessarily involved in all perception."[4] Here we thus see that *Leib*, next to being constituted, should be understood as a condition of possibility for the constitution of the spatiotemporal world. This "circle of constitution," which remained tacit in Husserl's work, has been explicitly addressed by Merleau-Ponty. Taking seriously the double bind between transcendental and worldly experience, he conceptualized subjectivity as embodied. The *Leib* thus takes the place of the transcendental subject, and the "I think" is substituted by the "I can." But since the *Leib* is constituted by means of sensations, it is not a pure transcendental condition. The circle of constitution—the *Leib* disclosing the world, while it is constituted by worldly sensations—marks the limits of transcendental reasoning indeed.

## From the *Körper-Leib* Distinction to Phenomenological Materialism

In *Phenomenology of Perception*, Merleau-Ponty described this ambiguous structure of the lived body as the condition for world disclosure by the concept of being in/to the world (*être au monde*): the body is part of the world while, simultaneously, being directed and related to the world. In his later work, *The Visible and the Invisible*, he uses the term "flesh" (*chair*) to indicate that the body for which the world appears is made of the same worldly fabric.[5] Here we see that if we take seriously the circle of constitution that is at stake in the *Leib* constitution, a strict distinction between *Körper* and *Leib* is not really tenable. The specific aspect of the *Leib* is first of all that it concerns the body that experiences itself as undeniably "here" and "mine" (so not as a thing). At the same time, however, this experience is never fully separate from the body's being a thing, its *Körperlichkeit*. *Leib* is thus not a sensing entity only, but a sensing entity that is embodied (*verkörpert*). As I have elsewhere explained in great detail, it is due to the embodiment or materialization of the *Leib* that embodied self-experiences—the embodied experience of "me-ness"—always go together with experiences of strangeness or otherness.[6]

Even though *Leib* should rather be understood as *Leibkörper* instead of some entity opposed to *Körper*, it is still helpful to preserve the *Körper-Leib* distinction as an analytic phenomenological tool. Indeed the distinction can serve to analyze the different dimensions and layers of embodiment in various contexts.[7] It is remarkable, however, that phenomenological studies that aim at criticizing the instrumental and objectified view of the body, such as in contemporary medicine, tend to use the *Körper-Leib* distinction as a "lived body" versus "objective body" contrast.[8] To employ the *Körper-Leib* distinction in such a way is to risk reestablishing dualism. Also, as the contemporary French philosopher Jean-Luc Nancy claims, phenomenological readings of the example of the two touching hands, which according to Husserl produces the *Leib* experience, run the risk of returning to a "primary interiority."[9] Indeed, if the "sensings" produced by touch sensations are merely considered as a zero point for world disclosure, one ignores that one needs to be in "exteriority," to be "outside" oneself, in order to touch oneself.

In his criticism of phenomenology Nancy mainly targets the transcendental aspirations still palpable in most phenomenological work, including that of Merleau-Ponty. Whereas phenomenology considers giving meaning or sense (*Sinngebung*) as a process that stems from individual sense-giving subjects, individual beings-in-the world, Nancy claims that the origin or beginning of sense-making consists of the worldly, nontranscendental fact of bodies, human and nonhuman ones, that coexist next to one another. Human existence is, according to him, conditioned by a fundamental *être-avec* (being-with) or *être-ensemble* (being-together). And this "being-with" involves the being with bodies, all kinds of bodies, whether they be inanimate, animate, sentient, speaking, thinking, having weight, and so on.[10] What all bodies have in common is that they are material and are extended: they occupy a certain place, which at that very moment cannot be occupied by another body. Bodies that are with one another therefore exist in the mode of what Descartes had called *partes extra partes*. They are next to one another, outside one another. As such they do not fuse or coincide but remain different.

Since Nancy considers the ontological "being-with" in terms of *partes extra partes*, his ontology entails a materialist view. But it is crucial to underline that he distances himself from mainstream materialism. For him, matter is not the same as substance or mass. Matter as substance or mass involves that which is self-containing and coinciding with itself. By contrast, Nancy writes, "'Matter' is not above all an immanent density that is absolutely closed in itself. On the contrary, it is first the very difference through which something is possible, as thing and as some."[11] In line with this, Nancy differentiates between a body belonging to a crowd (*foule*) and a body belonging to a mass, immediately adding that a body as mass is not worth the name "body."[12] The body as mass is the body of a mass grave; it is the body as cadaver; it is the body that does not sense anymore—the body as substance or self-coinciding mass. It is clear, then, that Nancy, like all phenomenologists, rejects the idea of the body as substance, yet at the same he claims that the body is material. The body is matter, but not in the sense of substance. It is matter in the sense of noncoincidence.

We could say that the plurality of material bodies that differ from each other forms the condition of possibility of a singular being in the world, even though Nancy would not use the term "condition of possibility," since he wants to employ only an "empirical logic, without transcendental reason."[13] While its incongruity had already surfaced in Husserl's analysis of the *Leib* and Merleau-Ponty's elaboration of the "circle of constitution," Nancy finally cancels transcendental reasoning altogether. In order to understand the singularity of sensing subjects, we should take seriously the materiality of given bodies. It is difference (or *différance*) that "constitutes" individual existence. Difference and noncoincidence are given with the *extra* of the *partes extra partes*. It is also through the *extra*, the being distinct of bodies, that world disclosure, and thus sense-making, takes place. For Nancy, world-disclosure is like a creation ex nihilo; there is no fundament for this creation other than the plurality of bodies that differ from each other. Therefore he claims, "The world no longer has a sense, but it *is* sense."[14] The world is sense for us, not because we are intentionally related to it but because we, embodied beings, are part of a plurality of bodies. As a self-declared critic of phenomenology, Nancy does away with the *Körper-Leib* distinction together with transcendental reasoning.

I believe, however, that Nancy's approach remains phenomenological since his descriptions of embodiment do justice to the different ways in which bodies exist. The only form of appearance that he does not acknowledge is the body as zero point for world disclosure. All bodies appear as material and extended. His thought, therefore, paves the way for a new position in phenomenology, which I call "phenomenological materialism."[15] It is because of his materialist focus that Nancy can do away with mainstream phenomenology's "neutral" view on the body. A material body is always marked, classed and, in our time of global markets, often "marketed": "a Bengali body bent over a car in Tokyo, a Turkish body in a Berlin trench, a black body loaded down with white packages in Suresnes of San Francisco."[16] Nancy's materialism thus allows for social-constructivist-(and Marxist-)oriented analyses of embodiment. But unlike social-constructivism, his materialism always remains attached to *experience*.

Material bodies touch one another. Being a (human) body therefore means being touched (*être touché*). In his autobiographical text *The Intruder*, Nancy nicely describes the different ways in which he experiences his "own" material body during the course of a chronic disease (heart failure) and during the recovery period after his heart transplant. This text shows the different ways in which he was touched by "strangeness." Of course, there is the strangeness that comes with the strange donor heart. But there is also the strangeness of the diseased heart—an organ that does not function anymore and that one might want to spit out. After the transplant, self-estrangement had to be induced by immunosuppressant drugs. Ironically, in Nancy's case, this suppression of his immune system led to the development of a cancerous tumor—yet another stranger or intruder. Even though the case of a heart transplant is an extreme one, Nancy uses it only to make clear that our material existence always comes together with various dimensions of strangeness and estrangement, even when we are completely healthy: "The intruder is nothing but myself and man himself."[17] Whereas phenomenology that maintains the *Körper-Leib* distinction prioritizes experiences of "ownness," phenomenological materialism enables a focus on strangeness and otherness. As such, it is in a better position to analyze and describe what happens when bodies are *touched by* joy or pain, by happiness or misery, by prosperity or misfortune.

## Notes

1. Thomas Fuchs, "Körper haben oder Leib sein," *Scheidewege: Jahresschrift für skeptisches Denken* 41 (2011): 122–37.

2. Maurice Merleau-Ponty, *Phenomenology of Perception* (1945), trans. C. Smith (London: Routledge, 1962).

3. Bernhard Waldenfels, "Körper-Leib," in *Esprit/Geist: 100 Schlüsselbegriffe für Deutsche und Franzosen*, ed. J. Leenhardt and R. Picht (Munich: Piper, 1989), 342–45.

4. Edmund Husserl, *Ideas Pertaining to a Pure Phenomenology and to a Phenomenological Philosophy, Second Book* (1952), trans. R. Rojcewicz and A. Schuwer (Dordrecht: Kluwer Academic, 1989), § 18.

5. Maurice Merleau-Ponty, *The Visible and the Invisible*, trans. A. Lingis (Evanston, Ill.: Northwestern University Press, 1964); see Donald Landes's entry on the flesh in this volume.

6. Jenny Slatman, *Our Strange Body: Philosophical Reflections on Identity and Medical Interventions* (Amsterdam: Amsterdam University Press, 2014).

7. Jenny Slatman, "Multiple Dimensions of Embodiment in Medical Practices," *Medicine, Healthcare and Philosophy* 17, no. 4 (2014): 549–57.

8. For example, Jennifer Bullington, *The Expression of the Psychosomatic Body from a Phenomenological Perspective* (Berlin: Springer, 2013).

9. Jean-Luc Nancy, *Corpus*, trans. R. A. Rand (New York: Fordham University Press, 2008), 128.

10. Jean-Luc Nancy, *Being Singular Plural*, trans. Robert D. Richardson and Anne E. O'Byrne (Stanford, Calif.: Stanford University Press, 2000).

11. Jean-Luc Nancy, *The Sense of the World*, trans. J. S. Librett (Minneapolis: University of Minnesota Press, 1993), 57.

12. Nancy, *Corpus*, 124.

13. Nancy, *Corpus*, 53.

14. Nancy, *The Sense of the World*, 8.

15. Jenny Slatman, "Is It Possible to 'Incorporate' a Scar? Revisiting a Basic Concept in Phenomenology," *Human Studies* 39, no. 3 (2016): 347–63.

16. Nancy, *Corpus*, 109–11.

17. Nancy, *Corpus*, 170.

# 30 The Look

William McBride

In the literature of phenomenology, the look, or the gaze (*le regard*, *der Blick*), is associated above all with Sartre's early philosophy. Of the four main parts of his *Being and Nothingness*, the first two deal, respectively, with his two familiar "regions of being," being-in-itself and being-for-itself, while the third focuses on a region that he considers incapable of being explained simply as some combination of the first two, namely, "being-for-others" (or "-for-another," the French pronoun *autrui* referring indefinitely to one or many).[1] The phenomenon of otherness, that is, *human* otherness, appears to be a fundamental ontological fact, but its reality calls for some sort of epistemological justification, at least for any philosopher—and there have been many such—who is tempted by solipsism, the view that I am, in some sense or other, ultimately alone in the world.

This temptation can be traced especially to Descartes and his *cogito*, a concept with which Sartre was unwilling to break at least in his early years, and one which continued to influence the Western philosophical mainstream well into the twentieth century, certainly including the philosophy of Edmund Husserl. (Descartes famously asked, for instance, how I could be sure that those human-like figures passing by outside my window are not mere automata.) Analytically oriented British philosophers who were Husserl's contemporaries were also haunted, in their own ways, by the "problem of other minds." Husserl attempted, notably toward the end of his *Cartesian Meditations*, to escape the charge of solipsism by exploring the experience of "the Other" and arriving at what he called an "intermonadic community." But Sartre contended that he had not succeeded in this endeavor and attributed a similar failure to Heidegger.

Sartre's solution through "the look," a solution which, he insists, is not to be thought of as a "proof," reflects his less intellectualist, more corporeal rendering of phenomenology. It begins with a reference to the experience of shame and is obviously influenced, as Sartre acknowledges at one point, by the moment in the biblical story of Adam and

Eve at which, having violated God's prohibition against eating of the fruit of the tree of the knowledge of good and evil, they notice for the first time that they are naked, and they feel ashamed. Shame is, then, "the original fall"; it is a paradigmatic response (though obviously not the only one possible—Sartre proposes arrogance as the alternative, opposite reaction) to the experience of being looked at by the Other, or Others. Sartre well illustrates it with the example of someone trying to ascertain what is taking place on the other side of a door, through the keyhole of which he is attempting to spy; then he hears, or thinks that he hears, footsteps further down the corridor in which he is standing, and he fears being discovered as a *voyeur*, being looked at. What is essential to the description here is not whether or not there really is someone coming down the corridor; rather, it is the awareness reawakened by this experience that we live in a world inhabited by Others, whose looks at us are ultimately omnipresent, inescapable, and unpredictable. The Scottish poet Robert Burns was right: I cannot see myself as others see me. And so the look constitutes my fundamental alienation and objectification, endowing me with a "nature" and exposing me to danger. As Sartre had already insisted in his earlier essay, *The Transcendence of the Ego*, the I, or what he came to call "being-for-itself," is nothing substantial in itself, but the "me" is a construct, endowed by others (or by me, in "the story I tell myself") with qualities as an object.[2] His exploration of the look in *Being and Nothingness* provides a more concrete, less abstract basis for understanding this idea.

A few marginal notes may be in order at this point. First, Western thought in general has tended to emphasize vision over the other senses. Consider Plato's myth of the cave and his comparison of the sun, which was for him the ultimate physical reality, with the Form of the Good, the highest Form; or consider the Christian metaphor of the All-Seeing Eye of God, which became a major symbol of the Masonic order. Sartre suffered from astigmatism in one eye beginning at a very early age, and eventually, near the end of his life, he became functionally blind, so that the phenomenon of seeing is likely always to have played an important role at least on the periphery of his consciousness. He enjoyed looking down from his room(s) at the city of Paris below, and his philosophy, arguably, sometimes falls into the "overview" mode of thinking that his longtime colleague Maurice Merleau-Ponty disparagingly called "la pensée de survol."

In any case, with his analysis of the look Sartre can be said to have taken an important step away from the classic Husserlian notion of intentionality and in the direction of lived experience. This analysis, in fact, makes more common cause with Hegel's approach to the Other, most notably in his "lordship and bondage" account of the struggle for recognition in the *Phenomenology of Spirit*, than with Husserl's approach, with the crucial qualification that Sartre emphatically rejects Hegel's idealism and ultimate reconciliation of conflicts at the stage of Absolute Knowledge. For Sartre, there exists an unsurpassable multiplicity of Others, which, as he says at the end of this long analysis, may appear as a synthesis, but only as a detotalized one. At the same time, Sartre's insistence on the centrality of the phenomenon of the look (which, he insists, does not literally reside in the eyes) helps him to reinforce several other important themes in his "phenomenological ontology" (as the subtitle of *Being and Nothingness* calls it): freedom (in the look, he says, I experience the infinite freedom of the Other), situation (the Other's look situates me both spatially and temporally), commitment (I exist as *engagé*), and consequently "historization" (as an event, the look is "a primary and perpetual fact"). There is an evident dark side in all of these themes. As object of the Other's freedom, Sartre says, I am enslaved and in danger. By situating me, the look defines me spatially and temporally. As committed, I appear limited and as having a certain nature rather than as pure freedom. And I cannot escape the *fact* of my position in history, much as I might wish to do so.

Among Sartre's contemporaries, the individual for whom the concept of the look was perhaps most important was Jacques Lacan. He acknowledged his debt to Sartre in this respect, agreeing particularly with Sartre's extension of the meaning of the gaze beyond the mere physical act of looking, but he shared neither the early Sartre's strong phenomenological orientation nor his ontology; Lacan's own field of interest and practice was psychoanalysis, and the single greatest influence on him was Freud. A well-known figure from the next generation of French thinkers, Michel Foucault, also made use of the idea of the look, in yet another context: that of surveillance. His work on the origins of the modern prison (and of modern disciplinary practices more generally), *Surveiller et punir*, makes good use of Jeremy Bentham's invention, the panopticon, in which prison corridors radiate out from a central tower where the guards sit and are able to look almost instantaneously at the activities of all the inmates, as a central trope. The etymology of Bentham's neologism *panopticon* points to the universalization of the look, or the gaze, in the prison setting—a concrete, historical realization of the enslavement that Sartre's analysis shows the phenomenon of the look to represent generally.

In film criticism, the gaze—as in "the male gaze" and "the female gaze"—has become a key concept. Its original use in this context is usually attributed to Laura Mulvey, who employed the notion of the male gaze primarily as a way of critiquing the objectification of women that occurs in so many of the film industry's products. The ambivalence of the meaning of the female gaze, on the other hand, has led some feminist film critics to eschew it.

This gender reference returns us to the field of philosophy, in which a number of feminist philosophers have referred to the (male) look as the principal vehicle to support male dominance and the subordination of women. One excellent example of this is Julien Murphy's essay "The Look in Sartre and Rich";[3] the late Adrienne Rich, the poet, was deeply influenced by the phenomenology of the look. In her early work, as Murphy shows, Rich accepted the notion of the look as oppressive and developed it especially with reference to women, but her later poetry makes more positive use of the look in the form of liberatory "feminist vision." Another philosopher in the phenomenological tradition who analyzed this phenomenon with great skill was the late Sandra Bartky, particularly in her work *Femininity and Domination*.[4] (It is perhaps worth noting that Bartky was strongly influenced not only by Sartre and by Simone de Beauvoir but also by the classical study of empathy undertaken by Husserl's student Edith Stein.)[5] The look, in this context, is the means by which the objectification of women is reinforced—very much in keeping with the spirit of Sartre's analysis of what he calls the "second attitude towards others," under which he includes indifference, desire, hate, and sadism. The male sexist aspires, to follow the Sartrean analysis along these lines, to capture the Other's (e.g., this woman's) freedom. But by reducing her to an object, a thing, he has failed totally in that aspiration: he is left with looking at the Other's eyes, nothing more.

Probably the most dramatic moment in this part of Sartre's account comes in an exceptionally long citation that he makes of a text from William Faulkner's novel *Light in August*. A mob of southern whites has castrated their black victim, Christmas, about whom Faulkner writes, "For a long moment he looked up at them with peaceful and unfathomable and unbearable eyes."[6] Even in this moment of extreme sadistic victimization, the Other's freedom, as expressed through his look, has escaped capture.

In fact, literature on race has also made much use of the notion. Ralph Ellison's *Invisible Man* explores the ways in which blacks in America are at once seen and disregarded. Frantz Fanon, to whose book *The Wretched of the Earth* Sartre wrote a famous preface, describes in another book (*Black Skin, White Masks*) his own experience of being seen in a train by a little boy, who says to his mother, "Look! A Negro!," and indicates that he is frightened. These treatments are deftly explored by Lewis Gordon, a Sartre and Fanon scholar, in his *Bad Faith and Antiblack Racism*.[7]

The entire part of *Being and Nothingness*, the account of "being-for-others," in which the discussion of the look occurs is an extremely important breakthrough in the evolution of phenomenology. It is a breakthrough shared in different ways by Sartre's colleagues Merleau-Ponty and Beauvoir, whereby the centrality of the corporeal, of the body, in the real world came to be fully acknowledged and opened to rigorous, systematic description. In *The Phenomenology of Perception*, Merleau-Ponty showed a better sense than Sartre of the ambiguities and paradoxes involved in looking at consciousness from the outside. Beauvoir, so influential on later feminist philosophers, made extensive use of the notion of the look in her analyses in *The Second Sex* of girls' and women's self-perceptions in response to the prevalence of the male gaze. Many years after the publication of these three seminal works within a few years of one another, Sartre, in a dialogue with interlocutors in connection with the Library of Living Philosopher volume on him, recalled his initial belief that Husserl's philosophy was a realism, an antidote to the idealism that still dominated French academic philosophy during Sartre's student years and immediately thereafter. But in fact it was Sartre and some of his contemporaries who brought about the redirection of phenomenology that endowed it with an affinity for the concrete that had previously been lacking, and Sartre's analysis of the look played a key role in this achievement.

It strikes me, somewhat as an afterthought but I think an important one, that the phenomenon of the look has become far more encompassing in our world than it was in Sartre's. The keyhole example, or even another one that he offers, in *Being and Nothingness*, of soldiers fearing detection by unseen enemy forces possibly located on a distant hill, is relatively pedestrian and old-fashioned when compared with the electronic surveillance devices that (shades of Foucault!) gaze upon so many human beings today, especially in urban areas, during so much of their daily lives—or the drones that monitor suspected "terrorists" in even the most remote areas of, for example, the Hindu-Kush Mountains. Shame is a relatively paltry emotion in comparison with the stark complementary terror that these automata (shades of Descartes!) inspire in their "intended" objects, in situations in which the very idea of intentionality has been virtually emptied of human content. We may well ask whether the meaning of the look requires serious revision in light of this increasingly common lived experience. Indeed, we may well ask whether, in this context, the very meaning of being human may require serious revision.

## Notes

1. See Kris Sealey's entry on being-in-itself, being-for-itself, and being-for-others.

2. Jean-Paul. Sartre, *The Transcendence of the Ego*, trans. F. Williams and R. Kirkpatrick (New York: Noonday Press, 1965).

3. Julien Murphy, "The Look in Sartre and Rich," in *The Thinking Muse.*, ed. J. Allen and I. M. Young (Bloomington: Indiana University Press, 1989).

4. Sandra Bartky, *Femininity and Domination: Studies in the Phenomenology of Oppression* (New York: Routledge, 1990).

5. Edith Stein, *On the Problem of Empathy*, trans. W. Stein (Washington, D.C.: ICS, 1989).

6. Jean-Paul Sartre, *Being and Nothingness*, trans. H. Barnes (New York: Washington Square Press, 1984), 526.

7. Lewis Gordon, *Bad Faith and Antiblack Racism* (Atlantic Highlands, N.J.: Humanities Press, 1995).

# 31 Mestiza Consciousness

Elena Ruíz

Gloria Anzaldúa's work is generative of multiple points of resistance to the complex legacy of colonial domination in women of color's lives. One of those points is her ontoepistemological concept known as *mestiza consciousness*, which she uses to "stretch the psyche horizontally and vertically" in order to accommodate the disjunctive phenomenological experiences of multicultural, borderland identities of women of color.[1] The concept develops significantly throughout her work and emerges as the term *conocimiento* in her post-*Borderlands* writings. It is related to her early transformative concepts of *la facultad, mental nepantilism, the Coatlicue state, Coyolaxauhqui imperative*, and later notions of embodied consciousness as spiritual activism. This entry will trace the development of the concept in Anzaldúa's writings and situate it as an example of phenomenological approaches to women of color feminisms and liberation epistemologies.

## Early Formulation: *Borderlands/La Frontera*

Anzaldúa's early writings center on her landmark publication, *Borderlands/La Frontera*, where the concept of mestiza consciousness is introduced. There, Anzaldúa gives a phenomenological description of life at the borderlands[2] for mestizxs (mixed-raced peoples descendant from imperial settler Iberians and American Indians). On her account, mestiza existence is permeated with internal strife, ambiguity, and contradiction that comes from being simultaneously positioned in many cultural contexts (such as the Indigenous, mestizx, Anglo) due to European colonization.[3] The strife is twofold. First, these contexts are often epistemically divergent, providing different social, metaphysical, and ontological interpretations of reality (with Western contexts dominating), which pull one in different hermeneutic directions on a daily basis. This pulling punctures the everyday flow of life and can be experienced as a clash, "un choque," that comes from having "two races in our psyche: the conquerors and the conquered," and additionally from having to navigate oppressive *internal* cultural norms like sexist racism in mestizx culture.[4] This can be debilitating for personal identity, especially if the norms and interpretive resources in the dominant culture do not accommodate flux and contradictory experiences.

According to Anzaldúa, living between and "straddling" different cultures is mentally and spiritually exhausting, since one is constantly navigating across cultures (the horizontal stretch) and within each one (the vertical stretch) in complex, often invisible ways (especially if one is marginalized, or "pushed out of the tribe for being different"). Being "in a constant state of mental *nepantilism*, an Aztec word meaning "torn between ways,"[5] la mestiza constantly "undergoes a struggle of flesh, a struggle of borders, an inner war" that is constitutive of a liminal, interstitial, borderland state of being—but in a potentially fragmented way that all too often results in existential paralysis. In a famous quote, Anzaldúa explains, "Alienated from her mother culture, 'alien' in the dominant culture, the woman of color does not feel safe within the inner life of her Self. Petrified, she can't respond, her face caught between *los intersticios,* the spaces between the different worlds she inhabits."[6] The result is often a negative self-interpretation, a devaluation of Indigenous and nonwhite culture, and a broader "tradition of silence" that harms intercultural (and especially queer intercultural) women of color in deep, long-lasting ways.

Anzaldúa's response is not to identify with either side of a cultural binary (Western/non-Western, Anglo/Mexican) historically responsible for mestizx identity but to sublate both terms and create a third option—a "New Mestiza" identity that is neither fully white nor Indigenous but breaks down existing paradigms to be able to acknowledge *all aspects* of Borderland experience. Hermeneutically, this will entail more than a creative redeployment of the existing interpretive resources in culture because the ontological elements being integrated into phenomenological experience are not *disclosable* in the dominant culture to begin with: "The new paradigm must come form outside as well as within the system."[7] Creative acts—art, poetry, rumor, myth, fictive stances and comportments drawn from a rehistoricized Mesoamerican pantheon—are thus all tools, self-made threads, if you will, the new mestiza can use for reincorporating corporeal intuitions and subaltern knowledges back into the fabric of lived experience. The goal is not an integrated Self without contradiction or ambiguity, but a more holistic perspective on existence that accommodates what imperial cultures historically use against colonized, marginalized peoples and women of color in particular. "By creating *a new mythos*—that is, a change in the way we perceive reality . . . *la mestiza* creates *a new consciousness.*"[8] Creating a new consciousness is not the same as establishing a new common ground through feminist consciousness raising or the self-insights Marxist ideological veil-lifting brings. There is no self-evident reality beneath the veil of ideology or universal patriarchy—no precolonial "home" to go to; for colonized peoples between cultures, the transformation requires both a prior transformation of the available resources of expression and the ability to be in between spaces that tolerate ambiguity and contradiction.

According to Anzaldúa, the first step in this process is "to take inventory" of the way we usually perceive the world and ourselves. Because the dominant way to perceive reality is structured through white, Anglo-European culture, language, and conceptual orthodoxies, the first step of mestiza consciousness is to dislodge the epistemic imperialism that licenses those ways of knowing as the only (or right) way to apprehend truth. At the heart of Western logical systems, she argues, is a "despotic duality" of Manichaean dualisms and binary logic. For Anzaldúa, a primary source of oppression lies in Occidental dualistic thinking, especially hierarchical binaries introduced by Spanish culture that forcefully eclipsed older, Mesoamerican conceptions of complementary dualisms and nonexclusionary binaries (particularly around those governing gender fluidity and Native American third sexes). On her account, "the work of *mestiza* consciousness is to break down the subject-object duality that keeps her a prisoner and to show in the flesh and through the images in her work how duality is transcended."[9] It is important to emphasize that Anzaldúa sees this new consciousness as a transformative, liberational tool that is hermeneutically radical yet also not created ex nihilo. It draws on corporeal intuitions and preexisting interpretive resources (unacknowledged by white, Anglo-dominant culture) that are able to gain articulation in "the images in her work," which in turn guide her back to those intuitions by affirming them. One of these key resources is what she calls *la facultad*. It is an intuitive form of corporeal knowledge that resembles a prereflective hermeneutics of suspicion, yet has epistemic import in the social articulation of experience. She writes, "La facultad is the capacity to see in surface phenomena the meaning of deeper realities, to see the deep structure below the surface. It is an instant 'sensing,' a quick perception arrived without conscious reasoning. It is an acute awareness mediated by the part of the psyche that des not speak, that communicates in images and symbols which are the faces of feelings. . . . The one possessing this sensitivity is excruciatingly alive to the world."[10] This intuitive reasoning allows one to acknowledge corporeal truths that run contrary to dominant interpretations of experience and official logics. To help loosen the grip of those logics, mestiza consciousness is built to question not just imperial logic but any form of "cultural tyranny" that impinges on individuals' ability to affirm all aspects of their identity. This is particularly important for Anzaldúa as a queer dark-skinned Chicana who lives with a disability on the Anglo side of the U.S.-Mexico border yet is culturally and linguistically marginalized on that side in multiple ways. Given these realities, in the early formulation of mestiza consciousness Anzaldúa has two primary foci: (1) the emphasis on what she calls "divergent" (epistemically plural) thinking versus "convergent"(dualistic/accepting cultural tyranny) thinking and (2) the need to "develop tolerance for contradiction and ambiguity" that runs contrary to the dominant, dualistic tradition rooted in Aristotelian logic and Greco-Roman metaphysical traditions.[11]

## Late Formulation: The Path to *Conocimiento*

In the later, post-*Borderlands* formulation of mestiza consciousness the term *conocimiento* takes precedence over *consciousness* while keeping key features of the new mestiza identity. In her posthumously published work, *Light in the Dark/Luz en lo Oscuro* (2015) Anzaldúa gives far more detailed accounts of what "instinctual knowledge and other alternative ways of knowing that fuel transformation" look like.[12] She retains a commitment to personal transformation but extends it more clearly to collective and political transformation and activism. The term *integration* is also pluralized to go beyond cultural integration to the broader role nature, and natural and religious symbolism, play in holistic, spiritual, and ethical life.[13] Thus the major shift is a metaphysical emphasis on the role of nature, worldly experience, and "the conditions of life" that help generate the catalyst for transformation to mestiza consciousness. Just seeing that psychic unrest and rigid dualisms are toxic for self-understanding is not enough. While this insight is important—she notes that "nothing happens in the 'real' world unless it first happens in the images in our heads"[14]—breaking through, making the actual "shift" in consciousness is paramount. Given this new emphasis, she outlines seven important steps on "the journey" or "path of *conocimiento*," which she defines as an "intuitive knowing" and "spiritual inquiry" that "questions conventional knowledge's current categories, classifications, and contents," especially through "creative acts."[15]

The first step is surviving fear. Like coping with the aftershocks of an earthquake,[16] it requires working through the natural fear that comes with catastrophes of meaning, natural disasters, and traumatic experience. The second stage is *nepantla,* where one is thrown after being "jerked from the familiar and safe terrain" by the earthquake—i.e., the clashing of cultures. It's a transitional space that is disorienting (because you're "living between stories") yet decenters the Self enough to allow a nondominant logical space in which to gain perspective, to "explore how some of your/other's constructions violate other people's ways of knowing and living."[17] Doing so is often a catalytic for depression, which is the third stage, "the Coatlicue depths of despair, self-loathing and hopelessness. Your refusal to move paralyses you, making you dysfunctional for weeks. In the fourth space, a call to action pulls you out of your depression."[18] The fifth stage is an Apollonian recentering of order and a renewed thirst for self-understanding. In it, one looks to traditional and nontraditional sources of knowledge to "reenvision the map of the known world, creating a new description of reality and scripting a new story."[19] The sixth space is engaged theory, where one applies the insights of the last stage to see if they are *livable*. Finally, in the seventh stage, the "critical turning point for transformation," one is able to "shift realities" and "develop an ethical, compassionate strategy with which to negotiate conflict and difference within self and between others" so that the end result is an integrated self that can form "holistic alliances," bridges between peoples, cultures, and oneself.[20] These "seven planes of reality" are not linear but representative of the kinds of spaces one travels through to enact "spiritual activism," a resistant epistemology that focuses on a "connectionist mode of thinking" that is nonassociative (because preestablished Occidental logical associations lead one *away* from the holistic connections necessary for well-being). Instead, it is based on a transformed receptivity—a new *phenomenological attunement* to what is usually left out as a possible way of understanding reality as plural, ambiguous, and many-sided. Thus, mestiza consciousness, like *conocimiento,* are bridges to help heal the gap between *felt experience* and the discursive realities that do not adequately acknowledge the phenomenological weight of those experiences.

## Critiques and Reception

There are two important critiques of mestiza consciousness. The first centers on the conceptual myopia of African traditions and black experience in Anzaldúa's account of mestizx identity (which has a strong tradition of antiblack racism alongside anti-Indigenous sexist racism in Latin America). There is a concern throughout critical race readings of her work that Anzaldúa tends to privilege a Mexican-Indigenous-Anglo identic triad to the exclusion of black identities (including Indigenous black identities). Sylvanna Falcón has argued that this myopia is unjustified, especially given the history of the transatlantic slave trade in Latin America and the experiences of U.S. Afro-Latinas with antiblack racism and its historical specificities.[21] What are Afro-Latinas to make of borderland/Borderland life? To address these issues, Falcón expands mestiza consciousness to a Du Boisian double consciousness, capturing antiblack racism in the lives of Afro-Latinas (and Afro-Peruvian women) who are also borderland beings, where antiracist frameworks often leave out the particularities of gendered racism. *Mestiza double consciousness* thus captures both axes of imperial and settler colonial domination on the lives of North-South, multicultural women of color.

The second critique charges that the concept of mestiza consciousness is still bound up in settler colonial thinking and primitivist discourses that work to disappear Native identities.

Anzaldúa often treats Indigenous history as part of an inherited, pre-Columbian imaginary that is not representative of the realities of many American Indian communities living today. She regularly primitivizes Indigeneity (particularly through her art) to rescue the cultural wellspring of Aztec, Maya, Inca, and Zapotec reciprocal dualisms that she associates with the metaphysical pluralism of in-between *nepantla* states. Yet she goes on to argue that the rise of an abstract, pre-Hispanic patriarchy (rather than colonialism) reversed this openness toward ambiguity to further bureaucratic goals of male predatory warfare between tribes.[22] As Andrea Smith argues, "Gloria Anzaldúa's *Borderlands*, the foundational text of borderlands theory, situates Indians and Europeans in a dichotomy that can be healed through mestizaje. Anzaldúa positions Indian culture as having 'no tolerance for deviance,' a problem that can be healed by the 'tolerance for ambiguity' that those of mixed race 'necessarily possess.' Thus a *rigid, unambiguous Indian* becomes juxtaposed unfavorably with the mestiza who 'can't hold concepts or ideas in rigid boundaries.'"[23] To clarify, Anzaldúa thinks the dichotomy between Indian and European can be healed through a *healed mestizaje*, which the concept of mestiza consciousness seeks to do. Yet the charge of settler thinking in the conceptualization of Indigenous identity is a serious problem that remains in Anzaldúan scholarship. With both critiques in mind, the concept of mestiza consciousness (and its adaptation in mestiza double consciousness) has become a key resource in women of color feminisms and Latina feminist philosophy in particular. As a key concept in liberation epistemology (in the Latin American philosophical tradition), mestiza consciousness can be seen as an epistemic resource hermeneutically marginalized communities produce in response to hegemonic interpretive spaces. As a phenomenological concept, it is situated in particular histories of resistance to colonial domination that speak to a specific praxis of survival for Borderland women of color and should not be taken as a prescriptive for all ways of inhabiting resistance to colonial domination.

## Notes

1. Gloria Anzaldúa, *Borderlands/La Frontera: The New Mestiza* (Aunt Lute Books, 1987), 101.

2. Anzaldúa defines *borderlands* in two ways: (1) as a geopolitical space generally associated with the Texas-Mexico borderlands (typically written as *borderlands* with a lowercase *b*) and (2) (written with a capital *B*) as a broader metaphorical space for working through the cultural, psychological, spiritual, and metaphysical realities of mixed-race peoples in North-South contexts and engaging the transformative potential of those realities. This broader notion of borders contributes to her theory of identity that is characterized by an intersectional, cultural multiplicity (as in being multiply positioned in different, often divergent cultural contexts while navigating the intersections of sex and gender, race and ethnicity, gender, class, and documentation status).

3. See Natalie Cisneros's entry on borderlands in this volume.

4. Anzaldúa, *Borderlands/La Frontera*, 52.

5. In her early writings the term *nepantla* is used to emphasize fricative ambiguity in existence or a sense of cultural displacement. In the later work, it focuses on a third, creative space that rejects dualisms and tolerates contradiction: "Living in nepantla, the overlapping space between different perceptions and belief systems, you are aware of the changeability of racial, gendered, sexual, and other categories rendering the conventional labelings obsolete." Gloria Anzaldúa, *Light in the Dark/Luz en lo Oscuro: Rewriting Identity, Spirituality, Reality* (Durham, N.C.: Duke University Press, 2015), 119.

6. Anzaldúa, *Borderlands/La Frontera*, 42.

7. Anzaldúa, *Light in the Dark/Luz en lo Oscuro*, 119.

8. Anzaldúa, *Borderlands/La Frontera*, 102, emphasis added.

9. Anzaldúa, *Borderlands/La Frontera*, 102.

10. Anzaldúa, *Borderlands/La Frontera*, 60.

11. In her middle and late writings, Anzaldúa builds on this concept through theories that perform what she calls "interventions that subvert cultural genocide" (that is, by allowing for the possibility of self-making and self-mapping in the wake of intergenerational violence against women of color). One strategy she typically deploys that has traces of mestiza consciousness is taking aspects of the devalued side of an Anglo-European binary (black/white, literal/nonliteral) and redeploying it in a way that subverts the stability of the binary or, in a way, "thirds" it. If "literal" is the dominant norm through which history is written, she takes the devalued side (nonliteral, fictive) and uses it to license personal and collective history that has been preemptively curated out of official (socially legible) history. Like *haciendo caras* (making faces), *autohistoria-teoría* is one such theory; see Gloria Anzaldúa, *Making Face, Making Soul/Haciendo Caras: Creative and Critical Perspectives by Women of Color* (San Francisco: Aunt Lute Books, 1990).

12. *Light in the Dark/Luz en lo Oscuro*, 121.

13. She writes, "Often nature provokes un 'aja,' or 'conocimiento,' one that guides your feet along a path, gives you el ánimo to dedicate yourself to transforming perceptions of reality, and thus the conditions of life. Llevas la precencia de éste conocimiento contigo" 2015, 115), meaning you carry the presence of this knowledge with you as an "ensouled" and sacred bodily knowledge (vs. innate cogito) that is primarily responsive to breath, animals, plants, spirits.

14. Anzaldúa, *Borderlands/La Frontera*, 109.

15. Anzaldúa, *Borderlands/La Frontera*, 119.

16. As an alternative to the teleological ascendance of the freed prisoner in Plato's allegory of the cave, Anzaldua depicts *el camino*, the path to *conocimiento* through a nonlinear set of natural metaphors and material conditions (earthquakes, assaults, depressions). It is also a challenge to the reductive cognitive bent of Descartes's *meditations*.

17. Anzaldúa, *Borderlands/La Frontera*, 122.

18. Anzaldúa, *Borderlands/La Frontera*, 123.

19. Anzaldúa, *Borderlands/La Frontera*, 123.

20. Anzaldúa, *Borderlands/La Frontera*, 123.

21. Sylvanna Falcón, "Mestiza Double Consciousness: The Voices of Afro-Peruvian Women on Gendered Racism," *Gender & Society* 22, no. 5 (2008): 660–80.

22. Her inclusive, integrative, "kneading" approach to personal identity often creates a problematic tri-valence between Anglo, Mexican, and Indigenous cultures that forecloses the *colonial genealogy* of hierarchical patriarchy as the source of gendered sexism in the Americas. At one point, she traces Mexican machismo to a universalized patriarchy rather than settler-colonial and imperial gender relations, noting that "before *the Aztecs* became a militaristic, bureaucratic state where male predatory warfare and conquest were based on patrilineal nobility, the principle of balanced opposition between the sexes existed" (*Borderlands/La Frontera*, 53, emphasis added).

23. Andrea Smith, "Queer Theory and Native Studies: The Heteronormativity of Settler Colonialism," *GLQ* 16, no. 2 (2010): 44.

# 32 Misfitting

Rosemarie Garland-Thomson

The idea of a *misfit* and the situation of *misfitting* elaborate a materialist feminist understanding of disability as a lived, situated experience in which the particularities of embodiment interact with their environment in its broadest sense, to include both its spatial and its temporal aspects. The critical concept *misfit* thus offers a strong materialist version of weak constructionist theory to further think through the lived identity and experience of disability as it is situated in place and time. The interrelated dynamics of fitting and misfitting constitute a particular aspect of world-making involved in material-discursive becoming. The concept of *misfit* advances critical disability theory about the social construction of disability in three ways: first, it accounts for the particularity of varying lived embodiments and avoids a theoretical generic disabled body; second, it clarifies feminist critical conversation about universal vulnerability and dependence; third, the concept of *misfitting* as a shifting spatial and perpetually temporal relationship confers agency and value on disabled subjects.

I propose the term *misfit* as a new critical keyword that seeks to defamiliarize and to reframe dominant understandings of disability.[1] *Fitting* and *misfitting* denote an encounter in which two things come together in either harmony or disjunction. When the shape and substance of these two things correspond in their union, they fit. A *misfit*, conversely, describes an incongruent relationship between two things: a square peg in a round hole. The problem with a misfit, then, inheres not in either of the two things but rather in their juxtaposition, the awkward attempt to fit them together. When the spatial and temporal context shifts, so does the fit, and with it meanings and consequences. Misfit emphasizes context over essence, relation over isolation, mediation over origination. Misfits are inherently unstable rather than fixed, yet they are very real because they are material rather than linguistic constructions. The discrepancy between body and world, between that which is expected and that which is not, produces fits and misfits. The utility of the concept of misfit is that it definitively lodges injustice and discrimination in the materiality of the world more than in social attitudes or representational practices, even while it recognizes their mutually constituting entanglement.

The theoretical utility of fitting and misfitting comes from its semantic and grammatical flexibility. Similar to many critical terms, *misfit* offers a layered richness of meaning. According to the *Oxford English Dictionary*, the verb *fit* denotes a relationship of spatial juxtaposition, meaning "to be of such size and shape as to fill exactly a given space, or conform properly to the contour of its receptacle or counterpart; to be adjusted or adjustable to a certain position." Moreover, the action of fitting involves a "proper" or "suitable" relationship with an environment so as to be "well adapted," "in harmony with," or "satisfy[ing] the requirements of" the specified situation. As an adjective, *fitting* means "agreeable to decorum, becoming, convenient, proper, right." *Fit* as an adjective also moves beyond simple suitability into a more value-laden connotation when it means "possessing the necessary qualifications, properly qualified, competent, deserving," and "in good 'form' or condition." In British slang, *fit* even means "sexually attractive or good-looking." *Fit,* then, suggests a generally positive way of being and positioning based on an absence of conflict and a state of correct synchronization with one's circumstances.

*Misfit,* in contrast, indicates a jarring juxtaposition, an "inaccurate fit; (hence) unsuitability, disparity, inconsistency," according to the *Oxford English Dictionary*. *Misfit* offers grammatical flexibility by describing both the person who does not fit and the act of not fitting. The verb *misfit* applies to both things and people, meaning "to fail to fit, fit badly; to be unfitting or inappropriate." This condition of mis-fitting slides into the highly negative figure of "a person unsuited or ill-suited to his or her environment, work, etc.; *spec.* one set apart from or rejected by others for his or her conspicuously odd, unusual, or antisocial behaviour and attitudes." Thus, to mis-fit renders one a *misfit.* Moreover, ambiguity between *fit* and *misfit* is intimated in a less prevalent meaning of *fit* as a seizure disorder or in a more traditional sense as what the *Oxford English Dictionary* explains as a "paroxysm, or one of the recurrent attacks, of a periodic or constitutional ailment."

Misfitting serves to theorize disability as a way of being in an environment, as a material arrangement. A sustaining environment is a material context of received and built things ranging from accessibly designed built public spaces, welcoming natural surroundings, communication devices, tools, and implements, as well as other people. A fit occurs when a harmonious, proper interaction occurs between a particularly shaped and functioning body and an environment which sustains that body. A misfit occurs when the environment does not sustain the shape and function of the body that enters it. The dynamism between body and world that produces fits or misfits comes at the spatial and temporal points of encounter between dynamic but relatively stable bodies and environments. The built and arranged space through which we navigate our lives tends to offer fits to majority bodies and forms of functioning and to create misfits with minority forms of embodiment, such as people with disabilities. The point of civil rights legislation, and the resulting material practices such as universally designed built spaces and implements, is to enlarge the range of fits by accommodating the widest possible range of human variation.

What we think of as disabilities emerge from a "mis-fit" between a body and its environment that is interpreted as inferiority on the part of the embodied subject and those around her. As such, *misfit* conceptualizes the ways of being and knowing that we think of as disabilities as minority forms of embodiment that do not conform to prevailing standards and expectations. The philosopher Jackie Leach Scully has recently characterized what I am calling misfitting as a mismatch between phenotype and habitus.[2] In this view, disability emerges from a discrepant fit between the distinctive individuality of a particular body and the totality of a given environment that the body encounters.

The layered meanings of *fitting* and *misfitting* are part of the ideological apparatus that assigns meaning to disabled and nondisabled identities. Being judged as fit, meaning both healthy and capable, is one trait associated with the privileged designation of able-bodied. To be fit means to be in good health, as in "fit as a fiddle." In our contemporary moment, of course, *fitness* and being *fit* refer to the achievement of a standardized attractive body through demanding activities that consumer culture requires us to take up as an investment in personal and professional self-improvement.

People with disabilities have historically occupied roles as outcasts or misfits as, for example, lepers, the mad, or cripples. One thinks of the iconic Oedipus: lame and blind, cast out for his hubris, patricide, and incest. People with disabilities become misfits not just in terms of social attitudes—as in unfit for service or parenthood—but also in material ways. Their outcast status is literal when the shape and function of their bodies come in conflict with the shape of the built world. The primary negative effect of misfitting is exclusion from the public sphere—a literal casting out—and the resulting segregation into domestic spaces or sheltered institutions. The disadvantage of disability comes partly from social oppression encoded in attitudes and practices, but it also comes from the built and arranged environment. Law or custom can and has produced segregation of certain groups; misfitting demonstrates how encounters between bodies and unsustaining environments also have produced segregation.

*Misfit*, then, reflects the shift in feminist theory from an emphasis on the discursive to an analytical focus on the material by centering on the relationship between flesh and environment. Misfitting is a performance in Judith Butler and Karen Barad's sense, in that agency is being enacted and subjectivity is being constituted. The performing agent in a misfit materializes not in herself but rather literally up against the thingness of the world. Misfitting focuses on the disjunctures that occur in the interactive dynamism of becoming. Performativity theory would rightly suggest, of course, that no smooth fit between body and world ever exists. Nonetheless, fitting and misfitting occur on a spectrum that creates consequences. To use the iconic disability access scene of misfitting as one illustration of those consequences: when a wheelchair user encounters a flight of stairs, she does not get into the building; when a wheelchair user encounters a working elevator, she enters the space. The built-ness or thing-ness of the space into which she either fits or misfits is the unyielding determinant of whether she enters, of whether she joins the community of those who fit into the space. Another iconic example of misfitting occurs when a Deaf sign language user enters a hearing environment.[3] Imagine, for instance, the extravagant full-body gesturing of the Deaf signer misfitting into a boardroom full of executives seated in contained comportment with moving mouths and stilled bodies conferring on important decisions.

Fitting and misfitting are aspects of materialization, as Butler has used the term, that literally ground discursive constructivism in matter.[4] Fitting occurs when a generic body enters a generic world, a world conceptualized, designed, and built in anticipation of bodies considered in the dominant perspective as uniform, standard, majority bodies. In contrast, misfitting emphasizes particularity by focusing on the specific singularities of shape, size, and function of the person in question. Those singularities emerge and gain definition only through their unstable disjunctive encounter with an environment. The relational reciprocity between body and world materializes both, demanding in the process an attentiveness to the thing-ness of each as they come together in time and space. In one moment and place there is a fit; in another moment and place a misfit. One citizen walks into a voting booth; another rolls across a curb cut; yet another bumps her wheels against a stair; someone passes fingers across the Braille elevator button; somebody else waits with a white cane before a voiceless ATM machine; some other blind user retrieves messages with a screen reader. Each meeting between subject and environment will be a fit or a misfit depending on the choreography that plays out.

The formative experience of slamming against an unsustaining environment can unsettle ours and others' occurrences of fitting. Like the dominant subject positions male, white, and heterosexual, fitting is a comfortable and unremarkable majority experience of material anonymity, an unmarked subject position that most of us occupy at some points in life and which often goes unnoticed. When we fit harmoniously and properly into the world, we forget the truth of contingency because the world sustains us. When we experience misfitting and recognize that disjuncture for its political potential, we expose the relational component and the fragility of fitting. Any of us can fit here today and misfit there tomorrow.

In this sense, the experience of misfitting can produce subjugated knowledges from which an oppositional consciousness and politicized identity might arise. So while misfitting can lead to segregation, exclusion from the rights of citizenship, and alienation from a majority community, it can also foster intense awareness of social injustice and the formation of a community of misfits that can collaborate to achieve a more liberatory politics and praxis. Indeed, much of the disability rights movement grew from solidarity born of misfitting. Even the canonical protest practices of disability rights, such as groups of wheelchair users throwing themselves out of chairs and crawling up the stairs of public buildings, act out a misfitting.[5] So whereas the benefit of fitting is material and visual anonymity, the cost of fitting is perhaps complacency about social justice and a desensitizing to material experience. Misfitting, I would argue, ignites a vivid recognition of our fleshliness and the contingencies of human embodiment. Misfitting informs, then, disability experience and is crucial to disability identity formation. The dominant cultural story of proper human development is to fit into the world and depends upon a claim that our shapes are stable, predictable, and manageable. One of the hallmarks of modernity is the effort to control and standardize human bodies and to bestow status and value accordingly.[6] Our bodies and our stories about them reach toward tractable states called *normal* in medical-scientific discourses, *average* in consumer capitalism, *ordinary* in colloquial idiom, and *progress* in developmental accounts.[7]

This refusal to face human contingency produces social bias toward people whose shapes, functions, and appearances witness unruliness in lived human embodiment. The transformations of bodies over time as they move through space and meet the world in ways that veer from the normal, average, or ordinary are identified with disability.

The stories we tell of the shapes we think of as disability are cast as catastrophe, loss, suffering, misfortune, despair, insufficiency, or excess and are thought to be countered through achievable states of embodiment such as *health* and interventions such as *cure*.

The concept of misfitting allows identity theory to consider the particularities of embodiment because it does not rely on generic figures delineated by identity categories. The encounters between body and environment that make up misfitting are dynamic. Every body is in perpetual transformation not only in itself but in its location within a constantly shifting environment. The material particularity of encounter determines both meaning and outcome.

Although *misfit* is associated with disability and arises from disability theory, its critical application extends beyond disability as a cultural category and social identity toward a universalizing of misfitting as a contingent and fundamental fact of human embodiment. In this way, the concept of misfitting can enter the critical conversation on embodiment that involves the issues of contingency and instability. Recently those concepts have been thoughtfully elaborated within feminist theory under the terms *dependence* and *vulnerability*. Such concepts allow us to put embodied life at the center of our understanding of sociopolitical relations and structures, subject formation, felt and ascribed identities, interpersonal relations, and bioethics. Conceptualizing human subjects as bodies ensures a materialist analysis that accounts for human particularity. Focusing on the contingency of embodiment avoids the abstraction of persons into generic, autonomous subjects of liberal individualism, what legal theorist Martha Albertson Fineman calls one of the foundational myths of Western culture.[8] The concepts of misfitting and fitting guarantee that we recognize that bodies are always situated in and dependent upon environments through which they materialize as fitting or misfitting.

More than a premise of unfettered freedom and autonomous agency posited by liberal individualism, the fact of human embodiment, I and others argue, bonds humans together into a social and political community of mutual obligation and responsibility. A relation of mutual dependence between body and environment is at the heart of fitting and misfitting. Vulnerability is a way to describe the potential for misfitting to which all human beings are subject. The flux inherent in the fitting relation underscores that vulnerability lies not simply in our neediness and fragility but in how and whether that flesh is sustained.

## Notes

1. My contribution to disability studies has been to provide four critical keywords: *extraordinary*, *normate*, *the stare*, and *freakery*: see Rosemarie Garland-Thomson *Extraordinary Bodies: Figuring Physical Disability in American Culture and Literature* (New York: Columbia University Press, 1997); Garland-Thomson, *Staring: How We Look* (Oxford: Oxford University Press, 2009); and Garland-Thomson, ed., *Freakery: Cultural Spectacles of the Extraordinary Body* (New York: New York University Press, 1996). A *keyword*, a term I borrow from Raymond Williams, is a single word that invokes an entire, complex critical conversation. Indeed, *normate* and *extraordinary* are no longer mine; they belong to disability studies in general. I see them used often uncited; sometimes I've heard them attributed

to other scholars. Like good children, they have successfully separated from their parent and are making mature contributions to the larger world. I hope *misfits* will answer a critical need as well.

2. Jackie Leach Scully, *Disability Bioethics: Moral Bodies, Moral Difference* (New York: Rowman and Littlefield, 2008).

3. I use the term Deaf here, following the convention that recognizes signing Deaf people as members of a vibrant cultural and linguistic minority group, rather than people characterized by a medically diagnosable hearing loss.

4. Judith Butler, *Bodies That Matter: On the Discursive Limits of "Sex"* (New York: Routledge, 1993).

5. For a detailed discussion of this example, see Joseph Shapiro, *No Pity: People with Disabilities Forging a New Civil Rights Movement* (New York: Times Books/Random House, 1993).

6. For discussions of normalcy and standardization of bodies, see, among many others, Ian Hacking, *The Taming of Chance* (Cambridge, U.K.: Cambridge University Press, 1990); George Canguilhem, *The Normal and the Pathological* (Cambridge, Mass.: MIT Press, 1991); and Lennard J. Davis, *Enforcing Normalcy: Disability, Deafness and the Body* (London: Verso, 1995).

7. Queer theory has similarly challenged the primacy of normal. Both disability and homosexuality are embodiments that have been pathologized by modern medicine. Robert McRuer has theorized this affinity most thoroughly in *Crip Theory* (New York: New York University Press, 2006), in his useful neologism *compulsory able-bodiedness*, which alludes to Adrienne Rich's germinal concept of *compulsory heterosexuality*. Adrienne Rich, "Notes towards a Politics of Location," in *Blood, Bread and Poetry: Selected Prose 1979–1985* (London: Little, Brown, 1984), 210–31. See McRuer's entry, "Compulsory Able-Bodiedness," in this volume. Also see Michael Warner, *The Trouble with Normal* (Cambridge, Mass.: Harvard University Press, 2000).

8. See Martha Albertson Fineman, *The Autonomy Myth: A Theory of Dependency* (New York: New Press, 2005); Fineman, "The Vulnerable Subject: Anchoring Equality in the Human Condition," *Yale Journal of Law and Feminism* 20, no. 1 (2008): 1–23.

# 33 Model Minority

Emily S. Lee

Since its creation by William Petersen in 1966, the model minority theory has been contested by almost the entire discipline of Asian American studies. As David H. Kim explains, "What makes the model minority myth a serious problem is that it continues to racialize Asians and as [Gary] Okihiro has pointed out, does so in a way that strategically keeps in play a host of negative perceptions."[1] Obviously the notion of a model minority has been much discussed and much debated. But in philosophy, specifically philosophy of race, political philosophy, and phenomenology, the notion of a model minority has not received much attention. This entry explores the topic through a phenomenological lens. In other words, it does not reconstruct the discussion about the concept's status as a theory or a myth but describes the experience of living in a world with this meaning structure.

Karen Hossfeld describes model minority theory as the belief that "lifestyle patterns and cultural values of some racial minority group (Asian) are more conducive to successful integration into the mainstream U.S. economy than those of other groups (African Americans and Latinos)."[2] Hossfeld challenges the accuracy of the theory; she points out that the group of Asian Americans that Petersen depicts as model minorities immigrated after the 1940s. The model minority did not form and does not describe the first wave of Asian immigrants into the United States. This is because the first wave of Asian immigrants were manual laborers. The Asian immigrants of the 1940–60s were professionals. The United States needed skilled labor during this period, and so admitted people from Asia with skilled labor. The success of the children of this immigrant population cannot be conceptualized as the success of the children of manual laborers economically climbing into the middle class; instead they were the children of middle-class professionals maintaining their parents' class status. Considering the inaccuracy of the model minority theory, what could be the reason for forwarding such a myth? Kim suggests "the Model Minority Myth is too inaccurate to be a truth and too harmful to be an error; rather, it is a tool of social stratification or political domination. In fact, it may be one of the greatest of the most recent inventions of White supremacy as a political system."[3]

One of the primary reasons for Kim's position that the model minority myth functions as a "tool of social stratification or political domination" is because the most dangerous consequence of the model minority myth is that it promotes *intraminority* conflict. Asian American scholars explain that belief in the myth promotes the idea that no institutional barriers exist to prevent economic advancement within the United States. Accepting this idea positions the minority populations who experience difficulty advancing economically as solely culpable for their "failure." Ultimately, the model minority myth pits Asian Americans against African Americans and Latin Americans. I think this remains the greatest danger of the myth and has been much discussed. But this essay expands upon the experience of being-in-the-world with this meaning structure.[4]

## Confessions of Being a Model Minority

I want to follow Hossfeld and Kim here in regard to the model minority myth, but I have to come out as a model minority, even as I do not believe in this stereotype or find the stereotype at all helpful in my life as an Asian American. I make this confession confident that my individual instantiation does not universalize the model minority myth as true about all Asian Americans. I make this confession in acknowledgment of the importance of phenomenological descriptions and the genre of autobiography. Autobiography functions as an important method through which the lives of minorities gain visibility, and such visibility is necessary to change dominant images of subjectivity. I choose to include my autobiographical confessions to illustrate the ambiguity of living with this meaning structure. Hopefully my autobiographical confessions do not simply draw attention to my personal self but turn attention to the social structural situation in which Asian Americans grapple with this stereotype.

My immigration was conditioned upon an aunt who married a white male, a member of the U.S. military occupying South Korea.[5] My aunt sponsored the immigration of her brother, my father. My family lost pretty much everything during the Japanese occupation of Korea and the subsequent Korean War. In other words, my parents are not educated, middle-class professionals. I became starkly aware of this when signing some papers to receive my doctoral degree. The graduate school asked about my parents' educational level, and it was in filling out this form that I fully understood the different levels of education between me and my parents.

I am left occupying an uncomfortable schism, explaining that the model minority myth does not describe the majority of the Asian American population, and still confessing that I fit the description. But this is the force of stereotypes—to hold a meaning structure in the world against which one's experiences must be interpreted.

## A Tool of Social Stratification or Political Domination

Let me turn to Kim's conjecture of how the myth serves as a tool of social stratification or political domination. Proponents of the model minority myth (both white and people of color) quickly point out that this is a positive stereotype. As a positive stereotype, many do not understand why the stereotype faces so much contestation from the Asian American community. The present research on stereotype stigma, especially in regard to race and gender stereotypes, demonstrates that when an individual hears a disabling statistic about her group identity, she internalizes the stereotype, ultimately impacting her performance.[6] Specifically, Glen C. Loury, an economist, argues that the existence of a racial stigma forecloses "productivity enhancing behaviors."[7] Following Loury's analysis of stigma, because the model minority stereotype is positive, hearing this stereotype could encourage "productivity enhancing behaviors," facilitating the educational achievements and economic mobility of Asian Americans. The existence of this "positive" stereotype as a meaning structure within the horizon of the world should enable Asian Americans. In other words, this stereotype should reassure me, as an Asian American, that I will inevitably rise in economic class, assimilate into the majority culture of the United States, and ultimately flourish.

To better understand the impact of the stereotype, let me introduce Maurice Merleau-Ponty's work for recognizing that embodiment conditions the subject's relation with the world. He argues that each of us has a corporeal schema that consists of "dynamic motor equivalents that belong to the realm of habit rather than conscious choice."[8] Frantz Fanon critically adopts and transforms Merleau-Ponty's discussion of the corporeal schema with reference to what Fanon calls the historico-racial schema. The historico-racial schema describes black people's embodiment grappling with the overdeterminations of all the stereotypes about their history, race, and body.[9] If other racialized populations develop a historico-racial schema, how does the model minority stereotype impact the embodiment of Asian Americans? As a positive stereotype, does it enable confidence in one's movements and actions? Does it provide certainty that the values exhibited in one's embodiment ultimately assure class mobility?

The model minority myth alone does not encircle the embodiment of Asian Americans. Asian American studies scholars point to the feminization of depictions of Asian American male embodiment. For men, associations of femininity counter career success, while Asian American females walk the fine line between the invisibility of docility and the characterization of being tiger-like at any sign of aggressivity. I find this line especially difficult to walk because any expression of authority is perceived as aggressive. Let me also add that the visibility of Asian American body features especially keeps prominent the status of foreigner, even if Asian Americans have resided in the United States since before 1900. Although there are third- and even fourth-generation Asian Americans, the population group never quite achieves being regarded as simply American. Specific to such foreignness, Asian American embodiment is associated with the comic.[10] Hence for Asian Americans, the stereotype of the model minority—even if taken to be purely positive—does not necessarily set the parameters for an uncontested positive historico-racial schema. The embodiment of Asian Americans is quite ambiguous because of the interaction with several other meaning structures. Moreover, the visibility of Asian American embodiment ensures the unavoidability of these meaning structures on an everyday basis.

Phenomenologically, I confess that the stereotype did not serve as a source of personal assurance. I read sociological studies in which some Asian American students described experiencing this stereotype as a source of self-confidence, but I experienced the stereotype as a burden, a source of anxiety and stress. I was astutely aware that not all Asian Americans succeeded; after all, I was growing up in the Bronx among other Asian American families barely making ends meet as small store owners. I came of age surrounded by evidence that not all Asian Americans climbed the economic ladder.

Homi Bhabha defines stereotypes as a method that the colonizers use to identify the colonized. Upon identifying the colonized, the stereotype functions to freeze the colonized, the other, as different, but yet entirely knowable. Bhabha's analysis of mimicry applied to the model minority myth suggests that naming this so-called feature of Asian Americans—that Asian Americans assimilate well because they share in the cultural values of white Americans—identifies Asian Americans as a hybridity. As a hybrid culture, Asian Americans are the same but not the same, and so still different from white Americans. The anxiety of the colonizers to remain in control through assumptions of knowledge is ever present in the need to reiterate and to keep the stereotype alive and persistent. Much as I appreciate Bhabha's analysis of stereotypes and mimicry, the model minority stereotype does not function only in this way, because all Asian Americans do not automatically and immediately comply with this stereotype.

Unique to this stereotype, the model minority myth predicts a possibility in the future. Therefore, it is not experienced as true in all periods of time; it is not frozen. And it is not inevitable; some do not achieve this status. So instead of being frozen, like most stereotypes, the myth functions similarly to the anxiety that John Zuern describes in "The Future of the Phallus." Zuern states that the embodied experience of possessing a phallus entails anxiety because of the expectations of the future from boys in becoming men. He explains the experience of the future "as a kind of strain on the body: the internal sense of forward orientation and anticipation in the face of . . . the 'horizon of expectations,' where the future is felt in the present as an anticipation that 'directs itself to the not-yet, to the nonexperienced, to that which is to be revealed. Hope and fear, wishes and desires, cares and rational analysis, receptive display and curiosity: all enter into experience and constitute it.'"[11] Because of the interpenetration of our bodies and the world, boys may experience the expectations of their future manhood as crippling. Within the horizon of a patriarchal society, men occupy positions with the privileges of normalization. But with the expectation of taking up certain futures comes the anxiety of not taking up these futures.[12] The emphasis of the model minority myth on the future, with its dialectical structure of expectations and anxiety of not taking up such futures, functions similarly to the embodied expectations of boys into manhood. In other words, the model minority myth can serve as a source of anxiety for Asian Americans. What if I am the Asian American who is not a model minority, the failed Asian American?

## The Centrality of Class in Assimilation

Perhaps most central to the looming anxiety of failure inherent in the model minority myth is class. I write elsewhere about the function of class in capitalist societies; I speculate that one may experience class as burdensome because of the emphasis on choice in the occupation of one's class level.[13] Because capitalism describes class as a matter of choice, as a direct result of effort and intelligence with just a droplet of luck, one is applauded or blamed for the class level one occupies. Under such circumstances, although the model minority myth emphasizes similarity in culture that facilitates assimilation, it centers on the achievement of class mobility. In other words, the effectiveness of the model minority myth relies upon the perpetuation of a capitalist narrative.

I wonder if the existence of the model minority stereotype contributes to the need for Asian Americans to desire wealth over other values in the twenty-first century. For without exhibitions of economic stability, Asian Americans falter as model minorities. Even without settling the question of whether Asian Americans internalize the stereotype, with the stereotype functioning as a meaning structure in the world, struggling with economic stability may be especially difficult to endure because of the existence of the stereotype. The stereotype promotes the perception that Asian Americans possess every opportunity for economic mobility, for success.[14] Under such circumstances, if one fails, it especially demonstrates one's economic, and therefore social, ineptness.

At the other extreme, Asian Americans who feel comfortably representative as model minorities, the assimilation practices necessary for class mobility may explain the mimicry of white behaviors. Kim writes, "The combination . . . of civic exclusion and racism, on the one hand, and the model minority myth, on the other hand, has led sociologist Mia Tuan to describe Asian Americans as trapped by the double bind of being an 'honorary White' and a 'forever foreigner.'"[15] Within this double bind, the honorary white status counters the foreign status. Assimilating through mimicry of white mannerisms offers the possibility of ceasing to be perceived as a foreigner and instead gaining acceptance and invisibility as the norm. But the visibility of Asian American embodiment ensures the constant play of the two identities of whiteness and foreigner.

I have yet to determine what the loyalties should be for hyphenated identities (not hyphenated in this book). If I am American, then the non-Asian practices in my household do not indicate some sort of "selling out" to whiteness. But if I am Asian, then such non-American practices portray signs of maintaining loose ties to some version of a traditional culture. This dualism suffers from clearly delineating Asian and non-Asian practices and casting such practices as static. Kim explains that there are degrees of assimilation.[16] Even if I follow Kim's possibility of hybrid assimilation, because we live in a society that normalizes the American practices, because we live in a state that incentivizes the American practices through promises of class mobility, I am concerned that in conceding to follow these practices, I am succumbing to the forces of normalization and capitalism. The only alternative I can foresee requires a reconceptualization of American practices. Being Asian American demands changes in understandings of American and Asian practices. In this sense, the hyphenation "Asian-American" does not depict the building of bridges but posits creating a new center. I hold onto the possibility of hybrid culturalism without desiring the invisibility of whiteness associated with the economic success of the model minority myth.

## Notes

1. David Haekwon Kim, "What Is Asian American Philosophy?," in *Philosophy in Multiple Voices*, ed. George Yancy (Lanham, Md.: Rowman and Littlefield, 2007), 241.

2. Karen Hossfeld, "Hiring Immigrant Women, Silicon Valley's 'Simple Formula,'" in *Women of Color in U.S. Society* ed. Maxine Baca Zinn and Bonnie Thornton Dill (Philadelphia: Temple University Press, 1994), 70.

3. David Haekwon Kim, "Shame and Self-Revision in Asian American Assimilation," in *Living Alterities: Phenomenology, Embodiment and Race*, ed. Emily S. Lee (Albany, N.Y.: SUNY Press, 2014), 110.

4. See Emily S. Lee, "The Ambiguous Practices of the Inauthentic Asian American Woman," *Hypatia: A Journal of Feminist Philosophy* 29, no. 1 (Winter 2014): 146–63.

5. Elaine H. Kim's autobiographical note expresses her pride in descending from a long line of "bad women." She points out that the women who risk everything to immigrate must have been escaping from their past. See "Appendix A," in *East to America: Korean American Life Stories*, ed. Elaine H. Kim and Eui-Young Yu (New York: Norton, 1996), 353–58. I am proud to list my aunt Leigh Parker in this long list of brave women who ultimately sponsored my immigration.

6. According to Sabrina Zirkel, "many studies have now documented the ways that stereotype threat can impair performances." She noted that in 1986, R.A. Gougis "found that African-American participants' performance faltered on a cognitive task when negative stereotypes about African-Americans were primed. Similarly, [C.M.] Steele and others have undertaken a series of studies that demonstrate decreased levels of performance when participants are asked to perform a task that measure[s] some aspect of a negative stereotype about themselves, as when African-Americans are asked to perform a task that will measure 'intellectual abilities.'" Sabrina Zirkel, "Ongoing Issues of Racial and Ethnic Stigma in Education 50 Years after Brown v. Board," *Urban Review* 37, no. 2 (June 2005): 110.

7. Glen C. Loury, *The Anatomy of Racial Inequality* (Cambridge, Mass.: Harvard University Press, 2002), 27.

8. Shaun Gallagher, *How the Body Shapes the Mind* (New York: Oxford University Press, 2005), 32.

9. Frantz Fanon, *Black Skin, White Masks*, trans. Charles Lam Markmann (New York: Grove Press, 1967), 111.

10. In the movie *500 Days of Summer*, the mere presence of an Asian American family served as comic relief.

11. John Zuern, "The Future of the Phallus: Time, Mastery, and the Male Body," in *Revealing Male Bodies*, ed. Nancy Tuana et al. (Bloomington: Indiana University Press, 1992), 61.

12. Zuern, "The Future of the Phallus," 66.

13. See Emily S. Lee, "A Problem with Conceptually Paralleling Race and Class: Regarding the Question of Choice," *Graduate Faculty Philosophy Journal* 39, no. 2 (2017): 349–68.

14. I wonder if the model minority stereotype exacerbated the number of suicides of Korean Americans during the great recession.

15. Kim, "Shame and Self-Revision in Asian American Assimilation," 111.

16. Kim, "Shame and Self-Revision in Asian American Assimilation," 104–5.

# 34 The Natural Attitude

Lanei M. Rodemeyer

To anyone who has read Husserl, his concept of the "natural attitude" appears to be a relatively simple—if not his *only* simple—concept. It describes our normal way of being in the world, taking things as they are: "By my seeing, touching, hearing, and so forth, . . . corporeal physical things . . . are *simply there for me*, 'on hand' . . . whether or not I am particularly heedful of them."[1] Beginning with the natural attitude, Husserl introduces his revolutionary new method, phenomenology.[2] But in doing so, he also distinguishes himself from other philosophers in important ways. First, the natural attitude is not a self-evident fact (as we see with many philosophers); rather it is a stance, an approach to how we experience things in the world. In his description of it, Husserl points out other attitudes, each of which takes up its own types of objects, each with its own essential rules.[3] Each attitude, then, is a very specific position that affects how we see things—and what we see. In the natural attitude, for example, we see real things that have causal relations and material effects on one another. In the arithmetical attitude, on the other hand, we see numbers, formulae, and mathematical relations. Numbers have neither causal nor material relations with one another, so when we are in the arithmetical attitude, we are not concerned with causation. Whatever attitude I take up at a particular moment, in other words, dictates what types of objects I am dealing with (e.g., material or numerical), as well as what types of laws govern the relations of those objects (e.g., causal or mathematical). The natural attitude, however, is special: it remains constantly in the background when I shift to other attitudes.[4]

Husserl's description of the natural attitude in his first volume of *Ideas* follows quite smoothly from his arguments presented earlier in the *Logical Investigations*, where he argues that different regions of objects function according to essentially different sets of laws (such as causal or mathematical laws).[5] In *Ideas*, however, he recognizes that it is not just by accident that consciousness is able to perceive these different regions of objects. Rather, consciousness is the *only* thing that is capable of transitioning between essentially disparate regions of objects—from the natural world to mathematical formulae to fantasy to theoretical concepts. For this reason, his project in *Ideas* becomes a focus on consciousness itself in order to determine what types of structures and laws are in effect there. In this move, Husserl distinguishes himself in a second, important way from many other philosophers: whereas debates about reality usually recognize only two possible regions, namely the material world and the world of ideas, Husserl recognizes that consciousness is reducible to *neither* of these worlds precisely because it is able to address, and shift between, both of them. In other words, consciousness is a dynamic stream of activity rather than either a material thing or an ideal concept. As such, it has its own rules according to which it functions.[6] Husserl identifies a "fundamental error" that can be seen cropping up in many philosophical and psychological theories: the tendency to conflate, reduce, or equivocate between our activity of consciousness and the object of which we are conscious.[7] When I imagine a unicorn, for example, there is a distinct difference between my activity of imagining (what I am doing) and the object I am imagining (the unicorn), and yet, when we speak of imagination, we do not usually take account of that distinction. Because Husserl's description of the natural attitude demonstrates how I can direct my gaze from one region of objects to another, however, it also allows me to recognize that my activity of imagining (in the region of consciousness) is not the same as the imagined unicorn (from the realm of fantasy objects). In fact, it is only through consciousness that different regions can be seen as having any relation at all to one another, which is why Husserl felt so compelled to examine consciousness for itself. To do so, however, he shifts to a stance that allows him to recognize these different regions of objects as well as consciousness itself; he takes up the phenomenological attitude.

In order to shift to the phenomenological attitude, Husserl makes an interesting move: he identifies a primary assumption underlying the whole natural attitude, namely, that we understand the objects we experience in the material world *to exist*. This presumption is in the background of all of our experience in the natural attitude; in other words, in the background of all of our everyday experiences, we are positing that things exist. Husserl calls this the "general positing" of the natural attitude.[8] In order to shift to the phenomenological attitude and focus on consciousness, though, we cannot allow this positing to inform or possibly taint our investigation, and so we must set it aside. Thus we "bracket" the general positing (of existence), neither denying nor affirming it, merely suspending it for the moment while we engage in phenomenology. This move is similar to any type of hypothetical or even fantasy attitude. In fact, as Husserl describes later in *Ideas*, our ability to bracket the thesis of existence is what makes it possible for us to engage in any type of fantasy or fiction at all, for if we could not remove ourselves from our presumption of existence, we would take every movie, play, novel, etc. to be real.[9] Once the general positing has been bracketed, Husserl then removes anything else that might affect his analyses of consciousness (the "phenomenological reductions"),[10] and finally, he moves to a description of consciousness itself.

It is interesting to note, however, that Husserl actually spends much of his time (almost half) in *Ideas* in the natural attitude. Part of the reason for this is that he needs to argue convincingly that the region of consciousness is worthy of serious investigation. But another reason, which dovetails with the first, is that many of the structures essential to consciousness are already evident in the natural attitude. (In fact, these structures can be found in *any* attitude.) Thus we see the cogitatio (act of consciousness) and the cogitatum (content of consciousness) already in the natural attitude, just as we were able to distinguish between the act of imagining and the unicorn being imagined in our example. The structures of cogitatio and cogitatum then become evident after the phenomenological reduction as noesis and noema, respectively. In this way, Husserl's description of the natural attitude serves several functions, even if they are not all apparent at first glance. First, it indicates our ability to shift to various attitudes, each of which takes up a different region of objects. Second, it demonstrates the importance of consciousness in addressing each of these regions and, thus, as an area of study for its own sake. Third, the natural attitude allows for a preliminary investigation of consciousness in that it already reveals many of the structures that become clear after the phenomenological reduction. These include the structures of cogitatio and cogitatum, the ability of consciousness to shift and direct its gaze toward various objects, structures, and regions, and the structure of consciousness itself as a dynamic flow of experiencing. Finally, it highlights our presumption of existence that remains in the background when we take up the natural attitude and, further, our ability to bracket that presumption as we move into the phenomenological attitude. It is important to note, however, that all of these insights are recognized in the natural attitude; we do not need to enter the phenomenological attitude in order to engage them.

The influence of Husserl's phenomenological approach, especially the importance of the natural attitude in offering clues to essential structures, is recognizable in Heidegger's "existential analytic of Dasein" in *Being and Time*. Although his understanding of phenomenology differs from Husserl's—for example, he focuses on linguistic clues and emphasizes how phenomena can be concealed as well as revealed—Heidegger maintains an important distinction between ontic and ontological levels of being. Similar to Husserl's "natural attitude," Heidegger's ontic level is a starting point in the "everyday" from which we are able to recognize significant aspects of our existence; these then point us to primary structures at the ontological level: "But the roots of the existential analytic . . . are ultimately *existentiell*, that is, *ontical*. Only if the inquiry of philosophical research is itself seized upon in an existentiell manner . . . does it become at all possible to disclose the existentiality of existence and to undertake an adequately founded ontological problematic."[11] It is only from the ontic level, as with Husserl's natural attitude, that we then shift to ontological insights.

While Merleau-Ponty takes issue with Husserl's move from the natural attitude to a purified, phenomenological study of consciousness, one could argue that the importance of Husserl's natural attitude—in all of the dimensions described above—remains at the core of Merleau-Ponty's *Phenomenology of Perception*. Merleau-Ponty contrasts a phenomenological approach against empirical and intellectual approaches in psychology. In doing so, he demonstrates that the essential laws of the empirical and intellectual attitudes fall short of accounting fully for such cases as the phantom limb: "The phantom limb is not the mere outcome of objective causality; no more is it a *cogitatio*. It could be a mixture of the two only if we could find a means of linking the 'psychic' and the 'physiological' . . . to each other to form an articulate whole."[12] Here the empirical and intellectual approaches run parallel to the material and ideal worlds that Husserl discusses. Similar to Husserl, Merleau-Ponty argues for a third position, in his case a phenomenological understanding of the living body which is able to address a multitude of psychological cases much more completely than either the empirical or the intellectual attitude alone. Without leaving the natural attitude, then, Merleau-Ponty is able to employ the phenomenological tools introduced by Husserl as a way to demonstrate the importance of phenomenology in issues of embodiment and psychology.

In *Being and Nothingness,* Sartre follows Husserl's lead in employing everyday experiences in order to identify the essential structures of consciousness that underlie them. His description of "bad faith," for instance, relies upon several examples, such as the waiter in the café and the woman on the date, in order to demonstrate that consciousness maintains a tension between being and nothingness, between immanence and transcendence. "Yet there is no doubt that I *am* in a sense a café waiter—otherwise could I not just as well call myself a diplomat or a reporter? But if I am one, this can not be in the mode of being in-itself. I am a waiter in the mode of *being what I am not.*"[13] In this way, Sartre, too, recognizes the importance of the natural attitude not only as a starting point for his work but also as a methodological approach useful for phenomenological and existential analyses.

Beauvoir's approach to the question "What is a woman?" in *The Second Sex* begins with a natural attitude stance that seeks to identify the structures in play that enable and support the oppression of women. Along with Merleau-Ponty, she employs phenomenology in a more practical sense: she seeks to identify oppressive structures not only at the social and institutional levels (although these are clearly important) but also within the oppressed subject herself, and within all subjects who participate in an oppressive society. "Every subject plays his part . . . through exploits or projects that serve as a mode of transcendence. . . . Every time transcendence falls back into immanence, stagnation, there is a degradation of existence into the '*en-soi*' . . . and of liberty into constraint and contingence."[14] Thus Beauvoir finds the natural attitude productive both as a starting point and as a methodological resource that she employs in her analyses of woman and women's oppression.

Given the fact that Husserl's "natural attitude" is neither just a self-evident fact nor a mere starting point but rather an approach that garners its own phenomenological insights, contemporary and critical approaches in philosophy today are able to employ it in a variety of effective ways—as can be seen in this volume. Phenomenological approaches to embodiment are able to recognize the body as more than mere material and, at the same time, not reducible to the conceptual level. This understanding is especially useful in analyses of gender and transgender, disability, and even raced embodiment, each of which can be taken up phenomenologically while remaining in the natural attitude. Using Husserl's approach, one can seek the structures underlying—or imposing themselves upon—these aspects of experience, and see how they intersect in subjective experience. Further, Husserl's method of beginning in the natural attitude in order to reveal important structures on another level—whether it is the level of consciousness, embodiment, or social discourses and institutions—is informative for critical approaches that take insights from the level of individual or community experience to theories of race and racism, gender and queerness, normativity, disability, etc. Simply put, the natural attitude is not just that. It is the first step to a phenomenological approach that is applicable to a multitude of contemporary issues—possibly in a way more productive than some traditional approaches, often providing insights that contribute to other methodologies, and allowing us to see how our own "attitudes" influence what we see.

## Notes

1. Edmund Husserl, *Ideas Pertaining to a Pure Phenomenology and to a Phenomenological Philosophy, First Book: General Introduction to a Pure Phenomenology (Ideas I)*, trans. F. Kersten (The Hague: Martinus Nijhoff, 1983), 51, emphasis in original.

2. Although there are several other philosophies under the heading of "phenomenology"—most notably Hegel's work and certain ancient Greek approaches—I am referring here more narrowly to the phenomenology initiated by Husserl and taken up in a variety of ways in contemporary Continental work.

3. Husserl, *Ideas I*, 54–55.

4. According to Husserl's description, the natural attitude is somehow both in the background as a ground to all other attitudes, and also necessarily distinct from them. I cannot address this tension here. See Husserl, *Ideas I*, 54–55.

5. Edmund Husserl, *Logical Investigations*, vol. 1, trans. J. N. Findlay (London: Routledge, 1970).

6. Husserl, *Ideas I*, 78–80.

7. Husserl, *Ideas I*, 92–94.

8. Husserl, *Ideas I*, 56ff.

9. See Husserl, *Ideas I*, 260ff. While the neutrality modification and fantasy have important distinctions, one needs the ability to neutralize doxic positings of existence before we can engage in acts of fantasy.

10. Husserl works through several reductions, but he tends to put them all under the umbrella heading of "the phenomenological reduction" (*Ideas I*, 66).

11. Martin Heidegger, *Being and Time*, trans. John Macquarrie and Edward Robinson (New York: Harper and Row, 1962), 34 (H 13–14), emphasis in original.

12. Maurice Merleau-Ponty, *Phenomenology of Perception*, trans. Colin Smith (London: Routledge, 1962), 77, emphasis in original.

13. Jean-Paul Sartre, *Being and Nothingness: A Phenomenological Essay on Ontology*, trans. Hazel E. Barnes (New York: Washington Square Press/Pocket Books, 1943), 103, emphasis in original.

14. Simone de Beauvoir, *The Second Sex*, trans. H. M. Parshley (New York: Vintage Books, 1989), xxxiv–xxxv, emphasis in original.

# 35 The Normate

Joel Michael Reynolds

Phenomena appear in relation to one's approach and method. The slogan of phenomenology, "Back to the things themselves" (*Zurück zu den Sachen selbst*), is in part a call to unlearn and unknow, to carry out a suspension, a bracketing (*epokhē*), that brings things to awareness not as they appear by habit, custom, or caprice, but from themselves.[1] This means that insofar as one holds cognition, consciousness, perception, and awareness to be irremediably embodied, one cannot bracket the body.[2] Critical disability studies scholars have argued that a central and ongoing misstep in phenomenological investigations of embodiment is the privileging of a particular type of body: the *normate* body.

I begin by situating the term *normate* within critical disability studies and the work of its coiner, Rosemarie Garland-Thomson. Drawing on Maurice Merleau-Ponty and Reiner Schürmann, I argue that *the normate is the hegemonic phantasm ableism carves out of the flesh*. The concept of the normate functions as a corrective and a call: a corrective relative to the "normal science" of phenomenology and a call for phenomenologies of non-normate embodiment. The normate attunes phenomenology to the lived experiences of disability and being in an ableist world.

## Ableism, Meaning, and Experience

At the outset of her seminal *Extraordinary Bodies*, Garland-Thomson notes the way in which disability functions as an "attribution of corporeal deviance."[3] She writes, "The narrative of deviance surrounding bodies considered different is paralleled by a narrative of universality surrounding bodies that correspond to notions of the ordinary or the superlative. . . . The meanings attached to physical form and appearance constitute 'limits' for many people."[4] I wish to tease out and expand upon three aspects of this passage as they relate to the role of the normate in Garland-Thomson's oeuvre. First, as a question of attribution and narrative, disability is constituted by and through the stories we tell ourselves about ourselves in general and our "bodyminds," to follow Margaret Price, in particular.[5] Disability cannot be understood outside of the centrality of its narrative role for the lived experience of selfhood, social identity, and, in a word, our being-in-the-world.[6]

Second, disability is a question of form, mode, and matter, all of which are cast as *deviant*—not just malformed or aberrant, but a de-viation, the loss or absence of way and of being. "Deviance" emerges in an *épistème* charged with both economic and moral facets: being wrong or lost in the world is taken to be blameworthy, and as such, it is a way of being that both represents and incurs a debt. This debt, in lockstep with nearly every religious tradition, is most often conceived as one borne through suffering. The ableist conflation of disability with pain, suffering, and disadvantage is at the core of deviance as a description of non-normate ways of being in the world.[7]

Third, disability cannot be thought outside of the triumvirate of the normal, natural, and normative, to follow Gail Weiss's apt formulation.[8] Albeit often vaguely defined and problematically deployed across multiple domains of knowledge production, these terms form an intricate tapestry of ideas and assumptions that underwrite commonsense notions of *how things ought to be*. That which is normal is that which is typical. That which is typical is natural, regular, common, and even universal. For example, this explains in part how it could be that homosexuality was medically pathologized and heterosexuality normalized until just a few decades ago and how it could be that the bodies of intersex children were mutilated as a matter of course in the name of "correcting" them until just a few years ago. The historically negative inertia of the *dis-* in disability constructs a tale of psychophysiological lack and loss that, in a perfect world, should not be. It is the fallacy and immorality of this inertia that Garland-Thomson lays bare.

Garland-Thomson's analysis of disability thus involves three central components: self- and social narratives, ontological deviance, and biopsychosocial typology. The concept of the normate threads the hermeneutic needle between nature and culture by broadly defining human difference in terms of a figure, an archetypal representation, of ability that serves to ground and orient people's sense of self. As she puts it, the normate is "the veiled subject position of the cultural self, the figure outlined by the array of deviant others whose marked bodies shore up the normate's boundaries. The term *normate* usefully designates the social figure through which people can represent themselves as definitive human beings. Normate, then, is the constructed identity of those who, by way of the bodily configurations and cultural capital they assume, can step into a position of authority and wield the power it grants them."[9] The normate is the tain of the mirror of ableism. It is the invisible mechanism that allows slippage from being to being-able, buttressing forces from toxic individualism to social eugenics.

The normate thus emerges in relief against both imaginary and concrete, perceived and real bodily difference. An able-bodied person talks loudly to someone in a wheelchair, spontaneously conflating nonambulation with hearing loss.[10] One job candidate is picked over another because they are perceived to be more attractive, conflating cultural ideals of beauty with labor-related abilities.[11] A majority of the Supreme Court argues that states have a right to forcibly sterilize the "feeble-minded" in institutions, conflating feeble-mindedness with both moral deviance and social flotsam.[12] In each case, though in differing ways, the judgment in question results from a confluence of natural and sociocultural determinates—both surreptitiously linking and taking as given the categories of the normal, natural, and normative. Neither found, nor created, but founded, the normate shapes how things are and ought to be from *behind the scenes*.

## Phenomenology and the Normate

We narrate our lives through horizons of ability: "I used to be able to hike that mountain." "I am much better at writing these days." "I'm learning how to cope with my past." Despite their diversity in form, content, and social significance, abilities are constituted *as* abilities through assumptions and fantasies concerning normality. For example, in considering myself a good friend, I likely never made explicit to myself the many abilities friendship requires: patience, discernment, loyalty, trust, flexibility, forgiveness, etc. I also may not have reflected upon the exemplar of friendship (the ideal friend) whose character, or *ēthos*, to invoke Aristotle, harmoniously bears out these many abilities, acting in the right way at the right time toward the right people. Yet it is all of these abilities, their complex interaction, and their melding in real or imagined exemplars that carve the horizon of my lived experience of myself as a friend as well as my ability to coherently narrate that experience to myself and others.

The normate can be understood as the *ultimate* ability exemplar, the exemplarity of which is shaped by and anchored in ableist assumptions that tell us how bodies are and should be. I here define ableism as the assumption that the "normal" or "typical" body is better than the abnormal body *because* it is normal. Ableism assumes the normal body to be the regulative paradigm of human corporeal form and behavior. In claiming that the normate is the hegemonic phantasm ableism carves out of the flesh, I am arguing that the normate is more than just a paradigmatic figure of normality. Following Schürmann's usage, a *hegemonic phantasm* functions as an ontological principle in the sense of a ground and origin: "In order to constitute the phenomenality of phenomena, in order to universalize them, a representational order must organize itself around a principle, a phantasmic referent measuring all representations. A hegemonic phantasm [*fantasme hégémonic*] so conceived not only directs us to refer everything to it, but has, furthermore, an endless supply of significations, that is to say, normative measures."[13] The normate is hegemonic in that it establishes a horizon of meaning that founds and organizes experience absolutely. It is a phantasm in that it appears absolute, while in fact being a construct, continually at risk of capitulation to the powers that be. As a hegemonic phantasm, the normate offers an endless supply of normative measures against which non-normate bodies will prove to be worth less or even worthless.

While it is tempting to index the ample experiences of ability, those of the "I can," to one's particular body, the "I can" is necessarily constituted by one's environment and the futures it affords. Ability expectations are culled not just from one's proprioceptive-kinesthetic experience of one's body, but from one's environment and social milieu. Insofar as the normate, ever furnishing normative measures, reigns over the scale, scope, and content of ability expectations, it shapes everyone's experience of embodiment. If, as Merleau-Ponty writes, the "body is the power for a certain world," then the normate orders and measures the interpretation and values of one's body and its powers or, more accurately, one's flesh.[14] The flesh, for Merleau-Ponty, names the thickness of embodiment, the enfolding of one within the folds of the world.[15] "Every relation between me and Being, even vision, even speech, is . . . a carnal relation with the flesh of the world [*un rapport charnel, avec la chair du monde*]."[16] To think through the problematic of the normate is to think through how this thickness and enfolding is always already shaped by a hegemonic phantasm of able-bodiedness, shaped by unjust ability expectations determining how bodies should be in the very recesses of how they are. As such, the normate is constitutive of the fleshly possibilities of experience.

To see how the concept of the normate can aid phenomenological inquiry, take the example of blindness. To the phenomenologist under the sway of the normate, blindness is experienced as a lack of sight. Speaking of Charles-Antoine Coypel's studies of blind men, Derrida writes, "Like all blind men, they must *ad-vance*, advance or commit themselves, that is, expose themselves, run through space as if running a risk. . . . These blind men explore—and seek to foresee there where they do not see, *no longer* see, or do *not yet* see."[17] Blindness is phenomenologically revelatory in unique respects, but it is often taken to be so primarily or solely in virtue of its relationship to sight—not as it is experienced in and of itself. Blindness reveals "human" lived experience through absence or lack of sight. That a lack, cessation, or breaking of a thing reveals its phenomenality is a commonplace in the phenomenological tradition. One need only think of Heidegger's famous discussion of the hammer in *Being and Time*, the existential and ontological meaning of which is revealed precisely through an analysis of its breakdown. Yet, does the experience of blindness in fact demonstrate itself through the "lack" of sight?

Take the account of John Hull, who writes about his experiences of late-onset blindness:

> First I believed that blindness was when you couldn't see because something had gone wrong with your eyes. Then I understood that blindness was a deprivation of knowledge for which alternative sources and kinds of knowledge would compensate. Gradually I came to see that blindness is a whole-body condition. It is not simply that your eyes have ceased to function; your whole body undergoes a profound transformation in its relationship to the world. Finally, I came to believe that *blindness is a world-creating condition.*[18]

Hull's description moves from an understanding of blindness cast in the logic of the ableist conflation—blindness as lack and suffering, as something "gone wrong"—all the way to a positive, generative, and rich form of life. To experience blindness as it appears from itself, Hull had to undermine the effect of the normate; he had to expel the hegemonic phantasm already figuring sight-as-ability/blindness-as-disability. Only then did he experience blindness as world-creating.[19] For Hull, the light of the normate blinded his experience of blindness. It is with such in-sights in mind that one can "see" how heeding and critically interrogating the role of the normate in lived experience would deepen and improve phenomenologies of embodiment of every sort.

## Non-Normate Futures

Garland-Thomson's work, in concert with thinkers across the field of critical disability studies and philosophy of disability, exposes and rebuffs the exclusions and injustices that situated and continue to situate the non-normate as second-class citizens or even subhuman.[20] For Garland-Thomson, disability is both the limit of *and* opening to understanding ability as an ever-present vector of lived experience and also sociopolitical power. "The experience of my flesh [*chair*]," Merleau-Ponty writes, shows that "perception does not come to birth just anywhere. . . . It emerges in the recess of a body [*le recès d'un corps*]."[21] The concept of the normate suggests that even the recesses of the body can harbor prejudicial assumptions. One's body assumes and installs itself as a standard for experience in a manner obstinate to reflection, as sighted assumptions about blindness so well exemplify. Insofar as phenomenological inquiry is irremediably embodied, the normate is a concept without which phenomenology risks the errors of ableism at every turn. By countering the toxic universality of the typical or standard body, the concept of the normate is indispensable for phenomenological inquiry committed to the call to behold phenomena as they appear from themselves.

## Notes

1. My gratitude to David M. Peña-Guzmán, Rebecca Longtin, and Gayle Salamon for feedback on earlier versions of this piece.

2. Maurice Merleau-Ponty, *Phenomenology of Perception*, trans. Donald A. Landes (Oxford: Routledge, 2011); Mark Johnson, *Embodied Mind, Meaning, and Reason: How Our Bodies Give Rise to Understanding* (Chicago: University of Chicago Press, 2017).

3. Rosemarie Garland-Thomson, *Extraordinary Bodies: Figuring Physical Disability in American Culture and Literature* (New York: Columbia University Press, 1997), 6.

4. Garland-Thomson, *Extraordinary Bodies*, 7.

5. Margaret Price, "The Bodymind Problem and the Possibilities of Pain," *Hypatia* 30, no. 1 (2015): 268–84.

6. David T. Mitchell and Sharon L. Snyder, *Narrative Prosthesis: Disability and the Dependencies of Discourse, Corporealities* (Ann Arbor: University of Michigan Press, 2001).

7. Joel Michael Reynolds, "'I'd Rather Be Dead Than Disabled'—The Ableist Conflation and the Meanings of Disability," *Review of Communication* 17, no. 3 (2017): 149–63. doi: 10.1080/15358593.2017.1331255.

8. Gail Weiss, "The Normal, the Natural, and the Normative: A Merleau-Pontian Legacy to Feminist Theory, Critical Race Theory, and Disability Studies," *Continental Philosophy Review* 48 (2015): 77–93.

9. Garland-Thomson, *Extraordinary Bodies*, 7.

10. S. Kay Toombs, "The Lived Experience of Disability," *Human Studies* 18 (1995): 9–23.

11. Tobin Siebers, *Disability Aesthetics, Corporealities: Discourses of Disability* (Ann Arbor: University of Michigan Press, 2010).

12. Buck v. Bell, 274 U.S. 200 (1927), written by Justice Oliver Wendell Holmes, Jr.

13. Reiner Schürmann, *Broken Hegemonies*, trans. Reginald Lilly, Studies in Continental Thought series (Bloomington: Indiana University Press, 2003), 11.

14. Merleau-Ponty, *Phenomenology of Perception*, 109, 137.

15. Maurice Merleau-Ponty, *The Visible and the Invisible*, trans. Claude Lefort (Evanston, Ill.: Northwestern University Press, 1968), 136–42, 248ff.

16. See Donald Landes's entry, "The Flesh of the World," in this volume. Also Merleau-Ponty, *The Visible and the Invisible*, 83–84.

17. Jacques Derrida, *Memoirs of the Blind: The Self-Portrait and Other Ruins*, trans. Michael Naas and Pascale-Anne Brault (Chicago: University of Chicago Press, 1993), 5–6.

18. John Hull, *On Sight and Insight: A Journey into the World of Blindness* (London: Oneworld, 1997), xii, my emphasis.

19. Joel Michael Reynolds, "Merleau-Ponty, World-Creating Blindness, and the Phenomenology of Non-Normate Bodies," *Chiasmi International* 19 (2018): 419–34

20. Rosemarie Garland-Thomson, "Misfits: A Feminist Materialist Disability Concept," *Hypatia* 26, no. 3 (2011): 591–609, doi: 10.1111/j.1527-2001.2011.01206.x; Rosemarie Garland-Thomson, "Disability Bioethics: From Theory to Practice," *Kennedy Institute of Ethics Journal* 27, no. 2 (2017): 323–39, doi: 10.1353/ken.2017.0020.

21. Merleau-Ponty, *The Visible and the Invisible*, 9.

# 36 Ontological Expansiveness

Shannon Sullivan

The term *ontological expansiveness* might sound abstract or esoteric, but it is a common phenomenon that occurs in the everyday lives of people with social privilege. Ontological expansiveness is a person's unconscious habit of assuming that all spaces are rightfully available for the person to enter comfortably. The space in question can be geographical—think neighborhoods, grocery stores, restaurants, churches, public parks, and so on—and in these cases, the movement in question means literally relocating one's body. Or the space in question can be linguistic, artistic, economic, and so on, and in that case the movement is more metaphorical (but no less bodily for all that). In each of these cases, the comfort is psychological and emotional, and the movement of expanding into a space involves a person's entire being as a psychosomatic unity—hence the adjective *ontological*. Whether literal or metaphorical, ontological expansiveness operates with an assumed right to enter and feel at ease in whatever space a person inhabits, and inhabiting a space in this way both shapes and is shaped by a person's individual habits. Because of the assumed right to psychological comfort, if something about a space makes an ontologically expansive person feel ill at ease, he tends to experience the situation as an unjust violation of his basic right to be and feel welcomed wherever he chooses.

I used masculine pronouns advisedly in that last sentence. While the concept of ontological expansiveness initially was developed to explain the racial privilege of white people[1]—a topic that I will address shortly—men also tend to have habits of ontological expansiveness. Those habits are a key component of traditional (white) masculinity in the Western world. Consider the example of manspreading. Manspreading occurs in crowded spaces, such as subway trains and airplane cabins, when a man sits with his legs spread wide enough to take up and/or block the seat(s) next to him. In 2014, the New York Transit Authority announced a campaign against manspreading, a man's "inalienable underground right" that has exasperated many female and other nonmale subway riders.[2] What is relevant about this particular example is not merely the masculine bodily habit of occupying more physical space than women and other feminized people are "allowed" to occupy. It also is many men's felt sense that this is a basic right that it would be inappropriate or unfair to deny them. As one man retorted unapologetically when being told about the Transit Authority campaign, "I'm not going to cross my legs like ladies do. . . . I'm going to sit how I want to sit."[3] This man effectively asserted that for him to give up his ontological expansiveness on the subway would be for him to feminize himself. Being a man means being able to take up as much space as one wants and not to have to justify doing so.[4]

The nature of the spatial "allowance" enjoyed by men is not legal or otherwise formal. It is not the case, for example, that there is a law in the United States (or elsewhere, to my knowledge) that grants men and denies women the right to spread their legs wide when sitting in public spaces. Manspreading and other forms of ontological expansiveness tend to be regulated informally, and this regulation primarily takes place via habit. Habit is a predisposition to engage with the world in particular ways that often are not consciously chosen. Habits are executed "without thinking," and they are as much physical and emotional as they are mental and psychological. (Indeed, these distinctions stop making sense in the case of habit.) Some habits are nonconscious but could easily become the object of conscious awareness once they are pointed out. These types of habits, such as the habit of taking the same route to work or school each day, are not as difficult to change as unconscious habits are. Unconscious habits tend to obstruct, resist, and undercut attempts to identify them, and thus they are more difficult to transform. These are habits that are personally and/or socially painful to acknowledge, as habits of male privilege and male domination generally are in twenty-first-century America.

This also is true for various habits of white class privilege and white domination of people of color, which tend to operate unconsciously in white people's lives nowadays. Ontological expansiveness is one such habit. White people tend to move and behave as if it is acceptable for them to go wherever they like, and this includes spaces that are predominantly nonwhite. While white people might choose not to enter nonwhite spaces, such as neighborhoods or churches that are majority black or Hispanic, this is because of their own choice (so the argument goes), not because they are restricted from or unwelcome in those spaces. If a white person wishes to enter a grocery store in a predominantly Hispanic neighborhood, for example, she should be able to do so without being made to feel uncomfortable or out of place. If she experiences a chilly climate or receives hostile glances from the people of color in the store, she might charge that she is a "victim" of reverse racism. In her view, her whiteness should not be a barrier to entering any space that she wishes to enter.

The charge of reverse racism in this example helps demonstrate how ontological expansiveness operates by denying the spatiality of situation.[5] As lived, spatiality is not the objective space of mathematically designated positions or locations, as it is for my pencil that is positioned four inches away from my coffee cup on the table. Lived spatiality is oriented via the spatiality of the intentional bodies moving and living in it. This orientation is personal in that it is the orientation of an individual's lived body, and it also is social in that lived spatiality is oriented collectively by the bodies and histories that give it meaning. The Hispanic grocery store in the earlier example is not primarily a point on an abstract grid of space that maps my hometown, e.g., with a longitude 35.28°N and latitude 80.66°W. While the objective space of the grocery store exists, it is secondary to the lived spatiality that gives it racial, ethnic, and linguistic meaning, which in this case serves as a respite from the whiteness of many spaces in the United States.

One of the defense mechanisms used to deny the existence of habits of ontological expansiveness is considering all space to be objective. Spaces are not racially oriented toward some people and against others, as the denial goes, nor are they racially magnetized to attract some people and repel others. Space is just space. It is like a container to move in and out of; it does not have anything to do with race or color. It is empty and thus colorless (in both senses of that term). This allegedly means that if a white person is uncomfortable in a Hispanic grocery store, it is because the Hispanic workers and customers antagonistically inserted the issue of race into the situation, not because a white person interrupted a refuge from whiteness. The white person did nothing wrong. Instead, the Hispanic people in the store discriminated against a white person by trying to keep her out of a public, neutral place.

We can see here a spatial version of white color blindness at work. Even though so-called color blindness tends to be invoked as a strategy for fighting racism, white people's claims to not see or notice race more often have the effect of allowing white class privilege and white supremacy to operate unnoticed. If a white person cannot or will not see race, then she is not able to see racism. (Indeed, I would argue that a white person's not seeing *racism*, rather than *race*, seems to be the unconscious goal of color blindness.) Being oblivious to the lived spatiality of racial situations and treating space as if it is merely a neutral container are ways for color blindness to operate in and through white people's racial habits. They allow white people to ontologically expand with impunity into any space they like, no matter the racial orientation of the space. White people's intrusion into spaces of color supposedly does not occur because those spaces were never infused with "color" in the first place.

The Hispanic grocery store example could involve a variety of different white people, including ones who probably do not think about race much at all. In contrast, one of the most striking and problematic forms of white ontological expansiveness is the ontological expansiveness of white antiracists, who assume that their antiracism gives them the right to enter into spaces and communities of color. Sara Ahmed provides an excellent example of this phenomenon as she recounts her attendance at a conference on sexuality whose list of speakers and participants was almost exclusively white.[6] During one breakout session, a caucus for people of color had been arranged, and Ahmed describes her relief at learning that a space had been made available for them to escape the exhaustion of swimming in a sea of whiteness. To her surprise, of the ten people who showed up at the caucus meeting, four were white. Even after the organizer handed out a description of the caucus that explained it was for people of color, the white people did not leave the meeting space. As the caucus began, the organizer asked all participants to take turns explaining why they had come, and the white people's reasons were telling. They were able to "giv[e] themselves permission to turn up at a black caucus" by means of the following reasons: "being interested in questions of race; a sense of solidarity, alliance, and friendship; a desire to be at a workshop rather than a traditional academic session; a belief that race didn't matter because it shouldn't matter."[7] As the six people of color tried in different ways to explain that they came to the caucus to be relieved of the presence of white people, one white person finally got the message and left, indicating bodily her understanding and acceptance of why she should leave. At least one of the other three, however, left in an aggressive manner, "saying that [the people of color] had made her unwelcome, forced her to leave."[8]

Ahmed's account of these forms of "caring whiteness" and "sorry whiteness" brilliantly reveals the ontological expansiveness at work in the four white participants' habits. These were white people who cared about issues of race and wanted to be in solidarity with people of color. They were white people who apologized for attending a session designed for people of color, indicating that on some level they recognized that a white person would be an intruder in the caucus, but that somehow their good intentions made them an exception. And yet their caring, apologetic demonstrations that they were good white people—not those bad ones who want to oppress people of color—were unconscious exercises of their ontological expansiveness. Their "care" became a way to justify entering a nonwhite space and to assume that they would be welcomed into that space by people of color. The fact that they were not welcome was experienced by at least one of the four white people as a wrong done to her. As a registered attendee, she allegedly had the right to attend whatever session she liked, and the fact that she was "forced" out of a session because of her race was unjust.

Ahmed's story helps illuminate connections between white people's ontological expansiveness and their psychological and emotional fragility when it comes to matters of race. As Robin DiAngelo explains, white fragility is "a state in which even a minimum amount of racial stress becomes intolerable, triggering a range of defensive moves."[9] White people generally are accustomed to not having to think about race or racism, and thus they have very little stamina to persist in situations that make them feel uncomfortable because of something related to their or another person's race. Their assumed entitlement to racial comfort is one of the key factors that contribute to white fragility,[10] and the white habit of ontological expansiveness enacts that entitlement spatially.

The result, as evidenced by the aggressive white conference participant, is an inability to undergo a racial experience in which one's whiteness is challenged. When such a challenge occurs, fragile white people tend either to lash out defensively or to flee, enacting a racialized version of the flight-or-fight response. In turn, white fragility tends to strengthen habits of ontological expansiveness, creating a vicious circle. The white person without sufficient racial grit or resilience is likely to demand her psychological and emotional comfort no matter what space she is in. She is accustomed to a certain amount of psychic freedom in which she does not have to devote any emotional or psychological energy to thinking about how to engage in situations that critically foreground her whiteness.[11] This frees up her energy to be spent on "things that matter" from a white class privileged perspective—that is, not race or racism—and forces the psychic labor of managing racial spaces onto people of color.

We encounter this transference of labor in Ahmed's description of the repeated, careful work that the six people of color had to do in the caucus meeting to convey their desire that it be a white-free space. This was valuable energy that would not have to be expended in this space if it were not for white people's ontological expansiveness. It also was precious time in a brief session spent by people of color managing intrusive white people, time that would have been better spent on the joy, relief, humor, and stories that Ahmed reports were exchanged and enjoyed after the white people finally left.[12] Here we see in a concrete way the toll that white habits of ontological expansiveness take on the psychosomatic health and overall well-being of people of color. The care that they often have to take managing white people's emotional lives, ensuring that white people feel comfortable, is time, energy, and psychic labor stolen from people of color's self-care, including care of communities, homes, families, and other spaces of color. One of the brutal ironies of ontological expansiveness is that even though it requires people of color to manage white people's emotional lives, making white people dependent on them, white people experience that management as their own, independent psychic freedom. The black and brown emotional labor that undergirds white psychic "freedom" tends to be invisible to white people and, moreover, to be interpreted by them as hostility on the part of people of color when people of color refuse to perform it.

Ontological expansiveness not only is a habit of socially privileged people that directly insulates them from discomfort and dis-ease. It also is a habit that indirectly has harmful effects on the bodies, lives, and relationships of subordinated people. I would surmise that this is true of all forms of ontological expansiveness, whether raced, gendered, or otherwise. Habits of ontological expansiveness can be thought of as producing micro-aggressions in the lives of subordinated groups and microkindnesses in the lives of dominant and privileged groups (and both microphenomena in the lives of many people who are complexly privileged and subordinated, such as middle-class white women, men of color, and able-bodied and heterosexual members of both those groups).[13] The little things that wound in one case unjustly pamper and cushion in the other, even as that cushioning makes privileged people psychically weak and prone to exhaustion when they step outside their privileged comfort zones. In small but powerful ways, the repeated effects of ontological expansiveness can accumulate into sedimented injustices that harm members of subordinate groups and warp members of privileged groups.

## Notes

1. Shannon Sullivan, *Revealing Whiteness: The Unconscious Habits of Racial Privilege* (Bloomington: Indiana University Press, 2006).

2. Emma G. Fitzsimmons, "A Scourge Is Spreading. M.T.A.'s Cure? Dude, Close Your Legs," *New York Times*, December 20, 2014, https://www.nytimes.com/2014/12/21/nyregion/MTA-targets-manspreading-on-new-york-city-subways.html.

3. Fitzsimmons, "A Scourge Is Spreading."

4. Unfortunately I do not have space here to discuss fully whether black men and other men of color are "allowed" to manspread to the same degree that white men are, but it is a topic worth further investigation. On the one hand, complaints about black men's manspreading show up occasionally online, for example, on an African American forum on Topix, no longer available: http://www.topix.com/forum/afam/TJ57UF50TUEOSCCNU/why-do-you-black-men-manspread-so-often, accessed June 10, 2017. On the other hand,

charges of manspreading appear to be part of the new Jim Crow, used to sweep up black and Latino men into the criminal justice system via minor infractions that (middle-class) white men would never be ticketed or arrested for: Christopher Mathias, "How Manspreading Arrests Highlight What's 'F**ked Up' about Broken Windows Policing," *Huffington Post*, May 28, 2015, https://www.huffingtonpost.com/2015/05/28/manspreading-arrest-broken-windows-policing_n_7462944.html. On the new Jim Crow, see Michelle Alexander, *The New Jim Crow: Mass Incarceration in the Age of Colorblindness* (New York: New Press, 2012). In the case of arrests for manspreading—as in many other cases—law enforcement has twisted (deliberately, it seems) the concerns of women of all races about men's sexism and male privilege into a racialized weapon to attack black men and perpetuate antiblack racism.

5. Maurice Merleau-Ponty, *Phenomenology of Perception*, trans. Colin Smith (London: Routledge, 1989), 100.

6. Sara Ahmed, *On Being Included: Racism and Diversity in Institutional Life* (Durham, N.C.: Duke University Press, 2012), 36–37.

7. Ahmed, *On Being Included*, 37.

8. Ahmed, *On Being Included*, 37.

9. Robin DiAngelo, "White Fragility," *International Journal of Critical Pedagogy* 3, no. 3 (2011): 54.

10. DiAngelo, "White Fragility," 60.

11. On psychic freedom and white fragility, see DiAngelo, "White Fragility," 62.

12. Ahmed, *On Being Included*, 37.

13. On racial microkindnesses, see Shannon Sullivan, *The Physiology of Sexist and Racist Oppression* (New York: Oxford University Press, 2015), 154–57.

# 37 Operative Intentionality

## Jennifer McWeeny

Maurice Merleau-Ponty took a seed from Edmund Husserl's phenomenology and brought it to full flower with his concept of operative intentionality (*l'intentionnalité opérante*). Variably referred to as "bodily intentionality," "motor intentionality," "latent intentionality," and "original intentionality,"[1] operative intentionality is a practical directedness toward the world that is not necessarily present to reflective consciousness but is instead made manifest in the daily operations of a person's life—in her movements, activities, bodily comportments, loves and hates, and modes of relating to herself and others. Merleau-Ponty insists that operative intentionality is "more ancient" than other forms of intentionality.[2] It is the structure through which a graspable and sensible world first emerges out of the ambiguity of experience; it is the mechanism that furnishes experience with its most original meaning.[3]

The concept of operative intentionality has opened phenomenology to fields like gender, critical race, queer, trans, and disability studies because it invites a reconsideration of the traditional assumption, exemplified in the works of Descartes, Kant, Husserl, and Sartre, that the character and structure of intentional experience is universal across bodies. If intentional experience is fundamentally operative, then it is synchronized with the practical possibilities afforded by a world. Moreover, if the practical possibilities for members of some social groups are different than for others due to the presence of oppressions such as racism and sexism, then their experiential possibilities might likewise be different. This implication is developed in the work of a diverse collection of critical social theorists, from Simone de Beauvoir, Frantz Fanon, and Michel Foucault to Sandra Bartky, Iris Marion Young, María Lugones, Lewis Gordon, S. Kay Toombs, and others.

The qualifier *operative* signals that Merleau-Ponty's concept parts ways with traditional conceptions of intentionality that associate the phenomenon with mind and interiority more so than with body and exteriority. This prevalent view is neatly captured in Franz

Brentano's claim that intentionality, which he defines as "reference to a content, direction toward an object . . . or immanent objectivity," is exclusive to mental phenomena.[4] The tendency to understand intentionality in Cartesian terms is further entrenched by its widespread association with a representationalist theory of mind, a direction first pursued by Brentano's students Alexius Meinong and Kasimir Twardowski as a means to guarantee the mind-independent status of intentional objects.[5] By contrast, Husserl, another of Brentano's students, rejects this move and instead affirms the ambiguity of intentional experience, which suggests that certain forms of intentionality, such as perception, present their object directly, without meditation; in a sense, the intentional object is both inside and outside the mind. This approach will eventually lead Husserl to describe what he refers to as a "functioning intentionality" (*fungigerende Intentionalität*) or a "living intentionality" (*lebendig Intentionalität*), both of which prefigure Merleau-Ponty's mature notion.[6] For example, Husserl writes, "The living intentionality carries me along; it predelineates; it determines me practically in my whole procedure, including the procedure of my natural thinking, whether this yields being or illusion. The living intentionality does all that, even though, as actually functioning, it may be non-thematic, undisclosed, and beyond my ken."[7]

Although Merleau-Ponty is directly inspired by Husserl's descriptions and lauds him for inaugurating this "enlarged notion of intentionality,"[8] he does not embrace Husserl's account without qualification. A working note to *The Visible and the Invisible* dated April 1960 clarifies his concerns: "The whole Husserlian analysis is blocked by the framework of *acts* which imposes upon it the philosophy of *consciousness*. It is necessary to take up again and develop the *fungierende* or *latent* intentionality which is the intentionality within being."[9] Once Merleau-Ponty turns toward those aspects of experience that are not our own acts—"that we have not constituted"[10]—his phenomenology is radicalized in that it allows for the possibility that my consciousness realizes meanings and perspectives that are not my own. How does operative intentionality reveal this possibility?

The core feature of operative intentionality is succinctly expressed in Merleau-Ponty's most famous phrase, "Consciousness is originarily not an 'I think that,' but rather an 'I can.'"[11] In operative intentionality a person's subjective perspective is not different from his body. This is aptly captured by Merleau-Ponty's refrain, "I am my body,"[12] and by his repeated references to the "body-subject" rather than a body *tout court*. In turn, a person's body is shaped by the world's contours in virtue of its practical activity. To perceive a hammer is already to sense my own hand; to watch another surveying a landscape is already to express the same faculties in myself. Because this systemic relation is always and everywhere already at work, Merleau-Ponty tells us that operative intentionality "only knows itself in its results";[13] when our feet miss the step, when our caresses are not returned, when we suffer from pain or illness, we become aware both of the practical directedness that orients and moves us and of certain aspects of the world that fail to meet our aims and reaches.

When intentionality is thus released from the boundaries of reflective thoughts and constituting acts, the question of the relationship between sociocultural context and intentional experience becomes more salient than it could have been before. It is unsurprising, then, that a number of contemporary theorists employ the concept of operative intentionality in order to account for behavioral and experiential patterns that are tied to particular kinds of socially categorized and politicized bodies. Iris Marion Young's landmark essay, "Throwing Like a Girl: A Phenomenology of Feminine Body Comportment, Motility, and Spatiality," provides a paradigmatic example of this approach. Young explains differences between masculine and feminine styles of throwing, sitting, leaping, and so on, by appealing, respectively, to two different types of operative intentionality: the confident posture of Merleau-Ponty's "I can" and what Young calls "inhibited intentionality," which she defines as a body's simultaneous enactment of "I can" and "I cannot"—a body's failure to commit fully to the activity at hand.[14] In a similar vein, S. Kay Toombs describes the experience of disability, and in particular her loss of upright posture due to multiple sclerosis, as a "permanent change in bodily intentionality."[15] Toombs recounts that as the disease progressed, her limbs stopped entertaining a number of practical possibilities that they once had. Additionally, and consistent with Merleau-Ponty's view, she describes how this shift in bodily intentionality is contemporaneous with a change in the way she experiences the world, as well as a change in how other people treat her. And yet her account goes beyond Merleau-Ponty's in drawing out the phenomenon's social and emotional dimensions. Toombs shows how shame, diminishment, and infantilization often accompany a frustrated or inhibited operative intentionality.[16]

Contemporary critical theory, and especially those branches that center on body politics, constitutes another lineage of operative intentionality. The idea that culture and power become inscribed on the body through disciplinary practices and subjectification presupposes an ontological mechanism that could ground this type of relationship between self and world. Judith Butler's notion of gender performativity, for example, holds that flows of power establish practical fields that corral bodies into habitual performances of either masculinity or femininity, and these patterns are mistakenly embraced as natural facts.[17] Likewise, Susan Bordo's analysis of anorexia nervosa draws upon Michel Foucault's conception of the disciplined body to explain how cultural ideals become "crystallized" in bodies through practical intentions that first appear to be illogical or self-sacrificing, but whose immanent sense is apparent when situated in sexist contexts where traits like masculinity, self-control, and mastery of the body are revered.[18] Whereas Young and Toombs attend to the social and political implications of cases where operative intentionality is frustrated or inhibited, Butler and Bordo focus on how a person's operative intentionality is tended, seduced, harnessed, and disciplined in the service of power, as well as on how people may resist the workings of power and its bodily inscriptions.

Perhaps the most significant way that operative intentionality has been used to develop both a social critique and a vision of liberation is reflected in Simone de Beauvoir's descriptions of women's experience in *The Second Sex*. Like Merleau-Ponty, she believes that theories should aim to "[recover] the original intentionality of existence."[19] However, she nonetheless emphasizes that women's experiences are not adequately explained by the maxim "I am my body." In an oft-cited passage, she explains, "Woman, like man, *is* her body; but her body is something other than herself."[20] Here Beauvoir is alluding to a kind of double intentionality lived by women in a sexist society where they are required to comport their bodies in ways that express someone else's subjectivity. Referencing Sartre's claim in *Being and Nothingness* that consciousness aims to "make itself be" (*se faire être*), Beauvoir explains that the situation of a girl under sexism is one of continually having to choose between making herself be and making herself a woman (*se faire femme*), neither of which is a desirable option. The constraints of this choice often lead a girl to make herself an object (*se faire objet*), an act that Beauvoir repeatedly associates with becoming a woman.[21] In making herself an object, a girl makes herself be by existing her body as the conduit of another's desires, by living her body as if it belonged to someone else. Consequently, this activity disrupts her capacity to experience her body solely as the locus of her own subjectivity. Instead, she experiences her body both as herself *and* as something other than herself. This situation of divided intentionality can explain why women often exhibit an inhibited intentionality, but the two forms are not identical. Inhibited intentionality reflects frustration within a unitary perspectival structure, whereas in *se faire objet* a woman's perspectival structure is multiple since her body lives two subjectivities at once.[22] This view integrates well with Monique Wittig's provocative claim "Lesbians are not women";[23] insofar as a girl refrains from making her body an object by removing herself from the practical and symbolic milieu of heteronormative patriarchy, she will fail to achieve the divided intentionality characteristic of the second sex.

Frantz Fanon's analysis of "the lived experience of the black man" also suggests a variability of experiential structure that derives from operative intentionality, albeit in a different way than Beauvoir's work does. In *Black Skin, White Masks,* Fanon explains that for a black man living in a racist and colonial society "consciousness of the body is solely a negating activity. It is a third-person consciousness."[24] In Beauvoir's account of woman's experience, a woman assumes another's desires and needs within her own perspective in the doubling act of *se faire objet*, but the black man is denied a perspective altogether under the weight of third-person ascriptions and anecdotes.[25] As Lewis Gordon writes, "Black bodies have an array of expressions predicated upon white views of blackness. . . . The body known as seen by others is linked to . . . the perspective of the body. What antiblack racism demands of the black body is for it . . . to be a body without perspective."[26] In this racist arrangement, the black man's own perspective dries up, desiccates into "an absolute density"; his "corporeal schema crumble[s]" in its immobility and recalcitrant facticity.[27] Fanon describes this race-specific intentional structure in terms similar to those Beauvoir uses to describe that which is sex-specific: "I took myself far off from my own presence, far indeed, and made myself an object [*me constituant objet*]."[28] And yet the two are not necessarily invoking the word *object* in the same way, since Fanon's sense refers to petrification or "thing-ification"[29]—the hardening of operative intentionality—and Beauvoir's points to a kind of bodily possession whereby one's operative intentionality is doubled, a portion of one's own experience directed by someone else's needs and desires.

From its first exposition in Merleau-Ponty's *Phenomenology of Perception* (and arguably earlier, in Husserl's intimations of the notion), the concept of operative intentionality has stood in an ambiguous relationship to phenomenology. In the first place, it is a continuation of the tradition from whence it was born because it calls for a return to the primacy of experience by attending to the first and most original moment of meaning. Alternatively, it is also a thread that threatens to unravel phenomenology's core belief in the universality and stability of experiential structure and the corollary ideas that consciousness is necessarily first-personal and inescapably (formally) individuated. In operative intentionality, intentionality is still the mark of the mental, but mind is not at all what we thought it to be; it is not merely inside the head but also out in the world and everywhere, in the fibers and surfaces of flesh as much as it is in reflective thought, in the social and cultural as much as it is in the private and individual. Paradoxically, it may well be this critical component of the concept that finally releases phenomenology from its Cartesian legacy and ushers in a new wave of thinking about what it is to live a consciousness that is intrinsically *bodily* in the strict sense of being unavoidably exposed to the world and others, capable of being transformed by them in constitutive rather than contingent ways. The more phenomenology gives serious and sustained consideration to the diverse experiences of diverse bodies—a project that is both opened and furthered by the idea of operative intentionality—the more quickly this next tide will come in.

## Notes

1. Although these terms are often conflated, *motor intentionality* and *bodily intentionality* appear to be subtypes of *operative intentionality* rather than its equivalent because they indicate specific kinds of practical directedness.

2. Maurice Merleau-Ponty, "The Philosopher and His Shadow," in *Signs*, trans. Richard C. McCleary (Evanston, Ill.: Northwestern University Press, 1964), 159–81, 165.

3. Maurice Merleau-Ponty, *Phenomenology of Perception*, trans. Donald A. Landes (New York: Routledge, 2012), lxxi, 407.

4. Franz Brentano, *Psychology from an Empirical Standpoint*, ed. Linda L. McAlister, trans. Antos C. Rancurello, D. B. Terrell, and Linda L. McAlister (New York: Routledge & Kegan Paul, 1973), 88, 89.

5. See Alexius Meinong, *On Assumptions*, trans. James Heanue (Berkeley: University of California Press, 1983); Kasimir Twardowski, *On the Content and Object of Presentations: A Psychological Investigation*, trans. R. Grossmann (The Hague: Martinus Nijhoff, 1977).

6. See Edmund Husserl, *Ideas Pertaining to a Pure Phenomenology and to a Phenomenological Philosophy. Second Book: Studies in the Phenomenology of Constitution*, trans. Richard Rojcewicz and André Schuwer (Dordrecht: Kluwer, 1989), 151–69; Edmund Husserl, *Formal and Transcendental Logic*, trans. Dorion Cairns (The Hague: Martinus Nijhoff, 1969), 157, 234–37; Edmund Husserl, *Cartesian Meditations: An Introduction to Phenomenology*, trans. Dorion Cairns (The Hague: Martinus Nijhoff, 1960), 77–80. Husserl's notion of passive synthesis is also integral to the idea of functioning intentionality. He insists, for example, that "anything built by activity necessarily presupposes, as the lowest level, a passivity that gives something beforehand" (*Formal and Transcendental Logic*, 78).

7. Husserl, *Formal and Transcendental Logic*, 235.

8. Merleau-Ponty, *Phenomenology of Perception*, lxxxii.

9. Maurice Merleau-Ponty, *The Visible and the Invisible*, trans. Alphonso Lingis (Evanston, Ill.: Northwestern University Press, 1968), 244. In "The Philosopher and His Shadow," Merleau-Ponty suggests that this radical or "audacious" direction is already present in Husserl's thinking.

10. Merleau-Ponty, "The Philosopher and His Shadow," 180.

11. Merleau-Ponty, *Phenomenology of Perception*, 139. See Husserl, *Ideas Pertaining to a Pure Phenomenology*, 234.

12. Merleau-Ponty, *Phenomenology of Perception*, 205.

13. Merleau-Ponty, *Phenomenology of Perception*, 453.

14. Iris Marion Young, "Throwing Like a Girl: A Phenomenology of Feminine Body Comportment, Motility, and Spatiality," *Human Studies* 3, no. 2 (1980): 137–56, 146.

15. S. Kay Toombs, "The Lived Experience of Disability," *Human Studies* 18, no. 1 (1995): 9–23, 16.

16. Toombs, "The Lived Experience of Disability," 19. For other relevant explanations of social patterns of experience that draw upon operative intentionality, see Sandra Bartky, *Femininity and Domination: Studies in the Phenomenology of Oppression* (New York: Routledge, 1990); M. J. Philpott, "A Phenomenology of Dyslexia: The Lived-Body, Ambiguity, and the Breakdown of Expression," *Philosophy, Psychiatry, & Psychology* 5, no. 1 (1998): 1–19; Gayle Salamon, "The Sexual Schema: Transposition and Transgender in Phenomenology of Perception," in *You've Changed: Sex Reassignment and Personal Identity*, ed. Laurie J. Shrage (New York: Oxford University Press, 2009), 81–97; Gayle Salamon, "The Phenomenology of Rheumatology: Disability, Merleau-Ponty, and the Fallacy of Maximal Grip," *Hypatia* 27, no. 2 (2012): 243–60; Jennifer McWeeny, "Liberating Anger, Embodying Knowledge: A Comparative Study of María Lugones and Zen Master Hakuin," *Hypatia* 25, no. 2 (2010): 295–315. Simone de Beauvoir, *The Coming of Age* (New York: Norton, 1996) is a classic example of this approach.

17. Judith Butler, "Performative Acts and Gender Constitution," *Theatre Journal* 40, no. 4 (1988): 519–31.

18. Susan Bordo, *Unbearable Weight: Feminism, Western Culture, and the Body* (Berkeley: University of California Press, 1993), 139–64.

19. Simone de Beauvoir, *The Second Sex*, trans. Constance Borde and Sheila Malovany-Chevallier (New York: Knopf, 2009), 55.

20. Beauvoir, *The Second Sex*, 41, translation modified.

21. This detail will likely be lost on readers of either of the English translations of Beauvoir's *The Second Sex* because neither renders the phrase consistently nor in its active construction, instead using locutions such as "to become object" (67) and "to be object" (302) from the Borde and Malovany-Chevallier translation, and "being made object," from Simone de Beauvoir, *The Second Sex*, trans. H. M. Parshley (New York: Knopf, 1953), 368. For other passages where Beauvoir employs the phrase, see the Borde and Malovany-Chevallier translation, 294, 295, 305, 363, 572, 653, 669, 688, 749.

22. For an elaboration of Beauvoir's theory of perspectival multiplicity, see Jennifer McWeeny, "The Second Sex of Consciousness: A New Temporality and Ontology for Beauvoir's 'Becoming a Woman,'" in *"On ne naît pas femme: on le devient . . .": The Life of a Sentence*, ed. Bonnie Mann and Martina Ferrari (New York: Oxford University Press, 2017), 231–73.

23. Monique Wittig, *The Straight Mind and Other Essays* (Boston: Beacon Press, 1992), 20.

24. Frantz Fanon, *Black Skin, White Masks*, trans. Charles Lam Markmann (New York: Grove Press, 1967), 110.

25. For a different account of ontological multiplicity that is tied to resisting multiple oppressions, see Maria Lugones, *Pilgrimages/*Peregrinajes*: Theorizing Coalition against Multiple Oppressions* (Lanham, Md.: Rowman & Littlefield, 2003). Lugones's concept of "'world'-traveling" is explained in chapter 50, this volume.

26. Lewis R. Gordon, *Bad Faith and Antiblack Racism* (New York: Humanity Books, 1995), 102.

27. Fanon, *Black Skin, White Masks,* 134, 112.

28. Fanon, *Black Skin, White Masks,* 112.

29. *Thing-ification* is a term Fanon finds in Aimé Césaire, *Discourse on Colonialism,* trans. Joan Pinkham (New York: Monthly Review Press, 2000), 42.

# 38 Perceptual Faith

Jack Reynolds

The philosophical idea of the "perceptual faith" is primarily indebted to Maurice Merleau-Ponty (1908–1961), deriving in particular from his unfinished book, *The Visible and the Invisible* (hereafter *VI*).[1] The concept has an enigmatic status, being both a kind of methodological program reminding us that we should not forget the significance of this "faith" as a condition for reflective thought, science, etc., and, perhaps because of this, also a problem for such thought, liable to lead to "transcendental illusions," dogmatism, and what has elsewhere been called the "myth of the given." In this entry, I will outline the underappreciated role that the concept of the perceptual faith has for Merleau-Ponty's late philosophy.

## Phenomenology and the "Given": Husserl and Merleau-Ponty's *Phenomenology of Perception*

Of course, the idea of the perceptual faith has antecedents within phenomenology and in Merleau-Ponty's own oeuvre prior to *VI*. Classical phenomenology has always been concerned with the idea of givenness (whether of perceptual or other forms), seeking an understanding of it that is "prior" to theoretical, scientific, and metaphysical constructions. Indeed, accessing the given in appropriate fashion is arguably the key goal of the phenomenological reduction and the famous Husserlian methodological injunction "to return to the things themselves," as well as Husserl's associated "principle of all principles," which holds "that every originary presentive intuition is a legitimising source of cognition."[2] The phenomenological trick, of course, is to access and then reflectively understand that "given" without falsifying it, which is no easy task on account of the seductions of what phenomenologists call the "natural attitude"—the fascination we have with the world and its objects, which paradoxically also blinds us to our mode of access to them and ensures that we encounter them within the terms of preestablished categories and modes of understanding. Although it is hard to achieve, however, once achieved it thereby grounds secure knowledge rather than constituting any sort of aleatory or paradoxical "perceptual faith."[3] For classical phenomenology, then, the "given" is not strictly a faith, or at least it is not recognized as such, but is rather more like a basic phenomenological datum that can be intuitively accessed through phenomenological training and practice and that can (among other things) provide the sciences with a secure epistemic foundation that is not circular in the manner that Husserl bemoaned regarding the respective efforts of psychologism and naturalism at the beginning of the twentieth century.

Now Merleau-Ponty is strongly indebted to Husserl, especially to his later work. He was an early reader of *Ideas II* and other texts at the Husserl archives in Leuven, and he famously characterized his own project in proto-deconstructive fashion as elaborating on Husserl's own "unthought." As this formulation indicates, however, Merleau-Ponty's commitment to key Husserlian ideas concerning the "given" and some of the methods for approaching it—e.g., intuition, eidetic reduction, etc.—are all nuanced and transformed in such a manner that his ultimate allegiance to Husserlian phenomenology is debatable, interpreted in profoundly different ways by scholars.[4] Indeed, most famously of all, Merleau-Ponty even declares in the preface of *Phenomenology of Perception* that the phenomenological reduction is impossible, and yet he continues to do phenomenology to good effect, albeit arguably in a hybrid and dialectical manner that is phenomenologically "impure" from a classical perspective. Nonetheless, in his early period, up to and including *Phenomenology of Perception*, Merleau-Ponty also espouses theses like the "primacy of perception" in an essay of that name, and advocates what he calls a "phenomenological positivism"—ideas that bear a close relationship to related formulations in Husserl. For Merleau-Ponty, at this time, to perceive is to organize an area of the visible, and this implicates him in a holistic understanding of perception rather than any sense-datum-style view in which the given just *is*. To a greater extent than Husserl, he also offers an account of perception wherein cultural, historical, and hermeneutical aspects are given significant attention (through the social and normative dimension of habits), and he more strongly emphasizes the activity of the perceiver and the tight interconnection of action, motility, and perception. Nonetheless, his primacy of perception thesis accords a nuanced version of the experientially "given" a basic epistemic significance for his early work. The perceived world is the origin of truth, we might say, even if truth cannot be reductively explained in terms of the former.

## Perceptual Faith in *The Visible and the Invisible*

Despite according greater attention to the *invisible* (cf. *VI* 229) and that which cannot be directly perceived, something close to this idea that the perceived world is the origin of truth also characterizes *The Visible and the Invisible* but is given a more paradoxical rendering that is methodological and (indirectly) ontological. Indeed, at one point the book was to be called "the origin of truth" (165), and while it is the intertwining between the visible and the invisible and associated ideas like the chiasm and flesh that are ultimately foregrounded here in this book's famous chapter 4, *VI* retains an emphasis on perception in its various modalities due to the idea of the perceptual faith, which has an important conceptual and structural role in the book. It serves as the starting point for the chapters "Reflection and Interrogation" and "Interrogation and Dialectics," with each of the subsection titles also explicitly referencing the idea in differing contexts. Chapter 1, for example, has the subsections "The Perceptual Faith and Its Obscurity," "Science Presupposes the Perceptual Faith but Does Not Elucidate It," and "The Perceptual Faith and Reflection," and chapter 2 has the subsections "Perceptual Faith and Negativity" and "Perceptual Faith and Interrogation." Chapters 3 and 4, by contrast, do not explicitly reference the perceptual faith in this structural/architectonic sense and only intermittently refer to it, perhaps indicating that its role as the key unifying theme for the text as a whole may not have worked in quite the way that Merleau-Ponty hoped it would, or that it had been usurped by other ideas, or that he simply had not yet tied together all of the elements of his manuscript given the book was unfinished when he died in May 1961. The first chapter will be our primary concern here.

## Reflection and Interrogation: The Perceptual Faith and Its Obscurity

As is typical of *VI*, which has the flavor of a *via negativa* or a "neither-nor,"[5] Merleau-Ponty begins the first substantial chapter by contending that the perceptual faith is not an opinion or judgement. It is not, as Françoise Dastur notes,[6] founded on reasons and judgments. Rather, it is held to be presupposed by any such justifications, and hence Merleau-Ponty says it is better described as a primordial "urdoxa," to borrow from Husserl, which makes possible both dogmatism and skepticism (*VI* 30), but also refers to our openness or "contact with being prior to reflection, a contact that makes reflection itself possible" (65). It is important to recognize, however, that this openness of the perceptual faith (88) is continually referred to as paradoxical (31). As with his famous claim from the *Phenomenology* that the most important lesson of the phenomenological reduction is the impossibility of any complete reduction, here we are told that philosophy cannot completely suspend or bracket the perceptual faith, part of which includes something akin to the natural attitude and a naive commitment to the world. As such, while Merleau-Ponty is sometimes criticized for what appear to be foundational appeals to the perceptual faith and to an intimate contact with being that precedes reflection, accusations of this sort ignore the paradoxical status of the perceptual faith, as well as Merleau-Ponty's related insistence that the perceptual faith is a problem for us.

Another way of seeing this is to recognize the close connection between the idea of the perceptual faith and another of the key terms and ideas of *VI*, the "hyper-dialectic," which is the focus of chapter 2. Merleau-Ponty's indebtedness to Hegel is a long story that cannot be done justice to here, but what Merleau-Ponty calls the good dialectic and contrasts with the "bad" or "embalmed" dialectic (*VI* 92, 94, 165), gives the perceptual faith a key role. The so-called good dialectic is characterized by attentiveness to the evidences of experience but is also conscious that every thesis is an idealization and therefore vigilant about its posits. The embalmed dialectic, by contrast, would be a repeatable or programmatic dialectic, akin to a scientific experiment that assumes it is uncontaminated by any vicissitudes concerning the inquiring subject, and is likewise neutral in regard to the particular singularities of the object under examination, proceeding inexorably in accord with a logic of history (or science). Merleau-Ponty highlights the political significance of this contingency against some (bad) construals of dialectics in earlier books, such as *Humanism and Terror* and *Adventures of the Dialectic*, but for our present purposes the point is just that philosophical reflection must continue to take the perceptual faith into account. And it must do so *not* by ignoring it or criticizing it from above as a version of what he calls "high-altitude thinking" (69), and *not* by making it a dogmatic axiom or a sort of epistemological foundation piece à la sense-data theories and the empiricist trajectory that he influentially criticizes in *Phenomenology of Perception*. At no point, for Merleau-Ponty, can the philosopher be epistemically sure that he or she has avoided this particular Scylla and Charybdis, just as a similar gesture governed his account and critique of empiricism and intellectualism in *Phenomenology*. Nonetheless, the hyper-dialectic that remains concerned with the perceptual faith appears (to Merleau-Ponty) as the best option, and, as would be expected of his dialectical account of this faith, it challenges any simple view of the perceptually "given." It is less a building block datum from which we accrue other reliable information and more a presupposition we cannot do without (normatively). As Merleau-Ponty puts a related point later on in the book, "the philosophical question is not posed in us by a pure spectator: it is first a question as to how, upon what ground, the pure spectator is established, from what more profound source he himself draws" (109). This "more profound source" is perhaps something akin to the chiasm and flesh that he describes in chapter 4, but it also involves the ongoing presupposition of the perceptual faith, which antedates oppositions between subjects and objects, selves and worlds. As he puts it, "The idea of the subject, and that of the object as well, transforms into a cognitive adequation the relationship with the world and with ourselves that we have in the perceptual faith. They do not clarify it; they utilize it tacitly, they draw out its consequences" (23). Here we can get something akin to Merleau-Ponty's rendering of Heidegger's being-in-the-world, but with perception playing a more important role, and with perception understood more broadly than simply visual perception but also including tactile, auditory, and olfactory "perception."

The perceptual faith is hence not something that is given apodictically, incorrigibly, etc. Rather, insofar as it is given at all, it is given ambiguously, to recall one of the key motifs of *Phenomenology of Perception*, which has been described by Weiss and others as a philosophy of ambiguity,[7] a term that recurs in the context of chapter 2's descriptions of his hyper-dialectical thought (*VI* 94). As such, Merleau-Ponty appears to agree with Deleuze and Leibniz on their famous overturning of Descartes: rather than having logical or perceptual access to the clear and distinct on the one hand, in contrast to the confused-obscure on the other, we have something more like the "clear-confused" on the one hand and the "distinct-obscure" on the other. The section, after all, is titled "The Perceptual Faith and Its Obscurity," and his basic claim is that we can neither readily translate this faith into theses nor ignore it. As Merleau-Ponty puts it, the "certitude, entirely irresistible as it may be, remains absolutely obscure; we can live it, we can neither think it nor formulate it, nor set it up in theses. Every elucidation brings us back to the dilemmas. . . . And it is this unjustifiable certitude of a sensible world common to us that is the seat of truth within us" (11).

## Science Presupposes the Perceptual Faith and Does Not Elucidate It

In this section, Merleau-Ponty considers potential rejoinders deriving from or inspired by science: in short, philosophical construals of science that would these days be called scientific naturalism. On such a view, the perceptual faith is ultimately little better than an illusion; the true is but the objective. Clearly he wants to guard against that conclusion with the idea of the perceptual faith, but not by simply accepting the opposite thesis, that the true is restricted to (or merely an elaboration of) the perceptual faith. He writes, "If the philosopher questions, and hence feigns ignorance of the world and of the visions of the world which are operative and take form continually within him, he does so precisely in order to make them speak, because he believes in them and expects from them all his future science" (*VI* 4). Any challenge that science poses to the perceptual faith (which is not equivalent to opinion or doxa, although it enables it) will take for granted some dimensions of experience, observation, connection with the world, etc. And the body remains key to this openness, even though Merleau-Ponty is rather less "thesis-like" concerning the primordiality of somatic or "motor" intentionality than he was in *Phenomenology*.

## The Perceptual Faith and Reflection

In the section on perceptual faith and reflection, Merleau-Ponty's aim is to explore the discontinuities that preclude any reflective or dialectical construal of the whole. Reflection aims to recuperate everything, including any putative antinomies between living and thinking, perceiving and judging, etc. The world becomes that which we think we perceive, liberated from what he calls bastard and unthinkable experiences (*VI* 31). Or, as he says later on, "The reflection recuperates everything except itself as an effort of recuperation, it clarifies everything except its own role" (33). Here I think we glean something like Merleau-Ponty's ongoing residual commitment to existentialism, and we might recall related ideas from *Phenomenology* against (a certain) Husserl: the world is not an "I think" but an "I can." His general concern here is that the perceptual faith is too readily transformed by reflection into a belief and thesis, or that it becomes tantamount to an epistemic given and therefore knowledge more than faith, in a manner that deprives perception of its ambiguous character, in both a descriptive and a normative sense. He cautions, however, that his remarks are not intended to disqualify reflection in favor of the unreflected and the immediate, or embrace some kind of fusion, a model that he criticizes in detail in chapter 3 (via a discussion of Bergson): "It is a question not of putting the perceptual faith in place of reflection, but on the contrary of taking into account the total situation, which involves reference from the one to the other" (35).

## The Perceptual Faith and Interrogation

In chapter 2, Merleau-Ponty has subsections on "perceptual faith and negativity" and "perceptual faith and interrogation." The focus of this material is on Sartre, his one-time close friend, and his antithetical model (a bad dialectic) of negativity versus positivity, of consciousness as nothingness opposed to the pure plenitude of being. To cut a long story short, Merleau-Ponty contends that such an account cannot recognize the ambiguity of the perceptual faith, and he argues that this is most apparent in Sartre's infamous treatment of other people via the Look. Indeed, part of the perceptual faith involves a commitment to our inextricable intertwining with others, but Sartre's phenomenology is accused of missing this, instead promulgating an agnosticism about the other (*VI* 79), "an anonymous faceless obsession," as Merleau-Ponty calls it (72). His concern in this chapter is more with ontology than with epistemology, but his general claim is that lived experience has a depth and significance that thought tries to do justice to, but cannot be properly comprehended via any thought of the pure negative (95). In many ways the central philosophical task is to interrogate the perceptual faith, but this is not because we may expect or receive answers in any ordinary sense (103). His discussion of chiasm and the intertwining in chapter 4 offers us the outlines of a new ontology that better acknowledges both the ineliminability of the perceptual faith and also the way it is a continual problem for us, leading to misconstruals and its own confabulation.

## Notes

1. Maurice Merleau-Ponty, *The Visible and the Invisible,* trans. A. Lingis (Evanston, Ill.: Northwestern University Press, 1964). Subsequent references to this work will be cited parenthetically in the text.

2. Edmund Husserl, *Ideas Pertaining to a Pure Phenomenology and to a Phenomenological Philosophy,* trans. F. Kersten (The Hague: Nijhoff 1982), §24.

3. On the question of the neglect of this internal struggle in Husserl, see Søren Overgaard, *Husserl and Heidegger on Being in the World* (Dordrecht: Kluwer 2004).

4. See Jack Reynolds, "Merleau-Ponty's Gordian Knot: Transcendental Phenomenology, Science and Naturalism," *Continental Philosophy Review* 50, no. 1 (2017): 81–104. This issue of the journal, guest-edited by Andrew Inkpin and me, explores some of these divergent receptions of Merleau-Ponty's work.

5. Cf. Jack Reynolds and Jon Roffe, "Neither/Nor: Merleau-Ponty's Ontology in 'The Intertwining/The Chiasm,'" in *Understanding Merleau-Ponty, Understanding Modernism,* ed A. Mildenberg (London: Bloomsbury 2018), 100–116.

6. Françoise Dastur, "Perceptual Faith and the Invisible," *Journal of the British Society of Phenomenology* 25, no. 1 (1994): 44–52.

7. See Gail Weiss, "Ambiguity," in *Merleau-Ponty: Key Concepts,* eds. R. Diprose and J. Reynolds (London: Routledge 2008) 132–41.

# 39 Public Self/Lived Subjectivity

Linda Martín Alcoff

The experience of a disjuncture between one's interior sense of self and the way one is viewed in public by others (especially by those with more dominant, mainstream, or higher-status identities) is a common theme in the writings of persons of color, LGBTQ folks, colonized populations, and people with disabilities. We might not even recognize our *self* in the projection that others have of us if there is a significant distortion effect. The question then arises, is our public self connected in any way to our "real" or lived self, our own sense of ourselves, or, perhaps, who we *really* are?

This essay will explore this question and the effects of the disjuncture between one's public self and one's lived sense of self. One might imagine that one's "public self" refers merely to publicly recognized identity categories, such as Latinx or female, and as such has only a superficial (and oppressive) relation to one's lived subjectivity or interior sense of self. However, post-Hegelian and phenomenological accounts of the self understand that one's public self (or how one is recognized by others) and one's lived subjectivity are co-constitutive elements of one's self-in-the-world. This idea shall be explained in what follows as a dialectical account of self formation.

The dialectical account does not reject the possibility that that there are conflicts between one's "exterior" and "interior" self, and so it can be useful to continue to talk of these two aspects of the self even though we take them to be related. I will begin by considering the implications of our sense of disjuncture between how we are seen by others and how we see ourselves on how we understand the formation of our self as a whole as we move between public and private spheres, familial and work environments, and out from beyond our neighborhoods or subcultures. Of course, we may well have multiple publicly recognized or acknowledged selves, quite distinct from one another, and not all of them may be equally oppressive or inaccurate to our own self-perception. And there is also the possibility, as discussed below, that a publicly recognized self can teach us some truths about our lived experience and in fact have more "truth-value" than our subjective sense of who we are. I will begin, however, with the issue of a disjuncture that is caused by marginalization and oppression.

The Cubana feminist philosopher Ofelia Schutte has described the dilemma of minoritized identity groups as a form of enforced "public erasure."[1] When my lived subjectivity or sense of self is unintelligible in the mainstream public domain, she suggests, I am *invisibilized*. Even more, she argues that in order to be able to function in a public domain that is hostile to women, Latinas, brown-skinned people, Spanish-speakers, etc., I must often perform the *invisibilization* myself, on myself. To gain credibility, achieve intelligibility, or simply to be included, the Latina is expected to perform in what Schutte calls a "North American voice." This means more than speaking in English: she must demonstrate her successful assimilation to norms of speech at multiple levels in order to display her mastery of "the language and epistemic maneuvers of the dominant culture, the same culture that in its everyday practice marks me as culturally 'other' than itself."[2] I am thus required to cover over my lived subjectivity, to engage in a pretense, and to participate in and reinforce the social oppression of my group as the price for recognition, inclusion, acceptance.

One might imagine this to involve merely the suppression of an accent, or of Spanglish, but it can also involve a manner of dress and comportment, the way I wear my hair, the decibel level of my laugh, my affective responses to people or events, my true thoughts and beliefs. In short, in hostile contexts, my lived subjectivity is inadmissible in public, and I must be on guard at every moment against slippage. While it may appear that the dominant mainstream is being inclusive of the visible Latina, what is being included is a carefully crafted and curated presentation. This requires an intensive hyper-self-consciousness, a form of "identity work," we might call it, unnecessary for those whose identities are more readily acceptable.

Consider the effects of this from the outside in. As Paul C. Taylor puts it, the "colonization of public meaning" produces "hegemonic ways of seeing [that] posit a hegemonic spectator that accepts and acquiesces to the requirements of these perspectives."[3] Hence, in order to create a palatable public self, I may come to adopt dominant perspectives on the bounds of palatability. I may become annoyed with friends or family who blow my cover, and thus slowly absorb, perhaps without intending to, the denigrating judgment of the dominant culture against people like me. This is a functional coping mechanism, not necessarily a moral flaw. But as a result, my selfhood changes. I seek out the assessments of dominant identity groups and respond to their judgments more than to those of my peers. I am calibrating my personality to gain a foothold in a larger public domain that is, in some cases, hostile, ignorant, and dismissive of my identity. If I can craft a public persona to gain social recognition of some important aspect of myself, however, the effect is that my identity changes. Successful dissembling over extended periods is bound to have deeper effects than I may originally intend.

Knowledge requires self-knowledge, numerous philosophers have argued, else we may be misled by our individual oversights and perspectival orientation. But self-knowledge also requires some manner of public confirmation. I may believe my lectures are scintillating, but a roomful of sleepy-eyed students tells another story. We look to the judgment of others not out of weakness or an undeveloped capacity for self-reliance but in order to gain a more accurate self-understanding. However, in social contexts that involve prejudice toward certain groups, this process becomes unreliable: I learn only how my dress, speech, and behavior generates a response that is a misrecognition. When this begins when we are young children, it is difficult to expect us to withstand the negative effects.

Call this account the "dialectical process of self-formation." Any given individual's personal characteristics, from confidence to charisma to the ability to tell a joke, have emerged through communal experiences, affected by whether one has had supportive audiences and positive interactions, or not.

Two further elements of this account need consideration here. The first concerns the intersectional nature of identities and concomitant variation in the public spheres to which any given individual has access. In most societies today, persons move between multiple communities, and their dialogical and dialectical encounters will be varied. It may be that my interactions closer to home—my family, my neighborhood, my religious community, my subculture—will express support and positive recognition, while social contexts I enter into further afield will be uncomprehending of various aspects of my identity, misreading my gestures or mistakenly guessing my motivations. However, the reactions could be reversed between interactions in the familiar and the farther afield: in some cases a lesbian may experience more positive forms of recognition the further away she travels from home. But the important point here is that my public or recognized self will vary by context so much so that, as Mariana Ortega puts it, we have "multiplicitous selves."[4] Though I may be silenced and misapprehended in one space, in another I may enjoy a profound sense of reciprocal understanding where my self-knowledge is given a more informed response. Such multiple variations can help us to resist the hegemonic aspirations of the "hegemonic ways of seeing" Taylor discusses.

This variability is part of what motivated W. E. B. Du Bois's conception of "double consciousness." In *The Souls of Black Folk*, published in 1903, Du Bois writes, "It is a peculiar sensation, this double-consciousness, this sense of always looking at one's self through the eyes of others, of measuring one's soul by the tape of a world that looks on in amused contempt and pity. One ever feels his two-ness,—an American, a Negro; two souls, two thoughts, two unreconciled strivings; two warring ideals in one dark body, whose dogged strength alone keeps it from being torn asunder."[5] Here, the variation, as with Schutte's description above, is a contestation between not simply different but contradictory representations: Du Bois goes so far as to suggest that these are not only unreconciled but unreconcilable. How could a white supremacist version of U.S. national identity reconcile with its excluded and despised minorities, groups whose history and thus very presence is a reminder of national injustice and a threat to national pride?

Double (or multiple) consciousness, then, follows not only from the differentiation of one's social spheres but from the political, economic, and cultural conflict between them. Mediation or coherence may be impossible, and yet the dialectical interplay could induce productive changes that may enable more inclusive and harmonious public domains of meaning if it can pierce hegemonic attempts at control and erasure. The representation of national-identity formations today are more varied and inclusive than when Du Bois wrote, and collective minority group movements can "recognize back": naming hostile climates, misrecognitions, misinformed judgments for what they are, and thus instigating more adequate representations.

In light of this discussion, we may be tempted to rename the "dialectical process of self-formation" a "multiple or pluralist process" because it involves in almost all cases relations between more than two. And it may be the case that the relations between multiple representations of public selves are not always conflictual and may be productive of new syntheses that improve the well-being as well as the political agency of lived subjectivity. Gloria Anzaldúa argues that, in fact, the proudly defiant "counterstance" to dominant cultures may fetishize opposition, circumscribing resistance to *reaction*. "At some point," she counsels, "on our way to a new consciousness, we will have to [occupy] both shores at once and, at once, see through serpent and eagle eyes." Or, she surmises, we might leave the dominant culture altogether "and cross the border into a wholly new and separate territory."[6] But the key to this fecund political imaginary is the decision "to act and not react," that is, to take a creative stance toward the possibilities of self-formation and self-understanding.

I will return to Anzaldúa's tantalizing proposal in a moment, but here I want to argue for retaining the dialectical account as one that does not lock us into opposition between reified alternatives or merely two sides. The idea of dialectics helpfully signifies the *dynamic co-constitution* of selves, resisting an interpretation as a happy pluralism or static juxtaposition. Just as Du Bois describes, the contestation between contradictory understandings of an identity category leads to struggle, whether overt or papered over. The concept of dialectics connotes such struggle, although, as Anzaldúa urges, we must not imagine that struggle as a simple conservation of current forms of identity.

The second element that needs further exploration here is to clarify the epistemic dimension of the disjuncture between a public self and a lived sense of interiority. We have already spoken to the need for some public epistemic confirmation of self-knowledge in order to determine whether one's self-perception has some truth-content. But can a phenomenology of the self be judged on epistemic grounds in general? And if so, should I give presumptive authority to my own sense of my self against those of others, whether these others are intimates close at hand or those farther afield?

These epistemic questions require us to clarify what is the referring term or object of knowledge here. There may be a truth about the way in which my public self is perceived in hostile contexts that has little reference to my ownmost self, my intellectual or moral characteristics, or my lived experience. The dialectical account developed here suggests, however, that our selves are never completely internal or interior. The critical epistemic question is not, therefore, simply a question about public or external *representations* of my self, nor is it exclusively a question about my *interior experience*. Rather, it is a question about my self-in-the-world, where "the world" is understood to be dynamic and multiply constituted. I not only experience my "self" differently in a supportive versus a hostile context; I manifest a different way of being, an expansive or retracted agency, a confidence that maximizes my capacities or a foreshortened reflexivity curtailed to survival of one sort or another. Inspired by Anzaldúa, both Edwina Barvosa and Ortega urge us to explore the "wealth of selves" any given individual can manifest in diverse contexts.[7] Thus the issue is not simply that I am misperceived, whereby we imagine that "I" to remain stable, but that my agential possibilities are significantly altered. Consider especially mixed-race, diasporic, transnational, and transgender identities here.

This account does not entail that the experience of "erasure," as we developed it from Schutte's work, never applies. So there remains the epistemic consideration of whether my understanding of my self, or another's understanding of my self, in any given moment, is an adequate or fair description. My public self may be represented, and experienced in different ways by various groups. It is possible that more than one representation has some truth content, that more than one describes some dimension that is truthful, and that my *self* is altered across contexts without being eclipsed.

Any given individual plays multiple social and relational roles: daughter, mother, employee, union member, consumer, voter, and so on. These indicate our relations to specific others, as members of a family, a workforce, a species that shares a planet or a water source with others. Focusing on each one foregrounds different aspects of my history, my social inheritance, my obligations, my choices and practices. Potentially, I can gain self-knowledge by attending to all of these; I need not decide between them to ascertain truths about my self.

Note, however, that the situation Du Bois describes is one full of intentional lies, misdirection, and omission. The problem he so acutely diagnoses in the multitude of his writings was not simply a mistaken representation at the discursive or ideational level but a coercive formation of selfhood with differential possibilities, benefits, and protections.

Consider, then, the problem of whiteness or maleness or any number of other forms of publicly recognized identity that have been produced through intentional lies and omissions. Here we have a dialectic of struggle in which self-knowledge is blocked by the control over subaltern perceptions. Lies of superiority go unchallenged by the enforcement of deference and the rewards given to the obsequious. Such a situation produces no double consciousness and no motivation for self-reflection or creative reformations. There is a kind of erasure occurring, but it is coming from one's closest peers. The public self of dominant groups may feel no abrasion from one's lived interiority, unless it is to feel some inadequacy to the persistent presumption of mastery. Hence the epistemic dimension of this dialectic is quite the reverse of the one Du Bois portrays. Rather than needing to deflect distorted external representations, the dominant need to welcome external viewpoints as a corrective. To champion a general epistemic privilege of the lived self over the public self is to disable the correction needed.

As our public spheres become more multilingual in a broad sense, containing multiple sensibilities, perceptions, and judgments, this can produce a newly felt anxiety for those whose public selves were in the past consistently portrayed in flattering terms. Now, dominant identities must negotiate a multitude of interpellations, some strongly critical. These require a response of one sort or another: an attempt to enforce their silence once again or a reappraisal of one's sense of self.

To summarize, I've argued that the exterior or publicly recognized self and our interior or lived sense of self exist in a dialectical relation to produce one's self-in-the-world. More correctly, we exist in multiple worlds, and the selves we can manifest are subsequently varied depending on the contextual conditions. The intersectional realities of increasingly pluritopic hermeneutic landscapes mean that most everyone will be negotiating multiple interpellations. However, these varied contexts are structured by power relations that affect the sphere of intelligibility and our likely self-knowledge. Not all face the same challenge to legibility or have the scope of their agency curtailed to the same degree.

On this dialectical account, it is impossible to be impervious to one's publicly recognized self, and it is possible to be mistaken in some significant measure about one's self-in-the-world. What are the implications of this claim on oppressed identities? Do relational theories of the self have worrisome implications for the right to self-name?

It is important to note that different forms of social identity require different analyses, even within an overall dialectical account. Not all processes of social construction are the same, nor are all socially constructed to the same degree. The right of a group to self-name needs to be grounded in a plausible metaphysical understanding of the process of self-formation, not simply in a liberal rights-based political theory, but also may be grounded in long histories of misrecognition and exclusionary processes of concept formation. Even if one's subculture allows for a proliferation of self-presentation and identity concepts, the requirement to be hidden or "discrete" constrains the production of new forms of social practice, interaction, and recognition that are part of the work of developing new ways of being and of being seen.

To counter the extreme hermeneutic injustice experienced by some groups, an epistemic deference is called for so that those with the requisite lived experience (internal and external) can lead the way to new concepts, terms, and definitions. They alone will have the thick and rich knowledge base from which to do meaningful theoretical work. Yet the very discussion and debate new understandings require will involve debates in which some individual and collective self-understandings may be challenged.[8] Improving social treatment, self-understanding, and the options for self-ascription will involve transformations in public domains, and these changes will affect the possibilities for our ownmost selves.

## Notes

1. Ofelia Schutte, "Cultural Alterity: Cross-Cultural Communication and Feminist Theory in North-South Contexts," in *Decentering the Center: Philosophy for a Multicultural, Postcolonial, and Feminist World*, ed. Uma Narayan and Sandra Harding (Bloomington: Indiana University Press, 2000), 47–66.

2. Schutte, "Cultural Alterity," 59.

3. Paul C. Taylor, *Black Is Beautiful: A Philosophy of Black Aesthetics* (Malden, Mass.: Wiley Blackwell, 2016), 59.

4. Mariana Ortega, *In-Between: Latina Feminist Phenomenology, Multiplicity, and the Self* (Albany, N.Y.: SUNY Press, 2016).

5. W. E. B. Du Bois, *The Souls of Black Folk*, ed. David W. Blight and Robert Gooding-Williams (Boston: Bedford Books, 1997), 38.

6. Gloria Anzaldúa, *Borderlands/La Frontera: The New Mestiza* (San Francisco: Aunt Lute, 1987), 78–79.

7. Edwina Barvosa, *Wealth of Selves: Multiple Identities, Mestiza Consciousness, and the Subject of Politics* (College Station: University of Texas Press, 2008).

8. Talia Mae Bettcher, "Trapped in the Wrong Theory: Rethinking Trans Oppression and Resistance," *Signs* 39 no. 2 (Winter 2014): 383–406.

# 40 Queer Orientations

Lauren Guilmette

How do we understand ourselves when we find ourselves on the outside of some set of norms, spaces, institutions, familial and/or cultural expectations, and what can be done with this experience of disorientation? The concept of "queer orientations" has been most fully developed by Sara Ahmed, signifying both "nonstraight sexual practices" as well as the disorientation of what is "oblique" more broadly.[1] She turns to the phenomenological tradition—particularly to Edmund Husserl and Maurice Merleau-Ponty—for their insights into what it means to "take up" an orientation, given that these are not neutral but *learned*, formed in a social space loaded with sedimented histories. "We have our bearings," Ahmed begins, and these include not only personal memories but cultural expectations of what bodies will do, such that what is presented as a choice of alternatives is often framed with a "right" way to turn at some juncture in life. Meanings are attached to the directions we take, as in the well-known association of "the left" (*sinister*) with deviation, "the East" with the exotic, over and against the "orthodox" right. As she writes, "The social depends in part on agreement about how we measure space and time, which is why social conflict can often be experienced as being 'out of time' as well as 'out of place' with others."[2] Orientations enable us to "find our way" and to "feel at home," yet these sites of familiarity can be more or less exclusionary of others who are not perceived to fit, and it is the status of these "other" orientations I want to explicate here.

Delineating Ahmed's concept through her interpretive use of phenomenology, I consider two questions for which Ahmed and others—especially Judith Butler and Rosemarie Garland-Thomson—provide insight. First, how widely does the term *queer* extend, and how does it function as a critical category? Second, what might be the ethical value of disorientation as a state of disrupting the tacitly encouraged (if not overtly normative) orientations of one's moment? Would disorientation then become a queer ethical ideal, and in what sense would disorientation be affirmed?

## Husserl's Not-So-Familiar Table

Ahmed draws on Husserl's first volume of his *Ideas*, where he describes the disruption of the "natural attitude" by which we ordinarily make sense of the world.[3] Husserl takes his writing table as his object, then allows his attention to wander to the unseen portions of his office and co-perceived surroundings of his summer home, with rooms where his children may now be playing.[4] In Husserl's description, to attend to this domestic space is to deviate from the reflective task at hand, and Ahmed writes, "Being oriented toward the writing table might ensure that you inhabit certain rooms and not others, and that you do some things rather than others."[5] With feminist theorists such as Virginia Woolf, Adrienne Rich, and Audre Lorde, Ahmed notes that the possibility of sitting down at the writing table—and thereby putting out of action the ordinary world—is foreclosed for many who cannot, in our present "political economy of attention," so easily set aside the demands of domestic life.[6] Furthermore, to be able to reflect at the writing table in this way requires that the table "open itself" to one's body as an object for use. While Ahmed criticizes Husserl for setting aside the familiarity of domestic uses—in order to attend to the flow of perception itself—she follows feminist phenomenologists such as Linda Martín Alcoff in finding Husserl's method "extremely useful" for engaging taken-for-granted values and norms; as Ahmed writes, "It allows us to consider how the familiar takes shape by being unnoticed."[7] Gail Weiss has also developed an account of Husserl aimed at the "de-naturalization of the natural attitude." This arises through the recognition of our natural attitudes as "themselves complex, dynamic constructions," which can shift "in response to specific social, cultural, and political encounters."[8]

## Heidegger's Hammer and Failed Orientations

Ahmed notes Heidegger's treatment of the table as both "a spatial thing" and a thing of occupational significance, one that allows us to *do* certain things.[9] She also briefly recounts his famous description of the broken or unusable hammer as no longer "ready-to-hand," which is formative for her own account of "failed orientations."[10] For Ahmed, the failure of a failed orientation may have as much to do with one's own relation to the tool as with the qualities of the tool itself, as when "a tool is used by a body for which it was not intended, or a body uses a tool that does not extend its capacity for action."[11] Ami Harbin helpfully elaborates the scene of Heidegger's hammer to describe experiences of bodily disorientation, which may break a sense of ease that we likely did not appreciate until its interruption, "when we are no longer able to recognize or interact with objects, people, or occasions in ways that were once habitual."[12] A failed orientation casts us out of this presumed ease; much in sympathy with Ahmed, Harbin finds that experiences of "disorientation" provide the conditions for coming to see our own orientations, enabling shifts of attention that can be morally and politically transformative.

## Merleau-Ponty's Queer Slant

Perhaps most central for the concept of "queer orientations" is Ahmed's use of Merleau-Ponty, who developed Husserl's later insights on touch[13] into a phenomenology of embodied perception. The body for Merleau-Ponty is not an object in space but is interactively submerged in a horizon which, far from neutral or objective, is loaded with "sedimented histories" formed through the habitual actions of the body.[14] Ahmed is drawn to Merleau-Ponty for his description of a series of spatial experiments, which tested one's capacity to "see straight," or reorient from a slantwise view, through the becoming-vertical of one's perspective. As he writes, when one sees the room "slantwise", "the general effect is queer."[15] One finds that one's spatial coordinates are not absolute but, rather, are shaped by the body's purposes, its "task and situation."[16] As Ahmed explains, for Merleau-Ponty this "queer" moment "must be overcome not because such moments contradict laws that govern objective space, but because they block bodily action."[17] While Merleau-Ponty's use of *queer* does not refer to sexuality, Ahmed claims that we can still appropriate his usage here for queer theory, following from its Indo-European etymology of "twisting": "Queer is, after all, a spatial term, which then gets translated into a sexual term, a term for a twisted sexuality that does not follow a straight line."[18] Ahmed thus reconsiders the normative significance of the vertical axis by which we "see straight" and reflects that this line is not absolutely given or fixed but is, rather, an effect of alignment. Thus, heteronormativity functions as a "straightening device" to reinforce the alignment of the body, by which "queer or wonky moments are corrected."[19]

Many feminist philosophers have found Merleau-Ponty's treatment of sexuality productive, insofar as sexual experience is *not* a distinct domain from bodily experience but is, rather, a mode of the body's *sensitivity*—feeling the nearness of others.[20] For Ahmed, this view situates "sexual orientation" as not just a matter of the object one desires but of how displaying the gestures associated with desiring such and such entails inhabiting the world differently.[21] In addition to Merleau-Ponty, Ahmed references Foucault here for his account of the production of the homosexual as a "species," "a type of person who 'deviates' from what is neutral," or straight.[22] Some critics have argued that the language of "sexual orientation" focuses too narrowly on the relation of desire and its object, turning to the terms of "sexuality" as a more fluid realm, but Ahmed counters that orientations matter in complicated ways, given how familial and social spaces are presently delineated—"in desiring certain objects *other things follow.*"[23] In this sense, Ahmed's *queer* does not primarily concern sexual desire but the social and institutional exclusions that have historically been effects of sexual and/or gender nonconformity, which shape how one can extend through public space—for instance, how to walk and comport one's body, and when and where it is acceptable to express affection to one's partner, while also noticing the unthinking intimacies of those who are "straight" and "cis" and thus can move through the world with ease.

## One Is Not Born but Becomes Straight

Paraphrasing Simone de Beauvoir, Ahmed writes of straightness as a matter of becoming: "One is not born, but becomes straight."[24] She builds upon Rich and Butler for an account of compulsory heterosexuality—normalized as a straight line leading toward "the other sex"—and observes that "subjects are required to 'tend toward' some objects and not others as a condition of familial as well as social love."[25] Referencing Butler on the formation of heterosexuality through the renunciation of the *possibility* of homosexuality, which "produces a field of heterosexual objects,"[26] Ahmed describes this "field" as the inheritance of the conventional family home, which demands its reproduction through the family line. "The heterosexual couple becomes a point along this line, which is given to the child as its inheritance or background. The background then is not simply 'behind' the child: it is what the child is asked to aspire 'toward.'"[27] In this field that treats the heterosexual and cisgendered couple as a social gift, the child is encouraged to display "straight tendencies."[28] Straightness in this sense entails that the contours of various spaces allow for the access and inhabitance of some bodies more than others.

Here we can begin to answer my first question, concerning how widely the term *queer* extends. Ahmed plays on the double meaning of *queer*, referring both to non-straight sexual practices and to an oblique perspective that might disorient a norm; for instance, she explores her own mixed-race identity as a queer orientation to whiteness, casting a critical angle on the desirability of its inheritance and reproduction.[29] While she recognizes that this expansive meaning of *queer* risks "losing the specificity" of sexual deviation, "it also sustains the significance of deviation in what makes queer lives queer."[30] On this question of the meaning of *queer* and its relation to *deviation*, I find Butler helpful. Still a bit skeptical in 1993 about the term's affirmative resignification, Butler argues that if *queer* is to retain its critical power as a site of resistance rather than repeating its historical meaning as a slur, theorists and activists must resist taking *queer* to represent a coherent or uniform identity.[31] Butler writes that *queer* can only be a term of affiliation and, at best, of collective contestation, "never fully owned but always and only redeployed, twisted, queered from a prior usage and in the direction of urgent and expanding political purposes."[32] If *queer* is, even in the narrower meaning of non-straight sexual practices, resolutely not a matter of *identification*, Ahmed proposes that we might instead understand *queer* as a matter of *orientation*—how we align and/or fail or refuse to align with straightness.[33] This queer critique of straightness takes inspiration from and, in turn, bears relevance for phenomenological studies of race, gender, and of disability.

## Queering the Corporeal Schema: The Misfit

For Merleau-Ponty, the situated body grasps its situation through the development of a corporeal schema, an ongoing process of meaning-making by which we become "flesh," realizing ourselves as objects for others as well as subjects. Fanon deepens Merleau-Ponty's analysis by attending to the constraints of racial categories on this meaning-making, the doubling of a "historico-racial schema" that exists alongside of, or over, his body schema.[34] In this superimposed schema—which Fanon views obliquely as both a mental health professional and a colonized subject—he negotiates the congealed meanings of a history he did not choose, which construct him "out of a thousand details, anecdotes, and stories." The white gaze filters Fanon's body through racialized habits of seeing—a parallel claim can be made for the homophobic and/or transphobic gaze under the heterosexual, cisgendered schema—and Fanon diagnoses these racialized habits as an "affective ankylosis": a numbing rigidity that makes one unreceptive to the pain of others.[35] Fanon's description of the colonized subject's "failed orientation" shows that disorienting experiences cannot be upheld as ethical in themselves. Perhaps this dehumanized state can be said to generate Fanon's insights, but it is in spite of and not because of it that he has the critical resources to respond.

Along these lines, Ahmed reflects on her experiences traveling with a last name that draws unwanted attention in airports, and she observes that some bodies can extend more easily than others through social spaces, while others are *stopped* and brought into question.[36] In her most recent book, she draws upon experiences of being a question for others: "To be asked 'Where are you from?' is a way of being told you are not from here," requesting an account of your foreignness.[37] Another, "What is your relationship?," brings to mind for Ahmed when she moved to a new home with her partner, with a neighbor inquiring if they were sisters.[38] The question "What is wrong with you?"—asked perpetually of (visibly) disabled subjects—demands "an account of oneself as an account of how things went wrong."[39] Questions like these entail more than an innocent curiosity, or rather, the innocence is a shiny surface that covers over a deep-seated desire to make sense of this perceived strangeness.[40] Such "violent curiosity" produces disorienting experiences that do *not* positively transform the one who asks but, more frequently, reinforce the asker's worldview while challenging the legitimacy of the one being asked. Disorientation cannot be a queer ethical ideal in this sense.

Here Garland-Thomson's concept of the "mis-fit" is a helpful resource for thinking about the disorientation of queer orientations, when and where that disorientation may be called "ethical."[41] This concept decenters the "able" body as the assumption for what "fits" in public space by recognizing that inaccessibility is "in the fit, not in the body." The "mis-fit" reveals a slippage in what is meant by *disorientation*: the disorientation of repeatedly mis-fitting in a physical, social, or institutional space is not the same as the disorientation of one who most always "fits" and, for a queer moment, mis-fits, thereby coming to realize that the ease with which one moves is not a natural given but a matter of the arrangement of space. We can speak of the latter as a queer ethical moment insofar it inspires a rearrangement, or at least a critical questioning of the existing arrangement and its presumptions. As Butler writes of the practice of critique, we are driven to interrogate the "historical conditions of experience" only after coming up against a tear in the fabric of our web of sense-making: "One asks about the limits of ways of knowing because one has already run up against a crisis within the epistemological field in which one lives."[42] Thus, while Ahmed describes disorienting experiences as vital moments that "throw the body from its ground" and upholds everyday experiences of disorientation as key sites of learning, she does not affirm disorientation as something that might be prescribed to others.[43] Rather than demanding deviation, an ethics of queer orientations asks what our orientation toward queer moments of deviation will be—in others and in ourselves—and to reflect on how we can inhabit the world in ways that give support to others who may register under the dominant schema as deviant or strange.

## Notes

1. Sara Ahmed, *Queer Phenomenology: Orientations, Objects, Others* (Durham, N.C.: Duke University Press, 2006), 161, cf. 107.

2. Ahmed, *Queer Phenomenology,* 13.

3. For more on the "natural attitude" see the entry in this volume by Lanei Rodemeyer.

4. Edmund Husserl, *Ideas: General Introduction to Pure Phenomenology,* trans. W. R. Boyce Gibson (London: Allen and Unwin, 1969), 101.

5. Ahmed, *Queer Phenomenology,* 30.

6. Ahmed, *Queer Phenomenology,* 32. See Virginia Woolf, *A Room of One's Own* (Orlando, Fla.: Harcourt, 1989); Adrienne Rich, *Of Woman Born* (London: Virago, 1991); Audre Lorde, *Sister, Outsider: Essays and Speeches* (New York: Crossing Press, 1984).

7. Ahmed, *Queer Phenomenology,* 37. Alcoff values Husserl's phenomenological reduction for taking distance "from the familiarity of the world," insofar as phenomenology does not purport to grasp the world of objects as they *really* are, but can study the world as we live it, as well as the structures of consciousness. Linda Martín Alcoff, "Phenomenology, Post-Structuralism, and Feminist Theory on the Concept of Experience," in *Feminist Phenomenology,* ed. L. Fisher and L. Embree (Dordrecht: Kluwer, 2000): 48. See Alia Al-Saji, "Bodies and Sensings: On the Uses of Husserlian Phenomenology for Feminist Theory," *Continental Philosophy Review* 43 (2010): 13–37. See also Talia Mae Bettcher's "When Tables Speak," *Daily Nous,* May 30, 2018, http://dailynous.com/2018/05/30/tables-speak-existence-trans-philosophy-guest-talia-mae-bettcher.

8. Gail Weiss, "De-Naturalizing the Natural Attitude: A Husserlian Legacy to Social Phenomenology," *Journal of Phenomenological Psychology* 47, no. 1 (2016): 4.

9. Ahmed cites Martin Heidegger, *Ontology—The Hermeneutics of Facticity,* trans. J. van Buren (Bloomington: Indiana University Press, 1999), 68.

10. Martin Heidegger, *Being and Time* (1927), trans. J. Macquarrie and E. Robinson (New York: Harper & Row, 1962), 75.

11. Ahmed, *Queer Phenomenology,* 51.

12. Ami Harbin, "Bodily Disorientation and Moral Change," *Hypatia: A Journal of Feminist Philosophy* 27, no. 2 (Spring 2012): 265.

13. Here Ahmed cites—and Merleau-Ponty builds from—Edmund Husserl, *Ideas pertaining to a Pure Phenomenology and to a Phenomenological Philosophy, Second Book,* trans. R. Rojcewicz and A. Schuwer (Dordrecht: Kluwer, 1989).

14. Ahmed, *Queer Phenomenology,* 56. See Judith Butler, "Performative Acts and Gender Constitutions: An Essay in Phenomenology and Feminist Theory," in *Writing on the Body: Female Embodiment and Feminist Theory,* ed. K. Conboy, N. Medina, and S. Stanbury (New York: Columbia University Press, 1997). See also "Horizons" by David Morris in this volume.

15. Maurice Merleau-Ponty, *Phenomenology of Perception* (1945), trans. C. Smith (London: Routledge, 2005), 289.

16. Merleau-Ponty, *Phenomenology of Perception,* 291.

17. Ahmed, *Queer Phenomenology*, 66.

18. Ahmed, *Queer Phenomenology*, 67.

19. Ahmed, *Queer Phenomenology*, 67. See "Heteronormativity" by Meghan Burke in this volume.

20. Merleau-Ponty, *Phenomenology of Perception*, 178–85. See Iris Marion Young, *On Female Body Experience: Throwing Like a Girl and Other Essays* (Oxford: Oxford University Press, 2005); Gail Weiss, *Body Images: Embodiment as Intercorporeality* (London: Routledge, 1999); Gayle Salamon, *Assuming a Body: Transgender and Rhetorics of Materiality* (New York: Columbia University Press, 2010).

21. Salamon's critical phenomenology of transphobia explores the slippage in cultural perceptions from trans girl to gay boy in the 2008 murder of fifteen-year-old Latisha King in Oxnard, CA, and the interpretation of her gender expression as itself sexually aggressive—a "panic-inducing provocation"—in the court proceedings that followed. Salamon observes that one juror understood Latisha's style of dress as "actually a form of taunting" the boy who would shoot her at point-blank range in their junior high school classroom. Gayle Salamon, *The Life and Death of Latisha King: A Critical Phenomenology of Transphobia* (New York: NYU Press, 2018), 5, 152.

22. Ahmed, *Queer Phenomenology*, 69. See Michel Foucault, *History of Sexuality, Volume One: The Will to Knowledge*, trans. R. Hurley (New York, Vintage, 1990).

23. Ahmed, *Queer Phenomenology*, 100.

24. Ahmed, *Queer Phenomenology*, 79. See Simone de Beauvoir, *The Second Sex* (1949), trans. C. Borde and S. Malovany-Chevallier (New York: Vintage, 2011).

25. Ahmed, *Queer Phenomenology*, 84.

26. Judith Butler, *The Psychic Life of Power* (Stanford, Calif.: Stanford University Press, 1997), 21.

27. Ahmed, *Queer Phenomenology*, 90.

28. Ahmed, *Queer Phenomenology*, 91–92.

29. Ahmed, *Queer Phenomenology*, 154.

30. Ahmed, *Queer Phenomenology*, 161.

31. Judith Butler, *Bodies That Matter: On the Discursive Limits of "Sex"* (London: Routledge, 1993), 226.

32. Butler, *Bodies That Matter*, 228. See also "Queer Performativity" by Sarah Hansen in this volume.

33. In this sense, Ahmed claims that one may "have a heterosexual orientation and not line up" to "straight" societal expectations, and likewise one may "have a 'nonhetero' sexual orientation and be straight in other respects," engaging recent queer critiques of "homonormativity" and the compulsory future-orientation of the reproductive family (*Queer Phenomenology*, 172). See also Lisa Duggan, *The Twilight of Equality: Neoliberalism, Cultural Politics, and the Attack on Democracy* (Boston: Beacon Press, 2003); Judith Halberstam, *In a Queer Time and Place: Transgender Bodies, Subcultural Lives* (New York: NYU Press, 2005); Lee Edelman, *No Future: Queer Theory and the Death Drive* (Durham, N.C.: Duke University Press, 2004).

34. Frantz Fanon, *Black Skin, White Masks* (1952), trans. R. Philcox (New York: Grove Press, 2008), 90–91. See Gayle Salamon, "'The Place Where Life Hides Away': Merleau-Ponty, Fanon, and the Location of Bodily Being," *differences: A Journal of Feminist Cultural*

*Studies* 17, no. 2 (2006): 103. See also "The Racial-Epidermal Schema" by Axelle Karera in this volume.

35. Alia Al-Saji, "A Phenomenology of Hesitation: Interrupting Racialized Habits of Seeing," in *Living Alterities: Phenomenology, Embodiment, and Race*, ed. E.S. Lee (Albany, N.Y.: SUNY Press, 2014), 141.

36. Ahmed, *Queer Phenomenology*, 139.

37. Sara Ahmed, *Living a Feminist Life* (Durham, N.C.: Duke University Press, 2017), 117.

38. Ahmed, *Living a Feminist Life*, 121.

39. Ahmed, *Living a Feminist Life*, 124. Ahmed cites Rosemarie Garland-Thomson, "The Story of My Work: How I Became Disabled," *Disability Studies Quarterly* 34, no. 2 (2014): 8.

40. See Lauren Guilmette, "The Violence of Curiosity: Butler's Foucault, Foucault's Herculine, and the Will-to-Know," *philoSOPHIA* 7, no. 1 (2017): 1–22.

41. Rosemarie Garland-Thomson, "Misfits: A Feminist Materialist Disability Concept," *Hypatia: A Journal of Feminist Philosophy* 26, no. 3 (2011): 594. See also "Misfitting" by Rosemarie Garland-Thomson in this volume.

42. Judith Butler, "What Is Critique? An Essay on Foucault's Virtue," delivered as the Raymond Williams Lecture at Cambridge University, May 2000, European Institute for Progressive Cultural Policies, http://eipcp.net/transversal/0806/butler/en/#_ftn1.

43. Ahmed, *Queer Phenomenology*, 157.

# 41 Queer Performativity

Sarah Hansen

The notion of queer performativity has its origin in Judith Butler's 1990 text *Gender Trouble: Feminism and the Subversion of Identity* and associated essays. Butler's early writings draw from and reimagine phenomenology in order to describe gender as performative, as a "stylized repetition of acts" rather than a stable natural ground or feature of identity. For Butler, gender amounts to the "mundane way in which bodily gestures, movements, and enactments of various kinds constitute the illusion of an abiding gendered self."[1] If these gestures, movements, and acts are arbitrary, it is possible to trouble gender, to break or subvert the repetition of a norm with a "different sort of repeating," a different style or form of gender performance. In conversation with *Gender Trouble*, Eve Kosofsky Sedgwick first formulates the term *queer performativity* in 1993, describing it as a "strategy for the production of meaning and being" that disrupts assumptions about identity and subjectivity.[2] Indeed, in the 1999 preface to the second edition, Butler shares that she underestimated the disrupting impact of her text. She did not know that *Gender Trouble* "would have as wide an audience as it has had . . . or that it would be cited as one of the founding texts of queer theory."[3] For Butler and others, performativity has exceeded its meanings in *Gender Trouble*, becoming a popular way to theorize queerness and to queer (as a verb) theory. Put differently, performativity not only makes sense of nonnormative queer sexualities; it also challenges normative practices of sense-making.

Perhaps because of Butler's engagement with phenomenology, questions about lived bodily experience have been especially generative of queer and queering readings of performativity. In her 1988 essay "Performative Acts and Gender Constitution: An Essay in Phenomenology and Feminist Theory," Butler develops an early account of gender performativity by reimagining Simone de Beauvoir's and Maurice Merleau-Ponty's phenomenological understandings of bodies and acts. When Beauvoir writes that "one is not born a woman, but, rather, becomes a woman," she relies on Merleau-Ponty's account of the body as a "historical idea." For Merleau-Ponty, the body is not merely material; it is also a historical process of "continual and incessant materializing of possibilities."[4] Rather than a stable natural ground of identity, gender is a mode of becoming. As Butler later puts it in *Bodies That Matter*, gender is a "process of materialization that stabilizes over time to produce the effect of boundary, fixity or surface." Extending Merleau-Ponty and Beauvoir, Butler goes on to describe how the actions that constitute gender are "socially shared and historically constituted."[5] The "I" that acts is not a disembodied agency that precedes and directs an embodied exterior.[6] Instead, the field of materializing possibilities and the meaning of particular performances is constituted by their social context and historical moment. While actions constitute gender, they are also constituted by gender as a socially and historically specific mode of disciplinary power. Here Butler is especially interested in the regulatory system of compulsory heterosexuality that reproduces gender categories on a broad cultural scale by compelling the enactment of gender norms. Drawing on a Foucauldian account of modern power and exploring the social practice of drag performance, Butler shows how vast movements of disciplinary power produce queerness as abnormal perversion *and* how queer individuals and communities subvert their own subjection, playing with the terms and styles of identity. As Patti Smith famously puts it, "Gender is a drag," in the double meaning of this phrase.[7] Gender is a process of play and performance *and* a materializing reflection of power relations that dominate and oppress.

To be clear, Butler's early engagement with phenomenology and performativity not only draws on a Foucauldian account of power to complicate the disembodied interior "I"; she also engages psychoanalysis to describe the shape of queer experience and queer resistance. Foucault's genealogical work consistently troubles the divisions of inside/outside and interiority/exteriority. For instance, in *Discipline and Punish*, Foucault rejects originary understandings of the subject that posit an interior essence or truth to be uncovered through structures of repression. In his view, modern power is not primarily repressive. It is disseminated and productive, subjecting bodies to "a system of constraints and privations, obligations and prohibitions," passing judgment on "drives and desires"; the "subject" of modern disciplinary power is fabricated through the play of dominations.[8] The soul, he dramatically announces, is the "prison of the body."[9] In *The History of Sexuality, Volume One*, Freud and Freudian leftists are identified as proponents of the erroneous repressive hypothesis. However, Butler finds resources in psychoanalysis to describe how queer subjects live and resist disciplinary power. In the Oedipal narrative, heterosexual identity is established through the prohibition against homosexual incest, melancholic grieving over the loss of the mother, and denial of the homosexual desire that necessitates that loss. From Butler's perspective, it is a culture of compulsory heterosexuality, and not the naturalness of heterosexual desire, that produces the melancholic heterosexual subject. For Butler, then, the Oedipal prohibition is not simply juridical. It is productive and disseminated in ways that are consistent with a Foucauldian understanding of power and which point to the possibilities of queer subversion. If heterosexuality is dependent on the disavowal of homosexuality, queering performances might unsettle its supposed naturalness, exposing vast discourses that reproduce heterosexuality and making space for different understandings of gender and sexuality. These possibilities of resistance are what have inspired intense queer interest in Butler's notion of performativity since the early 1990s. If gender is a series of performative acts, if it is something that is done or made, perhaps its binary and heterosexist meanings can be undone or unmade through acts of queer resistance and subversion.

Writing in the midst of performativity's enthusiastic uptake, Sedgwick's 1993 essay "Queer Performativity" explores *Gender Trouble*'s early reception alongside J. L. Austin's early notion of "performative utterance." In his 1962 text *How to Do Things with Words*, Austin defines performative utterances as a distinct class of utterances that not only describe or report but also *do*. Utterances like "I promise," "I bequeath," or "I do (take this woman to be my lawful wedded wife)" are actions as well as statements. Although Austin repeatedly returns to these examples, he ultimately suggests that performativity may be a feature of all utterances. As a distinct category, then, performative utterances may not exist. For Sedgwick, this suggests that performativity is "quite a queer category" because it "begins its intellectual career all but repudiated in advance."[10] Sedgwick also observes that Austin focuses on first-person cases that lend themselves to assumptions about the unity and authority of the speaking subject. She suggests that the second person verb-less utterance "Shame on you" more easily raises questions about the subject because it effaces the "I" and its agency. In her words, "Shame effaces itself; shame points and projects; shame turns itself skin side outside; shame and self-display, shame and exhibitionism are different interlings of the same glove; shame . . . is performative."[11] Austin's struggle with performativity betrays how shame poses identity as a question. Turned "skin side outside," there is no originary "performativity itself" to be found in Austin's or Sedgwick's text as shame makes and interrupts identity in a dislocating movement.

For Sedgwick, queer performativity's critique of identity challenges the affective emphasis on pride in mainstream LGBT politics and the psychoanalytic emphasis on melancholy in Butler's text. In Sedgwick's view, discourses of LGBT pride often strengthen normalizing power by attempting to exorcise shame and the questions of identity that it generates and legitimates. To be sure, Butler is generally critical of LGBT pride discourse and its commercial orientation in pride marches and parades. But her focus on melancholy and her psychoanalytic archive may not appreciate the force of Foucault's critique of the repressive hypothesis. At the close of her essay, Sedgwick argues that celebrations of "productive multiplicities of resistance" may be just so many sites for generating and proliferating more repression. And she mocks interpretations of Butler that involve "straining one's eyes to ascertain whether particular performances (e.g. drag) are really *parodic* and *subversive* (e.g. of gender essentialism) or *just uphold the status quo*. The bottom line is generally the same: kinda subversive, kinda hegemonic."[12] If queer performativity is "the name of a strategy for the production of meaning and being," these productions ought not twist back into the "recalcitrant knots" of identity politics.[13] According to Sedgwick, we cannot understand the politics of solidarity and identification without reckoning with the messy, slippery dynamics of shame.[14] Organized by melancholy, Butler's performative subject may underestimate these knots. At the very least, the reception of Butler's performative subject illustrates the kind of "good dog/bad dog" criticism that Sedgwick describes as a "premature domestication" of queer performativity.

In "Critically Queer," an essay published alongside "Queer Performativity" in the first issue of the journal *GLQ*, Butler attempts to respond to Sedgwick's wide-ranging commentary on performativity. She reiterates her claim that the "I" that queers gender is a kind of empty site of suspension akin to shame's question mark. Not surprisingly, though, questions about the "production of meaning and being" and the lived experience of performativity have continued to dominate discussions of *Gender Trouble* almost thirty years after its publication. In her recent book, *Notes toward a Performative Theory of Assembly*, Butler offers a performative account of street protest and argues that when bodies assemble in the streets, they open time and space "outside and against the established architecture and temporality of the regime" they oppose.[15] In effect, assembling bodies performatively enact new—more livable—modes of political life through the public exposure of their vulnerability. In this text, Butler complicates the location of the performative subject by exploring bodies in relation to spaces like the streets and parks where they gather. In and between assembled bodies, protests performatively enact meanings of where and who they are. While this is another illustration of Butler's claim that the performative "I" is not a disembodied agency, *Notes*'s hopeful program makes assumptions about the performative "we." For instance, it is unclear how assembled bodies have the generative power to vulnerably "stage our universal humanity."[16] And by focusing on the notion of the human, Butler misses an opportunity to explore the messy process of building collective power and bonds of solidarity. From Sedgwick's perspective, a celebration of shared humanity may be an instance of "persuading ourselves that deciding what we like or don't like about what's happening is the same thing as actually intervening in its production."[17]

In contrast to Butler's recent interest in human vulnerability, other writers have sought to reimagine the meaning and being of queer performativity beyond the species. In "Post-humanist Performativity: How Matter Comes to Matter (2003) and "Nature's Queer Performativity" (2012), Karen Barad argues that "performativity has been figured (almost exclusively) as a human affair; humans are its subject matter, its sole matter of concern."[18] In her view, this tendency obscures the role of the human/nonhuman binary in justifying racist and species-ist violence. It also leaves queer theory unequipped to challenge the ways that homophobia circulates in notions of "acts against nature." Drawing on her "agential realist account" of bodies as entangled in the world's performativity, Barad agrees with J. B. S. Haldane's claim that "the universe is not only queerer than we suppose, it is queerer than we can suppose."[19] She describes examples of nature's indeterminacies—from lightning to neuronal receptor cells in stingrays, to academics (a strange species), and atoms—in order to illustrate nature's queer subversion of "the notion of identity itself and its derivatives, including questions of causality, responsibility and accountability."[20] For Barad, Butler's limitation of performativity to the human realm ineluctably subscribes to a view of nature that bears all of the features of identity that she aims to question elsewhere. Reflecting on nature's queer performativity, its iterative materializations, Barad "interrogates the divisions that are at stake" in Butler's theory.

To be sure, Barad's agential realist account of nature has been criticized for not wholly appreciating the second half of Haldane's pithy comment about our queer universe. If the universe is "queerer than we can suppose," what does it mean to be a realist, to claim that one's queer reading of nature is specifically *real*? By what performative feat does one accomplish the objectivity enacted in claims to *the real*? This question raises a host of problems for Barad and for other "new materialist" theorists. But her playful reading of lightning, stingrays, and atoms points to a continuing interest in queer performativity as the "production of meaning and being." If *Gender Trouble* inspired readers to subvert naturalized, essentialist understandings of gender and sexual identity, it also opened innumerable questions about queer performance. Who is the "we" that queers streets in protest? Who is the queer subject among the uncountable numbers of indeterminate queer atoms? In 1993, Sedgwick worried about the "premature domestication of a conceptual tool whose powers we really have barely yet begun to explore." Today, queer performativity is wilder that Sedgwick or Butler may have anticipated.

## Notes

1. Judith Butler, "Performative Acts and Gender Constitution: An Essay in Phenomenology and Feminist Theory," *Theatre Journal* 40, no. 4 (December 1988): 519.
2. Eve Kosofsky Sedgwick, "Queer Performativity: Henry James and the Art of the Novel," *GLQ: A Journal of Lesbian and Gay Studies* 1 (1993): 11.
3. Judith Butler, *Gender Trouble: Feminism and the Subversion and Identity* (New York: Routledge, 1990), vii.
4. Butler, "Performative Acts and Gender Constitution," 521.
5. Butler, "Performative Acts and Gender Constitution," 530.
6. Butler, "Performative Acts and Gender Constitution," 521.
7. Quoted in Kate Bornstein, *My Gender Workbook* (New York: Routledge, 1998), 1.
8. Michel Foucault, *Discipline and Punish: The Birth of the Prison* (New York: Vintage Books, 1995), 11, 17.
9. Foucault, *Discipline and Punish*, 30.
10. Foucault, *Discipline and Punish*, 2.
11. Foucault, *Discipline and Punish*, 5.
12. Foucault, *Discipline and Punish*, 15.
13. Foucault, *Discipline and Punish*, 11.
14. Foucault, *Discipline and Punish*, 14.
15. Judith Butler, *Notes toward a Performative Theory of Assembly* (Boston: Harvard University Press, 2015), 75.
16. Thea Riofrancos, "Precarious Politics: On Butler's *Notes towards a Performative Theory of Assembly*," *Theory & Event* 20, no. 1 (January 2017): 266.
17. Sedgwick, "Queer Performativity," 15.
18. Karen Barad, "Nature's Queer Performativity," *Qui Parle* 19, no. 2 (Spring/Summer 2011): 122.
19. Quoted in Bruce Bagemihl, *Biological Exuberance: Animal Homosexuality and Natural Diversity* (New York: St. Martin's Press, 1999), 9.
20. Barad, "Nature's Queer Performativity," 147.

# 42 The Racial Epidermal Schema

Axelle Karera

Tracing lines of discursive inheritance between European and nonwhite thinkers remains a fraught enterprise. As is often pointed out, the inclination to treat the work of non-white philosophers as "derivative" of their white counterparts continues to determine their fate. Frantz Fanon is a case in point: the vitality of Fanon's work in philosophy—often Sartrean, regularly Freudian, Marxist, and Hegelian, or intermittently Lacanian or poststructuralist avant la lettre—is firmly linked to its inclusion in established European traditions. Though certain aspects of Fanon's psychoanalytic interventions—notably his work on the narcissistic inner workings of racially induced psychoneuroses—have led philosophers like David Marriott to identify a "crucial shift" towards psychoanalysis in Fanon's thought, I hope to show that his sustained engagement with the phenomenological tradition makes him a founding figure of critical phenomenology.[1] I attempt to do so by providing a close reading of several relevant passages in *Black Skin, White Masks.*

Fanon's conceptual (and personal) relationship to Jean-Paul Sartre is undeniable. It is important, however, to remember his dialogue with Maurice Merleau-Ponty. Within the very first pages of the famous fifth chapter of *Peau Noire, Masque Blanc*—"The Lived Experience of the Black"—Fanon explicitly replaces Merleau-Ponty's concept of "corporeal schema" with the "*schéma historico-racial.*" In fact, the first paragraph that introduces the notorious racist refrains of a traumatizing objectifying gaze already invokes the failure of Merleau-Ponty's concept. If the corporeal schema "gives us at every moment a global, practical, and implicit notion of the relation between our body and things" that informs us of our agential presence in the world, Fanon exposes us to a contrasting rupture between body and world or, perhaps more precisely, between a corporeality and the involuntary dissolution of the coherent corporeal schema.[2] To an important extent, Fanon's poignant cry in the face of this radical split between self and world also affirms Merleau-Ponty's corporeal schema in that it is ancestral and reciprocal and reveals a perpetual relation between body and world. "I came into this world anxious to uncover the meaning of things," Fanon writes, "my soul desirous to be at the origin of the world, and here I am an object among other objects."[3] Rather than finding the existential conditions under which one's body and the world join in a perpetual motion of reciprocal affection, the racialized body is forcefully relegated to the realm of mere "things" that occupy space differently than a body-subject would and is exposed to the instrumental will of another. Fanon's first explicit reference to the corporeal schema immediately follows his rejection of ontology's capacity to understand the being of the black. Ontology is unable, he argues, to come to terms with lived experience. Its explanatory power is unrealizable, radically canceled, wherever processes of racialization have objectified the black body.

Fanon refuses to concede to the universalizing gestures of a philosophy of existence unwilling to consider the irreducible singularity of the "lived experience" of racialized bodies. He points out, "In the white world, the man of color encounters difficulties elaborating his body schema [*schéma corporel*]. The image of the body is solely negating [*la connaissance du corps est une activité uniquement négatrice*]. It's an image in the third person."[4] Then he proceeds to describe the corporeal schema by describing the coming-into-being of a self, as a body, in a spatiotemporal world—a world constructed through its uninterrupted relation to this body. He makes sure, however, to point out that this spontaneous connection between body and world differs from what occurs in the context of domination. In nonrepressive circumstances, this formative relation between body and world is a "definitive" one "because it creates a genuine dialectic [*une dialectique effective*] between my body and the world."[5] The distinct corporeality of the black, which arrives as an unfortunate malediction, troubles the fundamental aspect of this dialectic. Rather than offering us, as Merleau-Ponty does, a corporeal schema that epitomizes the felicitous relational exchange between body and world, a second historical-racial schema is imposed on the skin (which is to say the body) of the racially captive. As Fanon writes, "Beneath the body schema, I had created a historical-racial schema. The data I used were provided . . . by the Other, the white man who had woven me out of a thousand details, anecdotes, and stories. I thought I was asked to construct a physiological self, to balance space and localize sensations, when all the time they were clamoring for more."[6] Hence the historical-racial schema is the result of mythologies endowed with the power to affix the racialized body to a historically contingent trajectory wherein its being-in-the-world is founded by a fundamental rupture between self and world. The racist myths also accomplish the work of creating a "black essence" in various dimensions of scientific, social, cultural, and political practices. This is why, after his recounting the imprisoning interpellation of the child's hailing—"Look! A Negro! *Maman*, look, a Negro; I'm scared!"—Fanon introduces the second characterization of his schema. As he tragically laments, "I couldn't take it anymore, for I already knew there were legends, stories, history. . . . As a result the body schema, attacked in several places, collapsed, giving way to an epidermal racial schema."[7] One might understand Fanon's articulation of this double schematization as representing two distinct moments in the distortion of the racialized being's corporeal schema. It is true that he posits the historical-racial schema as a direct corrective of Merleau-Ponty's corporeal schema. The historical-racial schema reminds us of the contingent nature of the corporeal schema.

Fanon also insists that we not ignore racism's usurpation of the black body's capacity to contribute to our historical world. For Merleau-Ponty, the body is free insofar as it acts and can transform the historically given, but as Fanon demonstrates, the black body's historical efficacy is amputated. But when one recognizes Fanon's own concept of the gaze as indissociably linked to his modification of the corporeal schema, one can see that the historical-racial and the racial epidermal are always two sides of the same coin. "*Maman*, look a Negro; I am scared!"[8] From this oft-cited passage, Fanon realizes the inevitable failure of his attempt to live unrestrained by the fact that his body, as Marriott rightly points out, is a "symbol of that which is always already given to be seen," that he remains "slave to an appearance of which he is not responsible, an imago whose 'cognitive' connotation is firstly prelogical and phobic, and that rests on an institutionalisation of stereotypical signs."[9] Indeed, Marriott is right to point to the "prelogical" characteristic of this child's gaze, his immediately phobic reaction to Fanon's presence and, more specifically, Fanon's appearance. It is equally important to remember that the racialized being's inner life is not immune to the insidious work of racism. Fanon warns us continually that the unidentifiable, unassimilable, and muddled structures of racialized subjectivity are such that one is always already a stranger to oneself—that the threat of alienation, and thus the complicated work of disalienation, is as much a matter of internal struggle as it is about fighting external oppressive circumstances. Alienating and disfiguring, the racial epidermal schema violently divides racialized subjectivity to such an extent that one can hardly provide an account of oneself. The existential synergy between myself and the other, which supposedly universally underlies the corporeal schema and eventually sediments a knowledge of myself as a practical agent, is annulled by the racist gaze. Instead, the black experiences his or her body from a fragmented vantage point. As Fanon recounts:

> In the train, it was a question of being aware of my body, no longer in the third person but in triple. In the train, instead of one seat, they left me two or three. I was no longer enjoying myself. I was unable to discover the feverish coordinates of the world. I existed in triple: I was taking up room. I approached the Other . . . and the Other, evasive, hostile, but not opaque, transparent and absent, vanished.

The racial epidermal schema explains the failure of Merleau-Ponty's concept in its attempt to provide an account of the co-constitution of self and world. It also reveals that, for the black, the conditions under which intersubjectivity yields self-knowledge are radically compromised. It may be tempting to account for the historical-racial and racial-epidermal stages of schematization as distinct moments in the lived experience of the black. However, the passage above, which comes directly after Fanon's first articulation of the racial epidermal schema—a passage in which he narrates black agency succumbing to the disastrous effects of a mythological racial history—suggests that epidermalization (*épidermation*) is not a distinct stage in the coming-into-being of the black.

Both the historical and the epidermal are part of the double process of disalienation.[10] Consider Fanon's first use of the term *epidermalization*, in *Black Skin, White Masks,* which appears within the first few pages of the introduction. Here Fanon insists that disalienation entails first and foremost a violent confrontation between the black and socioeconomic realities. We must thus view the black's inferiority complex not in individual but in sociohistorical terms. Importantly, Fanon describes racial inferiority complexes as dualistically structured and intertwined: first there is the economic level, then the epidermal. He describes the latter by using the psychological language of internalization. Epidermalization, therefore, is the internalization of sociohistorical myths, which are founded and nurtured by repressive economic conditions.

This is also where Fanon introduces his concept of sociogeny in response to what he deems insufficient with the psychoanalytic theories of phylogenetic and ontogenetic experiences. Freud, Fanon reminds us, had been reluctant to fully subscribe to phylogenetic inheritance in his diagnostic endeavors—the hypothesis according to which neuroses were understood by tackling the patient's prehistory, that is, the history that predates individual and retrievable occurrences in his or her life. Rather, Fanon points out, "Freud insisted that the individual factor be taken into account," and hence he "substituted for a phylogenetic theory the ontogenetic perspective."[11] For Freud, it was only when one had exhaustively considered all ontogenetic possibilities—i.e., experiences encompassed in one's immediate lifespan—that turning to phylogenetic experiences is necessitated. But for Fanon, individual experiences held little explanatory capacity for understanding the development of the black's alienation. By supplementing an established psychoscientific linguistic apparatus with the concept of sociogeny, Fanon reminds us that "unlike biochemical processes," society "cannot escape human influences."[12] Hence, he points out, "man is what brings society into being."[13] But unlike Merleau-Ponty, who conceives of a necessary synergy between the world (and thus the social) and the subject, Fanon is unwilling to accept that this relationship is intrinsically or inevitably easeful. More specifically, he insists that liberation cannot be achieved by attending to only one end of this relationship. In describing the relation between the subject and the world, he warns that "the gravest mistake would be to believe in their automatic [*mécanique*] interdependence."[14] Without denying their reciprocal connection, Fanon is careful to call attention to the limitation of assuming their necessary interdependence. This is why liberation for the black means necessarily fighting the battle on both grounds. Hence, while historical and individual dimensions of being can be distinctly apprehended in a racist society, it is only through the historical that one's skin color becomes significant. It is this structure of imposition by which the corporeal schema is replaced by a racial epidermal schema legitimized by the weight of "scientific truth" and fabricated historical facts that renders the lived experience of the black "overdetermined from the outside."[15]

Fanon will remain well-known for his unique ability to creatively and productively confront these and other dimensions of Western philosophical history. For a significant amount of time, the relevance of existentialism and phenomenology in both his work and his life has been of crucial interest for scholars in Fanon studies and critical race studies. Nonetheless it is vital to acknowledge that Fanon remained uncommitted to any given school of thought or any single philosophical method. He was suspicious of all teleological conceptions of emancipation. One can argue that one of the major ontological and practical implications of his work was the fact that the revolution was always already untimely, unpredictable, indefinitely deferred, and thus fundamentally irreducible to any institution, philosophy, or practical program—including those dictated by the dialectical impulses so characteristic of our hopes to "change" the world.

Marriott, for instance, claimed that Fanon had abandoned existential notions of liberation significantly earlier than readers have conventionally assessed and that, as early as *Peau Noire, Masques Blancs*, his notion of liberation was radically aporetic because for Fanon, according to Marriott, "the black subject [was] the thought of difference suspended between immanence and transcendence."[16] This observation, in my opinion, underscores the profound necessity for us to shift our comfortable inclinations to conceive of Fanon's work as a discourse of restitution, restoration, and regeneration. Unlike what many humanist readings have traditionally argued, the ongoing work of political transformation for Fanon is not a project of retroactive clarification whereby ethically corrupted sociopolitical categories are restored their proper meaning. Even though Fanon was drawn to and active in postwar debates over humanism, he conceived of political transformation as the quasi-impossible task of introducing invention into existence.

## Notes

1. See David Marriott, "Judging Fanon," *Rhizome: Cultural Studies in Emerging Knowledge* 29 (2016).

2. See "An Unpublished Text by Maurice Merleau-Ponty: A Prospectus of His Work," trans. Arleen B. Dallery, in *The Primacy of Perception and Other Essays on Phenomenological Psychology, the Philosophy of Art, History and Politics*, ed. James M. Edie (Evanston, Ill.: Northwestern University Press, 1964), 5.

3. Frantz Fanon, *Black Skin, White Masks*, trans. Richard Philcox (New York: Grove Press, 2008), 89.

4. Fanon, *Black Skin*, 90; Frantz Fanon, *Peau noire, masques blancs* (Paris: Editions du Seuil, 1952), 89.

5. Fanon, *Black Skin*, 91; Fanon, *Peau noire*, 89.

6. Fanon, *Black Skin*, 91.

7. Fanon, *Black Skin*, 92.

8. Fanon, *Black Skin*, 91; Fanon, *Peau noire*, 90.

9. David Marriott, "The Racialized Body," in *The Cambridge Companion to the Body in Literature*, eds. D. Hillman and U. Maude (Cambridge, U.K.: Cambridge University Press, 2015), 166.

10. Fanon, *Peau noire*, 8.

11. Here I return to the conventionally used translation of *Black Skin* by Charles Lam Markmann (New York: Grove Press 1967), 13.

12. Fanon, *Black Skin*, trans. Markmann, 13.

13. Fanon, *Black Skin*, trans. Markmann, 13.

14. Fanon, *Black Skin*, trans. Markmann, 13.

15. Fanon, *Black Skin*, trans. Philcox, 95.

16. Marriott, "Judging Fanon."

# 43 Racist Love

David Haekwon Kim

*Racist love* is a term of art coined in the midst of the Vietnam War and the many New Left and liberation movements of the 1960s and 1970s.[1] Asian American activists, writers, and scholars Frank Chin and Jeffery Chan introduced the phrase to thematize an undertheorized component of white supremacy and to explain a distinctive racialization pattern among Asian Americans.[2] Racist love is a kind of seduction strategy of white supremacy by which nonwhites are encouraged to accept their subordination and thereby receive a distorted form of positive accommodation, that is to say "love," within the oppressive system. Through an array of imposed sociopolitical measures and their own complicity, Asian Americans may be the only nonwhites who as a group are recipients of racist love. Within the accommodating structure of racist love, Asian Americans may be less likely to experience the sort of inner division and alienation that the literature in phenomenology of race has usefully highlighted in relation to other communities of color. The articulation of this viewpoint might seem distant from classical phenomenology. But in light of recent efforts in philosophy of race that highlight lived reality or underlying structures of social experience, phenomenology is capacious enough to accommodate the viewpoint of Chin and Chan and add its distinctive insights to their efforts.

This entry follows the increasingly commonplace practice of regarding white supremacy as more centrally a political system than a fringe ideology, say, of the KKK. In the beginning of their original statement, Chin and Chan assert, "White racism enforces white supremacy. White supremacy is a system of order and a way of perceiving reality."[3] The authors acknowledge not only that white supremacy is a political system but also that it has, broadly speaking, a phenomenology. In discussing racism as the enforcement structure of white supremacy, they discuss at length a range of interesting ideas concerning racial stereotypes. This is important for our purposes because they seem to regard stereotypes as modes of social perception that facilitate participation in systemic racial processes, a view that enables bridgework to more explicitly phenomenological ideas.

Recent phenomenology of race has shed much light on framing structures of racism that are at once ordinary and a part of the depth structure of subjectivity. Work by Linda Martín Alcoff, for example, has highlighted how our situated identities can be conceptualized in terms of embodied interpretive horizons. In a Gadamerian vein, she explains that a horizon is one's basic interpretive structure that renders the world intelligible through an immanent connection to that world, a connection in which the fundamental sense-making is generated from personal and collective histories and constituted by one's particular social positions.[4] Importantly, following Merleau-Ponty, she adds that the actual locus of the horizon is the body, the lived body, characterized by a kind of preunderstanding of and skillful attunement to the world and whose basic and prereflective structure underlies and permeates the more discursive operations of consciousness. In fact, the utterly basic and background nature of our embodied horizons is such that they are very difficult to articulate and assess, a point that will be useful to consider in the context of racial stereotypes. As she puts it, "If raced and gendered identities, among others, help to structure our contemporary perception, then they help constitute the necessary background from which I know the world. Racial and sexual difference is manifest precisely in bodily comportment, in habit, feeling, and perceptual orientation. Perceptual practices are tacit, almost hidden from view, and thus almost immune from critical reflection."[5] Returning to the work of Chin and Chan, racial stereotypes are ways of seeing the world that are holistic and complex in both meaning structures and political function, and in light of the foregoing we can think of these social perceptions as issuing from largely tacit embodied interpretive horizons. And just as phenomenology can add to their views, their particular way of talking about stereotypes in white supremacy can offer useful considerations for the phenomenology of race. They contend that "each racial stereotype comes in two models, the acceptable, hostile black stud has his acceptable counterpart in the form of Stepin Fetchit. For the savage kill-crazy Geronimo, there is Tonto. . . . For Fu Manchu and the Yellow Peril, there is Charlie Chan and his Number One Son. The unacceptable model is unacceptable because he cannot be controlled by whites. The acceptable model is acceptable because he is tractable. There is racist hate and racist love."[6]

There are a number of features worth highlighting here. First, on their view, the content of stereotypes is embedded in larger conceptual profiles that have a normatively dyadic complementation structure. Even if the paradigm of a racial stereotype involves negative attributions, perhaps tinged with animosity or contempt, the wider perspective of the typical racist also contains a complementing positive stereotype that is conceptually tied to the more commonly noted negative stereotype. So, in the racist interpretive horizon, there may be a notion of a "bad black" who is understood in terms of being violent or having criminal tendencies, but this will be harmonized with a notion of a "good black" who is understood to be, say, polite and deferential, or who otherwise appears to be supportive of the status quo or existing order. Relatedly, the authors seem to indicate, without elaborating, that the intentionality of the social perceptions that are stereotypes is not simply about character, personality, or bodily attributes—like being lazy or physically unattractive—but also about political relational attributes, like how tractable or unruly someone is vis-à-vis the social or political order. Therefore, although a "good black" may be deemed good because he lacks certain characterological traits commonly highlighted and despised in a racist subjectivity, he may additionally, and perhaps more significantly, be regarded as good because he does not resist or perhaps even aids the political system that is white supremacy.

Psychologists sometimes differentiate between descriptive stereotypes, like "Asians are socially passive or nondominant," and prescriptive stereotypes, like "Asians should be passive or nondominant."[7] These sorts of social perceptions can be matters of careful, discursive, though distorted reflection, and they can be prereflective, ordinary, spontaneous, and again distorted modes of immersive engagement with the world. Apart from the different logic of description and prescription, phenomenologically the two kinds of stereotypes operate differently. In descriptive stereotyping, insofar as the prejudice is strong, a nonpassive Asian may be presented unremarkably, and wrongly, to the perceiver's consciousness as Asian and passive. Encounters with enough counterexamples to the descriptive stereotype, that is, many nonpassive Asians, will potentially push the subject's racial hermeneutical presuppositions to be "brought up short" (as Gadamer describes the larger experiential genus). A primarily epistemic or doxastic revision takes place in which the subject simply modifies her descriptions of the social world. She thinks, "Well, I guess they're not like that, after all." But in the prescriptive stereotype, a nonpassive Asian person may be a provocation or unsettling of a perceiver's habits or habitual body, probably attended by negative or aversive feelings, in which the Asian person's apparent dominance troubles the perceiver's normative expectations and related comportment in the world. A subject might be bothered or resentful that an Asian person violates nondominance expectations, perhaps because the Asian person does not move aside on the sidewalk, roots vociferously for a losing team, resists one's butting into or controlling a conversation, sticks with apparent stubbornness to an unpopular proposal in a committee meeting, calls out someone's sexism or racism, or perhaps simply carries herself with unperturbable self-confidence. Unlike descriptive stereotypes, more than doxastic revision is salient; clearly, the subject is invested in Asians being socially passive. Feelings, desires, commitments, and projects are formative of the latter.

Chin and Chan are especially concerned with the latter phenomenon, the unsettling of habit, and this in relation to people's habit-constituting background sense of political structure and of broad behavioral or attitudinal patterns, real or imagined, of racialized peoples. In light of the good/bad complementarity being a configuring principle here, they add that those deemed to be "good" racial others, in terms of their hegemony or system affirmation, receive racist love, a twisted form of positive regard and accommodation in, though not liberation from, the racial hierarchy. For Chin and Chan, this should not be obscured by the more obvious phenomenon of racist hate. And to be clear, just as *racist love* is being used as a term of art, *racist hate* in this sense is neither standard emotional hatred nor about repulsive personal traits, even if there are many instances of racist hatred in the more conventional sense of the phrase.

A second feature of the interpretive horizon of racist love is that perceptions of a racialized group tend to be integrated in a broader, at least a triadic, interracialist conception.[8] Push hard enough, and one discovers that the racist subject has a view not just about "bad Latinos" but also about "good Asians." One of the most important instances of this phenomenon in twenty-first-century America is the model minority myth, in which Asians are deemed a minority to be emulated and blacks and other minorities criticized for their failure to follow the trajectory of Asians.[9] Importantly, given the dynamics of racist hate and love, the model minority myth can be viewed in terms of the (mis)attribution of more personally localized qualities, like industriousness and laziness, but also in terms of deference or resistance to systemic racism.

A third element concerns political function, specifically how white supremacy enhances its domination by extending racist love to people of color and having it reciprocated, as it were, when these subjects (1) accept the system-sustaining understanding of themselves and the world and (2) self-enforce the relevant prescriptive stereotypes. Although Chin and Chan do not put it this way, such a phenomenon is a distinctive species of Gramscian hegemony since it involves the subject populace being ideologically manipulated (i.e., following the racist common sense of their day) and thereby consenting, as it were, to conditions against their own interests (i.e., racial subordination). It is also in the ballpark of Foucault's panopticon concept since their view seems to posit a structure of social control becoming a principle of subject formation in a way that increases the efficacy of the environing system. As they put it, "The stereotype operates most efficiently and economically when the vehicle of the stereotype, the medium of its perpetuation, and the subject race to be controlled are all one."[10] So what does racist love and its reciprocation look like? Put another way, what does it look like for white supremacy to operate with enhanced efficiency? According to Chin and Chan, the racialization patterns of Asian Americans, in particular Japanese and Chinese Americans of the late twentieth century, reveal a reciprocity circle of racist love and thereby an increase in the efficiency of white racism.

On their view, a combination of imposed structures and collective complicity has generated this situation. The devastating consequences include an "utter lack of cultural distinction," "destruction of an organic sense of identity," and "complete psychological and cultural subjugation."[11] Among the specific deficiencies, they focus heavily on the absence of Asian American masculinity and the lack of Asian American literary sensibilities. The external impositions include deep, pervasive, and overt racism; racist legislation that prohibited immigration and denied equality and security in the U.S.; white Christian pacification ideologies that discouraged dissenting consciousness, beginning with massive evangelization campaigns in China; and the racial humiliation of early sojourners and coolie laborers, whose loathing of America caused them to destroy the material traces of their American heritage or archives. In terms of complicity, they note that even if physical and social survival was a past motive for reciprocating racist love, Asian Americans now have for the most part accepted ideologically a middle position in the racial hierarchy rather than rebelling against it. Two aspects of the complicity they dwell upon include collective self-contempt and the idea of the dual personality, where the latter is presented in a problematic gendered fashion.

Their discussion of self-contempt is somewhat unclear. At times, they seem to be referring to actual self-contempt experienced by many or most Asian Americans in virtue of believing the racist ideologies of racist love. But they also seem to use the expression as a term of art on the model of *racist love* and *racist hate*, where the real issue is not emotionality but support of the white supremacist order.[12] Whatever the case may be, it is crucial to consider what Chin and Chan think is indicative of collective self-contempt and whether the charge of self-contempt is appropriate. Here they focus a great deal on the absence of a distinctively *Asian American* identity, sensibility, linguistic style, and literary or more broadly cultural tradition. They argue that what comes under the heading of "Asian American" is not an organic synthesis of Asian and American elements but a schizophrenic vacillation or sense of discord between the "Asian" and the "American," which they thematize under the notion of the "dual personality."[13] Importantly, they contend that this problem has been greatly exacerbated by Asian American women authors of the mid-twentieth century who have published very popular books conceptually organized by the dual personality and whose popularity is due, they claim, to their pandering to a white audience whose understanding of Asian America is configured by the assumption of a deep alterity between Asia and America, the basis of the dual personality concept.

Although much can be said about these controversial claims, only a couple points will be raised. First, they never explore the possibility that the so-called dual personality, or some less skewed version of it, may actually be a common experiential structure, as opposed to a literary contrivance, for Asian American women (and men) of the mid-twentieth century. Second, they do not explain in the first place why Asian American experience cannot be capacious enough to include both an organic conciliation of the Asian and the American as well as more dualistic combinations of them.[14] Third, the blame they direct at these women is excessive, especially considering that there are many other sources of a lack of organically Asian American literary works and sensibilities, like a profoundly racist and Orientalist culture and Asian American men's inability or unwillingness to confront this culture in literary venues. Fourth, they express grave concern about the emasculation of Asian American men, but nothing about the hypersexualization of Asian American women. Their excessive blame of these women and their deep concern about Asian American men being emasculated indicate that they think resistance to racist love should have a masculinist structure.[15]

The foregoing account of racist love offers important considerations for the phenomenology of race. Much of the literature in phenomenology of race focuses on the conflicted twoness of Du Boisian double consciousness ("two warring ideals in one dark body") or Fanonian corporeal malediction ("Look, a Negro!"). Racist love reveals an important operation of white supremacy that does not generate conflictedness of an obvious kind. Indeed, it placates through accommodation, albeit partially and conditionally. Conceivably, some experiences of anti-Asian racism may even have their impact diminished by the framing effects of racist love. Also, the account of racist love raises the issue of whether racism is more generally characterized by intraracial splitting (good Asians vs. bad Asians, good blacks vs. bad blacks). Perhaps we are in the grips of theory, as it were, in thinking that racist consciousness typically operates by making skewed judgments about racial groups as a whole.[16] In addition, it raises the interesting methodological question of the potential virtues of triadic interracial analysis. Moreover, regardless of whether Chin and Chan's race diagnostic was right about the 1970s, it is an important question whether currently the Asian American community, which has changed considerably since that time, is caught in the grips of racist love. Finally, Chin and Chan's account offers not only a way to illuminate issues in Asian American racialization but to do so in a way that keeps a vital and constructive connection to elements that are often found in the so-called black/white binary and, through its problematic gendered discussion, highlights the importance of intersectionality.

## Notes

1. I am grateful to Gayle Salamon for insightful discussion and helpful editorial suggestions.

2. Frank Chin and Jeffery Paul Chan, "Racist Love," in *Seeing through Shuck*, ed. Richard Kostelanetz (New York: Ballantine Books, 1972), 65–79.

3. Chin and Chan, "Racist Love," 65.

4. Linda Martín Alcoff, *Visible Identities: Race, Gender, and the Self* (New York: Oxford University Press, 2006), 94–97. For other important work on this subject, see Gail Weiss, *Refiguring the Ordinary* (Bloomington: Indiana University Press, 2008); Lewis Gordon, *What Fanon Said: A Philosophical Introduction to His Life and Thought* (New York: Fordham University Press, 2015); Emily S. Lee, *A Phenomenology of Race* (unpublished manuscript).

5. Alcoff, *Visible Identities*, 126. On this subject, see also Alia Al-Saji, "A Phenomenology of Hesitation: Interrupting Racializing Habits of Seeing," in *Living Alterities: Phenomenology, Embodiment, and Race*, ed. Emily S. Lee (Albany, N.Y.: SUNY Press, 2014), chapter 6.

6. Chin and Chan, "Racist Love," 65.

7. See the helpful essay by Jennifer L. Berdahl and Ji-A Min that discusses this distinction and focuses heavily on the idea of Asians and nondominance: "Prescriptive Stereotypes and Workplace Consequences for East Asians in North America," *Cultural Diversity and Ethnic Minority Psychology* 18, no. 2 (2012): 141–52.

8. For an account of race that centralizes triadic interracialism, as well as issues of system affirmation or resistance (i.e., unruliness), see Falguni Sheth's *Toward a Political Philosophy of Race* (Albany, N.Y.: SUNY Press, 2009). Also see Claire Jean Kim's "The Racial Triangulation of Asian Americans," *Politics & Society* 27, no. 1 (March 1999): 105–38; David Kim and Ronald Sundstrom, "Xenophobia and Racism," *Critical Philosophy of Race* 2, no. 1 (2014): 20–45. Sumi Cho uses the notion of racist love to contextualize the Los Angeles uprising/riots in 1992: *Reading Rodney King, Reading Urban Uprising*, ed. Robert Gooding-Williams (New York: Routledge, 1993), chapter 13.

9. For more on this, see "Model Minority" by Emily Lee in this volume. Ellen Wu's *The Color of Success: Asian Americans and the Origins of the Model Minority* (Princeton, N.J.: Princeton University Press, 2015) is illuminating in terms of critical historical contextualization of so-called Asian success at the American Dream.

10. Chin and Chan, "Racist Love," 67.

11. Chin and Chan, "Racist Love," 66.

12. It is useful to think in terms of both actual emotionality and systemic structures in regard to self-contempt. And late twentieth-century and early twenty-first-century Asian American experience in this regard is much more complex than what Chin and Chan suggest. See my "Shame and Self-Revision in Asian American Assimilation," in Lee, *Living Alterities*.

13. Chin and Chan, "Racist Love," 76.

14. Appropriate here is the work of Mariana Ortega on multiplicitous selves. See her *In-Between: Latina Feminist Phenomenology, Multiplicity, and the Self* (Albany, N.Y.: SUNY Press, 2016).

15. A fitting reply is the following by Mari Matsuda: "I love my Asian brother, but I have lost my patience with malingering homophobia and sexism and especially using white racism as an excuse to resist change. You know, the 'I have to be Bruce Lee because the white man wants me to be Tonto' line." Mari Matsuda, *Where Is Your Body? And Other Essays on Race Gender and the Law* (Boston: Beacon Press, 1996), 155–56.

16. On normative considerations related to this point, see the interesting and important discussion by Lawrence Blum, *"I'm Not a Racist, but . . . :" The Moral Quandary of Race* (Ithaca, N.Y.: Cornell University Press, 2002), 30–32.

# 44 Sens/Sense

Keith Whitmoyer

> Le temps est le sens de la vie (sens: comme on dit le sens d'un cours d'eau, le sens d'une phrase, le sens d'une étoffe, le sens de l'odorat).
>
> Time is the sense of life (sense: as one says of the direction of a course of water, the meaning of a phrase, the feel of a fabric, the sense of smell).
>
> —PAUL CLAUDEL, *Art poétique*

*Sens*, the French cognate of our English word *sense* and *Sinn* in German, is a central concept for the phenomenological tradition as well as for more contemporary philosophies following in its wake.[1] The French and German terms are usually translated as "meaning," but in the case of the former it can also mean "feel" as well as "direction."[2] *Sens* names the texture, line, and curve of the phenomenon, as in the ancient Greek, φαινόμενον, the middle-passive participle of φαίνω, "to show,"[3] what in French is called the *il y a* and in German the *es gibt*. What shows itself, what there is, does so at the point where it has a certain figure, style, or modality, and from the phenomenological point of view, we may no longer speak of "objects," "things," or "beings" independently of the specific timbre and flavor through which they come into articulation, that is, independently of their *sens*.

For example, when I perceive an ordinary object, I tend to think of it as a reality indifferent to and independent of the profile of meanings that style and render it. In comporting myself with respect to the object in this way, however, I have already deployed a specific metaphysics in this relation, one that operates in the background and which allows the object to become visible in a definite, predetermined manner. Let us take this jar. It is an ordinary Mason jar of a relatively small size, cylindrical, made of clear, translucent glass with various fruits molded into its texture. It has a band-and-disc metal lid suitable for canning. Insofar as the jar makes itself known to me as an external and indifferent reality, the metaphysics that my attitude presupposes is an ordinary form of realism. And yet where is the justification for the realist metaphysics presupposed by my natural attitude toward things? How can I know that *to be* means *to be thus and not otherwise*? Phenomenology neutralizes these speculative anxieties by stipulating that we must not presuppose any one sense of what it means to be in our comportments toward what shows itself; rather, we must suspend our customary relations to things and attend closely to the complex of significations that allow beings to become what they are when we make space for the manifold sense through which the thing expresses itself. The jar I encounter here on the desk, before becoming an object of metaphysical speculation, first indicates, *zeigt an,* references, indeed "shows" the possibilities of its meanings, and in so doing articulates itself with the coloring and light of its sense. By showing itself as "container," it references the series of significations of what it might contain under the heading of preservation: vegetables, fruits, condiments, and so forth; it is thus not just any container, for it would be strange for it to contain a clean pair of pants. I could, maybe with some difficulty, wear it as a hat, and yet there is also something awkward about this proposal because "storing your clean pants" or "wearing on your head like a hat" are not what objects like this "are for." "To be for something," preserving in this case, means to be infused with systems of reference that point toward the manifold meanings of the thing, and hypothetical relationships take place only against a background of *sens* articulated in advance.[4]

Things, therefore, become what they are only thanks to the nexus of meanings they reference and project, and we recognize that our metaphysics, whether it is realism, idealism, or something else, is only ever the privileging of one sense of being over others. The jar that appears to the scientific gaze, a physicochemical reality, the consequent of antecedent natural causes subject to necessary laws, is a perfectly legitimate level of description, yet this is not quite the jar that I use in the process of making lemon chutney. The advance of phenomenology over the legacy of Western metaphysics is that the object of scientific description is only one sense among many. When we look at the world and ask about what we see, we need not privilege any one sense of its being but are, rather, invited to inquire into how there is any sense whatsoever. The jar that appears to the scientific gaze stands alongside the one that appears to the cook making use of it, to the poet, or even to the philosopher, and we understand that being becomes articulate in terms of so many *Ge-stellen,* so many ways of allowing things to enter into a process of revelation.[5] This is why it is impossible for the things that surround me to be completely devoid of sense, as if they were, as Husserl says, *bloße Sachen,* "mere things."[6] Painters have always known that things are never as inert nor as indifferent as some metaphysics may like to believe, for an art concerned with bringing being to light would be impossible if what is—color, line, even space and time—were devoid of *sens.* It is because being comes to us as a texture, a fabric, a flesh of meanings that artists can make the invisible visible and give the gift of speech to that which as of yet has no voice.

For the *sens* of the world to articulate itself, we must possess a power for orienting ourselves toward it. In French this is called *sentir,* usually translated as "sensing" or "feeling," but we must note that originally this word was the verbal form of *sens.*[7] To be capable of *sentir* is to possess a set of powers ready for *sens,* to be sensitive, to be sentient, to be sensible. At the point where we possess such powers, the world can call to us, and we are open to its echo, its vibration, and to its resistance and opacity. Already in Husserl, who is frequently criticized for reducing this openness to *Bewußtsein,* being-consciousness,[8] the place of *sentir* is the living body, the *Leib* in German as opposed to the *Körper*, the inanimate body of the object.[9] When I say that the jar is "here," I mean that it is within reach of my hand, that it reflects and refracts the light from the window in the specific way that indicates the time of day, the season, its direction, the weather, and it is my eye that allows these details to come into focus; if I pick it up and hold it, I feel its weight and density; the texture slides against the palm of my hand, illuminating the pattern of its surface, cold and hard, the smooth viscosity of glass that the hand immediately recognizes. All of this is apparent without the intervention of a judgment, and one would have to say that my comportment, my "intentional relationship" with respect to the glass is "operative," "prereflective," and "nonthetic."[10] The body is the site of these powers, which, like the eye, allows the world to become illuminated across so much distance, which needs only to open in order to clear a space in which things announce themselves. We sense because the specific style of things speaks to our bodies, which listen and release themselves, already positioned to welcome the encroachment of things as the sense of the world bleeds and seeps into us, organizing our πάθος, our "experience" and our suffering. Because our *sentir* dwells in the living body, we take a position with respect to things through judgments only belatedly, only in the wake of this more primary orientation toward things, and whatever judgments we make about the world, e.g., "This jar is sentimental and ugly," are parasitic upon our corporeal openness to the phenomena. Such openness would be impossible if we were not, in a profound sense, among things, if we did not belong to and with them, and if they did not already hold us in their grip. As we reach out toward the world with eye or hand, it welcomes us only at the point where we find that it already has us in its grasp; "the hold is held," as Merleau-Ponty says, and because of this *Ineinander*, because we are inscribed within the world's *sens* as it is inscribed on us, our view is never complete and our grasp never total.[11] The *sens* of the world slips from our *sentir*, incomplete as it escapes into the infinite depth of the horizon, awaiting touch and vision yet always just beyond them.

It is worth emphasizing that in French the concept of *sens* can also mean "orientation" or "direction." To have *sens* is to be embedded within a certain context of references that indicate the thing and which the thing also indicates, contexts which are invariably historical, cultural, and linguistic, and there is no thing that is not already encrusted with these hardened layers of signification and oriented by them. The jar, then, can never be "merely" a jar; rather it becomes what it is only through the layers of *sens* that constitute for it a place in which it remains rooted and from which it shines forth, perhaps a world of harvests, scarcity, and concern about the coming of winter. In its reference to a specific geographic, historical, and social context, the jar indicates so much other history, life in rural America perhaps, and therefore to the *Stiftungen*, the "institutions" or "initiations"[12] of meaning that organize such a life: agrarianism and industrialization, farmers and proletarians, bourgeois landowners, capitalism, exploitation, colonialism, racism, sexism, ableism, with all their variations and antitheses, stretching over the landscapes of a life, articulating and making it visible. The jar refers to this history of meanings that organize it and that come to make it the jar that it is, "this jar," and not another one. The things that populate our worlds are oriented with respect to these traces, and in this way there is something profoundly disingenuous, mendacious, and even violent in a metaphysics that longs for a being purified of its *sens*, purified of its orientation and history, that sees here only an "external object" in all its neutrality, innocence, and universality. Such romanticism is merely the privilege of metaphysics, which forgets these sedimentations and longs for the lost purity of being. Recognizing the primacy of *sens* with respect to what there is, we see that to be means to carry the weight and stain of such traces, to be a surface for so much text,[13] so many inscriptions and scars. To be is to be contaminated, to be marked: imprinted by the contour of history, culture, language, political economy, power, and the myriad ways in which the *sens* of what is gives birth to itself, what Husserl calls *Sinngebung*, "sense-genesis." In this way, everything is always more than it is, pointing toward its latent histories, unintended significations and consequences, and innocence, purity, universality, and neutrality are only so many metaphysical dreams; there is, rather, an excess of *sens*, even an ecstasy, an *ek-stase*, pointing toward the horizon of its as yet unrealized possibilities, toward the unknown frontier of the *sens* for which we struggle and wait, the sense of a world yet to come.

## Notes

1. I have in mind Deleuze, whose *The Logic of Sense* is clearly part of this tradition; Derrida, particularly his works on Husserl, *The Problem of Genesis in Husserl's Philosophy*, *Introduction to the Origin of Geometry*, and *Voice and Phenomenon*; Nancy's *Corpus* and *The Sense of the World*; and though maybe more subtle, I think we also find this in Foucault.

2. The German word *Bedeutung* is also sometimes translated as "meaning," e.g., Findlay's translation of Husserl's *Logische Untersuchungen*, which renders *Sinn* as "sense." Frege, importantly, wishes to demarcate a strict distinction between *Sinn* and *Bedeutung*, where *Sinn* is usually rendered as "sense" and *Bedeutung* as "reference," e.g., his *Uber Sinn und Bedeutung*, "Sense and Reference," though translating *Bedeutung* as "reference" seems to be a perhaps fruitful error. Husserl, importantly, insists on the interchangeability of these terms, contra Frege. See Edmund Husserl, *Logical Investigations I*, trans. J. N. Findlay (London: Routledge, 2001), 201. For further reading on Husserl and Frege see J. N. Mohanty, *Husserl and Frege* (Bloomington: Indiana University Press, 1982), as well as Robert Sokolowski, "Husserl and Frege," *Journal of Philosophy* 84, no. 10 (October 1987): 521–28. See also Nancy's discussion of the term's etymology in *The Sense of the World*, trans. Jeffery S. Librett (Minneapolis: University of Minnesota Press, 1997), 76–77.

3. This is why Heidegger insists on understanding the phenomenon as *das Sich-an-ihm-selbst-zeigen*, that which shows itself of and in itself. See Martin Heidegger, *Being and Time*, trans. John Macquarrie and Edward Robinson (New York: Harper and Row, 1962), 54.

4. Few have shown this more clearly than Heidegger in his discussion of tool use in *Sein und Zeit*. See Heidegger, "The Worldhood of the World," in *Being and Time*, 91ff. For a recent appropriation of Heidegger's discussion of tools in object-oriented ontology, see Graham Harman, *Tool Being: Heidegger and the Metaphysics of the Object* (Chicago: Open Court, 2002).

5. The term is used by Heidegger in *The Question concerning Technology*, usually translated as "enframing," sometimes rendered *Ge-stell*. This essay especially focuses on the "frameworks" through which the world is made visible and the "danger" associated with allowing one manner of articulation to become dominant. It is also worth noting that Heidegger quite purposively plays with various forms of the verb *stellen* (to place), i.e., *herstellen* (establish),

*bestellen* (put in order), *vorstellen* (to present), *verstellen* (to block), etc. See Martin Heidegger, *The Question concerning Technology and Other Essays*, trans. William Lovitt (New York: Harper & Row, 1977), 15.

6. See Husserl's discussion of this in *Ideas II*, § 11, "Nature as sphere of mere things," in *Ideas pertaining to a Pure Phenomenology and to a Phenomenological Philosophy, Second Book: Studies in the Phenomenology of Constitution*, trans. Richard Rojcewicz and Andre Schuwer (Dordrecht: Kluwer Academic, 1989). See also Merleau-Ponty's discussion of this in his only published text devoted specifically to Husserl, "The Philosopher and His Shadow," in *Signs*, trans. Richard C. McCleary (Evanston, Ill.: Northwestern University Press, 1964), 162ff.

7. The most well-known discussion of *sens* and *sentir* in phenomenology is Merleau-Ponty's in the chapter called "Le sentir" in *Phenomenology of Perception*. See Merleau-Ponty, *Phenomenology of Perception*, trans. Donald Landes (London: Routledge, 2013), "Sensing."

8. Next to which of course Heidegger places *Dasein*, "existence," literally "being-there."

9. Both *Leib* and *Körper* can be translated as "body" in English. *Körper* is from the Latin, *corpus*, which of course also means body and is the origin of our word "corpse." It is also used in the sense of corporeal: *Leibkörper*, for example, would be rendered as "corporeal body." *Körper* thus refers to the body in a formal, "anatomical" sense but also to the inert bodies of material entities like "interstellar bodies" or even "bodies of water." *Leib*, on the other hand, is of Old German origin and is a cognate of our word *life*. *Leib* is the word used more frequently by Husserl in his discussion of bodily intentionality in his *Ideas II* in reference to the body that we inhabit, live with, and live through. The translators of this text try to indicate this difference by rendering *Körper* as "body" with a lowercase *b* and *Leib* as Body with an uppercase *B*. While this may be unfortunate, there simply aren't equivalent words in English since we use *body* in both senses. See Husserl, *Ideas II*, especially chapter 3, "The Constitution of Psychic Reality through the Body," 151ff. See also "The *Körper/Leib* Distinction," by Jenny Slatman in this volume.

10. *Operative intentionality* is a term Merleau-Ponty claims to borrow from Husserl, which he opposes to *act intentionality*. See *Phenomenology of Perception*, 486. Operative intentionality, as Merleau-Ponty adds upon mentioning this concept in *La temporalité*, "is what Heidegger terms transcendence" (486). See "Operative Intentionality" by Jennifer McWeeny in this volume.

11. In *The Visible and the Invisible*, Merleau-Ponty defines this concept as follows: "The idea of chiasm, that is: every relation with being is simultaneously a taking and a being taken, the hold is held, it is inscribed and inscribed in the same being that it takes hold of." Maurice Merleau-Ponty, *The Visible and the Invisible*, trans. Alphonso Lingis (Evanston, Ill.: Northwestern University Press, 1964), 266.

12. In his lectures on institution, Merleau-Ponty uses this word to translate Husserl's term *Stiftung* in place of "constitution," the more recognizable translation. See Maurice Merleau-Ponty, *Institution and Passivity*, trans. Leonard Lawlor and Heath Massey (Evanston, Ill.: Northwestern University Press, 2010), 8, 76. In *The Visible and the Invisible*, Merleau-Ponty translates *Stiftung* as "initiation"; see *The Visible and the Invisible*, 243.

13. It is worth noting that while the concept of the trace within writing is most easily associated with Derrida, he pulls it directly from Husserl, specifically his introduction to the *Origin of Geometry*. See Derrida, *Husserl's* Origin of Geometry: *An Introduction*, trans. John P. Leavy Jr. (Lincoln: University of Nebraska Press, 1989).

# 45 Social Death

## Perry Zurn

There is a kind of living that feels like dying. There is a kind of life marked—relentlessly—by death. The term *social death* refers to this experience, this rhythm, this walled passage. By definition, social death may belong to whoever—or indeed whatever—lives and dies in a network of relation. Even when conceived of only anthropocentrically, then, the term must apply beyond that, because the human being lives and dies in nonhuman relation. Moreover, social death always occurs out of sync with physical death. As such, its temporality is unique. Social death is already and not yet, long begun and never finished, and one is never quite sure when it will strike; it is out of time. Given the way in which it eddies across existences and temporalities, social death is a chimerical, though no less powerful term.

Although the term appeared on the scene in the early nineteenth century, its use expanded considerably first in medical-thanatological literature, beginning in the 1960s, and then in sociological studies of slavery, starting in the 1980s. Within medical scholarship, the term refers to the death of a person (rather than a body), their meaning and function within their social networks. It may occur after the cessation of vital function, especially through rituals of mourning, or much earlier, as in the case of people who are terminally ill, suffer from dementia, or are comatose. Within sociological scholarship, the term refers to the death of a people group, their culture, history, and language. While it may involve the direct killing of bodies within that people group, it may also occur through the indirect assault on a group's vitality, as in, for example, forced migration or colonial education. Today the use of the term has expanded to refer quite broadly to the structural loss of human social function, whether at the macro level (e.g., war, imperialism, ostracization, or incarceration) or the micro level (e.g., teenage pregnancy, widowhood, chronic or terminal illness, or HIV/AIDS).

Social death becomes thinkable only when death itself becomes multiple and unmoored. Jacques Derrida is perhaps paradigmatic in his insistence on the indeterminacy of life and death. Death, in general, is a series of incommensurate, even provisional moments. Modern medicine continues to identify more and more lines across which "death" could be placed. The three most definitive are the functional cessation of the brain, the heart, and the lungs.[1] Life, likewise, is indeterminate; where it begins and ends is impossible to see cleanly or to state plainly. It is always more and less than itself. It is indeterminate, moreover, from *and because of* its other: death. Marking the multiplicity inherent in mortality, Derrida writes, "To deconstruct [the unity of] death . . . [is] to keep one's eyes open to what this word of death, this word 'death' means, to what one wants to make it say . . . [all while recognizing that] we don't know what [death] is, if and when it happens, and to whom."[2] It is the dream of deconstruction to deconstruct the most apparently indestructible, sacrosanct entity: death itself, but also, therefore, life itself. To deconstruct death/life means to put each back into question and to hold them there, refusing to settle the what and the how of it, the who and the why.

Some theoretical traditions, however, such as critical phenomenology and critical genealogy, will ask these questions relentlessly: What are the forces and symptoms of social death? How have they developed over time and crystallized into their current formulations? Who experiences social death? Why are those populations targeted over others? Critical phenomenology involves reflecting on the transcendental and material conditions of experience and restructuring the world to permit new experiential possibilities.[3] As such, critical phenomenologists have analyzed the roots of social death in the rupture of intersubjective capacities and explored new possibilities for personhood.[4] Critical genealogy, on the other hand, problematizes the emergence of present-day practices—of, for example, education, punishment, confession, or segregation—and, in doing so, provides the foundation for transforming them.[5] Critical genealogists have traced the sedimented practices and semiotic transfers that have led to the differential allocation of social death today. They have simultaneously undertaken a deconstruction of specific institutions built on the unequal distribution of life chances and a reconstruction of social networks calibrated to human flourishing.[6]

Perhaps the most "germinal"[7] text for the development of these phenomenological and genealogical considerations is Orlando Patterson's *Slavery and Social Death*.[8] In it, Patterson explores the extensive and intensive rituals by which slaves are rendered nonbeings. He distinguishes between intrusive and extrusive modes of social death, whereby slaves are either conceived of as already outsiders and therefore as not belonging, or they are found not to belong and therefore are made outsiders. In either case, social presence exists without full personhood and alienated from collective sense-making. Following Patterson's focus on black slaves, subsequent scholarship has traced the continued assignment of blackness to social death after emancipation. Caleb Smith, for example, finds in the civil death of incarceration a contemporary "counterpart" to the social death of slavery, historically targeting the same population.[9] Between slavery plantations and prisons, Loïc Wacquant identifies ghettos as an interim "ethnoracial enclosure," built on the same enervating forces of labor extraction and disenfranchisement.[10] Indeed, as Joshua Price argues, social death was never replaced by civil death, but lives on in the systemic violence, generalized humiliation, and natal alienation inflicted on incarcerated populations and, following Lisa Guenther, particularly those held in solitary confinement.[11] Finally, Lisa Cacho extends an analysis of social death to the racialized poor, who are constructed as "ineligible for personhood": "living nonbeings."[12] If, as Dylan Rodriguez states, "death is the social truth of imprisonment,"[13] this literature as a whole suggests that death is the social truth of living as a person of color in the U.S. today.

Continued systematization of the term *social death* has increased both its complexity and its generalizability. Claudia Card defines social death as the theft of meaning in life. That meaning is provided by social contexts and identities, themselves sustained through contemporary and intergenerational relationships or stolen through social alienation, isolation, violence, and destruction.[14] When either the bodies or the culture, history, and language that sustain a people group are assaulted, the group's social vitality is compromised.[15] As such, for Card, the project of social death is equally genocidal and ethnocidal. Damien Short, while granting both that social death is fundamentally racialized and that it debilitates cultures as much as it enervates bodies, demonstrates the important occlusion of land and ecosystems from these discussions. For Short, social death involves genocide, ethnocide, and, inescapably, ecocide.[16] The assault on a group's social vitality targets not simply kinship and citizenship, culture, history, and language, but also land and place. Expanding on Patrick Wolfe's claim that, for indigenous peoples, "land is life" and therefore "contests for land . . . are . . . contests for life,"[17] Short argues that when "peoples, who have a physical, cultural, and spiritual connection to their land, are forcibly dispossessed and estranged from their lands, they invariably experience 'social death.'"[18] Neither Card nor Short, however, waivers from the traditional anchoring of the social group in the human species. Their analyses are therefore anthropocentric, unable to account for the real possibility of social death—as the loss of social vitality—within a cross-species ecosystem.

Much as the literature restricts social death to human beings, it also assigns social death a limited temporality. That is, social death is typically characterized as complete, as permanent, as total. From Patterson to Card, scholars repeatedly refer to people as being "socially dead,"[19] indicating that the moment of death has occurred, has passed, is finished. Several scholars also assert that social death is "permanent."[20] This suggests not only that social death has definitively occurred but that it is irrevocably final. The social vitality that has been lost cannot be retrieved. Discursively conceiving social death as a total event, however, runs the risk of casting its subjects as "victims who lose their agency,"[21] as if nothing remains of their self-determination or resistance, their intersubjective selves or cultural creativity.[22] More fundamentally, the frame of totality is inconsistent with the very theoretical insight behind the term *social death* itself. If the moment of death must be multiplied to acknowledge forms of death beyond the physical, the moment of social death must itself be multiplied, or is already multiple, to account for the many ways that social vitality can be leached. Therefore, it is more appropriate to refer to the experience of social death or the projects and techniques of social death,[23] than to socially dead people. Indeed, as Ewa Ziarek insists, after aligning social death with the commodification process, there is always a remainder, an irreducible remnant from which forms of resistance may arise.[24]

Still, social death is even more ontologically diffuse and temporally extensive than as yet intimated. One of the best ways to elucidate this is through the literature on slow death and slow violence. Social death is, perhaps more often than not, a slow process; it involves less spectacular and catastrophic destruction than incremental, even understated forms of violence. As Lauren Berlant characterizes it, "Slow death prospers not in traumatic events, as discrete time-framed phenomena like military encounters and genocides can appear to do, but in temporal environments whose qualities and whose contours in time and space are often identified with the present-ness of ordinariness itself, that domain of living on, in which everyday activity; memory, needs, and desires; diverse temporalities and horizons of the taken-for-granted are brought into proximity."[25] Slow death goes all the way down, occurring in the microfibers of everyday life, the microphysics of insignificant interactions. While it can be deeply excavated in the present, the work of slow death is also flung far into the future, exponentially displaced and deferred. Focusing on climate change, Rob Nixon characterizes it as "slow violence" that "occurs gradually and out of sight, a violence of delayed destruction that is dispersed across time and space, an attritional violence that is typically not viewed as violence at all."[26] Whether traceable to the school-to-prison pipeline or legislated poverty, toxic drift, deforestation, or the thawing of the cryosphere, slow violence leaks across taxonomic boundaries and borderlands and entails an indefinite, perhaps even infinite deferral of effect and inheritance.

Given the many moments and forms of matter within and across which social death functions, greater attention might fruitfully be devoted to understanding exactly how the wound of social death bleeds. First, this work could begin by expanding the conceptual structure of the term itself. Instead of merely contrasting social death with social vitality, scholars might grant both that social life exists within social death and that social morbidity exists within social vitality. Prima facie, this structural expansion would allow future work to better account for forms of resistance to social death as well as cracks in social vitality—that is, the many little deaths that signal the healthy fluctuation of history, culture, and language. Second, this work could expand the referent of the term *social death*, broadening to whom or to what it applies and why. This second expansion would better equip scholars to account for how social death is differentially allocated across social identities, but also within transhuman lifeworlds. This, in turn, would cultivate a certain accountability to the vast number of existences and temporalities—as yet unidentified in the present and undecidable in the world to come—across which social death functions. Broadening analysis in these two ways would ensure increased attention to the specific arrangement of forces, the unique confluence of life forms, and the divergent temporalities that constitute a given slice of social vitality and morbidity, life and death. If ever there was a compelling brief for the impossibility and necessity of an ethical life, it is this. Indeed, from the perspective of social death, we are called to attend precisely to what is beyond our own possibilities of attendance—not unlike death itself.

## Notes

1. Jacques Derrida, *The Death Penalty,* vol. 1 (Chicago: University of Chicago Press, 2013), 242n19.

2. Derrida, *The Death Penalty,* 240.

3. Lisa Guenther, "A Critical Phenomenology of Solidarity and Resistance in the 2013 California Prison Hunger Strikes," in *Body/Self/Other: The Phenomenology of Social Encounters*, ed. Luna Dolezal and Danielle Petherbridge (Albany, N.Y.: SUNY Press, 2017), 47–74.

4. E.g., Lisa Guenther, *Solitary Confinement: Social Death and Its Afterlives* (Minneapolis: University of Minnesota Press, 2013), 15. See also Guenther's entry "Critical Phenomenology" in this volume.

5. Colin Koopman, *Genealogy as Critique: Foucault and the Problems of Modernity* (Bloomington: Indiana University Press, 2013).

6. Brady Heiner, "Excavating the Sedimentations of Slavery: The Unfinished Project of American Abolition," in *Death and Other Penalties: Philosophy in a Time of Mass Incarceration*, ed. Geoffrey Adelsburg, Lisa Guenther, and Scott Zeman (New York: Fordham University Press, 2015), 14–42.

7. Paul Taylor, "Bare Ontology and Social Death," *Philosophical Papers* 42, no. 3 (2013): 385.

8. Orlando Patterson, *Slavery and Social Death* (Cambridge, Mass.: Harvard University Press, 1982).

9. Caleb Smith, *The Prison and the American Imagination* (New Haven, Conn.: Yale University Press, 2009), 41.

10. Loïc Wacquant, "Deadly Symbiosis: When Ghetto and Prison Meet and Mesh," *Punishment & Society* 3, no. 1 (2001): 95–134; compare Eduardo Mendieta, "Plantations, Ghettos, Prisons: US Racial Geographies," *Philosophy & Geography* 7, no. 1 (2004): 43–59.

11. Joshua Price, *Prison and Social Death* (New York: Rutgers, 2015); Guenther, *Solitary Confinement*.

12. Lisa Cacho, *Social Death: Racialized Rightlessness and the Criminalization of the Unprotected* (New York: New York University Press, 2012), 6, 33.

13. As quoted in Brady Heiner, "Social Death and the Relationship between Abolition and Reform," *Social Justice* 30, no. 2 (2003): 98.

14. Claudia Card, *Confronting Evils: Terrorism, Torture, Genocide* (Cambridge, U.K.: Cambridge University Press, 2010), 237.

15. Card, *Confronting Evils*, 247.

16. Damien Short, *Redefining Genocide: Settler Colonialism, Social Death, and Ecocide* (Chicago: University of Chicago Press, 2016).

17. Patrick Wolfe, "Settler Colonialism and the Elimination of the Native," *Journal of Genocide Research* 8, no. 4 (2006): 387.

18. Short, *Redefining Genocide*, 36.

19. E.g., Patterson, *Slavery and Social Death*, 5, 34; Claudia Card, "Genocide and Social Death," *Hypatia* 18, no. 1 (2003): 74; Stephen Dillon, "Possessed by Death: The Neoliberal-Carceral State, Black Feminism, and the Afterlife of Slavery," *Radical History Review* 112 (2012): 121.

20. Price, *Prison and Social Death*, 5; Cacho, *Social Death*, 6.

21. James Snow, "Claudia Card's Concept of Social Death: A New Way of Looking at Genocide," *Metaphilosophy* 47, nos. 4–5 (2016): 622; Price, *Prison and Social Death*, 6.

22. See Nicholas T. Rinehart, "The Man That Was a Thing: Reconsidering Human Commodification in Slavery," *Journal of Social History* 50, no. 1 (2016): 28–50; John La Rose, "Unemployment, Leisure, and the Birth of Creativity," *Black Scholar* 26, no. 2 (1996): 30.

23. In the digital age, social death is perhaps less final than ever, insofar as the marks of social life live on and on.

24. Ewa Ziarek, "The Abstract Soul of the Commodity and the Monstrous Body of the Sphinx: Commodification, Aesthetics, and the Impasses of Social Construction," *Differences: A Journal of Feminist Cultural Studies* 16, no. 2 (2005): 88–115; Ewa Ziarek, "Bare Life on Strike: Notes on the Biopolitics of Race and Gender," *South Atlantic Quarterly* 107, no. 1 (2008): 89–105.

25. Lauren Berlant, "Slow Death (Sovereignty, Obesity, Lateral Agency)," *Critical Inquiry* 33 (2007): 759–60.

26. Rob Nixon, *Slow Violence and Environmentalism of the Poor* (Cambridge, Mass.: Harvard University Press, 2011), 2.

# 46 The They

## Nancy J. Holland

"In many ways Heidegger's chapter on . . . *the They*," Hubert Dreyfus claims, "is not only one of the most basic in the book, it is also the most confused."[1] There are two, somewhat interrelated reasons why Dreyfus considers Heidegger's discussion of the concept of "the They" in *Being and Time* to be "confused." On the surface level, the problem is that the German *das Man* has no direct correlate in English similar to the French *on*. "The They" has no clear meaning in English and so can open itself to a kind of paranoia about "them" or "the masses," a misunderstanding that prefigures a more profound confusion that I will discuss below. By contrast, "the one" has too many meanings in colloquial usage, from religious to romantic, that only confuse the issue more.

Yet what Heidegger means by *das Man* is relatively clear. Many aspects of our lives, from the grammar of the language we speak to how we use tools to the rules of etiquette and the laws we live under, aren't addressed to us as individuals but are understood or communicated to us impersonally as what "they" do in a particular situation or what "we" do or what "one" does (which is the sense of *das Man* and the French *on*). *Das Man* doesn't ignore a fire truck siren when driving. *On* says that word this way. One doesn't lick one's spoon, no matter how tasty the pudding. They say craft beers are overpriced. In order to exist in a social world, speak a common language, be recognized as a functional member of society, we must live by a set of social "norms" (Dreyfus's term, not Heidegger's) and do things as "they" do them.

That is why this concept is "one of the most basic" for Heidegger: "the They," not the "I myself," is "the 'subject' of everydayness."[2] This is, among other things, a profoundly anti-Cartesian (and by implication anti-Husserlian) move and hence at the core of the philosophical revolution Heidegger saw himself to be instigating.[3] He points out, "The word 'I' is to be understood only in the sense of a non-committal *formal indicator*, indicating something which may perhaps reveal itself as its 'opposite' in some particular phenomenal context of Being. In that case, the 'not-I' is by no means tantamount to an entity which essentially lacks 'I-hood' [*Ichheit*], but is rather a definite kind of Being which the 'I' itself possesses, such as having lost itself."[4] And what the I has lost itself in is, in the usual case, "the They." This is one of many ways Heidegger turns the Cartesian/ Husserlian understanding of the self on its head because, for him, "a bare subject without a world never 'is' proximally, nor is it ever given. And so in the end an isolated 'I' without Others is just as far from being proximally given."[5] Regardless of the ontic presence or absence of others like myself in my immediate surroundings or environment, my existence as Dasein requires a social context to give my actions, my language, and my "projects" meaning.

From this perspective, it is easier to understand the "confusion" noted above, namely, interpreting "the They" as "the masses" that the authentic individual must "free" himself or herself from or, more problematically, that he or she must free from their illusions.[6] Heidegger is, at times, quite clear about why this is an error: "By 'Others' we do not mean everyone else but me—those over against whom the 'I' stands out. They are rather those from whom, for the most part, one does *not* distinguish oneself—those among whom one is too."[7] "The They" is not something we can escape or be led out of. Later, he tells us that "proximally and for the most part Dasein is absorbed by the 'they' and is mastered by it." Even art and innovation can appear only on a background of the meaningful social context "the They" provides. In discussing "idle talk" (which "is not to be used here in a 'disparaging' signification"), he points out, "In [idle talk], out of it, and against it, all genuine understanding, interpretation, and communicating, all re-discovered and appropriating anew, are performed."[8] This is why the concept of "the They" is one of the "most basic" in *Being and Time*. "The They" makes authenticity possible.

This is clearer if one sees the usual (even in Heidegger) emphasis on authenticity versus inauthenticity in a broader context. At the very beginning of the section titled "Being-in-the-World" in *Being and Time*, Heidegger offers a more nuanced account of Dasein's relationship to the possibility of authenticity: "Mineness belongs to any existent Dasein, and belongs to it as the condition which makes inauthenticity and authenticity possible. In each case Dasein exists in one or the other of these modes, *or else it is modally undifferentiated*."[9] The possibility of this third, undifferentiated mode explains why existence in "the They" is not, in itself, inauthentic. In fact, it cannot be. Even authentic language, for instance, requires a shared, preexisting linguistic context that belongs to "the They." Dreyfus argues that "Dasein must always find itself in public practices . . . and this includes language."[10]

Moreover, even authentic Dasein remains in some ways and to some extent immersed in "the They." *Qua* Dasein, it continues to exist as *Mitsein* (being-with). Thus, Dasein continues to understand its experience and itself in terms of the social world around it: "Resoluteness, as *authentic Being-one's-Self*, does not detach Dasein from its world, nor does it isolate it so it becomes a free-floating 'I.'"[11] This is for two reasons. First, authenticity is not an attribute that, once attained, remains in place without any further effort (although this is one of many points on which Heidegger is not always as clear as one might wish). Rather, the temptation of inauthentic submersion in "the They" is a constant in the existence of even the most authentic and resolute Dasein. As Heidegger observes, "Dasein is already in irresoluteness, and soon, perhaps, will be in it again."[12]

At a deeper level, both Dasein's inability to be a "free-floating I" and its existence as "already in irresoluteness" result from the fact that "even resolute Dasein remains dependent upon the 'they' and its world." This dependence is, however, not submersion in "the They." If I achieve an authentic Being-toward-Death, for example, and create a "living will" accordingly, I will quickly become aware of how my social situation—both medical and personal—limits my options, as well as the extent to which the decisions I make at one time might change with shifts in medical practice and the law. "Resolution does not withdraw itself from 'actuality,' but discovers first what is factically possible; and it does so by seizing upon it in whatever way is possible for it as its ownmost potentiality-for-Being in the 'they.'"[13] Later Heidegger complicates this point by noting that Dasein "has been submitted to a 'world,' and exists factically with others. Proximally and for the most part the Self is lost in the 'they.' It understands itself in terms of those possibilities of existence which 'circulate' in the 'average' public way of interpreting Dasein today."[14] To push the submersion metaphor perhaps a little too far, "the They" can be seen as the ocean into which we are born. Authenticity, when achieved, does not allow us to fly free of the ocean, because the water is the source of our sustenance. Rather, authenticity allows us to float, half in, half out of the water, free of the illusion that only the ocean exists.

Once the twin specters of "the They" as "Them" or "the Masses" and of "the They" as necessarily inauthentic are laid to rest, it becomes possible to see the generative possibilities in the concept. We can see "the They" as that *against* which what is genuine and authentic is able to appear, an interpretation Heidegger suggests in the quotation about "idle talk" above. Taking this as the *primary* function of "the They," however, is only a more nuanced form of the error of thinking "the They" is to be disparaged in toto. More recent interpretations of how the concept of "the They" can be generative interpret it more positively as a means of making sense of the lived experience of those who travel or bridge between "worlds," in Heidegger's sense of the term. Alexander Ruch, in his reading of Simone de Beauvoir's *America Day by Day*, points out:

> If the everyday itself is seen as simply good, then we lose the critique that is essential to both Heidegger and Beauvoir . . . while if it is seen as merely bad, then authenticity becomes a melodramatic escape from the everyday, rather than a mode of living it. . . . The major difference between Heidegger and Beauvoir on the everyday is not to be found in their ideas of authenticity as a "modified grasp of everydayness," but in Beauvoir's attention to the grounded (ordinary) and social possibilities of authenticity, which Heidegger treats only melodramatically and abstractly in *Being and Time*.[15]

*Contra* Ruch, I would suggest Heidegger (at his best) falls somewhere in between these two extremes. As we have seen, while his work lacks the lyrical specificity of Beauvoir's, Heidegger also undercuts the romanticism of, say, Albert Camus by his awareness that we can be the free individuals we are only in a social context, against the background of a They-self, that gives our freedom meaning. Again, authenticity allows us to float, but not to fly.

Some feminists have used the concept of "the They" to understand the experience, not of those who literally travel, as Beauvoir did, "to there and back again," but of those who live on the borderlands, in the interstices between one "They" and another, that is, bi- or multicultural, bi- or multilingual code shifters of all varieties. One prime example of this line of argument can be seen in Mariana Ortega's "'New Mestizas,' 'World Travelers,' and 'Dasein': Phenomenology and the Multi-Voiced, Multi-Cultural Self."[16] Ortega invokes "the They" in Heidegger to explain how "in our everydayness we simply follow these norms and practices unquestioningly. Using [María] Lugones's terms, in our daily existence, in our interaction with others, we 'travel' our world with a certain ease that comes from already having a sense of what we have to do as teachers, friends, lovers, parents, or scholars, or whatever our role or situation is."[17] When Beauvoir comes to "America" or "the multicultural self" moves between a home culture and the dominant culture, however, "it does not have a sense of all the norms and practices of the new context which it now inhabits. Thus, it does not relate to the world primarily in terms of know-how, as we have seen Heidegger claims that we do."[18] Ortega juxtaposes Heidegger's concept of "the They" with Lugones's account of the "world" traveler and concludes that there is "a point of intersection between the two" because they both believe that "being completely maximally at ease or at home in the 'world' is not a positive phenomenon" because "it leads to a lack of self-understanding and a lack of responsibility," i.e., inauthenticity.[19] This makes world-traveling a key nexus of philosophical understanding. Ortega combines Heidegger's and Lugones's insights to give a rich phenomenology of the "new mestiza" who is constantly required to "world travel."

Although for the most part Lauren Freeman focuses on Dasein's *Mitsein* rather than "the They," in "Reconsidering Relational Autonomy: A Feminist Approach to Selfhood and the Other in the Thinking of Martin Heidegger," she, like Ortega, makes generative use of Heidegger's concepts. Freeman explores the synergy between Heidegger's thought and a feminist concept of "relational autonomy" found in the work of Lorraine Code, Evelyn Fox Keller, and others.[20] She presents "relational autonomy" as a feminist view that, rather than reject "autonomy" in the traditional/Kantian sense, redefines it so it is no longer understood to be the actualization of a preexisting essential self; "rather it is considered to be the exercise of skills that enable people to understand themselves, redefine themselves as needed, and direct their own lives."[21] Parallel to what I have said about Heidegger, this feminist view of autonomy underscores the need for interpersonal relationships and a broader social context to nurture and support its development. Freeman concludes that Heidegger and the feminists she discusses "share an important goal: overturning the traditional notion of a subject as an isolated, self-sufficient, atomistic individual and demonstrating that individuality requires, and is based upon, the individual's relation to, and at times even dependence on, others."[22]

As fascinating and productive as these lines of thought are, however, I would go further and suggest Heidegger's concept of "the They" can be an important, if not vital resource for resisting structures of domination and exclusion in its own right. Once we recognize that "the They" is where a society's racism, sexism, homophobia, etc. generally lurk, we can better understand why legal/judicial remedies and individual good intentions are never enough to eradicate them. Unless people can learn to see, for instance, how the way in which They/one/we think, speak, and view the world in the

U.S. allows discussions of rape to slide into discussions of how to gauge consent or discussions of racism to fade into discussions of civility (both of which center the needs of the perpetrator rather than those of the oppressed person), our society will never reach a state in which people are truly free or equal. A thorough study of social inequality from this perspective has the potential to become the matrix from which true social justice can arise.[23]

This suggests at least two reasons traditional interpretations of Heidegger tend to identify any reliance on "the They" with inauthenticity. First of all, an exclusive focus on the authentic/inauthentic dyad mirrors all the other hierarchical dualisms that have governed metaphysics since its inception in the West, a symmetry the concept of the "undifferentiated" disrupts in important ways.[24] Secondarily, as Freeman and others argue, the role of "the They," as described here, presents a significant challenge to the autonomy of the self-regulating individual that underlies most modern philosophy (and politics). To relegate "the They" to the realm of inauthenticity is to relegate to a morally inferior position those perceived to be insufficiently independent of social definitions, limitations, and stereotypes to qualify as the "self-made man" of classical liberal theory (see, for example, Jean-Paul Sartre's *The Respectful Prostitute*). The more complex picture I have tried to present here offers new possibilities for critical analysis both on the level of praxis, as suggested above, and on a metalevel that reveals the traditional interpretation of Heidegger to be part of the oppressive discourse so prevalent in the philosophical They of our time.

## Notes

1. Hubert L. Dreyfus, *Being-in-the-World: A Commentary of Martin Heidegger's* Being and Time, *Division I* (Cambridge, Mass.: MIT Press, 1991), 143.

2. Martin Heidegger, *Being and Time*, trans. John Macquarrie and Edward Robinson (New York: Harper, 1962), 150 (G114).

3. My understanding of the nature of this revolution is more fully explained in Nancy J. Holland, *Heidegger and the Problem of Consciousness* (Bloomington: Indiana University Press, 2018).

4. Heidegger, *Being and Time*, 151–52 (G116), translators' interpolation.

5. Heidegger, *Being and Time*, 152 (G116).

6. This appears to be roughly the argument, for instance, in Jill Hargis, "From Demonization of the Masses to Democratic Practice in the Work of Nietzsche, Heidegger, and Foucault," *Human Studies* 34 (2011): 373–92 (especially 380). Dreyfus attributes this side of the confusion about what he calls "the one" to the Kierkegaardian strain in Heidegger's thought (Dreyfus, *Being-in-the-World*, 143).

7. Heidegger, *Being and Time*, 154 (G118).

8. Heidegger, *Being and Time*, 210–13 (G167–69).

9. Heidegger, *Being and Time*, 78 (G53), my emphasis.

10. Dreyfus, *Being-in-the-World*, 241.

11. Heidegger, *Being and Time*, 344 (G298).

12. Heidegger, *Being and Time*, 345 (G299).

13. Heidegger, *Being and Time*, 346 (G299).

14. Heidegger, *Being and Time*, 435 (G383).

15. Alexander Ruch, "Beauvoir-in-America: Understanding Concrete Experience, and Beauvoir's Appropriation of Heidegger in *America Day by Day*," *Hypatia* 24 (2009), n14, emphasis in original.

16. Mariana Ortega, "'New Mestizas,' 'World Travelers,' and 'Dasein': Phenomenology and the Multi-Voiced, Multi-Cultural Self," *Hypatia* 16 (2001): 1–29.

17. Ortega, "'New Mestizas,' 'World Travelers,' and 'Dasein,'" 6–7.

18. Ortega, "'New Mestizas,' 'World Travelers,' and 'Dasein,'" 9.

19. Ortega, "'New Mestizas,' 'World Travelers,' and 'Dasein,'" 10.

20. Lauren Freeman, "Reconsidering Relational Autonomy: A Feminist Approach to Selfhood and the Other in the Thinking of Martin Heidegger," *Inquiry* 54 (2011): 361–83.

21. Freeman, "Reconsidering Relational Autonomy," 374.

22. Freeman, "Reconsidering Relational Autonomy," 379.

23. I offer a partial analysis in this vein with regard to the status of women in "'The Universe Is Made of Stories, Not of Atoms': Heidegger and the Feminine They-Self," in *Feminist Interpretations of Martin Heidegger*, ed. Nancy J. Holland and Patricia Huntington (University Park: Pennsylvania State University Press, 2001), 128–45. Another example (based on the work of Michel Foucault rather than directly on Heidegger) can be found in Ladelle McWhorter's brilliant *Racism and Sexual Oppression in Anglo-America: A Genealogy* (Bloomington: Indiana University Press, 2009).

24. For more on this, see Holland, *Heidegger and the Problem of Consciousness*.

# 47 Time/Temporality

Dorothea Olkowski

Edmund Husserl (1859–1938) is widely regarded as the founder of modern phenomenology, which he understood to be a rigorous science of what is given to intuition that proceeds by describing phenomena as opposed to providing causal explanations, the latter being the method of the natural sciences.[1] Husserl gave his initial lectures on time-consciousness in 1905. In the same year, Albert Einstein first presented his theory of special relativity, arguing that time is and must be an objective event independent of individuals.[2] This led shortly to the idea that space and time are a single frame of reference, now called "space-time."[3] The juxtaposition of these two theories characterizes many of the questions and conflicts surrounding the phenomenological understanding of time. Husserl's conception of time is oriented by his attention to the perpetual flux of consciousness such that no experience would even be possible without the consciousness of time.[4] By contrast, the scientific objective understanding of time, the time of nature and natural processes, is disconnected from experience and intuition.[5] Objective time presents itself in an idealized manner, from the point of view of an observer (actually a stopwatch or measuring device), which shows that events are always relative to a frame of reference, and that two events are simultaneous only within the same frame of reference—otherwise they are not.[6]

Phenomenology, Husserl states, concerns itself with "the *immanent time* of the flow of consciousness," and not with Objective time, the time of the world of experience.[7] In *The Phenomenology of Internal Time Consciousness*, Husserl's analysis of immanent temporal objects is articulated almost entirely in terms of sound.[8] The immanent temporal object appears in a continuous flux, like a wave, and the sound is continually different with respect to *the way in which it appears*.[9] Husserl is careful to distinguish between the sound that is actually heard and the duration in which the hearing takes place. Of particular importance to the analysis are the "running-off phenomena," which are modes of temporal orientation such as "now" and "past," so that "we know that it [the running-off phenomenon] is a continuity of constant transformations which form an inseparable unit."[10]

No running-off can reoccur; each begins as *now*; every subsequent phase of running-off is also a constantly expanding continuity of pasts; each now changes into a past, each of which sinks deeper into the past; each now passes over into retention and *every now changes continuously* from retention to retention, such that every now point is a retention for every earlier point and every retention forms a continuum.[11] The continuum of temporal consciousness is not the waning reverberation of the musical note that has just sounded; rather there is an ongoing transition and transformation of its mode of appearing, but as the temporal Object itself moves into the past, it becomes more and more obscure.[12]

Crucial to Husserl's account of running-off is that the phases of running off form a continuum that unifies the experience of temporality without the necessity of positing a transcendental subject, above or outside of it to unify temporal experience. Husserl's concept of retention distinguishes between the real sensation of a sound, a sensation that could be objectively measured, and the tonal moment in retention, which is *not actually present* but is *primarily remembered in the now*. "The intuition of the past itself . . . is an originary consciousness. . . . It is consciousness of *what has just been* and not mere consciousness of the now-point of the objective thing appearing as having duration."[13]

Ultimately Husserl differentiates at least three levels of temporality, three components of every temporal wave: (1) the individual objects of our experience in Objective time; (2) the manner in which objects appear in our consciousness; and (3) the absolute, temporally constitutive flux of consciousness.[14] In addition, Husserl accepts that there is a "pre-objectified time arising with sensations, which necessarily *founds* the unique possibility of an objectification of temporal positions."[15] For example, if bells begin to sound at some objectified external time, the sound also corresponds to the temporal point of the sound sensation; that is, they occupy the same temporal position.

Given his influence on later phenomenological philosophers, especially Maurice Merleau-Ponty (1908–1961), an account of phenomenological theories of time might want to consider not only Husserl but also Husserl's contemporary, Henri Bergson (1859–1941). Like Husserl, Bergson also challenged Einstein's view of physics and philosophy with respect to the nature of time. Einstein claimed that there is only one time, that of the physicists and mathematicians, and that any conception of time other than that of relativity does not exist because time is and must be an objective event independent of individuals.[16] Bergson did not object to relativity but insisted that it is possible for there to be a distinction between time perceived and time conceived, or real time and measured time.[17]

It took some years for even Einstein to clarify his ideas on the general theory of relativity for which there are "local time units whose different degree of dilation in different gravitational fields account for different measuring of time in two systems," even though these different measurements do not affect either the singularity or the irreversibility of the underlying structure—for example, that the departure will always precede the return.[18] It has been suggested that this comprehension of time and times in the general theory is not, after all, incompatible with Bergson's own conception of the variability of durations experienced, for example, by someone hallucinating, in comparison to another who is awake, even though they inhabit the same public time.

However, Bergson is critical of the tendency of science and philosophy to base their understanding of time on that of space as a series of static and homogeneous nows. By contrast, Bergson sets out the nature of time in terms of the fundamental concept of duration. He states, "Pure duration is the form which the succession of our conscious states assumes when our ego lets itself live, when it refrains from separating its present state from its former states . . . as it happens when we recall the notes of a tune, melting, so to speak into one another."[19] The past is not set alongside the present—as in the scientific conception of time—but permeates the present and cannot be distinguished from it in our intuition. At every moment, the past mingles with and enriches the present and the present "reflects itself at the same time as it forms the recollection of the old present." [20] This occurs because our nervous system is open to qualitative changes that permeate one another and form a heterogeneous, qualitative multiplicity.

Scholars have noted the similarity between Bergson's conception of time as duration and what is referred to as public or measured time in the novel *Mrs. Dalloway* by Virginia Woolf. Although the events of the novel occur on a single summer day, the time of the novel takes into account the flux of temporal consciousness, when the time of a character's thoughts is not uniform and expands or contracts in relation to the content of his or her reflections.[21] Thus the novel moves back and forth between objective, measured time, often expressed by reference to clocks, especially Big Ben in London, and the time of duration, that is, the fluctuating, unmeasurable time of the inner life of consciousness and reflection, as well as the recollection of past memories in the present and the intense and instantaneous thought of the future. Frequently, events that take but a short period of measurable time, such as an hour in the day of the protagonist, Clarissa, or Peter's brief recollection of his former life with Clarissa, are spread out over many pages of text. They may also cover many years of events and numerous different cities and countries, exemplifying the idea that the highly differentiated time of the stream of duration, of recollection and reflection, cannot be measured by the clock or the map.

Merleau-Ponty supports Bergson's conception of time in the face of criticism coming from Einstein and others.[22] He does so in part because he rejects both the classical scientific position of causal determinism, the idea that if given precise knowledge of Nature's elements (their positions and speeds), every future can be inferred, as well as the Cartesian idea that complexity can be decomposed into simples, the claim that the world's existence is extensive or spatialized and so excludes temporal becoming.[23] For Merleau-Ponty, "the subject is temporal by means of an inner necessity."[24] This is because the temporal horizons of objects come to our attention through the pre-objective hold that our body has upon the world. So parts of space coexist because, first, they are temporally present to the same perceiving subject and, prior to this, because they are "enveloped in one and the same *temporal wave*," the same temporal horizon "wedged in between the preceding and following one."[25] It is for this reason that time is the general field, a network of relationships within which we act, the place from which we form our commitments and assert our freedom.[26] The field of temporal relations that pass through the body of *someone* corresponds to Husserl's running-off phenomena, The past we have lived through, our experiences and perceptions, allow us to be the temporal wave that moves through the world.

In addition to this purely phenomenological line of thinking about the nature of time, Husserl's ideas also gave rise to a more existential phenomenology, beginning with his student Martin Heidegger (1889–1976). Heidegger situates his account of time in the context of an analysis of what he refers to as "Dasein," literally "being-there," that being whose essential nature is to question its own being and which is thoroughly temporal.[27] For Heidegger, this type of inquiry must precede that of the sciences, which remain "blind" if they have not "previously clarified the meaning of being sufficiently."[28] Since the meaning of being is temporality, the task, for Heidegger, is "to show that *time* is that from which Da-sein tacitly understands and interprets something like being at all."[29]

For Heidegger, time as we ordinarily conceive of it, that is, as a container of events (objective or natural time) as well as so-called world-time (roughly, the time of daily events that interest us, everydayness), does not capture what he means by time as a formal structure of Dasein's being or existence.[30] This "originary temporality," which Heidegger calls *ekstasis*, consists in an originary future (a potentiality or possibility projected into a future horizon), an originary past (called "thrownness" or "having been"), and an originary present ("being-alongside").[31] Together, these three modes constitute Dasein's existence as care, the manner in which any Dasein exists and discloses itself in the world among its most essential concerns. For the most part, Dasein exists in the worldly mode of "everydayness," a degenerate form of care, and "the monotony of everydayness takes whatever the day happens to bring as a change."[32] Care is defined in terms of Dasein's being-toward-death, the knowledge and acceptance of finitude, and Heidegger maintains that by taking over what it already was (thrownness) and resolutely opening itself to its potential, Dasein can be authentically itself in the face of finitude.[33] This means that Dasein does not simply get by in the everyday world, forgoing an awareness of temporality as care.

Although inspired by Heidegger, Jean-Paul Sartre's (1905–1980) conception of time in *Being and Nothingness* suggests a different orientation at work. To clarify this orientation, let us ask why Being is coupled with nothingness and not with time. Like Heidegger, Sartre asks about the relation between humans and the world. He finds that everywhere there is the real and "permanent possibility of non-being" and nothing more, yet nothingness is real only for human beings.[34]

When Sartre describes looking for his friend Pierre in the café, out of the possible infinity of persons who could be in the café, each one who is not Pierre is nihilated so as to move on to the next. What is described is a trajectory of nothingness, moving from point to point to point, from present to present, and each present is nihilated in order to reach the next. Sartre is witness to the successive disappearance of each of the objects he deliberately looks at, each of which detains him only for an "instant" before being nihilated as he moves on.[35] Sartre refers to this awareness, this deliberate or intentional act, as the "for-itself," which he identifies with temporality, which exists insofar as it has a future.[36] But unlike Heidegger, who situates temporality in Dasein's finitude, Sartre turns to an objective conception of time that returns us to Husserl's original division between objective time and time consciousness.

The for-itself apprehends temporality without any chance of modifying it as it unites each instant, passing from instant to instant in one and the same being.[37] However, as each present moment becomes past it passes into "facticity," the being of objects in the world. Thus, for Sartre, there is no difference between the past of the for-itself and the past of the world.[38] Yet even as the for-itself belongs to facticity through the past, it may still flee it through the present and the future.[39] Thus, for Sartre, time is the objective, formal form of universal time, the opening onto probabilities, but *also* the trajectory of one's own acts, the probabilities revealed to oneself, and thus the expectations we have of ourselves.

Simone de Beauvoir (1908–1986) formulates her own understanding of time and temporality. Acknowledging that it is future-oriented projects that give life meaning, she nonetheless remains dubious regarding the idea that existence founds itself moment to moment through the negation of what comes before. Beauvoir refers to this as the "absurdity of the clinamen," the concept of random events resulting from chance encounters.[40] She also argues that with age, our own past weighs us down so that the future we had freely chosen for ourselves has turned into a fact.

In spite of this, Beauvoir maintains that following "a more or less consistent line of conduct does not constitute slavery."[41] In *The Coming of Age*, she reaffirms the idea that life is based on self-transcendence, that is, projects oriented toward the future. Accepting that it is one's own life and not other people that set one up as objectified, it is "the books I have written, which now *outside me* constitute my works, and define me as their author."[42] Yet, when we make ourselves, when we take up a project in the world, that is how and when we make ourselves finite, and that is when we have only ourselves, our own past, our own skin to outstrip.[43] In other words, our own finished projects fall back into the realm of our own Other, and we are left, finite, always seeking the new, in order to be at all. Beauvoir claims that this "passionate heroism" is especially what the ageing must embrace, "delighting in a progress that must soon be cut short by death . . . carrying on, the attempt to outdo oneself in full knowledge and acceptance of one's finitude."[44]

One contemporary feminist philosopher has absorbed the phenomenological tradition and moved it forward by thinking about time in the context of race. Alia Al-Saji examines the structures of what she calls "racialized time" to determine how racism is temporally lived and constituted, as Sartre suggests, as a process of "othering."[45] Historically, this has involved the repression of the real past of colonized peoples and its replacement by stereotypes and colonized distortions, which are used to justify the need for present and future colonial domination.[46] Thus, a paradoxical temporal duality is set in place.

Al-Saji draws on a Beauvoirian perspective as well, noting that we come into a world that is always already there and that contains meanings sedimented through other lives so as to give us a sense of the world as real.[47] This world is thus intersubjective but also open to the creation of new possibilities. Racialization attempts to replace this temporalization with a world of truncated possibilities and also a sense of "lateness," wherein the field of possibilities has been defined and consumed by the dominant culture of whiteness.[48] This is an analysis that could also be adopted by feminists who are in search of an account of the limitations placed on women of all ethnicities and classes by the patriarchal past and present. In this regard, Al-Saji presents contemporary phenomenologists with a challenge to think about temporality in a social context beyond the abstract lived time of consciousness.

## Notes

1. Dermot Moran, "Introduction to Husserl," in *The Phenomenology Reader*, ed. Timothy Mooney and Dermot Moran (New York: Routledge, 2002), 7, 9.

2. Jimena Canales, *The Physicist and the Philosopher: Einstein, Bergson, and the Debate That Changed Our Understanding of Time* (Princeton, N.J.: Princeton University Press, 2015), 20.

3. Pedro S. M. Alves, "Objective Time and the Experience of Time, Husserl and Kant, in the Light of Some Theses of A. Einstein's Time-Theory" *Husserl Studies* 24, no. 3 (October 2008): 205–29, https://link.springer.com/article/10.1007/s10743-008-9039-1, 4.

4. Moran, "Introduction to Husserl," 60.

5. "Objective Time and the Experience of Time," 7.

6. Alves, "Objective Time and the Experience of Time," 21, 22.

7. Edmund Husserl, *The Phenomenology of Internal Time Consciousness*, trans. James S. Churchill (Bloomington: Indiana University Press, 1971), 23.

8. Husserl, *The Phenomenology of Internal Time Consciousness*, 40–46. This account is part of an earlier, full account of phenomenological conceptions of time.

9. Husserl, *The Phenomenology of Internal Time Consciousness*, 45.

10. Husserl, *The Phenomenology of Internal Time Consciousness*, 48.

11. Husserl, *The Phenomenology of Internal Time Consciousness*, 46–52.

12. Husserl, *The Phenomenology of Internal Time Consciousness*, 47.

13. Husserl, *The Phenomenology of Internal Time Consciousness*, 53–54.

14. Husserl, *The Phenomenology of Internal Time Consciousness*, 98.

15. Husserl, *The Phenomenology of Internal Time Consciousness*, 97.

16. Canales, *The Physicist and the Philosopher*, 20.

17. Henri Bergson, *Duration and Simultaneity*, trans. Mark Lewis and Robin Durie (London: Clinamen Press, 1999), 187.

18. Milic Capek, *Bergson and Modern Physics: A Re-interpretation and Re-evaluation*, Boston Studies in the Philosophy of Science, vol. 7 (Dordrecht: D. Reidel, 1971), 249.

19. Henri Bergson, *Time and Free Will: An Essay on the Immediate Data of Consciousness*, trans. F. L. Pogson (New York: Macmillan, 1959), 100.

20. Henri Bergson, *Matter and Memory*, trans. Nancy Margaret Paul and W. Scott Palmer (New York: Zone Books, 1988), 65–66; Gilles Deleuze, *Difference and Repetition*, trans. Paul Patton (New York: Columbia University Press, 1994), 80.

21. Robert Humphrey, *Stream of Consciousness in the Modern Novel* (Berkeley: University of California Press, 1954), 120.

22. Maurice Merleau-Ponty, "Bergson in the Making," in *Signs*, trans. Richard G. McCleary (Evanston, Ill.: Northwestern University Press, 1964), 182–91, 185.

23. Maurice Merleau-Ponty, *Nature: Course Notes from the Collége de France*, compiled by Dominique Séglard, trans. Robert Vallier (Evanston, Ill.: Northwestern University Press, 2003), 89.

24. Maurice Merleau-Ponty, *Phenomenology of Perception*, trans. Donald Landes (New York: Routledge, 2012), 432.

25. Merleau-Ponty, *Phenomenology*, 288. Only objective time is made up of successive moments.

26. Merleau-Ponty, *Phenomenology*, 483. "Your abode is your act itself. Your act is you. . . . You give yourself in exchange. . . . Your significance shows itself."

27. Robert J. Dostal, "Time and Phenomenology in Husserl and Heidegger," in *The Cambridge Companion to Heidegger*, ed. Charles Guignon (Cambridge, U.K.: Cambridge University Press, 1992), 141–69, 154–55.

28. Martin Heidegger, *Being and Time*, trans. John Macquarrie and Edward Robinson (San Francisco: Harper, 1962), 9.

29. Heidegger, *Being and Time*, 15.

30. William Blattner, "Temporality," in *A Companion to Heidegger*, ed. Hubert L. Dreyfus and Mark A. Wrathall (London: Blackwell, 2005), 316, 318.

31. Blattner, "Temporality," 319; Heidegger, *Being and Time*, 333, 334.

32. Heidegger, *Being and Time*, 339.

33. Heidegger, *Being and Time*, 303, 229.

34. Jean-Paul Sartre, *Being and Nothingness: An Essay on Phenomenological Ontology*, trans. Hazel E. Barnes (New York: Philosophical Library, 1956), 36.

35. Sartre, *Being and Nothingness*, 41.

36. Sartre, *Being and Nothingness*, 204; Maurice A. Natanson, *A Critique of Jean-Paul Sartre's Ontology* (Lincoln: University of Nebraska Press, 1951), 23.

37. Sartre, *Being and Nothingness*, 206.

38. Sartre, *Being and Nothingness*, 207.

39. Sartre, *Being and Nothingness*, 208.

40. Simone de Beauvoir, *The Ethics of Ambiguity*, trans. Bernard Frechtman (New York: Citadel Press, 1976), 25.

41. Simone de Beauvoir, *She Came to Stay* (New York: Norton, 1990), 103.

42. Simone de Beauvoir, *The Coming of Age*, trans. Patrick O'Brian (New York: G. P. Putnam, 1972), 373, emphasis added.

43. See Simone de Beauvoir, *All Men Are Mortal*, trans. Leonard M. Friedman (New York: Norton, 1992), and Beauvoir, *The Coming of Age*, 377–78.

44. Beauvoir, *The Coming of Age*, 410.

45. Alia Al-Saji, "Too Late: Racialized Time and the Closure of the Past," *Insights: Durham University Institute of Advanced Study* 6, no. 5 (2013): 2, 3.

46. Al-Saji, "Too Late," 6, 7.

47. Al-Saji, "Too Late," 8.

48. Al-Saji, "Too Late," 8.

# 48 Trans Phenomena

Talia Mae Bettcher

While trans people had been theorized since the late 1800s, particularly within the field of sexology,[1] by the 1950s a common view of the "transsexual" began to take shape. Through the work of Harry Benjamin[2] and Christian Hamburger et al.[3]—in the wake of the media explosion around Christine Jorgensen's transition—the notion of a recalcitrant sense of self that cannot be changed through mere psychiatric intervention and that required bodily transformation through surgical and hormonal intervention came into prominence. Meanwhile, work by John Money, John and Joan Hampson, and then Robert Stoller and Ralph Greenson produced the notion of "gender identity" (one's sense of being either male or female).[4] The formula of gender identity/body misalignment and the trope of "being trapped in the wrong body" thereby came to be closely associated with the idea of transsexuality, "gender identity disorder," and "gender dysphoria."

By the mid-1990s, trans studies exploded onto the scene. It was characterized by trans people beginning to theorize themselves, beginning to develop discourses that countered a pathologizing medical model.[5] Much of trans studies was closely associated with the burgeoning "queer theory" of the day, although some of it reacted to that association. While many of the questions addressed in trans studies were philosophical in character, most of the discussion occurred outside of the discipline of philosophy in what Butler has called "Philosophy's Other."[6] Certainly these discussions drew on philosophers such as Derrida, Foucault, Merleau-Ponty, and, of course, Butler herself. But the discipline of philosophy demonstrated next to no interest in trans issues. In fact, it is not until very recently that something like "trans philosophy" has even been identified within the discipline as such.

Nonetheless there are clearly philosophical questions that can be and have been posed when "thinking trans." One question, for example, concerns just how to characterize transphobia and trans-based oppression. While the dominant model has been the idea that trans people are oppressed through the focus on sharp binary divisions, I have argued that it is also important to consider the constitution of trans people as deceivers and pretenders and the role that an appearance/reality contrast plays in this. The imposition of a sharp binary is not the only kind of oppression that trans people face.[7]

There are several closely related questions around gender transition, gender identity, and gender dysphoria (or, as I prefer to call it, "discontent"). The first is prima facie ontological or perhaps semantic: What *is* a woman, and what *is* a man?[8] Does a transition really involve a movement from the one gender to the other? The second, closely related to the first, is epistemological: Are trans people *correct* in their self-identification?[9] Under what conditions might we be correct? Both can be subsumed under a more general question: How must things be in order for trans identities to be valid?

These questions can be given phenomenological import by considering the priority (or nonpriority) of phenomenology itself: Can a trans person's first-person experience of embodiment have the capacity to resignify their very body in case we adopt a phenomenological starting point?[10] Some other phenomenology-related questions that have been discussed include the following: How do we come to acquire gendered experiences of body in the first place?[11] To what degree are our discontented experiences of embodiment culturally mediated?[12] That is, how can something so intimate as these bodily experiences be informed by the significance of the body and its possibilities in a culture?

Perhaps the most essential starting question that a trans studies theorist could raise, it seems to me, is simply this: What *is* the phenomenology of "gender dysphoria"? How should it be understood?[13] The answer depends upon descriptive accuracy and thoroughness as an attempt to frame trans experience of gender discontent through various theoretical concepts. Prosser claims, for example, that "the image of wrong embodiment describes most effectively the experience of pre-transition (dis)embodiment: the feeling of a sexed body dysphoria profoundly subjectively experienced."[14] But is he right?

Let us first consider the appeal to an incongruence between conscious gender identity and various material realities as the foundation of trans gender discontent. I take a conscious sense of oneself as a woman or man to be part of one's general sense of who and what one is—including how one fits into the world. So a conscious self-identity includes a conception of what it means to be a woman or a man. Such a self-conception may, of course, be incongruent with the social/material reality in which one finds oneself: one may understand oneself to be a woman but be regarded by others as a man.

An appeal to this incongruence, however, proves unsuccessful in framing trans gender discontent insofar as gender self-identity is often one of the things that *gets* changed.[15] "I did not have the quintessential trans experience of always feeling that I should have been female," says Julia Serano. "For me, this recognition came about more gradually."[16] Some of us did not always know who we were—this was something we had to discover through struggle. We were raised to have one conscious gender identity—told that we were either a boy or a girl. And we came to believe it. Over a long and sometimes difficult process we had to undo these beliefs and adopt new ones. If this is so, then conscious self-identity cannot *anchor* the motivation to transition since it is sometimes actually *part* of the process.

Yet understanding the phenomenology of the transformation of gender self-identity may well prove to be an important task. According to Prosser in *Second Skins,* an autobiographical narrative is not only required as the defining symptom of transsexuality; it is also that through which subjectivity as transsexual is enabled. More than that, Prosser argues, autobiographical narrative serves an important function for transsexuals "posttransition" to heal the dissonance between past and present self through autobiography's retrospective and progressive features. Whether or not this is right, it is certainly the case that a new gender self-identity must play an important role in conferring intelligibility upon transition. For example, by including a "wrong body" narrative within one's gendered self-identity, one can locate oneself within an intelligible phenomenon, make sense of one's trans gender discontent and one's transition. And appeals of this type might also be useful in securing the legitimacy of one's identity to oneself and others.[17]

Accounts of trans gender discontent have, of course, commonly attempted to go beyond or beneath conscious gender identity by appealing to the notion of felt embodiment. This version of incongruence has turned on a contrast between first- and third-person perspective on the body. From the first-person perspective, the body is experienced from "within." One can be aware that one is standing, that one is moving, and so forth without having to see oneself or touch oneself in movement. One of the features of this experience of the body is that it is available only to oneself—nobody else experiences one's body in that way. From the third-person perspective, by contrast, the body is experienced from "without." One can see and touch one's body just as others can. That is, one can sense-experience one's body as it is available to others. By recognizing that one can experience the body in both of these ways as being of a particular sex or gender, we get a first- and third-person incongruence that is invoked to frame trans gender discontent. A trans man experiences his body as male "from within," while recognizing (and experiencing) that his body is seen and is experienced by others as female without.

Theorists such as Henry Rubin[18] and Prosser have appealed to this type of model in their formulations of trans discontent. For both, the phenomena of phantom limb experience and bodily agnosia (or anosognosia) figure prominently. The internal body image may include parts of the body that do not show up in third-person representation and that are not taken to be there materially, while other body parts may not be recognized despite their presence in the third-person register.

Rubin, for example, avails himself of the work of Merleau-Ponty in making sense of the experiences described above. He also draws on Sartre's three levels of bodily ontology.[19] The first level is characterized, for him, as trans experience of one's body "from the inside" (the body-for-itself), as sexed one way. The second level is characterized as the recognition that one's body, as accessible to others (the body-for-others), is sexed a different way. And the third level, one of profound alienation, is characterized by the first-person experience of one's body as an object for others, which Rubin uses to understand "a transsexual's painful realization that his flesh, his body-for-others is . . . not what he sees in his body image."[20]

Crucially in these formulations, the transition involves a literal change in the materiality of one's body through surgical or hormonal intervention. And the worry, pressed by Gayle Salamon in *Assuming a Body*, is the possible assumption that what is at stake is the blunt materiality of the body (rather than the material body as interpreted in some specific way) happily conforming to a body image that itself demands only some blunt material body. It's because our body and body parts *have* cultural meaning that they can come to have significance to us. Thus the cultural significance of the body needs to be centralized in understanding trans discontent. As Salamon argues, our very experience of felt body can be saturated with, highly sensitive to, cultural significance. This suggests the possibility of bodily experience resignifying the body. And it is certainly true that, at least for some trans people, gender discontent can be alleviated by the reinterpretation or recoding of body parts.

This recognition has a bearing on the explanatory question: insofar as trans discontent is understood as culturally mediated, it is difficult to maintain the view that the body is the sole source of the discontent, that trans people are "born this way."[21] Yet the question of how the discontent arises remains vexing. Salamon, for example, following Schilder,[22] proposes a body image that is developed over time, through memory, and that it is not uncommon for the body schema to misalign with the body as visual object, say. Yet it is difficult to see how a female body image could arise in environmental engagement with the world, when trans women as "boys" are not given opportunities to develop such an image.[23] To be sure, Salamon also emphasizes the importance of affective investment in one's body—and there need not be such a close tethering between internal felt sense and external engagement. Yet it remains unclear just what these affective investments are and how they might possibly arise. From a trans perspective, the "why" question can seem particularly mysterious: If one was raised to be one way, why is it that one's internal experience is quite another way? While we might well allow that the contrary investments are culturally saturated, their origin remains nonetheless mystifying.[24]

The main worry that I have with this entire model concerns its descriptive inadequacy. First, it exclusively focuses on embodiment experience: many binary self-identified trans men and women do not undergo any bodily changes at all. For them, a change in public gender self-presentation may suffice. A centralization of the body would require drawing a sharp theoretical line between those trans people who alter their bodies and those who do not.[25] This is evident in the works of both Prosser and Rubin. There we see a contrast between "transsexual" and "transgender" people. This contrast is particularly in play in Prosser's theory. As his work takes aim at Butler's early theories of gender,[26] he wants to distance himself from an emphasis on the "superficial" such as clothing and the visual manifestation of skin—the latter of which he sees as central to Butler's conception of psychic investment in body. By contrast, Prosser wants "depth." For him, this means focusing on the internal, first-person experience of being embodied—an experience for him that has little to do with gender presentation and little to do with visual representation of body.

This commitment to sharp theoretical difference is highly questionable, however, as both "kinds" of trans people self-identify strongly as men or women and "live their lives" accordingly. Indeed the line is highly permeable, with questions about bodily change confronting trans people in a way that is deeply personal and idiosyncratic.[27] Moreover, such an account appears to erase the role that gender presentation can play in the emergence of trans identity. Before transition one can don a gender presentation—which at the time is socially constituted as nothing but a costume—and nonetheless experience a sense of self-recognition. The incongruence model does not accommodate this phenomenon well.

Developing an account that gives due weight to gender presentation may require a deep rethinking of the subject/object contrast assumed by the incongruence model.[28] Gender presentation is a socially constituted appearance for others. And this suggests that an awareness of oneself as gender-presenting is rather like an awareness of oneself as an object for others (Sartre's third level). If this is so, however, it would make no sense to figure an incongruence between first- and third-person perspectives (or the first and second levels). Rather, it would seem to require two conflicting awarenesses of oneself as an object or potential object for others—an invalidating or "de-realizing" one and a validating or "realizing" one.

A second descriptive inadequacy of these accounts is the apparent abstraction from the violence and oppression of trans people and our resistance to it.[29] Might there be a phenomenology of trans oppression and resistance? What might it look like? The discontent theorized in the "wrong body" model is entirely disconnected from these questions. But perhaps there is a deep connection between the phenomenology of oppression/resistance and the phenomenology of the trans discontent that motivates gender transition.[30]

María Lugones posits the existence of multiple worlds in relations of contestation, oppression, and resistance.[31] Drawing on this idea, I have proposed that trans people can be constructed as one gender in one (dominant) world and as another gender in a resistant world.[32] For Lugones, this allows for the possibility of an *awareness of oneself* as multiple—that is, as both one person in one world and another person in another. How might the phenomenology of trans discontent learn from this? For example, while in the process of self-identity reconstruction, a trans person may experience the tug of "dueling narrative conceptions"—each one invalidating or explaining away the other. This may yield a liminal or double self-conception. More deeply, how might we formulate a phenomenology of liminality that takes heed of the trans experience of simultaneous "realization" and "de-realization" with regard to our appearances to others? Here Lugones's theories, and Latina feminist phenomenology more generally,[33] may prove especially instructive in theorizing a trans phenomenology. And the expectation, of course, is that trans phenomenology will also be able to lend some new illuminations in return.[34]

## Notes

1. Susan Stryker, *Transgender History* (Berkeley, Calif.: Seal Press, 2008).

2. Harry Benjamin, "Transvestism and Transsexualism," *International Journal of Sexology* 7, no. 1 (1953): 12–14.

3. Christian Hamburger, Georg K. Stürup, and E. Dahl-Iversen "Transvestism; Hormonal, Psychiatric, and Surgical Treatment," *Journal of the American Medical Association* 152, no. 5 (1953): 391–96.

4. John Money, Joan G. Hampson, and John L. Hampson "An Examination of Some Basic Sexual Concepts: The Evidence of Human Hermaphroditism," *Bulletin of the Johns Hopkins Hospital* 97 (1955): 301–19; Ralph R. Greenson, "On Homosexuality and Gender Identity," *International Journal of Psycho-Analysis* 45 (1964): 217; Robert J. Stoller, "A

Contribution to the Study of Gender Identity," *International Journal of Psycho-Analysis* 45 (1964): 220.

5. Sandy Stone, "The *Empire* Strikes Back: A Posttranssexual Manifesto," in *Body Guards: The Cultural Politics of Gender Ambiguity*, ed. Julia Epstein and Kristina Straub (New York: Routledge, 1991); Susan Stryker, "(De)Subjugated Knowledges: An Introduction to Transgender Studies," in *The Transgender Studies Reader*, ed. Susan Stryker and Stephen Whittle (New York: Routledge, 2004), 1–17.

6. Judith Butler, *Undoing Gender* (New York: Routledge, 2004).

7. Talia Mae Bettcher, "Trapped in the Wrong Theory: Rethinking Trans Oppression and Resistance," *Signs: Journal of Women in Culture and Society* 39, no. 2 (2014): 43–65.

8. Jennifer Saul, "Politically Significant Terms and the Philosophy of Language: Methodological Issues," in *Out from the Shadows: Analytical Feminist Contributions to Traditional Philosophy*, ed. S. L. Crasnow and A. M. Superson (Oxford: Oxford University Press, 2012); Talia Mae Bettcher, "Trans Women and the Meaning of 'Woman,'" in *Philosophy of Sex: Contemporary Readings*, 6th edition, ed. A. Soble, N. Power, and R. Halwani (New York: Rowman & Littlefield, 2012).

9. Talia Mae Bettcher, "Trans Identities and First-Person Authority," in *You've Changed: Sex Reassignment and Personal Identity*, ed. Laurie Shrage (Oxford: Oxford University Press, 2009), 98–120.

10. Gayle Salamon, *Assuming a Body: Transgender and Rhetorics of Materiality* (New York; Columbia University Press, 2010).

11. Jay Prosser, *Second Skins: The Body Narratives of Transsexuality* (New York: Columbia University Press, 1998); Salamon, *Assuming a Body*; Julia Serano, *Whipping Girl: A Transsexual Woman on Sexism and the Scapegoating of Femininity* (Emeryville, Calif.: Seal Press, 2007).

12. Salamon, *Assuming a Body*.

13. Prosser, *Second Skins*; Andrea Long Chu, "The Wrong Wrong Body: Notes on Trans Phenomenology," *TSQ: Transgender Studies Quarterly* 4, no. 1 (2017): 141–52.

14. Prosser, *Second Skins*, 69.

15. Talia Mae Bettcher, "Trans 101," in *Philosophy of Sex: Contemporary Readings*, 7th edition, ed. Raja Halwani, Sarah Hoffman, and Alan Soble (New York: Rowman & Littlefield, 2017), 119–38.

16. Serrano, *Whipping Girl*, 78.

17. Talia Mae Bettcher, *Realitymare: On Intimacy, Illusion, and Personhood. An Essay in Trans Philosophy* (Minneapolis: University of Minnesota Press, forthcoming).

18. Henry S. Rubin, "Phenomenology as Method in Trans Studies," *GLQ: A Journal of Lesbian and Gay Studies* 4, no. 2 (1998): 263–81.

19. Jean-Paul Sartre, *Being and Nothingness: A Phenomenology Essay on Ontology*, trans. Hazel E. Barnes (New York: Washington Square Press, 1993).

20. Rubin, "Phenomenology as Method," 271.

21. Bettcher, "Trapped in the Wrong Theory."

22. Paul Schilder, *The Image and Appearance of the Human Body* (New York: John Wiley and Sons, 1950).

23. Talia Mae Bettcher, "Through the Looking Glass: Transgender Theory Meets Feminist Philosophy," in *Routledge Handbook of Feminist Philosophy*, ed. Ann Garry, Serene Khader, and Allison Stone (New York: Routledge, 2017), 393–404; Bettcher, "Trans 101."

24. Bettcher, "Through the Looking Glass"; Bettcher, "Trans 101."

25. Bettcher, *Realitymare.*

26. Judith Butler, *Gender Trouble: Feminism and the Subversion of Identity* (New York: Routledge, 1990); Judith Butler, *Bodies That Matter: On the Discursive Limits of "Sex"* (New York: Routledge, 1993).

27. Bettcher, *Realitymare.*

28. Bettcher, *Realitymare.*

29. Bettcher, *Realitymare.*

30. Bettcher, *Realitymare.*

31. María Lugones, *Pilgrimages/Peregrinajes: Theorizing Coalition against Multiple Oppressions* (Lanham, Md.: Rowman and Littlefield, 2003).

32. Bettcher, "Trapped in the Wrong Theory."

33. Mariana Ortega, *In-Between: Latina Feminist Phenomenology, Multiplicity, and the Self* (Albany, N.Y.: SUNY Press, 2016).

34. Bettcher, *Realitymare.*

# 49 Witnessing

Kelly Oliver

*Witnessing* is defined as the action of bearing witness or giving testimony, the fact of being present and observing something; *witnessing* is from *witness*, to bear witness, to testify, to give evidence, to be a spectator or auditor of something, to be present as an observer, to see with one's own eyes.[1] The double meaning of witnessing—*eyewitness* testimony based on firsthand knowledge and *bearing witness* to something beyond recognition that can't be seen—is the heart of subjectivity. Whereas testimony is a spoken or written account of something seen or experienced, witnessing refers to the address-and-response structure of subjectivity itself, the very structure that makes testimony possible. The notion of subjectivity as witnessing is based on the fact that to be a subject is to be responsive to others and the world.

Edmund Husserl[2] maintains that subjectivity or consciousness is always consciousness of something. In other words, as conscious subjects we are always engaged with the world around us. Conceiving of subjectivity in terms of witnessing takes this engagement even further by proposing that the very possibility of consciousness itself is relational. It is not that there is a subject whose consciousness is an engagement, but rather there is no subject without engagement. The subject is a response to the world and others. So, unlike classical phenomenology, in which there is a subject first and then relationality, there is relationality first and only then is subjectivity possible. Furthermore, Husserl suggests that we come to know others through what he calls analogical reasoning, which is to say we reason that if when we do $x$ it means $y$, then when another person does $x$ it too must mean $y$. Conceiving of subjectivity in terms of the double sense of witnessing fills in the gap, so to speak, between the self and other, the subject and "its world." In fact, the world and others are no longer "for" the subject, nor are they given to it. Rather, the subject is constituted by its relationship to others and the world, and only through those relationships does it become a subject.

More specifically, it is through address and response that subjectivity is formed. In her early work, Cynthia Willett describes this address and response as the song and dance shared between mother and infant,[3] while in her later work she describes a call and response between animals, including human animals, as the basis of our thoroughly interrelational subjectivity.[4] Again, it is crucial to emphasize that the subject is not just in a relationship with others but appears to itself as a subject through its relationships with others.

What we gain from conceiving of subjectivity in terms of the double sense of witnessing is the addition of social context and historical situatedness, which are lacking in classical phenomenology. For example, Husserl asks us to bracket out empirical experience in order to deduce what is universal about consciousness. Witnessing, on the other hand, insists that all consciousness is situated, not just in space and time, but also in particular cultures and historical contexts. How we perceive the world and others is governed, if not determined, by our social and political context, including where we grew up, what we learned in school, whether or not our culture is racist or sexist or homophobic, what religion is dominant in our society or what religion we grew up practicing, etc. We cannot separate our social position from our subjectivity, In other words, we cannot deduce universal structures of consciousness by bracketing out the world.

Witnessing does this through its double meaning. On the one hand, it means seeing what is around you, what's there to be seen, both literally and figuratively. This aspect of witnessing corresponds to subject position. We are each located in a particular social and historical context to which we must attend, a context that is never devoid of power relations that affect what and how we know, and what and how we perceive the world. In this regard, the notion of witnessing that comes out of phenomenology prefigures contemporary social epistemology insofar as it already insists on the relationality of perception and knowledge and the power dynamics inherent in perception and knowledge.

On the other hand, witnessing also means bearing witness to something that cannot be seen. What cannot be seen is the very address and response structure of subjectivity and the deeply relational essence of each response-able being. That is to say, every living being is responsive to and dependent upon the world around it. Human beings are dependent upon the earth, plants, nonhuman animals, the atmosphere, the sun, etc. But we are also dependent upon each other. Human infants can't survive without care, many years of care. And dependency relations continue in various forms throughout our lives. In this regard, the notion of subjectivity as witnessing resonates with care ethics and other forms of relational ethics. But again, whereas care ethics and some other forms of relational ethics assume separate selves in dependency relations, witnessing proposes a thoroughly relation self such that the relationship comes first, and furthermore there is no self without the other.[5]

In addition, witnessing emphasizes the address-and-response structure that makes subjectivity possible. In their book *Testimony*, Shoshana Felman and Dori Laub, discussing Holocaust survivors, argue that the torture inflicted on concentration camp victims robbed them of the address-and-response structure of subjectivity and thereby rendered them fragmented subjects.[6] The attack was not just on the physical bodies of victims but also on the very possibility of maintaining relationships with others and therefore with themselves. Laub suggests that it was the inner dialogue that was damaged, and this inner dialogue is what makes us who we are; it is what makes us subjects. In addition, the inner dialogue is radically dependent upon outer dialogue, or actual address and response between people. But this address and response must open up the possibility of response and support one's sense of self rather than close it off and undermine it, like the Nazis did in the camps. The Nazis attacked the victims' sense of themselves as agents in the world.

With the double notion of witnessing, then, *subjectivity* refers to one's sense of oneself as an "I," as an agent, and *subject position* refers to one's position in society and history as developed through various social relationships. The structure of subjectivity is the structure that makes taking oneself as an agent or a self possible. This structure is a witnessing structure that is founded on the possibility of address and response; it is a fundamentally dialogic structure, in the broadest possible sense. Subject position, on the other hand, is not the very possibility of one's sense of oneself as an agent or an "I" per se, but the particular sense of one's kind of agency, so to speak, that comes through one's social position and historical context. While distinct, subject position and subjectivity are also intimately related. For example, if you are a black woman in a racist and sexist culture, then your subject position as oppressed could undermine your subjectivity, your sense of yourself as an agent. If you are a white man in a racist and sexist culture, then your subject position as privileged could shore up your subjectivity and promote your sense of yourself as an agent.

*Witnessing* as both subject position and sociohistorical context of subjectivity is a corrective to classical phenomenological theories of subjectivity that do not attend to history. While post-Husserlian phenomenologists such as Maurice Merleau-Ponty and Martin Heidegger formulated theories of relational subjectivity or subjectivity as inherently intersubjective, for the most part they neglected subject position conceived in terms of social-political context and how that context affects what we mean by subjectivity itself.[7] Even Emmanuel Levinas, who suggests that the subject is "hostage" to the other insofar as it comes into being in responsive relationships, and formulates a notion of ethical responsibility beyond recognition, arguably does not adequately account for subject position or politics in his postphenomenological philosophy.[8]

Following Levinas, but with a concern to connect ethics and politics, I develop the double notion of witnessing as a response to Hegelian recognition models of political and ethical subjectivity. Following Hegel, some contemporary critical theorists, particularly Axel Honneth, propose that subjectivity is developed through recognition from others.[9] I challenge the recognition model by arguing that recognition always presupposes a power dynamic wherein one individual or group confers recognition on another.[10] Given that the power relation is built into the notion of recognition, I argue that recognition is pathological when it comes to discussing oppression. That is to say, the recognition model requires that the oppressed seek recognition from their oppressors, the very people who have been withholding recognition from them in the first place. Relating this problematic back to the witnessing model of subjectivity, we could say that the oppressors deny a healthy or robust address-and-response dynamic to those who are oppressed and thereby undermine their subjectivity. In fact, I argue that oppression does just that: it undermines one's sense of oneself as a subject.[11] Thus the recognition model does not adequately account for differential subject positions and therefore proposes a pathological form of subjectivity that risks perpetuating rather than overcoming oppression.

Witnessing is a process of address and response that radicalizes Hegel's insight that subjectivity is constituted intersubjectively and takes us beyond recognition to the affective and imaginative dimensions of experience, which must be added to the politics of recognition. Most important, the double meaning of witnessing as both eyewitness testimony and bearing witness to what cannot be seen points to the tension at the heart of subjectivity that opens up the possibility of considering both social-political context and the intersubjective constitution of subjectivity, namely the tension between ethics and politics.

Ethics requires that we treat each individual being as singular and unique. Otherwise we cannot do it justice. Politics requires that we treat everyone equally and develop universal laws or policies. How can we possibly do both? There is a fundamental tension between ethics and politics, singular and universal. The double sense of witnessing is an attempt to account for both the singular and the universal, the unique subjectivity of each and the shared subject positions of groups. Witnessing does not attempt to resolve this tension but rather to stay with the tension and make it productive in thinking through a more ethical politics, that is to say, a politics more attuned to the singularity of each being.

In my own work, what started as a dialogic theory based on the address-response structure of subjectivity has evolved to include not just human beings or other linguistic beings but also all responsive living beings.[12] If we are by virtue of our ability to respond, which necessarily develops only through our relationships with others, then we are obligated to our founding possibility, namely our responsive relationships. We have a responsibility to open up rather than close down the possibility of response from others, including nonhuman living beings. As Levinas says, we are responsible for the other's response (although he doesn't include nonhuman animals in his ethics). Witnessing, then, entails a new radical way of approaching ethics as response ethics wherein we are responsible not only for our actions and our beliefs and even for the other's response but also for what we do not and cannot know, what we do not and cannot recognize. In this way, witnessing as response ethics demands that we remain vigilant to the ways in which even our attempts to be just and fair, to do the right thing, may exclude or silence some others we have not yet considered or recognized as members of our moral community. Witnessing beyond recognition, then, is not only a theory of subjectivity and subject position but also an ethical politics that requires that we continually investigate our own exclusionary or violent practices and take responsibility. Our responsibility comes from our response-ability, or our ability to respond. And that is the crux of response ethics based on the double sense of witnessing that brings together the singularity of each with the plurality of those with whom we share a world, and ultimately all of those with whom we share our one and only planetary home, the earth.

In this way, witnessing ethics as response ethics can take us beyond human-centrism and toward consideration of the ways in which all of the creatures of the earth, and the earth itself, respond. Within response ethics, political and moral subjects are constituted not by their sovereignty and mastery but rather by address and response. Extending the analysis of witnessing, address and response (broadly conceived) are the basis of earth ethics grounded on cohabitation and interdependence. And the responsibility to engender response, or facilitate the ability to respond, in others and the environment is the primary obligation of response ethics.

In sum, phenomenological meaning both requires social bonds and emerges through social bonds, which are tied to particular spaces or places and times or histories. The relationality of social bonds, including bonds to places and histories, makes meaning possible, even while meaning emerges through relationships. The dynamic of meaning as both constituted by and constituting our relationships is akin to the *witnessing* structure of response-ability, the structure of address and response. Living creatures are responsive, and an earth ethics promotes our responsibility to open up, rather than close off, the response-ability of others, their ability to respond.

## Notes

1. Oxford University Press, OED Online, June 2017.

2. See the following by Husserl: *Cartesian Meditations: An Introduction to Phenomenology*, trans. Dorion Cairns (Dordrecht: Kluwer Academic, 1950; *Ideas: General Introduction to Pure Phenomenology*, trans. Dermot Moran (New York: Routledge, 2012); *Ideas Pertaining to a Pure Phenomenology and to a Phenomenological Philosophy*, trans. R. Rojcewicz and A. Schuwer (Dordrecht: Kluwer Academic, 1989).

3. Cynthia Willett, *Maternal Ethics and Other Slave Moralities* (New York: Routledge, 1995).

4. Cynthia Willett, *Interspecies Ethics (A Serious Ethics with a Comic Twist)* (New York: Columbia University Press, 2014).

5. See especially Carol Gilligan, *In a Different Voice: Psychological Theory and Women's Development* (Cambridge, Mass.: Harvard University Press, 1982); Nel Noddings, *Caring: A Feminine Approach to Ethics and Moral Education* (Berkeley: University of California Press, 1984); Eva Feder Kittay, *Love's Labor: Essays on Women, Equality and Dependency* (New York: Routledge, 1999).

6. Dori Laub and Shoshana Felman, *Testimony: Crises of Witnessing in Literature, Psychoanalysis and History* (New York: Routledge, 1992).

7. Martin Heidegger, *Being and Time*, trans. John Macquarrie and Edward Robinson (New York: Harper Perennial, 2008); Maurice Merleau-Ponty, *Phenomenology of Perception*, trans. Colin Smith (New York: Routledge Classics, 2002).

8. See the following by Levinas: *Totality and Infinity*, trans. Alphonso Lingis (Pittsburgh, Pa.: Duquesne University Press, 1961); *Otherwise Than Being, Or Beyond Essence* (1974), trans. Alphonso Lingis (Dordrecht: Springer, 1991).

9. G. W. F. Hegel, *Phenomenology of Spirit*, trans. A. V. Miller (Oxford: Oxford University Press, 1977); Axel Honneth, *The Struggle for Recognition: The Moral Grammar of Social Conflicts* (Cambridge, Mass.: MIT Press, 1992).

10. Kelly Oliver, *Witnessing: Beyond Recognition* (Minneapolis: University of Minnesota Press, 2001).

11. Kelly Oliver, *The Colonization of Psychic Space: Toward a Psychoanalytic Social Theory* (Minneapolis: University of Minnesota Press, 2004).

12. Kelly Oliver, *Animal Lessons: How They Teach Us to Be Human* (New York: Columbia University Press, 2009); Kelly Oliver, *Earth and World: Philosophy after the Apollo Missions* (New York: Columbia University Press, 2015).

# 50 World-Traveling

Andrea J. Pitts

Since its introduction in 1987, María Lugones's concept of world-traveling has had a significant impact on philosophical discussions related to a number of important phenomenological themes. These themes include questions of embodiment, spatiality and movement, historicity and temporality, interpersonal communication and meaning, and questions of selfhood. Lugones's initial articulation of the concept originally appeared in an essay titled "Playfulness, 'World'-Travelling, and Loving Perception" (1987), and was later republished in a slightly modified version in her 2003 book, *Pilgrimages/*Peregrinajes*: Theorizing Coalition against Multiple Oppressions*, along with an extended introduction that discussed several core concepts within the essay.[1] Generally speaking, *world-traveling* refers to experiential shifts—both willing and unwilling—between differing "worlds" of sense and meaning. What precisely Lugones means by "world" in world-traveling and *who* is doing the traveling are important questions, which I return to later. For now, it is important to highlight some of the major contours that appear in her description of the concept and to briefly discuss the context in which she developed the notion. First, I outline Lugones's main articulation of world-traveling, then I briefly describe some overlapping themes between world-traveling and phenomenological approaches to experience, embodiment, and motility. I conclude with some critical responses to the notion of world-traveling and briefly highlight some novel directions through which contemporary readers can potentially extend the concept.

One important place to begin examining the concept of world-traveling is Lugones's framing of the experiences that brought her to the notion. Notably, she situates her essay within the need to "understand and affirm the plurality in and among women."[2] She also writes that two forms of "coming to consciousness" made her articulation of the approach possible.[3] First, she describes her shifting sensibilities regarding her relationship with her mother, namely, that she wants to explore her "failure to love [her] mother" as a problem that can be addressed, to some extent, via world-traveling.[4] Second, she describes her "coming to consciousness as a woman of color" and her gradual recognition of the failures among women to love one another across racial and cultural differences.[5]

To understand the two "failures" that prompted Lugones to propose world-traveling, we must briefly discuss the conception of "loving perception" that undergird both examples. "Loving perception" is a phrase utilized by the feminist theorist Marilyn Frye in her 1983 essay "In and Out of Harm's Way: Arrogance and Love." Frye uses the concept to articulate loving perception as a contrast to "arrogant perception." Arrogant perception is a worldview that places an individual's own desires, needs, and beliefs at a teleological center, from which the desires, needs, and beliefs of others become secondary or subservient. Frye writes, "The arrogating perceiver is a teleologist, a believer that everything exists and happens for some purpose, and he tends to animate things, imagining attitudes toward himself as the animating motives."[6] Frye's articulation of this relationship primarily takes place between men and women; Lugones's interpretation of arrogant perception expands this criticism to the relationships between women. Specifically, she describes how "being taught to be a woman" in the United States and in Argentina entails this form of arrogant perception, and she claims that women learn to be "both the agent and the object of arrogant perception."[7] Her "coming to consciousness" in the ways described above thus arises from her recognition that she has treated her mother as an object to meet her own needs, and that she mistook this relationality with her mother as a form of love. Additionally, while in the United States, Lugones came to realize that both white/Anglo men and white/Anglo women engaged in practices of arrogant perception to relate to people of color. She writes that white/Anglo men and women could "remain untouched, without any sense of loss" through their engagements with people of color, and that "a part of racism is the internalization of the propriety of abuse without identification."[8] Lugones thereby expands Frye's articulation of arrogant perception by interpreting the processes through which structural features of racism and white supremacy are enacted in the everyday interactions between white people and people of color.

Willful world-traveling, then, becomes a practice that seeks to respond to arrogant perception. To perceive others lovingly, rather than arrogantly, Lugones follows Frye's claim that "one must consult something other than one's own will and interests and fears and imagination" and proposes that this form of "consultation" is world-traveling.[9] Lugones writes in response to her arrogant perception of her mother:

> Loving my mother also required that I see with her eyes, that I go into my mother's world, that I witness her own sense of herself from within her world. Only through this travelling to her "world" could I identify with her because only then could I cease to ignore her and to be excluded and separate from her. We are fully dependent on each other for the possibility of being understood and without this understanding we are not intelligible, we do not make sense, we are not solid, visible, integrated; we are lacking. So travelling to each other's "worlds" would enable us to *be* through *loving* each other.[10]

Note Lugones's use of an affirmation of being in this sentence. World-traveling—in this case a willful attempt to relate to another's "world"—underscores the fundamental interdependency of meaning-making ("we are not intelligible, we do not make sense") and embodied perception of one's self and others ("we are not solid, visible, integrated"). In this vein, Lugones's concept of world-traveling highlights a core ontological commitment to intersubjectivity and a rejection of solipsistic forms of selfhood, perception, and experience. Such a commitment places her alongside other feminist and phenomenological theorists who have highlighted these features as well, including, for example, Simone de Beauvoir, Frantz Fanon, Maurice Merleau-Ponty, Emmanuel Levinas, and Iris Marion Young.

To elaborate what she means by "world," Lugones clarifies that a world must "be inhabited by some flesh and blood people."[11] This characteristic of "worlds," she states, contrasts her notion with other, more utopian or logical valences of the term. Notably, in the introduction to *Pilgrimages/*Peregrinajes, she provides an extended explanation of "worlds." Unlike the philosophical distinction between actual and possible worlds common within Anglo-American analytic modal logic, metaphysics, and philosophy of language,[12] Lugones offers her conception of "actual worlds" to highlight the "heterogeneous," "co-temporaneous," and "multiple" ways in which human social life is organized. She states that a world can be an actual society, be a portion of a particular society with just a few inhabitants, be incomplete or in the process of being constructed, and have inhabitants who may or may not understand how a given world constructs them.[13] Worlds are also, in her words, "multiple, intersecting, co-temporaneous," and "permeable."[14] Moreover, in the introduction to *Pilgrimages*/Peregrinajes, she specifies that *historicity* is a core feature of "worlds" in the sense she intends.[15] She argues that rather than referring to certain gestures of political resistance as indicative of a *possible* world whereby some injustice is imagined as having been overcome—the example she explores is a series of acts aimed to resist confining norms that necessarily associate women with domestic labor—she proposes instead that committing to the "flesh and blood" inhabitants of actual worlds offers a stronger stance on the heterogeneous and historical characteristics of our social lives. Resistant acts, she proposes, should be connected to actual worlds in which oppression and injustice do not function as the constitutive ordering principles. Locating resistant acts within such "worlds" requires developing an understanding and appreciation for those sites of valuation, belonging, and worth that sustain marginalized communities both historically and in the present. Moreover, such worlds may be "historically muted or distorted," and the existential characteristics of such worlds may be hard to convey or communicate to others due to systemic imbalances of power.[16]

One potential illustration of Lugones's conception of worlds can be found in the description of the legacy of queer and trans activism against prisons by the prison abolitionist organizer Tourmaline (formerly Reina Gossett): "Too often, in abolitionist movements, we imagine that trans lives have just started to exist, that there is no legacy of trans people engaging in abolition. We often do not know or retell how trans people organized around state violence and the PIC [the prison industrial complex], like the Street Transvestite Action Revolutionaries organizing against police violence alongside the Black Panthers and the Young Lords."[17] Gossett's commentary on histories of queer and trans communities working against prison expansion and the surveillance and policing of people of color demonstrates something akin to locating "worlds" in Lugones's sense. The collective efforts and experiences of Street Transvestite Action Revolutionaries like Sylvia Rivera and Marsha P. Johnson become constitutive of a "world" within the 1970s radical movements of New York City that strove for queer and trans liberation beyond reformist and neoliberal framings of LGBTQ life. Locating such worlds, then, becomes important for contemporary queer and trans organizers working against the prison industrial complex by helping to locate our contemporary efforts to extended networks of resistant acts and histories of meaning-making.

These gestures toward communicative struggles and their connection to the heterogeneity of the social fits well within Lugones's later work on "complex communication" and on building coalition across communities of color.[18] Lugones affirms a commitment to the plurality of worlds, due, in part, to the need to historicize resistance, and to make conceptual space for forms of experience in which people who are often subjected to dismissal, condemnation, and neglect are treated as active subjects. In this sense, Lugones addresses the experience of being oneself beyond the arrogant perception of others, and "worlds" bear a close relationship to the lived experiences of oppressed peoples. In her words, affirming a plurality of worlds is important because it "is true to experience even if it is ontologically problematic."[19]

To clarify *unwilling* experiences of world-traveling, we can turn more specifically to what Lugones states regarding her notion of "traveling." She draws from the work of Janet Wolffe and Caren Kaplan to critique conceptions of mobility and movement as "unbounded."[20] Alongside these thinkers, she views conceptual and metaphorical utilizations of unbounded movement, including discourses of nomadism and exile, as failing to "decenter masculinity," and she states that "it is only men of a certain class and race who are in a position to exercise their mobility without restriction."[21] She also asserts that due to the constitution of worlds through the arrogant perception of white/Anglo needs, desires, and interests, for example, many people of color are forced to "travel" to worlds in which they are both viewed by others and view themselves as limited, unhappy, confused, unplayful, or as "not at ease." Being at ease, according to Lugones, is to "know the norms . . . all the words . . . [and] all the moves" and to be "confident" in oneself in the world.[22] To not be at ease is, then, to not have this familiarity, fluency, and comfort in a given world. Returning to the example of the relationship between white/Anglo women and women of color, Lugones argues that white/Anglo women construct worlds in which Latinas view themselves as contradictory beings. In her particular example, Lugones describes herself as someone who views herself and who is viewed by her friends as playful, but she is also someone who is unplayful in other worlds. The latter way of being is due both to her nonintentional and intentional enactment of the stereotype that Latinas are "serious" or unnecessarily "intense."[23] She proposes that Latinas find themselves in between worlds of sense, meaning, and material possibility that require their construction in ways that contradict what they may know and affirm about themselves. Thus, world-traveling can also be understood as compulsory, alienating, and painful, and this connects her work to critical articulations of racial and gender oppression.

In light of this brief overview of both willing and unwilling forms of world-traveling, we can draw several points of convergence between world-traveling and traditional phenomenological areas of study. As mentioned, Lugones's concept is richly invested in notions of intercorporeal and intersubjective dependency. Like classic phenomenologists such as Merleau-Ponty and Beauvoir, she appears quite critical of notions of liberal individual subjecthood and the possibility of developing proprioceptive awareness in absentia from other corporeal beings. Other readers of her work have interpreted world-traveling alongside the foundational texts of Edmund Husserl and Martin Heidegger, as well as those of Merleau-Ponty.[24]

Another interesting overlap within phenomenological traditions emerges between Lugones's conception of world-traveling and theorizations of resistance and agency found within the black existentialist tradition. Recall Lugones's statement that her conception of "worlds" is drawn explicitly from experience and that one's sense of oneself in a world in which one is affirmed by others can be radically distinct from how one is treated in another world. Interestingly, it appears that this formulation of a plural conception of selfhood does not rely on a part-whole relationship. One's relationship to oneself in oppressive conditions is not a part of some total conception of self that includes all their other (nonoppressed) parts. There is no total version of oneself, on her reading. Furthermore, any attempt to amalgamate worlds is incomplete as well. Along these lines, we can draw resonances between Lugones's concept of world-traveling and writings within black existentialism.[25] Consider, for example, Fanon's statement in response to Sartre's critique that Négritude is merely "a phase in the dialectic" toward a more universal form of liberation.[26] Fanon's response to this patronizing claim from his white interlocutor is that "black consciousness is immanent in itself. I am not a potentiality of something; I am fully what I am. . . . My black consciousness does not claim to be a loss. It *is*. It merges with itself."[27] Accordingly, both Fanon and Lugones assert that one's consciousness as a racialized person cannot be reduced to a part-whole relationship between white existential framings of being and subjecthood that would require separation from black valorization and history. Freedom, embodiment, and so on, on this reading, need not be disconnected from one's material relations within specific cultural and historical communities. Rather than strive to move beyond or away from blackness or Latinidad (i.e., because they are understood as inhibiting or naive), these facets of being are always already fully instantiated in one's experiences of one's own consciousness and conceptions of self. One's racial or ethnic identity is not a piece of a larger whole, but is already full of meaning, value, and significance that inform one's conceptions of oneself.

Last, it is important to note the numerous critical responses to Lugones's conception of world-traveling, many of which focus on world-traveling practices enacted by members of dominant groups. For example, some theorists have argued that world-traveling, when done by white people, can result in a problematic sense of ontological expansiveness, which is, as Shannon Sullivan has described it, "a way of being in the world (often nonconscious) in which [white people] presume the right to occupy any and all geographical, moral, psychological, linguistic, and other spaces." [28] Other theorists have proposed that world-traveling may enable privileged Western feminist researchers to exoticize, romanticize, or otherwise objectify non-Western women.[29] Some theorists have also criticized Lugones for presenting world-traveling as a one-sided practice that fails to require trans-worldly reciprocity.[30]

Many critics of Lugones's work, however, also find much value in the concept of world-traveling, and a number of theorists have sought to augment or expand her articulation of the concept to refine its theoretical utility. One such expansion can be found in the work of Mariana Ortega.[31] While Ortega is careful to note several major problems regarding Lugones's form of ontological pluralism for the self/selves that world-travels (e.g., questions regarding the continuity of multiple "realities" and questions regarding the relationship between one's own selves across worlds), she revises Lugones's concept by proposing what she calls *existential* pluralism.[32] This form of pluralism is contrasted with Lugones's view that world-traveling requires a plurality of selves. Rather, on Ortega's reading, existential pluralism is "the lived experience of the self, including the existential sense of understanding myself as an 'I,' a sense of how I am faring in worlds, and the multiplicity of my experience in terms of the ways I understand myself."[33] This conception of selfhood serves to explain the experience of multiple understandings of oneself, but without the ontological commitment to multiply existent selves, i.e., selves which must be connected in the relevant ways for continuity of experience by oneself and others. Ortega's interpretation of selfhood is then importantly able to maintain the existential sense of multiplicity between worlds of sense and material possibility that were at the heart of Lugones's framing of the concept.

It is important to note that the various threads of Lugones's conception of world-traveling that I have highlighted here also aid in emphasizing facets of her later work in decolonial theory.[34] While her later work develops macronarratives regarding modern/colonial world-systems and the widespread distribution of Eurocentric conceptions of embodiment, labor, race, and so on, subtle aspects of her earlier work can be seen woven throughout. Specifically, Lugones's conceptions of agency and subjectivity developed through the notion of world-traveling become malleable and productive resources for theorizations of the tensions described by colonized subjects who are caught between multiple worlds of meaning and sense. World-traveling, then, offers a further resource that enables work examining how Eurocentrism has framed and continues to frame subjectivity, embodiment, and value, and that can provide a critical tool that enables us to search for worlds in which decolonial sites of love, history, and relationality are possible.

## Notes

1. María Lugones, "Playfulness, 'World'-Travelling, and Loving Perception." *Hypatia* 2, no. 2 (1987): 3–19; María Lugones, *Pilgrimages/*Peregrinajes*: Theorizing Coalition against Multiple Oppressions* (Lanham, Md.: Rowman & Littlefield, 2003).

2. Lugones, "Playfulness, 'World'-Travelling, and Loving Perception," 3.

3. Lugones, "Playfulness, 'World'-Travelling, and Loving Perception," 3; Lugones, *Pilgrimages/*Peregrinajes, 77.

4. Lugones, "Playfulness, 'World'-Travelling, and Loving Perception," 5; Lugones, *Pilgrimages/*Peregrinajes, 79.

5. Lugones, "Playfulness, 'World'-Travelling, and Loving Perception," 3, 5; Lugones, *Pilgrimages/*Peregrinajes, 77, 79.

6. Marilyn Frye, "In and Out of Harm's Way: Arrogance and Love," in *The Politics of Reality* (Trumansburg, N.Y.: Crossing Press, 1983), 67.

7. Lugones, "Playfulness, 'World'-Travelling, and Loving Perception," 5; Lugones, *Pilgrimages*/Peregrinajes, 79.

8. Lugones, "Playfulness, 'World'-Travelling, and Loving Perception," 5; Lugones, *Pilgrimages*/Peregrinajes, 79.

9. Lugones, "Playfulness, 'World'-Travelling, and Loving Perception," 8; Lugones, *Pilgrimages*/Peregrinajes, 85.

10. Lugones, "Playfulness, 'World'-Travelling, and Loving Perception," 8; Lugones, *Pilgrimages*/Peregrinajes, 85–86, original emphasis.

11. Lugones, "Playfulness, 'World'-Travelling, and Loving Perception," 9; Lugones, *Pilgrimages*/Peregrinajes, 87.

12. See David Lewis, *On the Plurality of Worlds* (London: Basil Blackwell, 1986); W. V. O. Quine, *From a Logical Point of View* (New York: Harper and Row, 1953); Saul Kripke, *Naming and Necessity* (Oxford: Basil Blackwell, 1980).

13. Lugones, "Playfulness, 'World'-Travelling, and Loving Perception," 10; Lugones, *Pilgrimages*/Peregrinajes, 87–88.

14. Lugones, *Pilgrimages*/Peregrinajes, 16.

15. Lugones, *Pilgrimages*/Peregrinajes, 24–25.

16. Lugones, *Pilgrimages*/Peregrinajes, 25.

17. Che Gossett, "Abolitionist Imaginings: A Conversation with Bo Brown, Reina Gossett, and Dylan Rodríguez," in *Captive Genders: Trans Embodiment and the Prison Industrial Complex*, 2nd edition, ed. Eric A. Stanley and Nat Smith (Oakland, Calif.: AK Press, 2015), 367. For an extension of Lugones's conception of world-traveling within trans philosophy, see Talia Mae Bettcher, "Trapped in the Wrong Theory: Rethinking Trans Oppression and Resistance," *Signs* 39, no. 2 (2014): 383–406.

18. See, for example, María Lugones, "On Complex Communication," *Hypatia* 21, no. 3 (2006): 75–85, María Lugones, "Multiculturalismo radical y feminismos de mujeres de color," *Revista Internacional de Filosofía Política* 25 (2005): 61–76, reprinted in English as "Radical Multiculturalism and Women of Color Feminisms," *Journal for Cultural and Religious Theory* 13, no. 1 (2014): 68–80; María Lugones, "Toward a Decolonial Feminism," *Hypatia* 24, no. 4 (2010): 742–59.

19. Lugones, "Playfulness, 'World'-Travelling, and Loving Perception," 11; Lugones, *Pilgrimages*/Peregrinajes, 89.

20. Lugones, *Pilgrimages*/Peregrinajes, 17. Caren Kaplan, "The Politics of Location as Transnational Feminist Critical Practice," in *Scattered Hegemonies: Postmodernity and Transnational Feminist Practices*, ed. Inderpal Grewal and Caren Kaplan, 137–52 (Minneapolis: University of Minnesota Press, 1994); Caren Kaplan, *Questions of Travel* (Durham: Duke University Press, 1996); Janet Wolff, "On the Road Again: Metaphors of Travel in Cultural Criticism," *Cultural Studies* 7, no. 2 (1993): 224–39.

21. Lugones, *Pilgrimages*/Peregrinajes, 17.

22. Lugones, "Playfulness, 'World'-Travelling, and Loving Perception," 12; Lugones, *Pilgrimages*/Peregrinajes, 90.

23. Lugones, "Playfulness, 'World'-Travelling, and Loving Perception," 13–14; Lugones, *Pilgrimages*/Peregrinajes, 92.

24. See Gail Weiss, *Refiguring the Ordinary* (Indianapolis: Indiana University Press, 2008); Mariana Ortega, "'New Mestizas,' 'World' Travelers,' and *'Dasein'*: Phenomenology and

the Multi-Voiced, Multi-Cultural Self," *Hypatia* 16, no 3 (2001): 1–29; Mariana Ortega, *In Between: Latina Feminist Phenomenology, Multiplicity, and the Self* (Albany, N.Y.: SUNY Press, 2016); Jacqueline M. Martinez, "Culture, Communication, and Latina Feminist Philosophy: Toward a Critical Phenomenology of Culture." *Hypatia* 29, no. 1 (2014): 221–36.

25. See, for example, black existentialists such as Anna Julia Cooper, Richard Wright, Frantz Fanon, Audre Lorde, Kathryn T. Gines, Lewis R. Gordon, LaRose Parris, George Yancy, and Donna Dale-Marcano.

26. Frantz Fanon, *Black Skin, White Masks*, trans. Richard Philcox (New York: Grove Press, 2008), 111.

27. Fanon, *Black Skin, White Masks*, 114.

28. See Shannon Sullivan, "White World-Traveling," *Journal of Speculative Philosophy* 18, no. 4 (2004): 302. See also Shannon Sullivan, "The Racialization of Space: Toward a Phenomenological Account of Raced and Antiracist Spatiality," in *The Problems of Resistance: Studies in Alternate Political Cultures*, ed. Steve Martinot and Joy James (New York: Humanity Books, 2001), and the entry by Sullivan in this volume.

29. See Christine Sylvester, "African and Western Feminisms: World-Traveling the Tendencies and Possibilities," *Signs* 20, no. 4 (1995): 941–69.

30. See Weiss, *Refiguring the Ordinary.*

31. See Ortega, "'New Mestizas'"; Ortega, *In Between.*

32. Ortega, *In Between*, 89–102.

33. Ortega, *In Between*, 102.

34. Lugones, "Toward a Decolonial Feminism"; María Lugones, "Heterosexualism and the Colonial/Modern Gender System," *Hypatia* 22, no. 1 (2007): 186–219.

# Contributors

**Linda Martín Alcoff** is a professor of philosophy at the City University of New York. She is a past president of the American Philosophical Association, Eastern Division. Recent books include *Rape and Resistance* (2018); *The Future of Whiteness* (2015); and *Visible Identities: Race, Gender and the Self* (2006), which won the Frantz Fanon Award for 2009; and the coedited volume *The Routledge Companion to the Philosophy of Race* (2018).

**Alia Al-Saji** is an associate professor of philosophy at McGill University. She is the author of "Decolonizing Bergson: The Temporal Schema of the Open and the Closed" (2019); "A Phenomenology of Hesitation: Interrupting Racializing Habits of Seeing" (2014); and "The Racialization of Muslim Veils: A Philosophical Analysis" (2010).

**Debra Bergoffen** is George Mason University Emerita Professor of Philosophy and American University Bishop Hamilton Philosopher in Residence. Her writings include "From the Shame of Auschwitz to an Ethics of Vulnerability and a Politics of Revolt" (2019); "The Misogynous Politics of Shame" (2018); *Contesting the Politics of Genocidal Rape: Affirming the Dignity of the Vulnerable Body* (2011); and *The Philosophy of Simone de Beauvoir: Gendered Phenomenologies, Erotic Generosities* (1997).

**Talia Mae Bettcher** teaches philosophy at California State University, Los Angeles. She is the author of "Trapped in the Wrong Theory: Rethinking Trans Oppression Resistance" (2014); "When Selves Have Sex: What the Phenomenology of Trans Sexuality Can Teach about Sexual Orientation" (2014); and "Evil Deceivers and Make-Believers: On Transphobic Violence and the Politics of Illusion" (2007).

**Megan Burke** is an assistant professor of philosophy at Sonoma State University and is the author of *When Time Warps: The Lived Experience of Gender, Race, and Sexual Violence* (2019); "Beauvoirian Androgyny: Reflections on the Androgynous World of Fraternité" (2018); and "Love as a Hollow: Merleau-Ponty's Promise of Queer Love" (2016).

**John D. Caputo** is the Thomas J. Watson Professor of Religion Emeritus at Syracuse University and the David R. Cook Professor of Philosophy Emeritus at Villanova University. He is the author of twenty books in hermeneutics, postmodern Christianity, phenomenology, deconstruction, and theology, including *Hermeneutics: Facts and Interpretation in the Age of Information* (2018); *Hoping against Hope: Confessions of a Postmodern Pilgrim* (2015); *The Folly of God: A Theology of the Unconditional* (2015); *Truth* (2014); and *The Insistence of God: A Theology of Perhaps* (2013).

**Natalie Cisneros** is an associate professor of philosophy at Seattle University. Her recent work appears in *Hypatia: A Journal of Feminist Philosophy*; *Radical Philosophy Review*; and *Active Intolerance: Michel Foucault, the Prison Information Group, and the Future of Abolition* (2015).

**Patricia Hill Collins** is Distinguished University Professor Emerita of Sociology at the University of Maryland, College Park. Her award-winning books include *Black Sexual Politics: African Americans, Gender, and the New Racism* (2004) and *Black Feminist Thought: Knowledge, Consciousness, and the Politics of Empowerment* (1990, 2000).

**Duane H. Davis** is a professor of philosophy at the University of North Carolina, Asheville. He is the coeditor of *Merleau-Ponty and the Art of Perception* (2016, with William S. Hamrick) and the editor of *Merleau-Ponty's Later Thought and Its Practical Implications: The Dehiscence of Responsibility* (2001).

**Rosalyn Diprose** is Emeritus Professor of Philosophy at the University of New South Wales, Sydney. Her book publications include *Arendt, Natality and Biopolitics* (with E. P. Ziarek, 2018); *Merleau-Ponty: Key Concepts* (coedited with J. Reynolds, 2008); and *Corporeal Generosity: On Giving with Nietzsche, Merleau-Ponty and Levinas* (2002).

**Helen A. Fielding** is an associate professor of philosophy and women's studies and feminist research at the University of Western Ontario. She is the coeditor of *Feminist Phenomenology Futures* (2017) and *Time in Feminist Phenomenology* (2011).

**Rosemarie Garland-Thomson** is a professor of English and bioethics at Emory University, where she teaches disability studies, bioethics, American literature and culture, and feminist theory. She is the author of *Staring: How We Look* (2009) and several other books. Her current project is "Embracing Our Humanity: A Bioethics of Disability and Health."

**Moira Gatens** is Challis Professor of Philosophy at the University of Sydney. She is a fellow of the Academy of the Humanities and the Academy of the Social Sciences in Australia. She was a Fellow at the Wissenschaftskolleg Berlin in 2007. In 2010 she held the Spinoza Chair at the University of Amsterdam. In 2011 she was president of the Australasian Association of Philosophy. She has research interests in social and political philosophy, feminist philosophy, early modern philosophy, and philosophy and literature. She has a book on Spinoza and George Eliot forthcoming.

**Lewis R. Gordon** is a professor of philosophy at the University of Connecticut, Storrs; honorary president of the Global Center for Advanced Studies; and the 2018–19 Boaventura de Sousa Santos Chair in Faculty of Economics of the University of Coimbra, Portugal. He is the author of *Fear of Black Consciousness* (forthcoming); *Disciplinary Decadence* (2006); and *Existentia Africana* (2000).

**Lisa Guenther** is Queen's National Scholar in Political Philosophy and Critical Prison Studies at Queen's University in Canada. She is the author of *Solitary Confinement: Social Death and Its Afterlives* (2013) and coeditor of *Death and Other Penalties: Philosophy in a Time of Mass Incarceration* (2015).

**Lauren Guilmette** is an assistant professor of philosophy at Elon University. Her research areas include feminist and queer theory, continental philosophy, and affect theory. Her publications include "The Violence of Curiosity: Butler's Foucault, Foucault's Herculine, and the Will-to-Know" (2017) and "The Age of Paranoia: Teresa Brennan's Posthumous Insights for the Present" (2019).

**Sarah Hansen** is an assistant professor of philosophy at California State University, Northridge, whose writings have appeared in *Philosophy Today*; *Foucault Studies*; *philoSOPHIA: A Journal of Continental Feminism*; *Journal of French and Francophone Philosophy*; and the *International Journal of Feminist Approaches to Bioethics*. Hansen is coeditor of *New Forms of Revolt: Essays on Kristeva's Intimate Politics* (2017).

**Nancy J. Holland** is Professor Emerita of Philosophy at Hamline University. Her most recent books are *Heidegger and the Problem of Consciousness* (2018) and *Ontological Humility: Lord Voldemort and the Philosophers* (2013).

**Axelle Karera** is an assistant professor of philosophy and African American studies at Wesleyan University. Her areas of specialization are twentieth-century continental philosophy, the critical philosophy of race, and the environmental humanities. She has published in the *Critical Philosophy of Race* journal and is currently working on her first book, "The Climate of Race: Blackness and the Pitfalls of Anthropocene Ethics."

**David Haekwon Kim** is an associate professor of philosophy at the University of San Francisco. He has published widely in the philosophy of race, decolonial thought, and comparative philosophy. His current research is on East-South decolonial dialogue, focusing on shared political struggle and resources for theoretical hybridity in the wider South or non-West.

**Tamsin Kimoto** is a Ph.D. candidate in the Department of Philosophy at Emory University. Their research interests include trans* studies, Women of Color feminisms, and social and political philosophy.

**Donald A. Landes** is an associate professor in the Faculté de philosophie at Université Laval in Québec, Canada. He is the author of two books, *Merleau-Ponty and the Paradoxes of Expression* (2013) and *The Merleau-Ponty Dictionary* (2013). He is also the sole translator of the recent English version of Merleau-Ponty's *Phenomenology of Perception*.

**Emily S. Lee** is a professor of philosophy at California State University at Fullerton. Her research interests include feminist philosophy, philosophy of race, and phenomenology. She writes on phenomenology and epistemology in regard to the embodiment and subjectivity of women of color. She is the editor of *Living Alterities: Phenomenology, Embodiment, and Race* (2014) and *Race as Phenomena: Between Phenomenology and Philosophy of Race* (2019).

**Scott Marratto** is an associate professor of philosophy at Michigan Technological University. He is the author of "Alterity and Expression in Merleau-Ponty: A Response to Levinas" (2017); "Blind Narcissism: Merleau-Ponty and Derrida on the Line" (2016); and *The Intercorporeal Self: Merleau-Ponty on Subjectivity* (2012).

**William McBride** is the Arthur G. Hansen Distinguished Professor of Philosophy at Purdue University. His works include *The Philosophy of Marx* (reprinted in 2015); *From Yugoslav Praxis to Global Pathos: Anti-Hegemonic Post-Post Marxist Essays* (2001); and *Sartre's Political Theory* (1991).

**Robert McRuer** is a professor of English at George Washington University and the author of *Crip Times: Disability, Globalization, and Resistance* (2018) and *Crip Theory: Cultural Signs of Queerness and Disability* (2006).

**Jennifer McWeeny** is an associate professor of philosophy at Worcester Polytechnic Institute. She is the coeditor of *Speaking Face to Face: The Visionary Philosophy of María Lugones* (2019, with Pedro DiPietro and Shireen Roshanravan) and the coeditor of *Asian and Feminist Philosophies in Dialogue: Liberating Traditions* (2014, with Ashby Butnor). She is the editor in chief of *Simone de Beauvoir Studies.*

**Eduardo Mendieta** is a professor of philosophy, the associate director of the Rock Ethics Institute, and affiliated faculty at the School of International Affairs and the Bioethics Program at Penn State University. He is the author of *The Philosophical Animal* (forthcoming); *Global Fragments: Globalizations, Latinamericanisms, and Critical Theory* (2007); and *The Adventures of Transcendental Philosophy* (2002). He is also coeditor of the *Cambridge Habermas Lexicon* (2019, with Amy Allen); of *Habermas and Religion* (2013, with Craig Calhoun and Jonathan VanAntwerpen); and of *The Power of Religion in the Public Sphere* (2011, with Jonathan VanAntwerpen). He is the 2017 recipient of the Frantz Fanon Outstanding Achievements Award.

**Charles W. Mills** is Distinguished Professor of Philosophy at the CUNY Graduate Center. He is the author of six books, most recently *Black Rights/White Wrongs: The Critique of Racial Liberalism* (2017).

**David Morris** is a professor of philosophy at Concordia University, Montreal. His work seeks to advance phenomenological philosophy, especially in relation to the natural and human sciences, and with special attention to the role of temporality and the openness of being in nature and experience. His most recent book is *Merleau-Ponty's Developmental Ontology* (2018).

**Ann V. Murphy** is an associate professor of philosophy at the University of New Mexico in Albuquerque. She is the author of *Violence and the Philosophical Imaginary* (2012).

**Shannon M. Mussett** is a professor of philosophy at Utah Valley University. She specializes in existentialism, German idealism, feminist theory, and aesthetics. She is coeditor of *Beauvoir and the History of Philosophy from Plato to Butler* (2012) and *The Contradictions of Freedom: Philosophical Essays on Simone de Beauvoir's "Les Mandarins"* (2006).

**Kelly Oliver** is the W. Alton Jones Distinguished Professor of Philosophy at Vanderbilt University. She is the author of sixteen scholarly books and four novels, the editor of eleven collections, and has published more than one hundred scholarly articles. Her work uses phenomenology and psychoanalysis to critically engage contemporary social issues.

**Dorothea Olkowski** is a professor of philosophy, director of humanities, and director of the Cognitive Studies Program at the University of Colorado, Colorado Springs. She has been a Fellow at the University of Western Ontario, Rotman Institute of Philosophy and Science, the Australian National University in Canberra, and UC Berkeley. She is the author or editor of ten books and more than a hundred articles, including *The Universal (In the Realm of the Sensible)* (2007); *Postmodern Philosophy and the Scientific Turn* (2012); and *Feminist*

*Phenomenology Futures* (2017, with Helen A. Fielding); *Deleuze and Guattari's Philosophy of Freedom* (2019, with Eftichis Pirovolakis); and *Deleuze, Bergson, and Merleau-Ponty, The Logics and Pragmatics of Affect, Perception, and Creation* (forthcoming).

**Mariana Ortega** is an associate professor in the departments of philosophy and women's, gender, and sexualities studies and an affiliate in Latina/o Studies at Pennsylvania State University. She is coeditor of *Constructing the Nation: A Race and Nationalism Reader* (2009, with Linda Martín Alcoff); author of *In-Between: Latina Feminist Phenomenology, Multiplicity, and the Self* (2016); and coeditor of *Theories of the Flesh, Latinx and Latin American Feminisms, Transformation, and Resistance* (forthcoming with Oxford University Press, with Andrea J. Pitts and José Medina).

**Diane Perpich** is a professor of philosophy and the founding director of the Program in Women's Leadership at Clemson University. She is the author of *Phenomenological Contributions to Social Ontology* (forthcoming) and *The Ethics of Emmanuel Levinas* (2008).

**Andrea J. Pitts** is an assistant professor of philosophy at University of North Carolina, Charlotte. Their publications appear in *IJFAB: The International Journal of Feminist Approaches to Bioethics*; *Hypatia: A Journal for Feminist Philosophy*; and *Radical Philosophy Review*. Pitts is also coeditor of *Beyond Bergson: Examining Race and Colonialism through the Writings of Henri Bergson* (2019) and *Theories of the Flesh: Latinx and Latin American Feminisms, Transformation, and Resistance* (2019).

**Mark Ralkowski** is an associate professor of philosophy and honors at George Washington University. He is the author of *Plato's Trial of Athens* (2018) and *Heidegger's Platonism* (2009); the editor of *Time and Death: Heidegger's Analysis of Finitude* (2005); and the coeditor of *Plato at Syracuse* (2019).

**Jack Reynolds** is an associate dean (research) and a professor of philosophy at Deakin University, Australia. He is most recently the author of *Phenomenology, Naturalism and Science: A Hybrid and Heretical Proposal* (2018).

**Joel Michael Reynolds** is an assistant professor of philosophy at the University of Massachusetts, Lowell, and the Rice Family Fellow in Bioethics and Humanities at the Hastings Center. He is the author of *Ethics after Ableism: Disability, Pain, and the History of Morality* (2019) and coeditor of *The Disability Bioethics Reader* (forthcoming).

**Lanei M. Rodemeyer** is an associate professor at Duquesne University. Her publications include *Lou Sullivan Diaries (1970–1980) and Theories of Sexual Embodiment: Making Sense of Sensing* (2018); "Husserl and Queer Theory" (2017); and *Intersubjective Temporality: It's about Time* (2006).

**Elena Ruíz** is an assistant professor of philosophy and global studies at Michigan State University. Her work has appeared in *Feminist Philosophy Quarterly*, *Hypatia: A Journal for Feminist Philosophy*, and *The Oxford Companion to Feminist Philosophy*.

**Gayle Salamon** is a professor of English and gender and sexuality studies at Princeton University. She is the author of *The Life and Death of Latisha King: A Critical Phenomenology of Transphobia* (2018) and *Assuming a Body: Transgender and Rhetorics of Materiality* (2010).

**Kris Sealey** is an associate professor of philosophy and codirector of the Black Studies Program at Fairfield University. Her most recent publications can be found in *Critical Philosophy of Race*; *Hypatia: A Journal for Feminist Philosophy*; and *Levinas Studies: An Annual Review*. She is the author of *Moments of Disruption: Levinas, Sartre, and the Question of Transcendence* (2013). Her current book project investigates the unfolding of community formations in decolonial contexts, and offers creolization as a conceptual tool through which such formations might be theorized.

**Jenny Slatman** is a professor of medical humanities in the Department of Culture Studies at Tilburg University, the Netherlands. She has published widely on issues of embodiment in art, expression, and contemporary medical practices. Her publications include *Our Strange Body: Philosophical Reflections on Identity and Medical Interventions* (2014) and *L'expression au-delà de la représentation: Sur l'aisthêsis et l'esthétique chez Merleau-Ponty* (2003).

**Shannon Sullivan** is a professor of philosophy and health psychology and the chair of the philosophy department at UNC Charlotte. Her recent publications include *White Privilege* (2019); *The Physiology of Sexist and Racist Oppression* (2015); and *Good White People: The Problem with Middle-Class White Anti-Racism* (2014).

**Ted Toadvine** is the Nancy Tuana Director of the Rock Ethics Institute and an associate professor of philosophy at Pennsylvania State University. He is the author of *Merleau-Ponty's Philosophy of Nature* (2009) and the editor of *The Merleau-Ponty Reader* (2007) and *Eco-Phenomenology: Back to the Earth Itself* (2003), among other works.

**Gail Weiss** is a professor of philosophy at George Washington University. She is the author of *Refiguring the Ordinary* (2008) and *Body Images: Embodiment as Intercorporeality* (1998) and has edited or coedited several volumes on Merleau-Ponty and embodiment, including "The Ethics of Embodiment," a special issue of *Hypatia: A Journal of Feminist Philosophy*.

**Keith Whitmoyer** is an adjunct assistant professor at Pace University. He is the author of *The Philosophy of Ontological Lateness* (2017) and "The Caprice of Being: αἰών and φύσις in Merleau-Ponty, Heraclitus, and Deleuze" (2017). Additionally he is guest coeditor (with Elodie Boublil and Galen Johnson) of a special issue of the *Journal for the British Society for Phenomenology*, "Phenomenology and Vulnerability."

**Shiloh Whitney** is an assistant professor of philosophy at Fordham University. She researches at the intersection of feminist philosophy, twentieth-century French philosophy, and phenomenology. Her work can be found in the journals *Hypatia: A Journal for Feminist Philosophy*; *Philosophy and Social Criticism*; *Chiasmi International*; *Journal of Phenomenological Psychology*; *Southern Journal of Philosophy*; *Journal of Speculative Philosophy*; and *PhaenEx*.

**Kyle Whyte** holds the Timnick Chair in the Humanities and is a professor of philosophy and community sustainability at Michigan State University. Recent publications include "Indigenous Science (Fiction) for the Anthropocene: Ancestral Dystopias and Fantasies of Climate Crises" (2018); "Critical Investigations of Resilience: A Brief Introduction to Indigenous Environmental Studies and Sciences" (2018); and "What Do Indigenous Knowledges Do for Indigenous Peoples?" (2018).

**Cynthia Willett** is the Samuel Candler Dobbs Professor of Philosophy at Emory University. She has coauthored *Uproarious: How Feminists and Other Subversive Comics Speak Truth* (2019, with Julie Willett) and authored *Interspecies Ethics* (2014); *Irony in the Age of Empire: Comic Perspectives on Freedom and Democracy* (2008); *The Soul of Justice: Racial Hubris and Social Bonds* (2001); and *Maternal Ethics and Other Slave Moralities* (1995).

**George Yancy** is a professor of philosophy at Emory University and Montgomery Fellow at Dartmouth College. Yancy is the author, editor, and coeditor of more than twenty books. He is known for his influential essays and interviews at the *New York Times'* philosophy column, "The Stone." He has twice won the American Philosophical Association's Committee on Public Philosophy's Op-Ed Contest. Yancy's most recent books include *Buddhism and Whiteness: Critical Reflections* (2019, with Emily McRae); *Educating for Critical Consciousness* (2019); *Backlash: What Happens When We Talk Honestly About Racism in America* (2018); *Race: 34 Conversations in a Time of Crisis* (2017); and the expanded second edition of *Black Bodies, White Gazes* (2017). Yancy is also Philosophy of Race Books Series Editor at Lexington Books.

**Perry Zurn** is an assistant professor of philosophy at American University. He is the coeditor of *Active Intolerance: Michel Foucault, the Prisons Information Group, and the Future of Abolition* (2016), *Carceral Notebooks 12* (2017), and *Curiosity Studies: A New Ecology of Knowledge* (forthcoming).

# Index